Ohio Canal Era

∴

A CASE STUDY OF GOVERNMENT
AND THE ECONOMY, 1820–1861

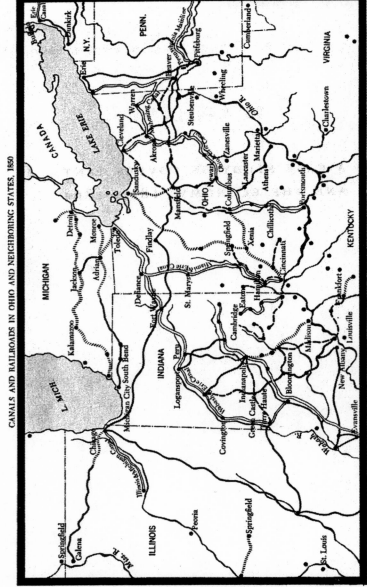

CANALS AND RAILROADS IN OHIO AND NEIGHBORING STATES, 1850

HISTORICAL AND PHILOSOPHICAL SOCIETY OF OHIO

From the Liberty Hall and Cincinnati Weekly Gazette, May 9, 1850

||||||||| Railroads constructed ========= Railroads under construction
········· Railroads surveyed ————— Canals operating

OHIO CANAL ERA

A Case Study of Government
and the Economy, 1820–1861

HARRY N. SCHEIBER
Foreword by Lawrence M. Friedman

OHIO UNIVERSITY PRESS · ATHENS

Ohio University Press, Athens, Ohio 45701
ohioswallow.com
© 1968, 1987, 2012 by Harry N. Scheiber
Foreword © 2012 by Lawrence M. Friedman

Printed in the United States of America
Ohio University Press books are printed on acid-free paper ∞ ™

20 19 18 17 16 15 14 13 12   5 4 3 2 1

Library of Congress Cataloging-in-Publication Data

Scheiber, Harry N.
    Ohio canal era.

    With a new foreword by Lawrence M. Friedman
    With a new preface by the author
    Bibliography: p.
    Includes index.
    1. Canals—Ohio—History—19th century. 2. Canals—Government policy—Ohio—
History—19th century. 3. Railroads—Ohio—History—19th century. 4. Railroads and
state—Ohio—History—19th century. 5. Ohio—Economic conditions. I. Title.
HE395.047S3   1987   386'.48'09771   86-23800
ISBN 978-0-8214-1979-3 (pbk.)
ISBN 978-0-8214-4403-0 (electronic)

Third printing 2012
Second printing 1987
First printing 1968

Grateful acknowledgment is made to the Harvard University Press for permission to
incorporate materials, in Maps II.A and II.B of this volume, from George Rogers Taylor
and Irene D. Neu, *The American Railroad Network, 1861–1890.* (Copyright © 1956 by the
President and Fellows of Harvard College.)

For Jane

Acknowledgments

IN THE COURSE of research for this study, I was the beneficiary of the generosity with which American scholars characteristically respond to requests for aid and counsel. Paul Wallace Gates, who directed my graduate studies at Cornell University, provided me with a critique of my doctoral dissertation on Ohio's transport policies, and it became the agenda for a considerable program of additional research. I am grateful to him for his continuing interest, his many incisive suggestions, and his friendly prodding. Others at Cornell to whom I owe a special debt are Curtis P. Nettels and Douglas F. Dowd.

Substantial portions of this study were read in draft form by Peter J. Coleman of the University of Illinois (Chicago), Jere Daniell of Dartmouth College, Miss Miriam Gallaher of the Center for Advanced Study in the Behavioral Sciences, and Mrs. Fannia Weingartner, all of whom contributed to what felicity of style may be evident. I have profited greatly, too, from many discussions of the substance of this work with Edward Chase Kirkland, Roger H. Brown, Morton Rothstein, and Herbert G. Gutman. Others who have aided me generously in various ways are James P. Baughman, Allan G. Bogue, Robert W. Fogel, Lawrence Friedman, Carter Goodrich, Eugene Litwak, Stewart Macaulay, Walter R. Marvin, Roger L. Ransom, George Rogers Taylor, Paul P. Van Riper, and Francis P. Weisenburger.

In the course of research in Ohio, I had in addition the benefit of association with James H. Rodabaugh of Miami University, whose insights color many passages of this study. Henry Caren and Bruce Harding, both formerly of the Ohio Historical Society staff, were trenchant critics; they also shared with me their thorough knowledge of the Ohio State Archives. Mrs. Elizabeth Martin, Mrs. Marion Bates, and Mr. Kenneth Duckett of the Ohio Historical Society Library staff all extended genuine hospitality as well as expert aid during my year in residence there. Those who have had occasion to use the other libraries where I worked will readily appreciate my great indebtedness to the staffs of the Western Reserve Historical Society, the Cincinnati Historical Society, Columbia University's Special Collections, the Cornell University Regional History Collection, the Ohio State University Library, the Ohio State Library, and the U. S. National Archives. The staff of Baker Library in Dartmouth College, and particularly Miss Virginia Close, have given invaluable assistance as well. Mrs. Robert Wells, Mrs. Agnes Page, and Mrs. Beth Strack provided tireless, cheerful aid in typing.

The funds that supported my research were provided by several scholarly organizations, and I owe thanks to the Social Science Research Council, for a year's fellowship; the American Association for State and Local History, for a summer grant; and Resources for the Future, Inc., for a grant to Dartmouth College that financed research on the role of engineers in public-investment decisions, some of which material appears here. During a treasured period of residence as a Fellow of the Center for Advanced Study in the Behavioral Sciences, while I also held a fellowship of the American Council of Learned Societies, I was able to reconsider the study and undertake some major revisions. Generous aid by the Center's staff made it possible to do so while I was deeply engaged in other concerns as well; and special thanks are due the director emeritus of the Center, Ralph W. Tyler, and Preston Cutler and Mrs. Jane Kielsmeier. I am grateful also to Dartmouth College for several grants in support of research.

My colleagues in the History Department at Dartmouth have provided an exciting milieu for research and have extended their assistance in many ways. Ian MacKenzie, director of the Ohio University Press, and Mrs. Susan Schulman have also made many contributions to this work.

The editors of *Ohio History, The Political Science Quarterly,* and *The Business History Review* have kindly granted permission to use in Chapters 1, 3, and 10 materials drawn from my articles in those journals. Thanks are due Mrs. Joan Erdman for the index.

Neither funds for research nor even the scholarly community's extraordinary generosity would have seen this work through to completion, had it not been for the indispensable help and patient forbearance of my wife, Jane Lang Scheiber, and the resourceful (and unique) contributions of Susan and Michael.

H. N. S.

Contents

TABLES   xi

MAPS AND CHARTS   xiii

ABBREVIATIONS   xiv

FOREWORD BY LAWRENCE M. FRIEDMAN   xv

PREFACE   xix

PREFACE TO THE 1987 EDITION   xxiii

BIBLIOGRAPHIC NOTE, 1987   xxvii

BIBLIOGRAPHIC NOTE, 2012   xxxi

PART I. THE STATE ENTERPRISE, 1820–1850   1

CHAPTER

1. *Toward a Canal Policy, 1820–1825*   7

2. *Construction and Finance, 1825–1833*   36

3 *Administration of the Enterprise, 1825–1833*   61

4. *Egalitarian Ideals and Pressure for Expansion, 1825–1838*   88

5. *The Public Works and Mixed Enterprise, 1836–1845*   120

6. *Financing Expansion, 1836–1845*   140

7. *Administration: Change and Adjustment, 1833–1850*   164

PART II. THE COURSE OF ECONOMIC CHANGE, 1820–1851   183

8. *The Canals in the Economy, 1820–1840*   187

9. *The Transportation Revolution: Second Phase,*
   1840–1851   212
10. *State Rate-Making and Market Allocation,*
    1827–1851   247

PART III. BEGINNING OF THE RAILROAD
           AGE: TO 1861   269

11. *Competition and Response: The Ohio*
    Railroads, 1826–1861   275
12. *Transportation and Economic Change,*
    1850–1860   318
13. *Conclusion*   353

APPENDICES:
1. *The Sources of Capital*   371
2. *Tolls on the Ohio Canals*   380
3. *Tonnage of Canal Commerce*   387
4. *Estimating "Indirect Returns"*   391

BIBLIOGRAPHY   398

INDEX   423

Tables

2.1.	PURCHASERS OF OHIO BONDS, 1825–32	39
2.2.	SPECIFICATIONS OF CONSTRUCTION: MIAMI AND OHIO CANALS, 1833	43
2.3.	EXPENDITURES FOR CONSTRUCTION, 1825–33	54
5.1.	ANNUAL DISBURSEMENTS FOR CANAL CONSTRUCTION, 1833–45	128
5.2.	PRINCIPAL OHIO TRANSPORTATION LINES, 1845	134
6.1.	PURCHASERS OF OHIO BONDS, 1836–39	143
6.2.	PURCHASERS OF OHIO BONDS, 1840	148
6.3.	OHIO CANAL DEBT, 1850	155
8.1.	PRINCIPAL COMMODITIES IN OHIO CANAL TRADE AT CLEVELAND, 1832–51	193
8.2.	PRINCIPAL COMMODITIES IN OHIO CANAL TRADE AT PORTSMOUTH, 1833–51	195
8.3.	PRINCIPAL COMMODITIES IN MUSKINGUM IMPROVEMENT TRADE AT HARMAR (MARIETTA), 1841–51	197
8.4.	PRINCIPAL COMMODITIES IN MIAMI CANAL TRADE AT CINCINNATI, 1833–51	202
8.5.	PRINCIPAL COMMODITIES IN WABASH & ERIE CANAL TRADE AT TOLEDO, 1841–51	204
9.1.	AVERAGE ANNUAL CLEVELAND WHEAT AND FLOUR RECEIPTS, 1837–51	218
9.2.	SELECTED OHIO EXPORTS FROM LAKE ERIE AND OHIO RIVER PORTS, 1843, 1851	226
9.3.	SELECTED OHIO EXPORTS, BY INDIVIDUAL PORT, 1843	228

9.4.   SELECTED OHIO EXPORTS, BY INDIVIDUAL
       PORT, 1851   229
9.5.   VALUE OF TRADE AT MAJOR OHIO PORTS,
       1832–52   232
10.1. OHIO CANAL CHARGES IN THE NEWARK-
       CLEVELAND TRADE, 1850   260
11.1. OHIO RAILROAD MILEAGE COMPLETED AND
       TOTAL IN OPERATION, 1847–60   284
11.2. ESTIMATES OF OHIO RAILROADS' OPERATING
       RECEIPTS AND EARNINGS, 1839–59   295
11.3. REVENUES AND AGGREGATE TONNAGE, OHIO
       STATE CANALS, 1849–60   302
12.1. EXPORTS AND PROPORTION RECEIVED BY CANAL,
       1851, 1860   321
12.2. MAJOR CINCINNATI EXPORTS, 1846–50, 1856–60   322
12.3. EXPORTS OF OHIO, 1857–58   326
12.4. VALUE OF OHIO AGRICULTURAL EXPORTS,
       1852–58   329
12.5. STATISTICS OF OHIO AGRICULTURE, 1849, 1859   330
12.6. OHIO MANUFACTURING INDUSTRIES, BY GROUPS,
       AND SHARE IN STATEWIDE TOTAL MANUFAC-
       TURING OUTPUT, 1850, 1860   341

Appendices

1.   HOLDERS OF RECORD, 1840, OHIO BONDS
     ISSUED, 1825–39   371
2.   TOLLS ON OHIO CANALS, 1827–58   380
3.   TONNAGE OF CANAL COMMERCE, 1850–60   387

Maps

Distribution of Ohio population in 1820   12
Canal routes surveyed during 1822–1825, and
   approved in 1825   18
Proposed canals and railroads, 1825–1846; and
   completed canals   96
Transportation and population growth, 1830–1850   234
Ohio railroads, 1851   288
Ohio railroads, 1861   291
Changes in Ohio population and farmland valuation,
   1850–1860   334

Charts

Figure 3.1.   Canal Commission Organization   63

Abbreviations used in Notes

AR — *Annual Report*
ASTC — *Annual Statement of the Trade and Commerce of Cincinnati*
BFC — Board of [Canal] Fund Commissioners
BPW — Board of Public Works
CC — Canal Commission (Board of Canal Commissioners)
CHS—Cincinnati Historical Society
HPSO — Historical and Philosophical Society of Ohio
MVHR — *Mississippi Valley Historical Review*
OAHQ — *Ohio Archaeological and Historical Quarterly*
OH — *Ohio History*
OHQ — *Ohio Historical Quarterly*
OHS — Ohio Historical Society
OSA — Ohio State Archives (Ohio Historical Society)
OSL — Ohio State Library
WRHS — Western Reserve Historical Society

Foreword

OHIO CANAL ERA: *A Case Study of Government and the Economy, 1820–1861* (1969) is, in my view, a tremendous achievement. It was, at the time of publication, a signal contribution to economic history; and it was also—or would come to be seen as—a major contribution to socio-legal history, a field in which Harry N. Scheiber would later be one of the leading players. Professor Scheiber was and is a historian, trained in history, with a doctorate in history. But he was already, at the time, aware of, and influenced by, the pioneering work of J. Willard Hurst and the Wisconsin school of legal history—a school of thought that directed attention to state and local government, to the way the legal system actually operated on the ground, and to its relationship to the market and to the American economy.

In hindsight, we can fit *Ohio Canal Era* into the historiography of legal history. We see it now as a monumental and still definitive study of law and the economy in an American state. But in its day, the book was, first and foremost, a study of *government* and the economy. It followed in the line of work begun by such scholars as Scheiber's adviser at Cornell, Paul Wallace Gates, and also Oscar Handlin and Mary Handlin, Louis Hartz, and others—scholars who were engaged in close, careful, and insightful study of state and local government in the nineteenth-century economy.

In reality, the two streams of scholarship—legal and economic history—were sisters under the skin. The very first sentence of the preface to *Ohio Canal Era* announces, "To channel private energies and to affect the course of economic change, Americans of the early nineteenth century employed the power of government at all levels." The phrase "to channel private energies" would immediately remind legal historians of one of Hurst's most famous phrases, "the release of energy." The phrase comes from *Law and the Conditions of Freedom,* Hurst's seminal book of 1956.

Hurst and the economic historians exploded the myth of a golden age of laissez-faire in the early nineteenth century—the myth that this was a period when, by reason of ideology, government played no role in the economy, and the pure free market was sovereign. Rather, research showed that government—but mostly state and local government—did play a vital role in the economy. Not much of what government did looked like regulation in the modern sense. There was a lot of law about banks and insurance companies—and infrastructure in general. The point was to unleash economic "energy" in an age that believed in progress. This was the Hurstian theme, and it was also a theme that pervaded this study of the era of canal building in Ohio.

Subsidies for canals and later railroads were genuinely popular. The law, responding to those in society whose opinion counted for something, was less interested in protecting "vested" rights than in trying to coax, bribe, and stimulate the growing economy. This was not mere ideology; it meant money, growth, prosperity to large numbers of people. For this reason, the law of the early nineteenth century stressed "dynamic" over "static" property rights. It stressed enterprise; it stressed rules of property and land law that worked, that produced, that moved the economy forward. What was "static" was often labeled as "monopoly"; and the image was of an obstacle, something to be overcome. The men who labored to create the Ohio canal system believed in the march of civilization; they believed in development, in American advancement toward a brighter, more prosperous future. They were Hurstian to the core.

To fit this book into its proper historical slot does not mean that this study was in any way derivative. Quite the contrary: it was fresh and original. And it rested on a firm foundation of close and careful research—comprehensive, deep, and thorough. On the surface, the subject might seem rather unpromising. The canal period in Ohio was brief. The passion for canal building rose like a rocket, flourished, and then declined; within forty years it had come and gone. It was killed by politics, by changes in demography and economics—and above all by the rise of the railroads.

In Scheiber's hands, however, the period takes on much greater historical significance. This is a book rich in insights. It is also a prime study of political history, and in addition, of administrative history. On the political side, we learn, for example, how the original canal program was expanded far beyond the original intention. Between 1836 and 1838, the legislature authorized more canals and river-improvement projects, and gave "large-scale state aid to private companies engaged in canal, railroad, and turnpike construction" (p. 88). As Scheiber explains, this explosion of government largesse was a response not so much to economic needs as it was to "egalitarian ideology," which "so thoroughly pervaded American political thought" that it generated a "corollary that all members of the community should share *equally* in the benefits that government might provide." Thus the test of the legitimacy of a policy "tended to be how well it diffused material benefits," rather than "preconceptions about either *laisser-faire* or interventionism" (p. 90). The "parochial pursuit of local ambition" overwhelmed any notion of planning (p. 356). As a result, canal after canal was authorized and built. This political insight, very plainly, is still relevant to an understanding of American legal, economic, and social development.

Ohio Canal Era is written in clean, supple English. What might have been a rather dry exercise in the history of infrastructure comes vividly to life in these pages. I direct the reader, for example, to the wonderful description of life on the canal, a lively passage that makes the canal era seem almost palpable and (in addition) explains why canals flourished—and why they fell from grace (p. 235).

Ohio Canal Era was a major study by a historian who had already made a considerable contribution to legal and economic history and who was embarked on what would prove to be a long and extremely fruitful career, particularly in socio-legal history. At the time the book was published, Harry Scheiber was a professor of history at Dartmouth College. He later moved to the history department at UC San Diego, and then, in 1980, to the Law School of UC Berkeley. There were many reasons why he felt this move was attractive; but it also represented a decisive commitment to American legal history. For more than twenty-five years now, he has worked and written in the Berkeley environment. This is a law school environment, of course, but a law school with a strong commitment to interdisciplinary research. This environment was well suited to his style of scholarship. His major interests were now focused on environmental law—in particular, ocean resources; on American constitutional history, especially its structural elements—federalism in particular; and on civil liberties. The work on the law of the sea and related matters is particularly notable; it is interdisciplinary, comparative, and reflects strong ideas about right and wrong. A case in point is a powerful essay on the regulation of whaling, published in 2000.

For Scheiber, history does more than reconstruct the past. It explores traditions that often illuminate questions people face in contemporary times. His work is history as a kind of social science. Modern problems and dilemmas are part of his mandate. This is implicit in *Ohio Canal Era,* and explicit later on. Over the years, Professor Scheiber has trained a whole generation of socio-legal scholars, some of them also historians. They share an enriched view of what legal history is or ought to be— Harry Scheiber's view. History is not just finding out what happened a long time ago. It is not even just about assessing and explaining what happened. History is more than a buried city. It is a big book of data, about people, how they lived and thought, how they defined problems and tried to solve them. It is a record of society's collective memories— good memories and bad memories. In an age in which myths, legends, and illusions about the American past create so much loud noise in the public sphere, Harry Scheiber's brand of history seems more necessary than ever. *Ohio Canal Era* is a paragon, a superb example, of the best that this historiography has to offer.

Lawrence M. Friedman
Stanford University School of Law

Preface

TO CHANNEL private energies and to affect the course of economic change, Americans of the early nineteenth century employed the power of government at all levels. In pursuing these purposes, they invoked a great variety of policy devices which ranged from adjustments in water law through regulation of corporations all the way to grants of public subsidies and the use of government-owned, government-operated enterprises. Moreover, to a perhaps surprising degree, they made the states the focus of their efforts—attempting to formulate their collective interests as New Yorkers, or Ohioans, or Virginians—and they expected their state governments to devise policies that would serve diverse pluralistic interests within the state community.

Recent scholarship has established that the states' transportation policies carried a special significance in the pre-Civil War era. For with few exceptions, the pursuit of economic policy in other areas was through limited types of action that required little in the way of public expenditures or elaborate administrative effort: the states distributed public resources to private interests, as in land grants to corporations; they expedited private use of resources, as with permissive water and timber-use law; they extended legal privileges and immunities, as with limited liability; or else they regulated activity in the public interest, as with banking laws. But in the area of transportation, many states implemented policy aims by what I shall term "outright public enterprise," by establishing public agencies to build, finance, and operate costly transport facilities such as canals. The financial requirements for such enterprises were enormous, and taxes necessary to finance them would fall upon every citizen. Moreover, transportation projects would confer greater advantages on some regions and certain economic interests than on others. Men deliberated at length the costs and benefits of transport investment, and they brought engineering expertise heavily to bear on their public-investment decisions. As a result, these decisions tended to be much more deliberate and considered than many other policies whose adoption involved lower "visible" costs.

The state transport investments were important because they filled a great gap in the structure of the economy. The Federal government had chosen to play only a secondary role in the planning and development of transportation, and yet such "internal improvements" were essential to growth. Therefore state investment in canals and other facilities made a crucial contribution to American economic development in the pre-Civil War years.

This book, which is a case study of an American state government and its role in economic development, emphasizes one issue that has not been fully explored in the historical literature: the problem of the operative public enterprise. Concentrating upon the Ohio case has permitted close scrutiny of day-to-day bureaucratic functioning, and has revealed how operations of the agencies responsible for canal construction and finance touched every important economic interest in the state. Though the creation, financing, and management of one of pre-Civil War America's major public enterprises provides the focus, I have attempted to introduce comparisons with the experience of other states. In addition, I have sought to consider in some detail aspects of policy and administration—for instance, the interplay of banking, public banking policy, and state finance—which may well have been comparable to developments in other states, but which scholars have generally overlooked. Attention is given as well to the more traditional subjects of analysis: the dynamic political process, ideology, statute law, the role of the courts, and the broad setting of business-governmental relationships.

One cannot treat the achievements and failures of state government, as it responded to critical transportation problems of the day, exclusively in terms of policy and administration. For one must ask how consistent state policies were with the social and political values of the electorate; and also, what was the long-term impact of transport policy on the economy. Thus I have given considerable attention to the remarkable transformation of the Ohio economy from 1820 to 1861, and especially to the effects of transport innovations. In 1820 Ohio had barely gone beyond the frontier stage of development, except in a few settled areas along the Ohio River and its major tributaries; yet by 1861 it had become one of the nation's leading states in population and in industrial and agricultural development. Distinguishing the effects of transportation from the many other factors operative in the complex processes of economic growth is difficult enough in any event; complicating the task here is the need to place Ohio's development within the larger framework of national and international economic changes. In dealing with this interpretive problem, I have attempted to draw from the available data on institutional changes, as well as from such surviving nineteenth century statistics as appear reliable. Attention has also been given to Ohioans' contemporary assessments of how well their expectations had been realized by the state's public transport investments; for it was on the basis of their own perceptions that they predicated changes in their public policies, and indeed changes in their definition of "commonwealth interest."

As a book concerned with the intersecting effects of policy-making, public administration, and economic development, this study does not assert a single thesis. Rather it offers the reader a set of related propositions concerning localism, political ideology, and partisan cleavages as they affected the making of policy; the character of entrepreneurship (the innovative functions of organizational leaders) in public undertakings, and the sources of strength and weakness in a functioning state bureaucracy; the impact of legal process and administration upon the economy; and the influences shaping statewide and regional economic change during four hectic decades of development.

A delegate to Ohio's 1850 constitutional convention ably articulated the premises on which a generation of men in the state had based economic policies, when he declared that government was established for "two great ends." The first, of course, was the protection of the citizen "in the enjoyment of his inalienable rights." Second was a purpose that required positive state action: "The earth is to be subdued, the necessaries of life created, its conveniences and adornments to be secured"; and the society's "efforts for improvement are also to be encouraged." These, he declared, "are the great operative duties of government. . . . The common weal, the public good, is the great end."*

What follows, then, is a study of "the great operative duties of government" as expressed and implemented in one of pre-Civil War America's leading innovative states. The focus is positive state government, interacting with the economy, under conditions of rapid development.

* Ohio Constitutional Convention, 1850, *Debates and Proceedings* (Columbus. 1851), 1267.

Preface to the 1987 Edition

WHEN THIS study of state enterprise and the antebellum economy was first published, there was a growing divergence of views among American scholars in the field of economic history about how to approach their research. Some of them, myself included, regarded it as imperative that studies of economic change should seek to integrate evidence of institutional development, policy-making process, and law with evidence relating more strictly to economic resources and their mobilization in the marketplace. Others, mainly economists doing history, instead regarded institutions, law, and government policy only as a "given." They were persuaded that "hard" economic analysis, concerned with quantifiable measures of production and distribution of goods in the market, was sufficient for an understanding of the forces that transformed the American economy in the antebellum years.

This difference of viewpoint became acute in the 1970s. Indeed, for a time it seemed unlikely that some prominent economic historians would ever again concern themselves or their students with such questions as the mobilization of state enterprise or other forms of intervention, the administration or financing of such public enterprises, the political ideology and localistic rivalries (among other forces) that manifested themselves in the struggle for economic advantage amidst rapid economic change, or the role of entrepreneurial decision-making in governmental institutions as they affected and responded to private economic interests. All the foregoing questions, of course, were at the heart of the research inquiry that resulted in this book on Ohio's antebellum canal era. As its subtitle indicates, it is a case study of government and the economy; but I was not seeking to subordinate altogether to the study of governance and institutions the analysis of agriculture, commerce, or industrialization. On the contrary, such analysis was also an integral, core concern of the book.

Unlike so many of my colleagues in the field of economic history in those days, I did not regard government policy, law, administration, and politics as things to be treated under the marvelous heading, *ceteris paribus*, as if they were the contents of some kind of magical conceptual holding tank. Nor did I think that a very useful understanding of the institutional dimensions of agriculture, manufacturing, transportation, commerce, and banking—or of the dynamics of change in these sectors—could be achieved if one put into practice in research the view, then very chic, that the only things worth study were the phenomena one could quantify.

In the last few years, we have witnessed a softening and narrowing of this dichotomization in the field of economic history. First of all, there has been a change of view among some of the figures in economic history who fifteen years ago were single-mindedly dedicated to the idea that legal rules and institutions could be held static in the background when one set out to reconstruct the history of economic change. Now, many of these scholars have accepted that the seductive abstraction called "the market" was not autonomous; they concede that, in the real world, institutions and law mattered, and that in fact they shaped, constrained, and channeled market processes. They acknowledge, although belatedly, that we must analyze conscious political decision-making, the allocation of public investment funds, and the shifting (and highly purposive) definition of property rights, privileges, and immunities by legislatures and courts as forces that have much to do with the structure of the market and its distributive or redistributive impact on society.

Second, at the same time—thanks especially to the prior work, from the 1940s to 1960s, of a small but brilliant group of pioneering scholars, including Paul Wallace Gates, Willard Hurst, Oscar Handlin and Mary Handlin, Milton Heath, and Carter Goodrich—there has been a distinct renaissance of interest among historians in what has become known as "legal-economic history." Historians of law who formerly were interested primarily (or exclusively) in the doctrinal issues of constitutional history have now become concerned with understanding the social and economic functions of law, with legal process, and with such issues as the definition of rights, the centralization of power in the federal system, the allocative effects of law, the relationship of law to technological development, and the identification of "winners and losers" in the dynamics of legal and economic change. The refreshing rediscovery by economists that policy and institutions do matter after all, and the parallel renaissance of interest among historians in legal systems and process conceived more broadly than as a subject bounded by judicial doctrine, hold out the prospect of a convergence and reintegration of the field of economic history with mainstream interpretive concerns of historians.

It is an interesting commentary on how far this convergence of interests and reintegration have gone already that this book—and also related articles of mine, published after *Ohio Canal Era* appeared—are as often characterized in review essays and literature surveys as examples of "legal history" as they are characterized as "economic history." The province of legal history has become so broad today that it is hard indeed to discern the conceptual line that distinguishes it from "governmental history" writ in its largest dimensions.

If *Ohio Canal Era* has something to contribute, after the passage of some years, to this emergent reintegration of scholarship on government and the economy, I hope it will be found in two of the book's conceptual features. The first is the effort that was made to systematically relate public enterprise, law, and institutional change to the economy—not stopping with theoretical conjectures about impacts, or with statistical data, but going on to tracing relationships through the study of archival correspondence, business records, the local press, and other contemporary evidence bearing on impacts.

The second feature of the book germane to continuing studies is the attempt that was made to probe deeply into the history—social, political, economic, and legal—of substate regions and communities. This was undertaken as a way of checking generalizations, testing hypotheses about institutions and the dynamics of economic relationships, and painting in more vivid colors than would otherwise be possible on the canvas of historical reconstruction. As I proceeded with the research and shaped the analysis for *Ohio Canal Era*, over many years, I reached a point at which rarely did I encounter in manuscript or printed sources any unfamiliar names in the records of activity of entrepreneurs, political leaders, major landowners, or public officials. Similarly, the geography, developmental history, and local problematics of economic development or business enterprise had become familiar subjects for certainly every county, and probably every major town or rural farm region, in the state over four decades' time. Other subjects that figured in this history—the technology of canal design and contemporary concerns in hydraulic engineering, New York and London bankers and their firms, canal forwarding companies and agents, state engineers, the proprietors of mills, and the river merchants—became equally familiar.

All this is said not in a spirit of self-congratulation but only to suggest that whatever success in analysis this book may represent stands largely on that sort of intimate familiarity with institutional nuances, personalities, networks of kinship and influence, and geographical idiosyncracies. Without it, it would have been unlikely that the research would have opened windows into such developments as the uses and subsidy effects of the eminent domain power in law; the administrative allocation of markets through the setting of canal tolls on a purposefully discriminatory basis, in blatant (and unchallenged) violation of the Commerce Clause doctrines of the Marshall Court; the importance of waterpower facilities associated with canal construction and water-supply in shaping the location of manufacturing; the many faces of the competition between railroads and canals in the 1850s; or the ways in which entrepreneurial experience and influence carried over, and overlapped, between the public and private sectors. Whether the results, in the case of this book, warranted the effort is something the reader will judge; but as a matter of methodology in historical research, I think the results of this sort of research approach are worth striving for as an ideal. It is, I am certain, an indispensable element of what gives such enduring importance to books such as the studies by Willard Hurst on the Wisconsin lumber industry, Stephen Salsbury on the Massachusetts railroad policy, or Paul Wallace Gates on antebellum land policy and agriculture.

This book did not represent a methodological or conceptual breakthrough at its appearance. For as Hugh Aitken, an extraordinarily learned scholar of the North American economy, wrote in his review in *Business History Review* 44 (1970) when the work first appeared, *Ohio Canal Era* should properly be appraised as a study that built systematically on the contributions of others—an extension of earlier studies of antebellum government and the economy that comprised a "remarkable example of the cumulative buildup of historical knowledge." I hope that I may have extended in a persuasive and useful way the conceptual terms and boundaries of that literature, in addition to contributing toward an understanding of federalism as a working system, of state government as an actor in the economy, and, above all, of the wholeness of patterns of economic change in those years of hectic development.

I am especially pleased and grateful to the Ohio University Press that publication of this reissue edition comes in what is not only the nation's constitutional bicentennial but also the two hundredth year of the Northwest Ordinance—the great document that established a basic part of the legal framework for the historical developments recounted here.

HARRY N. SCHEIBER

The University of California
Berkeley, April, 1987

Bibliographic Note, 1987

The methodological issues and controversies of the 1970s in American economic history are discussed in Stephen Salsbury, "Economic History Then and Now," *Agricultural History 53* (1979). A perceptive analysis and overview, written when division in the field was nearly at its height, was provided by James Soltow, "American Institutional Studies: Present Knowledge and Past Trends," *Journal of Economic History 31* (1971). See also Stephen Salsbury and Harry N. Scheiber, "Reflections on George Rogers Taylor's *The Transportation Revolution,*" *Business History Review 51* (1977); and, for more recent analysis, see Scheiber, "Regulation, Property Rights, and Definition of 'The Market,' " *Journal of Economic History 41* (1981).

The emergence of legal-economic history and linkages (and reintegration) with economic history are treated in Donald Pisani, "Promotion and Regulation: The Constitution and the American Economy," *Journal of American History* (1987, in press); Scheiber, "At the Borderlands of Law and Economic History," *American Historical Review*

75 (1970); and Willard Hurst, "Old and New Dimensions of Research in U.S. Legal History," *American Journal of Legal History 23* (1979). The full scope of the new legal history, embracing social and economic change as well as positive government in the large, is illustrated in two major scholarly works in the new genre: Lawrence M. Friedman, *A History of American Law* (2nd edition, New York: Simon and Schuster, 1986); and Willard Hurst, *Law and Social Order in the United States* (Ithaca, N.Y.: Cornell University Press, 1977).

Since the original publication of this book, a number of studies have appeared that concern public enterprise, canal and railroad transport, and early nineteenth-century economic change in the West. They include two books on Old Northwest canal projects: Paul Fatout, *Indiana Canals* (Purdue University Studies; West Lafayette, Ind., 1972); and John N. Dickinson, *To Build a Canal: Sault Ste. Marie, 1853–54 and After* (Columbus: Ohio State University Press, 1981). A narrative history with abundant material in detail on Ohio and Old Northwest railroads is John F. Stover, *Iron Road to the West: American Railroads in the 1850s* (New York: Columbia University Press, 1978). Other transport studies include my own, "The Transportation Revolution: Urban Dimensions," in *Towards an Urban Ohio*, ed. John Wunder (Columbus: Ohio Historical Society, 1977); and articles by Ralph D. Gray, Ronald Shaw, and myself in the symposium volume *Transportation and the Early Nation* (Indiana Historical Society, 1981).

The persistence of the flatboat traffic and its contributions to antebellum regional development are treated in the quantitative study by Erik F. Haites, James Mak, and Gary M. Walton, *Western River Transportation: The Era of Internal Development, 1810–1860* (Baltimore: The Johns Hopkins University Press, 1975). Trends in volume and composition of river commerce, and also the flatboat trade's business structure and practices are the main themes of my essay, "The Ohio-Mississippi Flatboat Trade," *The Frontier in American Development: Essays in Honor of Paul Wallace Gates*, ed. David M. Ellis (Ithaca, N.Y.: Cornell University Press, 1969). Richard T. Farrell, "Internal Improvement Projects in Southwestern Ohio, 1815–34," *Ohio History* 80 (1971), fills in some interesting detail on the history of promotional efforts in the region centering on Cincinnati.

On general economic history of the West, important new publications include the essays by the distinguished economic historians Robert Gallman and William N. Parker, and others, in *Essays in Nineteenth-Century Economic History: The Old Northwest* (Athens: Ohio University Press, 1975); and the collection of articles by the leading student of agrarian history in Ohio, Robert L. Jones, *History of Agriculture in Ohio to 1880* (Kent, Ohio: Kent State University Press, 1983).

My own writings pursuing various themes from this book include "Federalism and the American Economic Order, 1789–1910," *Law and Society Review 10* (1975); and "Xenophobia and Parochialism in the History of American Legal Process," *William and Mary Law Review 23* (1982), exploring aspects of federalism and state policy. Also, two studies that deal on a small canvas with topics derived directly from this book are "The Pennsylvania and Ohio Canal: Transport Innovation, Mixed Enterprise, and Urban Commercial Rivalry," *Old Northwest 6* (1980), examining the history of a "mixed enterprise" corporation, a type of firm much neglected in the literature although important in many states before 1860; and "Public Canal Finance and State Banking in Ohio, 1825–1837," *Indiana Magazine of History 65* (1969), exploring the subject of linkages between banking and the public transport enterprise, as suggested by Nathan Miller's earlier study of New York State's management of Erie Canal funds. In "Land Reform, Speculation, and Governmental Failure: The Administration of Ohio's State Canal Lands, 1836–60," *Prologue: The Journal of the National Archives 7* (1975), I have considered the rather dismaying history of state land administration and its consequences for settlement and state finances; the record, as to both efficiency and vision, is in very stark contrast to that of the canal commissioners and the fund managers in the period before 1837.

"Alfred Kelley and the Ohio Business Elite," *Ohio History 87* (1978), was the Ohio Canal Sesquicentennial Lecture given in Cleveland, on an occasion memorable for the author because it involved a nostalgic journey through the oldest sections of the Ohio Canal dams and locks preserved in a then newly opened national park. In "Patterns of Public Enterprise: Government Intervention and the American Economy, 1790–*1986*," *Annali di Storia Dell'Impressa* (Italy, 1987, in press); "Doctrinal Legacies and Institutional Innovation: Law and Economy in American History," *Law in Context 2* (1984); and, earlier,

"Government and the Economy," *Journal of Interdisciplinary History* 3 (1972); and "Public Economic Policy and the American Legal System," *Wisconsin Law Review* (1980), I have tried to relate issues of government and economy to larger concerns in American legal and economic history.

Bibliographic Note, 2012

OHIO'S PLANNING, construction, and operation of a major public transportation system constituted one of antebellum America's most compelling examples of boldly interventionist state-level public policy, resulting in a far-reaching impact on the national economy as well as on the state's own economic development. Recent scholarly writings—discussed below—have analyzed a broad range of intriguing variations, from one state or region of the country to another, in the style of public economic policies and their implementation. Taken as a whole, these studies comprise a robust challenge to the odd (but politically potent) survival in current-day political debates of the "laissez-faire myth." This amazingly durable myth is supportive of its champions' antigovernmental ideology, expressing the view that nineteenth-century economic growth was the product of market forces unimpeded by any meaningful state intervention. As such, that myth embodies a serious misreading of the nation's constitutional tradition (which in fact gave doctrinal support to regulatory and other interventions), and equally it is a distortion of the forces that shaped America's economic development and institutions.

In *Ohio Canal Era,* as is true generally in the rich literature of legal-economic history in the states, historic antecedents and continuities are identified that provide a much more complex portrayal of both the policy history and the impact of state activism on patterns of economic change. Moreover, state-level policies functioned in a dynamic interaction with the national government's interventionist policies, the most notable being protective industrial tariffs, banking services and regulation, maintenance of labor force growth through open immigration, use of the U.S. Army Corps of Engineers for surveys and for river and harbor improvements, and deployment of public lands to subsidize enterprises (including the canal projects in Ohio) and more generally to shape settlement and development in the West.

An analysis of the major interpretive issues bearing on the legal-economic history of the states' role in development is undertaken in my essay "Economic Liberty and the Modern State" in *The State and Freedom of Contract,* edited by Harry N. Scheiber (Stanford: Stanford University Press, 1998). The more comprehensive history of legal change in relation to social and political development has been delineated persuasively in the many uniquely original writings of James Willard Hurst, of which his book *Law and Social Order in the United States* (Ithaca: Cornell University Press, 1977) requires reiterated mention here. Valuable insights as to the roles of government in the antebellum era are also abundantly present in the classic work by Lawrence M. Friedman, *A History of American Law* (3rd edition, New York: Simon and Schuster, 2005). Scheiber, "Private Rights and Public Power: American Law, Capitalism, and the Republican Polity in Nineteenth-Century America," *Yale Law Journal* 107 (1997), discusses the character and limits of another important aspect of intervention, the regulatory power, and comments on the scholarly literature, in particular William J. Novak's book, *The People's Welfare: Law and Regulation in Nineteenth-Century America* (Chapel Hill: University of North Carolina Press, 1996). Charles Sellers, *The Market Revolution: Jacksonian America, 1815–1846* (New York: Oxford University Press, 1991), is a broad-ranging work not specifically concerned with either the Old Northwest region or the public transport enterprises, yet it is valuable for its provocative portrayal of deep changes in political culture and popular moral sensibilities in the canal era.

Several important, specialized research studies have been published since the previous edition of *Ohio Canal Era* appeared. In the recent literature of legal-economic history, a work of unique importance is Tony A. Freyer's *Producers versus Capitalists: Constitutional Conflict in Antebellum America* (Charlottesville: University Press of Virginia, 1994). This work analyzes public policies and legal change on a foundation of carefully crafted comparative analysis of the record in four states: Delaware, New Jersey, Maryland, and Pennsylvania. Significant differences in policy outcomes and judicial doctrines are considered, with an emphasis on identifying winners and losers among specific economic interests, and among social groups or classes. Moreover, Freyer systematically integrates key aspects of America's national constitutional development with the substantive history of state policies and patterns of interventionism.

John Majewski, *A House Dividing: Economic Development in Pennsylvania and Virginia before the Civil War* (New York: Cambridge University Press, 2000) similarly employs systematic comparison to demonstrate how divergent local circumstances and differences in state-level politics and economic structure influenced differences in public economic policies. This pioneering work focuses on the policies and the processes of economic change in Cumberland County, Pennsylvania, and Albemarle County, Virginia, providing minute and brilliantly revealing detail that in turn illuminates the differences that emerged in the nature and success (or failure) of state and local policies for development. As happened in Ohio, especially with regard to Cincinnati and its hinterland, in Pennsylvania the dynamic interrelationship of transport expansion, agricultural settlement and production, and the patterns of state and private investment served as an engine for urban-based industrialization. Despite a similar popular enthusiasm in Virginia for policies that would promote economic growth, a congeries of factors, not least the presence of slavery and plantation agriculture, worked against industrialization in that state. Majewski found that the popular support for interventions crossed political lines, enlisting both Jacksonian and Whig factions—a pattern that we have observed also prevailed in Ohio well into the late 1840s.

The author also casts fresh light on how investors and the electorate generally expressed a faith in "commonwealth" ideas supportive of intervention—a question to which I have given attention, from the standpoint of evolving legal doctrines, in "Public Rights and the Rule of Law in American Legal History," *California Law Review* 72 (1984).

L. Ray Gunn, *The Decline of Authority: Public Economic Policy and Political Development in New York State, 1800–1860* (Ithaca: Cornell University Press, 1988) provides an intriguing analysis of what he terms "competing strategies of legitimacy" that were expressed in policy debates as the state underwent a progressive democratization of political life and ideologies. Gunn argues that this democratization process eventually undermined support for government's capacity to pursue autonomous interventionist strategies. Gunn investigates a broad spectrum of specific policy areas in New York, offering a rich empirical matrix for framing comparisons of the legal and cultural environment of enterprise in other states—a challenge that remains to be taken up if we are to have an even fuller picture of the antebellum era.

Ronald E. Shaw, *Canals for a Nation: The Canal Era in the United States, 1790–1860* (Lexington: University Press of Kentucky, 1990) is a welcome addition to the historical literature on the American canal states, offering an excellent survey in depth of the major developments. John L. Larson, *Internal Improvement: National Public Works and the Promise of Popular Government in the Early United States* (Chapel Hill: University of North Carolina Press, 2001) usefully complements Shaw's book and other studies of state policy. Larson focuses exclusively on the early decades of the Republic and offers insights on the promotional ideology and politics that were mobilized to support national projects. Thus Larson expands on themes explored in valuable earlier studies by Ralph D. Gray and Carter Goodrich.

An insightful thesis on how the federal structure of governance and political culture influenced comparative patterns of railroad development—and in a larger sense influenced industrialization—is presented in Colleen A. Dunlavy, *Politics and Industrialization: Early Railroads in the United States and Prussia* (Princeton: Princeton University Press, 1994). For one region of Ohio, Matthew Bloom, "Creating Connections: Economic Development, and Use, and the System of Cities in Northwest Ohio during the Nineteenth Century" (Ph.D. dissertation, Bowling Green State University, 2009) advances significantly our knowledge of state chartering and local government assistance to transport projects in Toledo and Lucas County, taking the story of regional transportation and urban-industrial development down to the modern period. H. Roger Grant, *Ohio on the Move: Transportation in the Buckeye State* (Athens: Ohio University Press, 2000) is a popular history that includes a brief chapter on the canal era.

Cultural and art historians have written on how canals reflected the aspirations and values of an earlier age. Their interest is manifested in two fine books dedicated to images of the Ohio canals: Frank Nelson Wilcox, *The Ohio Canals: A Pictorial Survey* (Kent, Ohio: Kent State University Press, 1969), a book of drawings and paintings; and Jack Gieck, *A Photo Album of Ohio's Canal Era, 1825–1913* (revised edition, Kent, Ohio: Kent State University Press, 1992). The latter study complements *Ohio Canal Era* in bringing to light photographs that portray the post–Civil

War period of decline for the canals. New essays on the subject are collected in *Canal Fever: The Ohio & Erie Canal from Waterway to Canalway,* edited by Lynn Metzger and Peg Bobel (Kent, Ohio: Kent State University Press, 2009).

Concerned principally with cultural and social history, emphasizing New Yorkers' ideas of progress associated with internal improvements, is Carol Sheriff, *The Artificial River: The Erie Canal and the Paradox of Progress, 1817–1862* (New York: Hill and Wang, 1996). Several themes that will be familiar to readers of *Ohio Canal Era,* such as the issues raised by eminent domain takings, are explored in a fresh way in the New York context. Sheriff also provides illuminating discussion of laborers on the canals and the cultural impact on local communities of canal building and operations. Kim M. Gruenwald, *River of Enterprise: The Commercial Origins of Regional Identity in the Ohio Valley, 1790–1850* (Bloomington: Indiana University Press, 2002) is a valuable study of the Ohio River trade's structure both before and during the canal era. Gruenwald puts together from business archives and other sources a detailed reconstruction of the web of business firms and personal entrepreneurial connections that sustained the trade and linked to the trade network on the canal lines.

The broader question of Old Northwest regionalism has attracted the attention of historians in recent years, reviving a theme once central in the historiography of Ohio and of the early nineteenth century as exemplified in the classic work of R. Carlyle Buley and of Beverley W. Bond, Jr., and in a different way the influential contributions of Frederick Jackson Turner. Among recent works on this subject, not specifically concerned with transport development or state enterprise yet useful for understanding vital aspects of temporal and geographic contexts, are Malcolm J. Rohrbough, *The Trans-Appalachian Frontier: People, Societies, and Institutions, 1775–1850* (1978; 3rd edition, Bloomington: Indiana University Press, 2008), an ambitious history that has had a seminal influence on the revival of Old Northwest regionalism studies; David A. Hamer, *New Towns in the New World: Images and Perceptions of the Nineteenth-Century Urban Frontier* (New York: Columbia University Press, 1990); and Andrew R. L. Cayton and Peter S. Onuf, *The Midwest and the Nation: Rethinking the History of an American Region* (Bloomington: Indiana University Press, 1990), with detailed critical commentary on the historical literature.

Andrew R. L. Cayton, *Ohio: The History of a People* (Columbus: Ohio State University Press, 2002), and George W. Knepper, *Ohio and Its People* (3rd edition, Kent, Ohio: Kent State University Press, 2003) are brief survey histories that incorporate findings from recent scholarship. Even after the passage of so many years since its publication, the monumental series *The History of the State of Ohio,* edited by Carl Wittke, requires special notice. Three books in that series deal with periods that embraced the canal era: William T. Utter, *The Frontier State, 1803–1825* (Columbus: Ohio Historical Society, 1943); Francis Weisenburger, *The Passing of the Frontier, 1825–1850* (Columbus: Ohio Historical Society, 1941); and Eugene H. Roseboom, *The Civil War Era, 1850–1873* (Columbus: Ohio Historical Society, 1944). Few studies of American state and local history have stood the test of time as well as they, and all three remain an indispensable source.

PART I

THE STATE ENTERPRISE

1820-1850

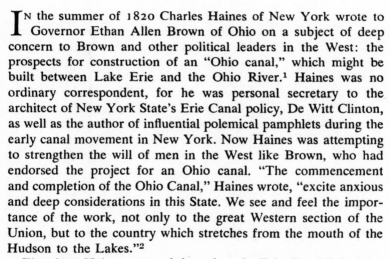

IN the summer of 1820 Charles Haines of New York wrote to Governor Ethan Allen Brown of Ohio on a subject of deep concern to Brown and other political leaders in the West: the prospects for construction of an "Ohio canal," which might be built between Lake Erie and the Ohio River.[1] Haines was no ordinary correspondent, for he was personal secretary to the architect of New York State's Erie Canal policy, De Witt Clinton, as well as the author of influential polemical pamphlets during the early canal movement in New York. Now Haines was attempting to strengthen the will of men in the West like Brown, who had endorsed the project for an Ohio canal. "The commencement and completion of the Ohio Canal," Haines wrote, "excite anxious and deep considerations in this State. We see and feel the importance of the work, not only to the great Western section of the Union, but to the country which stretches from the mouth of the Hudson to the Lakes."[2]

Elsewhere Haines asserted that when the Erie Canal linked the Hudson's waters with Lake Erie at Buffalo, it would "unite the two most populous and powerful sections of the nation, and form one of the strongest safeguards of the union, that either state or national policy is capable of devising."[3] An Ohio canal, Haines said to Brown, would be "a continuation" of the Erie Canal "into the heart of a fertile territory, capable of sustaining from ten to fifteen millions of people. . . . When Ohio resolves to make her Canal from the Lakes to the Ohio River, and is willing to pledge her credit for the means of accomplishing the undertaking, it will be done."[4]

But could it be done? The question was hardly new to Ethan Allen Brown; for like Haines, he had long pondered the prospects of such an enterprise.[5] A Lake Erie-to-Ohio River canal, he thought, would provide a vital link in the chain of communications that might bring America to the threshold of a new age. Such a canal would end the West's isolation from the states on the Atlantic Coast; no longer would the nation be fragmented, as it was in 1820 despite the nationalistic sentiments that the War of 1812 rekindled. In more immediate terms, Brown hoped that a canal connecting the Ohio Valley with the Great Lakes and the Erie Canal (which was then under construction) would permit Ohio's farmers to realize cash profits on exports of their surplus crops to the East—something they had been unable to do for more than a year because of the banking panic of 1819 and the depression that had paralyzed the West's commerce ever since.

As he prepared a reply to Haines, however, Brown's sense of the harsh realities overcame the optimism born of a vision. He found the strength of private enterprise crushed in his state, he wrote; and the public revenues were strained by a depression that had cut into the already slender tax base. "The aspect of affairs," he concluded, remained "rather gloomy." He could not see the means: "We are compelled to view the accomplishment, and even the commencement, of the Ohio Canal, as more remote than our more sanguine wishes had once imagined it to be."[6]

It must have come hard for Brown to admit this fact since from the mid-1790's—when the Federal government crushed the Indian menace in the West and made its policy for disposal of the public lands attractive to migrants seeking farms—up to 1819 the record of economic growth in his state had been spectacular. The Anglo-French wars after 1793, and then the War of 1812, had resulted in inflation of food prices in world markets; and consequently the West had exported its flour, cured meats, whiskey, and grain by way of New Orleans to the Atlantic coast, to Europe, and to the Indies. When war ended in 1815, crop failures delayed Europe's recovery, and food shortages continued. At home there was a boom, fed by reckless expansion of bank credit and land hunger that drove men westward. "The tide of emigration, which had been restrained by the war," wrote an early historian of the state, "now poured into Ohio. Speculation, stimulated by every incentive, ran into wild and extravagant excesses."[7] By 1820 the population of Ohio was nearly 600,000. The principal concentrations of settlement were all in the Ohio Valley and in the valleys tributary to the Ohio, in the southern half of the state, where farmers could reach the New Orleans markets by way of flatboats. The northern half of Ohio, where streams flowed down to Lake Erie and did not offer access to a cash market, remained only sparsely settled. Even so, the pace of development was swift: between 1815 and 1819 banking credit in Ohio expanded rapidly, and urban and rural real-estate prices spiraled upward. Growth seemed to be a permanent condition.[8]

But it could not continue. When the nationwide financial panic struck in 1819, Ohio's banks were virtually wiped out. During the business depression that ensued, western prices fell precipitously. Sales of public lands in Ohio ceased, and men who had bought large tracts on speculation or small farms as homesteads from the Federal government on credit now faced loss of their property. "Farming yields no profit," Governor Brown wrote. "Money is very scarce, and will continue so until our debts abroad are paid."[9] Merchants in Ohio had bought large quantities of manufactured goods from the East and Europe on credit, waiting until the next year's crop was sold to obtain the means for payment. But the price collapse in 1819 rendered "the next year's crop" practically worthless: although the land continued to produce abundantly, it was impossible to ship produce down the long river route to New Orleans, then to the East or foreign markets, and still make a profit. "The failure of our merchants to meet their payments to their correspondents in the Eastern cities and New Orleans," one Cincinnati observer declared, "put an entire stop to all commercial intercourse between the Eastern and Western countries that is not based upon a cash foundation."[10] The river wharves fell quiet. The factories in western towns ceased working, as an entire generation of Ohio industrial entrepreneurs was caught in "one general ruin."[11] The general mood of despair was reflected in Brown's poignant reply to Charles Haines, that the means were simply not available to finance the canal project that he believed could end the economic crisis in Ohio and the West.

NOTES

1. Charles Haines to Brown, Aug. 4, 1820, Ethan Allen Brown Papers, OSL.
2. *Ibid.* On Haines' role in New York canal politics, see Ronald E. Shaw, *Erie Water West: A History of the Erie Canal* (Lexington, Ky., 1966), 402 *et passim.*
3. Haines, ed., *Public Documents relating to the New-York Canals* (New York, 1821), x *et seq.*
4. Haines to Brown, Aug. 4, 1820.
5. Brown's early role in the Ohio canal movement is treated in Chapter 1, *infra.*
6. Brown to Haines (draft copy), Sept. 20, 1820, Brown Papers, OSL.
7. Salmon P. Chase, *Sketch of the History of Ohio* (Cincinnati, 1833), 34. William T. Utter, *The Frontier State* (Columbus, 1942) treats fully the question of economic growth in Ohio from 1803 to 1825. On the heavy migration from the East after 1815 (which contemporaries termed the "Ohio fever"), see Lewis D. Stilwell, *Migration from Vermont* (Montpelier, 1948), 128–136.
8. See Richard C. Wade, *The Urban Frontier* (Cambridge, 1959), 162ff. Not all the war-nurtured manufacturing industries survived after 1815. For a comment on some that did not, see "The Mississippi Valley in 1816 through an Englishman's Diary," ed. O. L. Schmidt, *MVHR*, XIV (Sept. 1927), 149.
9. Brown to Jonathan Dayton, Feb. 4, 1821, Ethan Allen Brown Papers, OHS. A Chillicothe speculator wrote that he could not compute the value of his extensive lands "as there is no money in the country to purchase it." (Amasa Delano to Jabez Hammond, Dec. 6, 1820, Delano Family Papers, Dartmouth College Library.)
10. "A New Englander's Impressions of Cincinnati in 1820," ed. R. R. Wulsin, *Bulletin of the Hist. and Phil. Society of Ohio,* VI (1949), 121.
11. Quoted in Wade, *Urban Frontier,* 59.

CHAPTER I

Toward a Canal Policy
1820-1825

WHEN the 1819 panic first struck, many in Ohio blamed the banks for the crisis, and they were taken by surprise when the depression continued into 1821 and then 1822. But the crucial problem of the West was in fact not banking but transportation. For only improved transport facilities could provide what one Cincinnati editor correctly perceived as the solution: "a steady and adequate market for produce."[1] Two decades of inflated wartime prices had obscured the more fundamental difficulties which threatened to retard long-term economic growth in the West. As Ohio's political leadership came to recognize this fact, men like Ethan Allen Brown gave more sustained attention to the prospects of improving transportation, and especially to the project for a canal between Lake Erie and the Ohio River.[2]

It came naturally enough to seek government action in a crisis of this kind. Much as *laisser-faire* ideas may have been debated and occasionally exalted in the early nineteenth century, Americans were well accustomed to using their state governments to remove bottlenecks that hindered economic growth.[3] Ohio was no exception, and evidence of a positive attitude toward state intervention in the economy abounded in the statute books. Even before Ohio's admission to the Union in 1803, the territorial legislature of the Old Northwest had asserted commonwealth interests in important areas of economic life. Some territorial laws had been designed to regulate enterprises deemed essential to the prosperity of agriculture, as for instance a statute of 1799 that required millers to keep on hand standard measures of volume and specified the rates a miller might charge. After 1803 the state's legislature set bounties on the hides of wolves, to aid in protecting livestock; it permitted municipal governments to regulate local markets and required them to oversee the fencing of livestock; it required construction of locks at private dam sites on navigable streams; and it brought order into the terms of commerce by instituting standard weights and measures. Perhaps the most far-reaching measure of early economic policy was a banking law of 1816, designed both to assert state power over bank operations and to enhance the public revenues. The law required newly chartered banks to issue a portion of their capital stock to the state, and thereby assured the state a proportion of any profits.[4]

But the most sustained attention was given to the problem of transportation: the Ohio legislature provided for financing of local roads, regulated bridges and ferries, issued charters to private companies for turnpikes and other facilities, permitted river-improvement and bridge companies to run lotteries, granted local governments the right to exercise eminent domain for road construction, and required two days of labor on the public roads from able-bodied males over age 21, or else commutation of the road service at one dollar per day. Nevertheless, this wide range of policies did not yield much in tangible benefits. The key problem was lack of capital. The total tax revenues of the state government itself amounted to $200,000 annually during the decade before 1820; and since most of this was required to support general-purpose government, little was left to finance roads and other transport improvements. Moreover, the private companies that were granted charters to build turnpikes, bridges, and other facilities faced the problem of deficient capital. As a result, few of them built at all, and those that did could seldom maintain their works in good repair. Nearly all the money expended on public road construction came from the Three Per Cent Fund—obtained from the Federal government under terms of the statehood compact, which had provided for 3 per cent of the proceeds of public land sales in Ohio to be paid to the state—and in all this fund amounted to only $170,000 up to 1815.[5]

Even the Three Per Cent Fund did not lead to the construction of major highways. For each year the legislature parceled out the money to each county, never concentrating funds on a few major highways, never adopting an overall statewide road plan, never establishing priorities. Thus the fund was dissipated. And the process whereby this had occurred gave vivid evidence of the power of localism in Ohio state politics: in every session of the legislature, each member struggled to increase his local district's share of the state revenues. His constituents expected it of him, and the fact that the state revenues were so limited intensified the rivalry over appropriations.[6]

With so many obstacles to transportation improvement, the settlers in Ohio remained dependent mainly upon the navigable rivers and streams. Most of the population before 1820 therefore clustered along the Ohio River and in the valleys of streams tributary to the Ohio, where farmers could reach an outside cash market by way of the Ohio and Mississippi rivers.[7] So long as prices had held up under unusual wartime conditions, there had been profits in shipping downriver to New Orleans. But even before 1819, when prices finally collapsed, the rivers and the New Orleans route had burdened western commerce with severe problems. The state's surplus farm produce was shipped southward almost exclusively by flatboats prior to 1820. Farmers and small country merchants built their own flatboats, 30 to 90 feet long and 12 to 25 feet wide. As a rule of thumb, they figured a cost of a dollar per foot for the lumber, and when the boat reached its downriver destination it was broken up and the wood sold for 25 to 75 cents a foot, depending on local market conditions.[8] Nearly every young man in the villages of early Ohio went downriver at least once in his teens, either as a deckhand on the family boat or as a paid hand—earning perhaps fifty dollars for the trip—on a neighbor's craft. Thousands of these boats went downriver each year, and hundreds were lost on snags, bars, or ice floes; others overturned while attempting to run the treacherous falls of the Ohio near Louisville; a few "disappeared" when hired hands sold the cargo for their employer and made off with the proceeds.[9] If he was fortunate and made it safely to the lower Mississippi's waters, the boatman had to contend with the climate, for the heat and humidity subjected foodstuffs to rapid spoilage. New Orleans itself was an uncertain market in any case. Its warehouse and port accommodations were inadequate, and because all the West's produce came downriver on the same freshets, market gluts were the common condition. Shipping service to New Orleans was erratic, so that the gluts were aggravated by frequent lack of cargo space for export to Atlantic or overseas markets. Even if the boatman could dispose profitably of his produce at New Orleans (or possibly at one of the towns or plantations upriver from the port city), and could recapture some of his investment by selling the boat for lumber, he still faced the arduous task of making his way back home up the Mississippi Valley. Few could afford steamboat passage, which became available on a regular basis after 1817, and the overland journey required traveling through swampy regions that harbored brigands and where malaria was an ever present danger. Some returned to Ohio via Baltimore, Philadelphia, or New York; this was especially true of the merchants, who bought their goods for the next season in the East and then went overland across the mountains, returning home three months or so after their departure for New Orleans.[10]

The upriver trade, which brought eastern dry goods and manufactures, southern cotton and hemp, and other products north to the commercial cities of Ohio, was even more expensive and difficult. Keelboats, driven by long poles, operated regularly on the upriver route, and by 1820 the steamboats were being used more frequently for high-value merchandise. Yet the costs of transportation remained high, and in towns like Cincinnati the buying power of the dollar for purchase of merchandise from the East or South was small indeed.[11] A flow of goods came overland through the Appalachians: the National Road to Wheeling was opened in 1818, and by 1820 a Pennsylvania turnpike from Philadelphia to Pittsburgh was carrying wagon traffic between the seaboard and the West. But again the costs of transportation remained high.[12] The new roads made emigration easier and did permit some high-value western products, mainly furs, hides, and whiskey, to be sent eastward by wagon. But the only sizable western export sent to market by the roads was livestock on the hoof. Cattle drives from the Scioto Valley and eastern Ohio to Philadelphia produced some spectacular individual fortunes in Ohio, yet they involved costs and risks that ruined many men in the trade. For the export of the principal western staples—meat, flour, and grain—the region remained dependent on the rivers and New Orleans. Except for its contributions through the Three Per Cent Fund and the National Road (built with funds realized from the proceeds of land sales, and not by direct appropriations), and through construction of postal roads and military highways, the Federal government contributed little to the solution of western transportation problems. Ohio in 1820, as before, remained dependent on its own resources.[13]

For the business leaders and state politicians who hoped to see internal improvements built in Ohio, the political conditions in 1820 were not much more promising than fiscal circumstances. To undertake a major state investment, on the scale of a lake-to-river canal project, meant above all to combat the influence of localism in the legislature. For in every region the citizenry felt a strong attachment to their local interests: they kept up unremitting pressure for state appropriations that would benefit their own districts, and they viewed with jealousy any projects designed to benefit other areas of the state.

Among the principal regions of the state, the Miami country, north of Cincinnati, was the most populous and wealthy. By 1820 more than 100,000 settlers lived there, the farmers working rich land that produced each year perhaps 250,000 bushels of wheat in addition to nearly 500,000 bushels of corn (fed to hogs) and a considerable quantity of other grains. The focus of the Miami Valley's commerce was Cincinnati, which with its population of 7,000 was already one of the largest cities west of the Appalachians. It was the site of "about 1,500 buildings, most of which are of brick," one traveler wrote. It boasted "a large and stately court-house, brick and framed churches, . . . three brick market-houses, an elegant Lancasterian Seminary," and factories manufacturing textiles, furniture, meat, candles, and a score of other products.[14] The townspeople were mainly concerned with improving the Ohio River, to perfect their communications with the south. When the idea of a lake-to-river canal within Ohio was presented in Governor Brown's administration, the Cincinnatians appeared, on the whole, quite ready to subordinate the

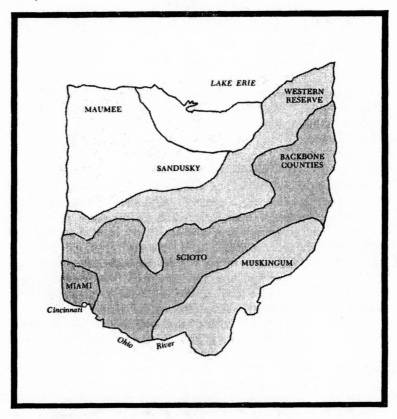

DISTRIBUTION OF OHIO POPULATION, 1820
(Major regions of the state are shown.)

Less than 2 per square mile   18 to 45 per square mile

2 to 6 per square mile   45 to 90 per square mile

6 to 18 per square mile

Source: *Twelfth Census of the U.S. (1900):* Statistical Atlas, plate 2.

Map 1-A

entire question and use state funds to build instead a Falls Canal near Louisville.[15]

A second major center of settlement was the Scioto Valley, along a major tributary of the Ohio River upstream from Cincinnati. To this area in south-central Ohio had come southern uplanders, planters, and a sprinkling of Yankees and Pennsylvanians. They produced wheat, corn, and livestock, and although they undertook direct trade in livestock with the east, they relied almost exclusively on the rivers for their export of flour, whiskey, corn meal, and other products. In the Scioto country, settlers were concerned chiefly with improvement of the Ohio River, with the development of communications between central Ohio and the river, and with local roads.[16]

On the thinly settled Lake Erie shore the tiny villages vied with one another for harbor improvements, designation as Federal customs ports, and state appropriations for roads to the interior. In eastern Ohio, beyond the Pennsylvania boundary, was the "backbone district" of the state with many settlers from Pennsylvania. They were heavily engaged in the commercial production of wheat. Their principal interest was to gain access to Baltimore by the way of that city's Chesapeake & Ohio Canal Company project, with prospects for extending the National Road westward into Ohio, and with manifold projects for local roads.[17]

Everywhere in the state, however, a striking characteristic of the society was "the extraordinary animation with which the people . . . flung themselves into political activity," and especially the consistency with which they pursued local and regional ambitions through the medium of politics.[18] It was indeed a society of expectant capitalists, and men in each region seemed to assume that their own communities would grow and prosper only if they could steal a march upon rival communities. Development was regarded as a race, a desperate struggle. And this was understandable enough. For in the early phase of growth, wilderness areas were first being settled, new towns were being laid out, and the region as a whole was starved for capital. Investment by an eastern capitalist in one town or region seemed to be at the expense of another; every new family that settled elsewhere was regarded as one lost to its rivals; the growth of commerce or manufacturing at one center seemed a threat to similar growth elsewhere.

In the Federalist and early Jeffersonian years, Ohioans had enlivened their politics with the pursuit of ideological and national-party aims, but when the spirit of national partisan conflict waned after 1815, the spirit of localism gained new force in the state. It was in this political milieu, in which every policy proposal in the legislature must be put in the crucible of localism, that the transportation problem would have to be debated.

Because localism militated against orderly planning in the allocation of state resources, to fashion a solution to the transportation problem of the commonwealth required astute political statesmanship. The first man to approach it was Thomas Worthington, elected governor in 1814. Worthington was one of the wealthiest men in the state, a planter and merchant who built a local business complex of his farming and commercial activities at Chillicothe, the seat of economic life in the Scioto Valley. A Virginian who had helped lead the Jeffersonian struggle against the Federalist political establishment in territorial days, Worthington had served with distinction in Congress before his election as governor, and in Washington he had become one of the foremost spokesmen for Federally supported internal improvements in the West.[19]

As governor, Worthington urged that Ohio improve her roads and highways systematically, giving priority to the strategic commercial routes used most heavily to export farm products, instead of dissipating the public's limited resources on a multitude of local roads. Although he failed to reform the legislature's view of road policy, he did make a major contribution by his continual reiteration that a comprehensive state transportation policy was crucial to Ohio's economic future. He did not, however, confine himself to the question of roads. For when the New York State assembly first discussed De Witt Clinton's Erie Canal plan, Worthington urged the Ohio legislature to contribute financial support. Considering the difficulties that Ohio then faced in financing even a limited road program, it was unrealistic to expect appropriations in aid of a New York canal; and the Ohio legislature responded only with a public-spirited resolution wishing New York well. But at least Worthington had given public exposure to the Erie Canal idea, and in the process he publicized the potential economic benefits of the New York project for Ohio and the West.[20]

Worthington's successor as governor was Ethan Allen Brown, who took up the cause of internal improvements soon after his election in 1818. No less than Worthington, Governor Brown understood that the Erie Canal would open a trade route of great significance to Ohio, and in his first message to the legislature Brown asserted that Ohio should build its own canal to link the Ohio River and Lake Erie. Thereby the densely settled regions, in the southern half of the state on streams tributary to the Ohio River, would obtain access to the New York canal. In the legislature, Brown's friends promptly introduced bills providing funds for the necessary engineering surveys. But zealous in their pursuit of local ambitions, the lawmakers burdened the survey appropriation bill with amendments requiring the engineers to include various specified localities and routes when they ran their surveys, and finally the entire proposal was voted down.[21] At a time when the state's revenues were barely sufficient to support a system of poorly maintained local roads, rival local ambitions thus blocked a canal policy for the state as a whole. Individual legislators might recognize the desirability of a lake-to-river canal, but each feared that allocating state resources to such a mammoth project would end all practical hopes of financing local projects of special importance to his own constituents.

Some of those who opposed Brown's plan, however, argued that the Federal government and not the state should finance such large-scale improvements. Others believed that a private company should be chartered to build a lake-to-river canal, a view that Brown deplored both because sufficient private capital probably could not be obtained, and because he felt that so important a project should not be permitted to pass out of public control.[22]

In order to skirt the dual obstacles of fiscal conservatism and localistic rivalries, Brown shifted course in 1819. Instead of emphasizing the canal project, he recommended internal improvements by the state in general terms only. And later, when the legislature itself debated a lake-to-river canal, Brown urged Congress to provide financial aid for its construction. Specifically, he suggested a canal from the Scioto Valley northward to the lake, running through the unsettled Congressional lands between Columbus and the lake shore. Brown proposed that Congress sell Ohio four million acres of land at a low price, so that the state

might sell the land at a profit after the canal was built, thereby
defraying construction costs. Although the legislature appropriated
funds for a canal survey, it made the survey contingent on such a
land grant from Congress. The state's Congressional delegation
worked to obtain a land grant on these principles, but without
success, and the surveys were not conducted.²³ In the 1820–21
session of the Ohio legislature, Brown once again requested appropriations for a survey. But though a bill to accomplish it might
have won approval, friends of the scheme decided not to press
for a vote, fearing that "the murmurs and alarms of a large
minority" might offset any good that a survey would do.²⁴

In his December 1821 message to the legislature, Brown proposed a canal survey for the fourth consecutive year. The assembly this time appointed a special committee to study the question,
selecting Micajah T. Williams of Cincinnati as chairman. As a
journalist and local politician, Williams had long been an ardent
proponent of active state planning of transport improvement.²⁵
His committee's report reflected his conviction that a lake-to-river
canal was the essential prerequisite to economic recovery in Ohio.
It declared that New York's progress on the Erie Canal and the
British record proved that canal construction would be feasible
and would diffuse "wealth, activity and vigor" throughout the
state. The committee strongly urged, too, that the canal be built
as a state enterprise. The record of New York in building its great
canal was cited as "practical refutation of the doctrine which has
so long prevailed, that the public could not accomplish works of
this kind so cheap as a corporation." As for engineering practicability, the report stated that a canal from the Scioto Valley
to the lake, via either the Sandusky River or the Black River,
probably could be supplied with sufficient water. As for financing,
the committee urged an appropriation for surveys; then, once
"scientific inquiry" had determined the precise location and estimated costs, the legislature might decide whether or not the canal
should be built.²⁶

The Williams Committee Report was a public document in the
broadest sense, its arguments being directed as much to the electorate as to the legislature. It catalogued comprehensively both
the direct and indirect benefits that a canal would provide; and

it sought to refute the doubts, especially concerning engineering feasibility and financing, that skeptics had expressed in earlier debates. As expected, the report was given wide attention in the press, and it introduced the canal proposal as a practical and immediate question of state policy.[27] At the same time, however, the report was vague enough to avoid arousing local jealousy. Probably for this reason, the legislature was disposed to take favorable action. In January 1822 a bill was enacted providing for surveys of five possible routes from the Ohio River to Lake Erie. It established a canal commission of seven members to direct the surveys, and authorized the commission to engage an expert civil engineer.[28]

The commissioners appointed by the legislature represented a broad cross-section of the state's commercial and regional interests. Named were Ethan Allen Brown, recently elected to the U. S. Senate; Alfred Kelley of Cleveland, a banker, lawyer, and real estate speculator; former governor Thomas Worthington of Chillicothe; Ebenezer Buckingham, a wealthy merchant and salt manufacturer of Putnam, a town near Zanesville in the Muskingum Valley; Benjamin Tappan of Steubenville, lawyer and former federal judge; Isaac Minor of Madison County in west-central Ohio, also a former member of the judiciary; and Jeremiah Morrow of Warren County in southwest Ohio, farmer and one-time Congressman. All seven had been active in politics and several were members of the legislature. Moreover the broad range of their business activities—in most cases some combination of land speculation, banking, manufacturing, farming, and commerce —gave the commissioners an informed sense of the need for transportation improvement. Although some members of the legislature believed a seven-man commission to be too large, a wide geographical representation had been deemed necessary to allay local jealousies and to "effect the object and get the bill through."[29]

Despite some personal frictions, the commissioners early reached a consensus among themselves that a canal project was indispensable. Instead of being confined to scientific inquiry, therefore, their work took on an increasingly political character. In its private deliberations, the board gave fully as much attention to producing a canal plan that was *politically* realistic as it did to

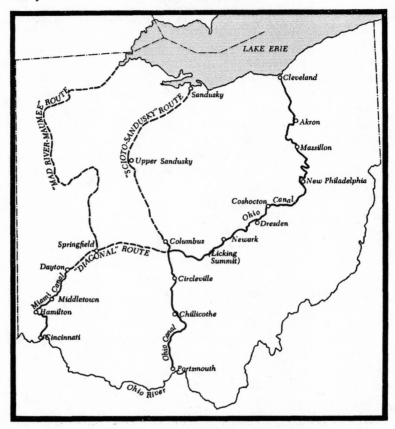

Canal routes surveyed, 1822-25, and approved, 1825

— — — Routes surveyed and considered, 1822-1825

———— Canal routes approved for construction, 1825

NOTE: Preliminary surveys were also conducted for two additional routes between Coshocton and Lake Erie (Ohio Canal route), one to a point east of Cleveland, one to a point west of Cleveland, on the lake. The "Mad River-Maumee" route, a projected extension of the Miami Canal, was a preliminary survey only.

Map 1-B

questions of engineering. Originally the legislature had established the commission to serve as a fact-finding agency. But the commissioners soon assumed a different role: they became actively committed to the goal of producing a politically acceptable canal plan, and they soon began to function as a pressure group, engaging in publicity and lobbying at the state capital on behalf of a specific policy. As such, the canal commission became similar to the private organizations that had developed the initial popular support for canal programs in New York and Pennsylvania. In those states, groups of private citizens had formed to consider transport projects of common concern to various local communities and interest groups; and out of their efforts had come compromise plans for state-financed public works. In Ohio there was no concerted private effort on the part of communities and groups interested in a canal policy. From the beginning, the quest for a politically workable plan was linked with the task of scientific inquiry, and the commission itself was the arena in which local interests were taken into account and molded into a policy for the commonwealth. Because the canal commissioners chose to perform this role, political acumen would be critical to their ultimate success or failure.[30]

THE SURVEYS, 1822–23

One of the board's first decisions in 1822 was agreement that the projected lake-to-river canal should pass through as many settled regions of the state as possible. Toward this end, the commission hoped to prove the practicability of a "diagonal canal." With its southern terminus at Cincinnati it would run north through the Miami Valley, and then cross eastward to the Scioto region; thence turn northward to Lake Erie somewhere near the Muskingum River, with a branch line running from the main trunk to the Ohio River near Steubenville. But this "very grand design" was soon abandoned when initial surveys proved that there was insufficient water to build a line across the southern foothills lying athwart the route between Cincinnati and the Scioto region.[31]

With the cooperation of Governor De Witt Clinton of New York, the Ohio commission engaged James Geddes, a senior engineer on the Erie Canal staff and one of the nation's most prominent engineers.[32] Geddes conducted careful instrument surveys of two routes: one from the Scioto Valley directly northward across the Scioto-Sandusky portage, thence down the Sandusky to the lake; the second, from the Scioto eastward to the upper Muskingum River, and then northward to Lake Erie by way either of Black River or Cuyahoga River. Presenting his findings to the legislature in January 1823 the canal commission urged additional surveys, declaring that "in a matter of such high importance to the state, nothing should be left to conjecture." Like the Williams Committee Report a year earlier, the commission's document catalogued the advantages of the canal—asserting that indirect economic returns, in the form of higher farm prices and reduced import costs, would be incalculable, and that any debt incurred for the project would seem as "light and trivial" as the Revolutionary War debt appeared in retrospect, compared with "the great blessings" involved.[33]

The general assembly complied with the request for additional appropriations. Micajah T. Williams was appointed to succeed Commissioner Morrow, who had been elected governor; the commission was instructed to name two of its members as "acting commissioners," to serve in a supervisory capacity and spend full time in the field; and the board was given funds to hire another engineer to replace Geddes, who had returned to New York. In addition, the legislature instructed the commission to investigate how the canal project could best be financed.[34]

Because construction of the Erie Canal was reaching its climax at this time, the Ohio commission found it impossible to engage a civil engineer to succeed Geddes. Thrown back on their own resources, the commissioners sent Alfred Kelley to New York, where he examined the Erie Canal line "very minutely" between Rochester and the Hudson River, and where he "ascertained from the Commrs., Engineers, and contractors the cost of performing the various kinds of work . . . as well the contract price as the actual cost. Also the manner of constructing the various aquaducts, culverts, embankments, &c. &c."[35] Commissioner

Tappan, a stout old-line democrat, objected that any surveyor "of ordinary good judgment and discretion" could lay out a canal line; nevertheless, the commission financed additional visits to the Erie Canal for Micajah Williams and a Dayton surveyor, Samuel Forrer, who had been engaged to work for the commission.[36]

In June 1823 the commission appointed Micajah Williams and Alfred Kelley, who were to become the central figures in the Ohio canal enterprise over the next decade, to serve as the acting commisisoners. With the aid of their field staff, Kelley and Williams accomplished three major engineering tasks in 1823: they carefully gauged the streams in the Sandusky-Scioto portage region, tentatively concluding that the water supply was inadequate for a canal; they made further surveys of the Scioto-Muskingum-Lake Erie line, favored by Geddes the previous year; and they struck out on a new course, locating a line from Cincinnati northward to the Maumee River and thence east to the river's mouth (at the present location of Toledo) on Lake Erie. Reviewing the field surveys, the entire commission accepted the need to abandon the Sandusky route. This was done reluctantly, for all believed that "on this route there would be less difficulty in uniting the public feeling and opinion than on [any] of the others."[37] In late autumn, the prominent Erie Canal engineer David S. Bates was asked to review the commission's findings. Bates concurred in the view that the Sandusky route was an "extremely doubtful" prospect, and he asserted that either of the two remaining routes might be feasible.[38]

Presenting their own findings and those of Bates to the legislature, the canal commission also reported the results of inquiries at New York as to the possibility of financing canal construction. Appended to the board's report were letters from William Bayard, Cadwallader Colden and other New York financiers, from each of whom came "very flattering assurances" that Ohio would be able to market its state bonds in the East on favorable terms, just as New York State had been doing since 1817.[39]

Publication of the commission's report to the 1823–24 session of the legislature produced "a thrilling effect" at Columbus.[40] Indeed, it aroused sufficient enthusiasm to overbalance even the local jealousies aroused by abandonment of the Sandusky route.

Sensitive to political dangers, the commissioners pleaded that they had been dispassionate and impartial in all their deliberations: "The members of the board," they wrote, "have uniformly felt disposed to yield something of their local sentiments and wishes, in order to unite cordially in accomplishing an object which they deem essential to the honor and prosperity of the state. . . . There has been a concurrence of opinion in the direction of all our principal operations."[41] To cap the argument, they shrewdly suggested that a second canal might be built from Cincinnati northward less than seventy miles to Dayton, through the densely settled Miami Valley.[42] In this way, they played on the local ambitions of Cincinnati's large delegation in the legislature, whose support appeared essential in view of rising hostility from the Sandusky country.

With publication of the January 1824 report, it became obvious that all the surveys to date favored the Scioto-Muskingum-Lake Erie route. Meanwhile, the Cincinnati-Dayton canal was gaining support as an ancillary project. The resultant coalition of local interests was strong enough to secure enactment of a bill appropriating funds for further surveys. But to allay discontent in the regions threatened with frustration of their hopes for canal facilities, the legislature further required the commission to engage an experienced engineer to supervise the final surveys, to draw up estimates of construction costs, and to provide a distinterested comparison of the varying merits of the several routes.[43] Leaders of the canal movement privately admitted that further surveys were approved by the legislature only because the question of specific routes had been left open, indeed "studiously avoided" in debates on the floor. Had it been otherwise, they believed, "the whole fabrick would . . . have gone by the board."[44] The persistence of localistic jealousies lent increased urgency to the ensuing year's task of locating specific routes, leading to presentation of a final program to the legislature.

Throughout 1824 the canal commission worked to produce a final report and recommendations by the winter, when the legislature would meet. All its hopes were pinned on successful location of a canal on the Scioto-Muskingum-Lake Erie route. The key engineering question was whether the water supply would permit a canal to penetrate the divide on the Licking Summit between the Scioto and the Muskingum watersheds. But engineering questions were also political questions. Design of a deep cut through Licking Summit, Micajah Williams wrote in March, *"must be done,* whatever the cost may be," for this route would "tie together the *interests* of the two great valleys of Scioto and Muskingum."[45] Devising a strategy of construction "whatever the cost may be," on any one route, had not originally been conceived by the legislature as the canal commission's concern. But so had political realities affected the commissioners' activities.

To assure that the board's final recommendations would carry the weight of scientific authority, Williams implored Governor Clinton to lend the Ohio commission an eminent Erie Canal senior engineer.[46] Geddes proved unavailable, and so it fell to David S. Bates to return and review the canal commission's work. During the summer of 1824, the actual field surveys were directed by staff engineers in Ohio. Bates arrived in the autumn, and immediately went to the Sandusky region again to gauge the streams there. His findings confirmed his earlier view that they were inadequate to sustain canal navigation. But he found that the engineers had indeed solved the problem of the Licking Summit, and approved their plan for an elaborate deep cut at the summit requiring construction of an extensive reservoir.[47] At some point in early 1824, the commission apparently decided that a second canal between Cincinnati and Dayton was politically no less essential than finding a way to penetrate the Licking Summit divide. Surveys were run from Cincinnati, and the final plans there were also approved by Bates. As the report to the legislature took shape, Bates endorsed as well the full long-line canal plan, from the Scioto to a point south of Columbus, through Licking Summit to the Muskingum's headwaters, and then northward *via* any one of three alternative routes (the final choice to be determined later) to the Lake Erie Shore.[48]

On Micajah Williams' principle that if the people were well informed "their representatives will act accordingly," the commissioners conducted an active publicity campaign for the emergent canal plan.[49] Throughout 1824 Kelley and Williams kept newspaper editors informed on the progress of surveys, always couching their reports in most optimistic terms. Thomas Worthington contributed to the board's political effort in southern Ohio by writing a series of newspaper articles, widely reprinted, which set forth the advantages and anticipated benefits of canal construction in carefully reasoned, often eloquent arguments. Meanwhile other members of the commission worked to marshal popular support in their home localities.[50]

As soon as the specific terms of the commission's impending report became evident, opposition to the project crystallized. It was concentrated, as might have been expected, in the Sandusky Valley and in the river counties of eastern Ohio, neither of which would benefit from the projected canals. Spokesmen for these regions questioned the technical competence of the commission; they accused individual commissioners of "perpetual efforts . . . to prejudice and prepossess the public mind in favor of one general route, and against others"; and they denounced the entire board as "a band of speculators, intent upon aggrandizing themselves at the expense of the public."[51] But while the tone of the opposition became more venomous, enthusiasm for the project gathered strength in towns and regions which did expect to benefit from the proposed canals. The press gave close attention to the progress of the surveys, and friendly editors faithfully reported the publicity statements issued by the canal commissioners, predicting benefits of cheaper navigation, improvement in land values, and provision of new waterpower sites, if the state were to build canals.[52] As the autumn elections approached, one journalist asserted that "every representative . . . ought to be chosen in reference to this canal," declaring the canal question "greatly more important to us . . . than who shall be President."[53]

The outcome of state contests for the legislature gave little indication of how the canal commission's proposals would fare at Columbus. Many representatives were elected who had made no commitments for or against canals, and ominously there were many who had gone on record as opposed to any large new expenditures by the state.[54] The uncertainty deepened because the canal commission's report was not ready when the legislature convened in late December.[55] But two developments contributed toward dispelling the clouds of doubt that shrouded the canal plan. First, Governor Jeremiah Morrow threw his full support to the canal commission, on which he himself had served. Anticipating that opponents of the report would attempt to discredit the engineering competence of the board, Morrow urged the legislature to place full confidence in the judgment of David Bates, the Erie Canal engineer who had advised the board; and he exhorted the assembly to provide for financing of the canal enterprise by revision of the state's antiquated tax system.[56] The second development, which was even more important in generating support for the forthcoming commission report, was the publication in mid-December of the Erie Canal's financial record for 1824. This showed that canal tolls on the partly completed New York canal exceeded interest costs on the state debt by more than $50,000. Jubilantly, supporters of the Ohio canal scheme declared it a "convincing and undeniable demonstration, not merely of the practicability of constructing so noble and everlasting a work, but also the benefits that resulted from it."[57] Meanwhile, Governor Clinton of New York—whose fame for his brilliant role in the Erie Canal enterprise lent exceptional weight to his opinion —declared before his legislature in Albany that an Ohio canal could be financed in the eastern money market "on easy and satisfactory terms."[58] Moreover, Clinton provided the Ohio canal commissioners with a letter asserting his optimism about the possibility of financing, a document that they apparently circulated to good effect at Columbus.[59]

Against the background of rising optimism at Columbus in early January, the canal commission finally produced its report.[60] Its recommendation, fully endorsed by David Bates, was for construction of two canals. The main "Ohio Canal" was planned to run up the Scioto Valley to a point south of Columbus, thence to the east where it would meet the tributaries of the Muskingum. From there, the commission declared, it might run to Lake Erie either along the Black River or down the Cuyahoga. The report estimated the cost of construction at $2.8 million to $4 million. The second canal, termed the "Miami Canal," was planned on a 66-mile route from Cincinnati through Middletown to Dayton, at an estimated cost of $673,000. Once state finances permitted, the commission asserted, the state might readily extend the canal northward to the Maumee River, near the Michigan and Indiana borders, and run down the Maumee to Lake Erie.

In a second set of recommendations, the board asked for establishment of a newly constituted canal commission to supervise construction of the canals and, once completed, their operation. It proposed that the agency be authorized to seize lands and materials for the canal, to establish the specific locations along generalized routes recommended in the report, to engage engineers and other staff, and to establish tolls and regulate traffic on the completed works. But financing of the public works, the board asserted, should be left to a separate commission, empowered to issue bonds backed by the credit of the state. The concept of separate agencies for administering finance and construction was founded on the example of New York, which had adopted such a system eight years earlier, upon authorizing the Erie Canal project.[61]

The report also proposed a major tax revision, which would assess lands *ad valorem,* instead of merely classifying lands without reference to market value, as was then the system. *Ad valorem* taxation not only would increase state revenues, but would also place a larger (and fairer) share of the tax burden on localities where land values rose quickly because of the canals. Finally, the report recommended creation of a sinking fund to pay the principal on the canal debt, the fund to be accumulated from a special state canal tax on land and by allocation of other revenues as needed.

In addition to specific recommendations, the commission set forth full and detailed arguments for the larger policy. It predicted that both canals would be profitable enterprises in time. The proposed Miami Canal would tap a large existing trade, and would therefore produce large revenues and profits from the day it opened. The Ohio Canal, on the other hand, would give the densely settled Scioto Valley a route for inexpensive transportation to New York; but in the central and northern portions of the state, it would have a developmental effect, promoting settlement in a sparsely populated region and permitting commercialized agriculture to take hold. The commission also set forth its views on state *vs.* private enterprise, asserting that construction by a private corporation "of citizens or foreigners, as may happen," would be inconsistent "with the dignity, the interest, or the convenience of the state." Projects crucial to the public interest should not be "parcelled out into monopolies." The commission also said that the state could command the necessary capital in eastern money markets better than could any private company. Justifying state borrowing for canal construction, the commission declared that the commonwealth would gain in two ways over the long run: the canals would be worth more "as merchantable stock," once completed, than they would cost; but there would also be substantial indirect benefits to shippers, merchants, consumers, and other private interests by virtue of lower transportation costs. This doctrine of "indirect benefits" was an important element of the argument for a canal in 1825. As will be seen, it would prove no less persuasive when others called for additional public works expenditures in later years.

Publication of the commission's final report inaugurated a debate in the legislature as momentous as any in the state's history. Opponents of the program attacked the recommendations on several counts, but their objections fell into four broad categories.[62] First, they deplored construction of the Cincinnati-Dayton canal as part of the plan. That was a strictly local improvement, they declared, and as such it betrayed the high-toned declarations of the canal commission that it spoke for the entire commonwealth. Second, some opponents objected that the report proposed the vesting of unnecessarily broad powers in the agency to be established to supervise construction. They demanded that the precise locations, and not merely the general route, of each canal should be specified in any bill. "We are acting in the dark," one representative complained, urging against yielding sovereign powers of the legislative to a board of administrators not responsible to the people. Third, the opposition questioned the fiscal soundness of the project. One member concentrated on the cost estimates prepared by the engineers, asserting that actual costs would run as high as 12 million dollars. Others expressed doubt that the proposed tax revision would in fact yield increased revenues, objecting as well to the board's prediction that toll revenues on the Cincinnati-Dayton would be sufficient to amortize the debt incurred to build it. Fourth, the opposition asserted the positive value of delay. They pointed out that the commission's final report had been published after the legislature had convened. With concrete proposals at hand, let the representatives go back to their constituents and test public sentiment. Then, in the following legislative session, "if the fever shall then be raging . . . for canalling, as the friends of this policy state to us . . . it does now," the assembly could act accordingly.[63] Most significantly, however, the opposition did not lean to any extent upon *laisser-faire* doctrine—an argument that some champions of the canal program had anticipated. Canal advocates and their critics instead seemed to agree that state activism was an appropriate means of undertaking internal improvements on the scale projected.[64] When the actual vote came on bills that incorporated all the commission's recommendations, the opposition was revealed as a sectional bloc. In the senate, only two votes were cast against the measure, both by men from counties distant from the proposed public works. In the house of representatives, thirteen negative votes were recorded—again, all by men from the "bypassed" counties.[65]

Thus large majorities in both houses supported legislation that embodied all of the canal commission's principal recommendations. By an act of February 3, 1825, the Ohio system of taxation was put on an *ad valorem* basis, with a state board of equalizers appointed to review assessments by local officials. And by what became known as the "1825 canal law," an act of February 4, the assembly authorized construction of two canals: the Miami Canal from Cincinnati to Dayton; and the Ohio Canal, to be built on the Scioto-Muskingum-Lake Erie route. The canal law also incorporated the administrative organization that the commission had proposed for management of construction and financing. A new canal commission of seven men was appointed to supervise the actual building and operation of the canals. The legislature named to the new board six of the old commissioners—Worthington, Tappan, Beasley, Minor, Kelley and Williams—and also a new member, John Johnston, a former Federal official and farmer residing at Piqua in the upper Miami Valley.[66] The board was authorized to appoint up to three "acting commissioners," to be paid a *per diem* salary and expenses and to supervise work in the field; the other members of the board would be compensated only for expenses.

In addition, the February 4 law established a "board of canal fund commissioners," empowered to "make all arrangements relative to obtaining loans and the payment of interest thereon, and [to] the transfer, transmission, and deposit of moneys, as they may deem conducive to the public interest." The board was authorized to borrow $400,000 in 1825 and $600,000 each year in 1826 and 1827, by issuing bonds and pledging "the full faith and credit" of the state as security for payment of interest and principal. Appointed as fund commissioners were Brown and Buckingham of the old canal commission, and also Allen Trimble, a prominent politician from southwestern Ohio. Despite their awesome duties, the commissioners were apparently expected to operate on a shoestring: they were given no appropriation for a staff and were to be compensated only for actual expenses.

Enactment of the tax revision and canal laws marked the climax of the canal movement in Ohio. Although it still remained to be learned whether funds for construction could actually be procured, the political struggle was now over. An explanation of the large majorities won by the canal measures in the legislature must take some account of the fact that many affirmative votes were cast by representatives of "by-passed" districts. This was partially attributable, no doubt, to the enactment of a bill authorizing extensive improvements of a state road from Columbus to Sandusky—the route once considered for the lake-to-river canal and the scene of growing popular opposition to the canal program. In addition, similar road appropriations were made for the eastern portion of the state, where local political spokesmen and journalists were complaining bitterly about the canal locations. Equally significant, no road funds were appropriated in the 1824–25 session for counties that were on the projected canals. Then too, the power of political patronage through grants of offices and favors may have brought some of the early opponents into "the snare of the intriguers," as one critic charged.[67]

In the last analysis, however, it was not crass political trading at Columbus that assured the success of the canal measure. Rather it was the shrewd linking of the canal bill with a tax reform that promised to throw a large part of the state's financial burden upon the localities that would benefit from canal construction; the equally important decision to recommend the Dayton-Cincinnati canal, which won over the large Cincinnati and Miami Valley delegations; the weight of Governor Clinton's public statements and the sensational financial success of the Erie Canal; and, not least, the unanimity with which the canal commissioners themselves resolved personal differences and threw their individual prestige behind the final program.

Appointment of the canal commission in 1822 had brought together a group of able business and political leaders. They shared a common understanding of the state's economic problems which predisposed them to favor construction of a public canal system. Inspired by the example of the Erie Canal and identifying themselves with the national movement for internal improvements, they hammered out a policy that was both politically acceptable and consistent with the needs and resources of the state. In these respects, their policy was conservative. Yet it was also bold and visionary, for they proposed an enterprise of far greater magnitude than any previously undertaken in the West, and comparable to the pioneering Erie Canal enterprise in one of the eastern seaboard's wealthiest states. In the long run, the commission's boldness, rather than its conservatism, would have the more telling influence on the climate of public opinion in the state. Although the reckless expansion of the state's public works a decade later would derive in part from the boom psychology that became prevalent in the mid-thirties, it would also reflect a revival of public attitudes fostered by the canal commission itself during the initial period of canal promotion in Ohio.

NOTES

1. *Liberty Hall and Cincinnati Gazette*, May 18, 1824; see also William T. Utter, *The Frontier State* (Columbus, 1942), 284ff.

2. Brown's activities and the internal improvements movement in Ohio are treated *infra*, pp. 15–20. See also John S. Still, "Ethan Allen Brown and Ohio's Canal System," *OHQ*, XLVI (Jan. 1957), 22–43, a full and incisive account.

3. Oscar Handlin and Mary E. Handlin, *Commonwealth: A Study of the Role of Government in the American Economy —Massachusetts, 1774–1861* (New York, 1947); James Willard Hurst, *Law and the Conditions of Freedom in the 19th Century U. S.* (Madison, 1964), Chaps. 1–2; Carter Goodrich, *Government Promotion of American Canals and Railroads* (New York, 1960); and Gerald D. Nash, *State Government and Economic Development . . . in California* (Berkeley, 1964), 10–26.

4. Beverley W. Bond, *The Civilization of the Old Northwest* (New York, 1934), 409–10 *et passim;* Bond, *The Foundations of Ohio* (Columbus, 1941), 412, 417, 443–44; Utter, *Frontier State,* 35, 147–48, 203, 268ff.; Thomas S. Berry, *Western Prices before 1861* (Cambridge, 1943), 140, 147ff.

5. Utter, *Frontier State,* 203; William F. Gephart, *Transportation and Industrial Development of the Middle West* (New York, 1909).

6. Alfred B. Sears, *Thomas Worthington, Father of Ohio Statehood* (Columbus, 1958), 204; Harold E. Davis, "The Economic Basis of Ohio Politics, 1820–1840," *OHQ,* XLVII (Oct. 1938), 303ff.

7. See accompanying Map 1–A, for population distribution; also, Francis P. Weisenburger, *Passing of the Frontier* (Columbus, 1943), Chap. 1.

8. Cases were recorded of boats selling for as low as $16 in New Orleans (1820), but this was unusual. Berry, *Western Prices,* 24; see also George R. Taylor, "Agrarian Discontent in the Mississippi Valley," *Journal of Political Economy,* XXIX (1931), 476, on average costs during 1800–1810; and Utter, *Frontier State,* 177.

9. See Richard L. Power, *Planting Corn Belt Culture* (Indiana Historical Society Publications, XVII, Indianapolis, 1953), 146–47; Paul W. Gates, *The Farmer's Age* (New York, 1960), 174–78; and the full study of boating down the rivers in Leland D. Baldwin, *The Keelboat Age on Western Waters* (Pittsburgh, 1941).

10. R. C. Downes, "Trade in Frontier Ohio," *MVHR*, XVI (1930), 467–94; and Utter, *Frontier State, passim.*

11. See relative prices at Cincinnati for eastern and western goods, 1824–26 and 1844–46, in Berry, *Western Prices*, 120.

12. *Ibid.*, 86ff.; Arthur L. Kohlmeier, *The Old Northwest as the Keystone of the Arch of Federal Union* (Bloomington, 1938), 1–13.

13. On the failure of movements for Federal aid, cf. Curtis P. Nettels, "The Mississippi Valley and the Constitution, 1815–29," *MVHR*, XI (Dec. 1924), 332–57; Goodrich, *Government Promotion*, 36ff.

14. C. W. Ogden, *Letters from the West* (1821), in R. G. Thwaites, ed., *Early Western Travels* (Cleveland, 1904–07), XIX, 35.

15. Richard C. Wade, *The Urban Frontier* (Cambridge, 1959), 328; Paul Fatout, "Canal Agitation at Ohio Falls," *Indiana Mag. of Hist.*, LVII (Dec. 1961), 279–310. In 1821 one Cincinnatian complained bitterly that interest in a lake-to-river canal in Ohio was diverting attention from the Falls Canal (J. N. to Ethan Allen Brown, Dec. 20, 1821, Brown Papers, OSL.)

16. Sears, *Thomas Worthington*, 124–127.

17. Randolph C. Downes, *History of Lake Shore Ohio* (3 vols., New York, 1952), I, *passim;* Kenneth E. Davison, "Forgotten Ohioan: Elisha Whittlesey, 1783–1863" (Ph.D. dissertation, Western Reserve University, 1953), on Whittlesey and harbor improvement controversies. The special interests of eastern Ohio were reflected in James Shriver, *An Account of Surveys and Examinations . . . relative to the Projected Chesapeake and Ohio and Ohio and Lake Erie Canals* (Baltimore, 1824), 73–74, 98ff.

18. Saul Elkins and Eric McKitrick, "A Meaning for Turner's Frontier," *Political Science Quarterly*, LXIX (Sept. 1954), 336.

19. Sears, *Thomas Worthington*, 124–28.

20. *Ibid.*, 202–207.

21. Still, "Ethan Allen Brown and Ohio's Canal System," 22ff.

22. *Ibid.*, 24. At one point Brown shifted his view and said he thought a private corporation might "prosecute the work with vigor," whereas public construction probably would be "long in its accomplishment." (Brown to Jonathan Dayton, Feb. 4, 1821, Brown Papers, OHS.)

23. Still, "Ethan Allen Brown," 23–29.

24. Brown to Dayton, Feb. 4, 1821, Brown Papers, OHS.

25. H. N. Scheiber, "Entrepreneurship and Western Development," *Business History Review*, XXXVII (Winter 1963), 346–49.
26. *Report of the Committee on Canals* (Columbus, 1822), 3, 14, and *passim*.
27. Samuel Forrer, MS. sketch of life of Williams, dated 1860, in Micajah T. Williams Papers, Ohio State Library (OSL).
28. John Kilbourne, *Public Documents Concerning the Ohio Canals* (Columbus, 1828), 27. The routes specified were (1) from the Ohio River up Scioto to Sandusky River and Sandusky Bay; (2) from the Muskingum at its juncture with the Ohio across Cuyahoga-Muskingum Portage and down Cuyahoga River to Cleveland; (3) from the Muskingum to the lake via Black River; (4) from the Mahoning's junction with the Ohio to Grand River and then to the lake; and (5) from the Ohio River at Cincinnati northward to Maumee River and the lake.
29. Alfred Kelley to Brown, Feb. 3, 1822, Ethan Allen Brown Papers, OSL. On the commissioners, see Still, "Ethan Allen Brown"; Sears, *Thomas Worthington;* Scheiber, "Ebenezer Buckingham," *Museum Echoes*, XXXIII (Dec. 1960); unsigned note on Jeremiah Morrow, *Bulletin of the Hist. and Phil. Soc. of Ohio*, VI (Oct. 1948), 164–65; *Dictionary of American Biography*, on Tappan; and pp. 74–75, *infra*, on Kelley.
30. For a detailed study of the canal commission and its surveys, see Scheiber, "The Ohio Canal Movement," *OHQ*, LXIX (July 1960), 231–56. On the role of private promotional groups in other states, see citations, *ibid.*, 232, n. 3.
31. Alfred Kelley to Brown, May 31, 1822, Brown Papers, OSL; Brown to Kelley, July 24, 1822, Ohio Canal Commission Papers, Ohio State Archives (hereafter cited CC Papers).
32. De Witt Clinton to Allen Trimble, Feb. 26, 1822, Clinton to Geddes, March 30, 1822, De Witt Clinton Papers, Columbia University Library.
33. *Report of the Canal Commissioners*, January 3, 1823 (Columbus, 1823), 5, 8, 9–11; *Canal Report Made by James Geddes* (Columbus, 1823), 9ff.
34. Still, "Ethan Allen Brown," 38–39.
35. Kelley to T. Worthington, May 20, 1823, Thomas Worthington Papers, OSL; also, Williams to Brown, Feb. 3, 1823, Brown Papers.
36. Tappan to Williams, March 11, 1823, Williams Papers, OSL;

also, Buckingham to Worthington, Jan. 3, 1824, Thomas Worthington Papers, OHS.

37. Williams to Worthington, Sept. 19, 1832, Worthington Papers, OSL; also, Canal Commission Minute Books, entry of Sept. 19, 1823 (MSS., Records Room, Ohio Dept. of Public Works, Columbus).

38. *Report of the Board of Canal Commissioners, January 21, 1824* (Columbus, 1824); Bates's report is in *ibid.*, Appendix.

39. Williams to Brown, Jan. 24, 1824, Brown Papers, OSL; also, Kilbourne, *Public Documents*, 53–55.

40. Forrer, MS. sketch, cited n. 27.

41. *Report* . . . *January 21, 1824*, p. 6.

42. *Ibid.*, 26.

43. By the same act of the legislature, the board was expanded to eight members, Nathaniel Beasley being appointed to represent the district between the Scioto and the Miami. (Williams to Kelley, Feb. 25, 1824, CC Papers; Williams to Brown, Feb. 22, 1824, Brown Papers, OSL.)

44. R. D. Simons to Brown, Feb. 26, 1824, Brown Papers, OSL.

45. Williams to Brown, March 7, 1824, *ibid.*

46. Williams to Clinton, March 7, 1824, Clinton Papers.

47. *Report of the Canal Commissioners, January 10, 1825* (Columbus, 1825), *passim;* Buckingham to Worthington, Sept. 28, 1824, Worthington Papers, OHS; Bates to Kelley, Oct. 1, 10, 18, 1824, CC Papers.

48. Buckingham to Brown, Dec. 27, 1824, Brown Papers, OSL.

49. Williams to Brown, March 15, 1824, *ibid.*

50. *Liberty Hall and Cincinnati Gazette*, Aug. 21, Sept. 3, Oct. 5, 1824; Downes, *History of Lake Shore Ohio*, I, 106.

51. Sandusky, *Clarion*, Aug. 14, Sept. 4, 1824; Delaware *Patron*, Sept. 23, 1824; *Clarion*, Jan. 22, Feb. 12, Apr. 30, 1825. On the leadership of sectional opposition, see Scheiber, "Ohio Canal Movement," 247–48.

52. *Liberty Hall and Cincinnati Gazette*, Aug. 27, 1824.

53. *Ibid.*, Oct. 25, 1824; see also Williams to Kelley, Oct. 18, 1824, CC Papers.

54. Jacob Blickensderfer to Kelley, Oct. 22, 1824, CC Papers; William Doherty to Brown, Dec. 12, 1824, Brown Papers, OSL.

55. Buckingham to Brown, Dec. 27, 1824, Brown Papers, OSL; also, Alfred Kelley to his wife, Nov. 27, 1824, in Albert L. Cummings, *The Alfred Kelley House . . . and Some Family Letters* (Columbus, 1953), 42.

56. Kilbourne, *Public Documents,* 102.

57. Columbus *Gazette,* Dec. 18, 1824. Buckingham wrote that the news "produced . . . excitement not only in the Legislature, but in the community in general." (Letter to Brown, Dec. 27, 1824, Brown Papers, OSL.)

58. *Liberty Hall and Cincinnati Gazette,* Jan. 28, 1825. Clinton had promised Williams that he would make such a statement. (Clinton to Williams, Dec. 4, 1824 [marked *"Private"*], Clinton Papers.)

59. "I have no doubt but that loans may be obtained on the credit of your State amply for the construction of the work," Clinton wrote (*ibid.*). See also Kelley to Clinton, Jan. 20, 1825, Clinton Papers, acknowledging the usefulness of Clinton's letters.

60. The report is cited, n. 47, *supra.*

61. When the board formulated its proposals, it apparently had in hand a letter from Clinton urging organization of two separate agencies, along the lines followed in New York State. (Clinton to Worthington, Dec. 14, 1824, Clinton Papers.)

62. This analysis is based upon a reading of the debates, as reported in Columbus *Gazette,* Jan. 29–Feb. 24, 1825.

63. *Ibid.,* Feb. 8.

64. This is not to say that private construction had never been considered. In correspondence with Ohio promoters of the canal project, De Witt Clinton had since 1818 discouraged all thought of building a lake-to-river canal by private enterprise. Only the state itself, Clinton reiterated, could finance the project. (See Clinton to Steele, June 24, 1818, Clinton Papers; Brown to Clinton, May 29, 1820, Brown Papers, OHS; Brown to Col. Haines, Feb. 7, 1821, Brown Papers, OSL.) For a public letter advocating private construction, see Cleveland *Herald,* Jan. 14, 1825.

65. The canal bill was enacted Feb. 3 and the taxation bill on Feb. 4, 1825 (documented copies in OHS). The voting was reported in several newspapers; I have used Sandusky *Clarion,* Feb. 5, 1825.

66. On the new canal commission, see Chap. 3, *infra.*

67. Blickensderfer to Kelley, March 27, 1825, CC Papers; Kelley to Brown, March 11, 1825, Brown Papers; *Liberty Hall and Cincinnati Gazette,* April 19, 1825; Columbus *Gazette,* Dec. 23, 1824, Feb. 15, 1825; Delaware *Patron,* Feb. 24, 1825; Sandusky *Clarion,* Aug. 13, 1825.

CHAPTER 2

Construction and Finance
1825-1833

ENACTMENT of the February 1825 canal law was a political triumph, but formidable obstacles to the project's success lay ahead. Chief among these was the urgent problem of financing. The canal commission had received assurances and encouragement from eastern financiers, and of course New York State had proved that an American state government could borrow capital for canal purposes in both domestic and foreign money markets. But Ohio in 1825 had less than half the population of New York in 1815, when the first of the Erie Canal bonds had been sold, and Ohio's public revenues were considerably smaller.[1] Even if funds could be obtained, moreover, considerable doubt remained as to whether Ohio could command engineering and managerial talent sufficient to design and build the canals successfully. Opponents of the 1825 canal plan still insisted that the surveys had been deficient and water supplies overestimated. If such charges were accurate, or if the electorate lost enthusiasm for the project as the effects of increased state indebtedness and taxation were felt, the legislature might well order retrenchment, curtailing construction on one or both projected canals.[2] Indeed, until construction was actually completed eight years later, the canal commissioners would be haunted by the specter of millions borrowed to finance nearly four hundred miles of ditches which might be unable to sustain navigation, or might need to be abandoned when only half completed.

The legislature had taken two steps, however, that greatly enhanced the prospects of successful financing. First, it appointed men of high standing and ability to the three-man board of fund commissioners given responsibility for obtaining loans and managing canal funds. They were Ethan Allen Brown, now a United States Senator, whose long-standing friendship with De Witt Clinton and prominence in public life lent unusual prestige to the board; Ebenezer Buckingham, a former canal commissioner and one of Ohio's wealthiest businessmen; and Allen Trimble, a leading figure in state politics. Trimble's tenure on the board was brief: he resigned in 1826 when elected speaker of the state senate. But his successor, Simon Perkins, was equally distinguished. The Ohio agent for the Connecticut Land Company, Perkins was also a leading Ohio banker; and like Brown, he enjoyed a wide range of business contacts in the financial community of the East.[3]

Apart from appointing able commissioners, the legislature placed the full faith and credit of the state behind the authorized bond issues. This assured potential bond purchasers that if the construction effort foundered, or if the canals produced inadequate revenues, the general taxing power of the state would be employed to pay interest and principal on the canal debt. De Witt Clinton had advised that if Ohio backed its bonds in this way, it would "satisfy the most scrupulous capitalists."[4] The accuracy of Clinton's prediction would need to be tested at once. For immediately after the canal law passed, the fund board solicited subscriptions to the authorized $400,000 bond issue of 1825 among the banks of Ohio, hoping thereby to obtain concrete evidence of support within the state for the project; but the banks responded negatively, and the fund board then turned to the "scrupulous capitalists" of the East.[5]

The continuing uncertainty as to whether Ohio bonds could find a market stimulated opponents of the canal plan to continue their fight. Having failed to influence the legislature, they now held public meetings in the "neglected" regions (by-passed by the projected canals), where popular opposition to the canal plan was strongest. They issued public resolutions asserting that the bond issues violated the state constitution, and rushed copies of such

statements to eastern newspapers in the hope of frightening off
potential investors and defeating the loan.[6]

But more deeply rooted influences favored the fund board's
mission in the East. In the first place, the leading merchants and
bankers of New York recognized well the potential value of an
Ohio canal in expanding their trade into the West. According to
Charles Haines, the prominent New York publicist for canals, it
had long been taken for granted "that New York capital would
sustain [the Ohio] enterprise."[7] There was also the matter of
profits that might be made from dealing in Ohio bonds. Many
New York businessmen—among them John Jacob Astor, William Bucknor, and the partners of Prime, Ward & King—had
reaped handsome gains from buying Erie Canal bonds and resell-
ing them later in England and America. The profitability of
their investments in New York canal bonds had reflected recent
changes in the structure of international capital flows: on the
strength of profits made earlier in British canal stocks, English
investors had since 1822 bought several hundred thousand dollars'
worth of Erie Canal bonds directly from the New York fund
board, but had also bought bonds at premium prices from Prime,
Ward & King and other early purchasers of the New York issues.
Moreover, the great rise in New York City's foreign trade
since 1815 had increased commensurately the resources of her
money brokers and investment banking firms. These houses used
Erie Canal bonds as security for lines of credit from the major
banking firms of London, to help finance New York's foreign
commerce. These factors lent buoyancy to the eastern money
market generally, but the year 1825 was especially auspicious for
a new American bond issue because a sudden rise in U. S. exports
was temporarily reversing the normally unfavorable trade balance.[8]

With these influences favoring its quest for capital, the Ohio
fund board in April 1825 sought bids on its $400,000 bond issue.
Even the most optimistic friends of the Ohio project were sur-
prised when several New York capitalists each offered to take
the entire issue. The board accepted the highest bid, 97½ (that
is, 97½ cents on the dollar of redemption value), on bonds
yielding 5 per cent interest payable semiannually in New York,
from the banking firm of Rathbone & Lord. (See Table 2.1.)

TABLE 2.1

ORIGINAL PURCHASERS OF OHIO BONDS, 1825–1832

PURCHASER	1825	1826	1827	1828	1830	1832
Rathbone & Lord	400,000	180,000				
Lewis Cass		20,000				
John J. Astor		800,000		342,000		
Prime, Ward & King			100,000	170,000	400,000	100,000
Bank for Savings, N. Y.			200,000			
Wm. Woolsey, Thos. Biddle *et al.*			900,000			
Wm. Woolsey				65,000		
Thos. Biddle				278,300		
Wm. G. Bucknor				112,500	200,000	
Others				232,200		
Totals	400,000	1,000,000	1,200,000	1,200,000	600,000	100,000
Premiums	—10,000*	8,475	77,580	48,840	105,420	24,000

* Discount

Source: List of purchasers, ms. transfer book, Ohio State Archives. For premiums, see Bogart, *Internal Improvements,* 56.

This meant that the fund board agreed to an effective interest rate of slightly over 5 per cent on the $390,000 that Rathbone & Lord paid.[9] The terms compared favorably with those obtained by New York in its initial Erie Canal bond issue a decade earlier, and Ohio's success demonstrated that a western state could indeed hope to emulate the Empire State in canal construction.[10] No less important for Ohio's future financing prospects, however, was the fact that a prominent New York investment house had lent its prestige to the project and acquired a stake in its completion: for the debtor-credit relationship, in such cases, gave the borrowing government an ally on Wall Street, with an interest in maintaining the market price of the state's paper. For the time being, then, the days of anxiety were over.

With funds assured, the new canal commission, which was in charge of construction, moved quickly to perfect its building plans. Shortly after the legislature passed the canal bill in February, the board had organized its staff and appointed Micajah Williams and Alfred Kelley as "acting commissioners" to oversee the actual work of construction in the field.[11] The principal policy issue ostensibly unresolved in April was the formal selection of a route for the Ohio Canal between the Muskingum River and Lake Erie. The legislature had given the commission discretion to select either of two routes. It is clear from the board's records, however, that in February at the latest the commissioners decided to build on the Cuyahoga Valley route to a lake terminus at Cleveland. This information was suppressed for three months, apparently to encourage private donations of land from Cuyahoga Valley landholders who thought they might influence the board's decision. Not until May was selection of the route to Cleveland announced publicly.[12]

At their policy meeting in May, the commissioners also decided that "specifications as to the manner of construction of the New York canals be adopted for the Ohio canals."[13] The dimensions of the main canal channels were thus to be 26 feet width at the base, 40 feet at the water line, and 4 feet depth from the water line. Like the Erie Canal, the Ohio canals were to be designed for navigation by boats towed by horses or mules driven on a towpath built along one side of the line. Because animal-drawn boats moved slowly, at about 3 to 5 miles an hour, they set up only a gentle wash as they moved—an important factor, affecting how heavily embankments of the canal channel must be constructed. Had the commissioners attempted instead to accommodate steamboats, they would have needed to specify much more massive embankments than those on the Erie Canal. Dimensions of the channel's "prism" (in this case 26 by 40 by 4 feet) also had important economic ramifications. In the first place, they dictated the maximum width of boats that could be run through the line. To pass one another in transit, boats must be built less than half the width of the channel; in practice, canal boats in Ohio later would be constructed about 60 to 75 feet long and 14 feet wide, giving them cargo capacity of up to 60 tons. The boats would turn around at basins built at the official canal ports, where toll collectors would be stationed; and at the larger ports the basins would have to be large enough to permit construction of warehouse and wharfage facilities around their perimeter. (At Cleveland, for instance, the basin would be 120 feet wide and nearly a quarter mile in length.) Dry docks for the repairing of boats might also be located at the basins.

A crucial limiting factor that affected the dimensions was water supply. The larger the prism, the greater the amount of water needed per mile of length. Also relevant was the volume of water held by locks that passed the boats from one level of the line to another; for each time a lock was used, the water it held passed down the channel below, and the lock would be refilled from the line above. Relevant too, of course, was the anticipated density of traffic on the line, dictating the number of times the locks would be used daily. The locks on the Ohio Canal were designed to lift an average of 9 feet each, and on the Miami, 8 feet. The length of the locks, which dictated the maximum length of boats, was 100 feet. Their width, however, was 25 feet, so that locks in series could not accommodate two-way traffic simultaneously, as the main channels did.

Essential to maintaining orderly navigation, in canal technology, was the control of water flow. Thus the commission would need to build reservoirs where water supply from the natural streams was highly variable according to the season of year. On level stretches of the main lines where water flow was normally heavy, guard-gates would be built across the canal channel: they were watertight (or nearly so) and would be opened to pass boats through or to regulate water flow down the line. The other main installations needed were aqueducts—which surprisingly enough were usually built of wood—to carry the navigational channel over natural streams; and bridges and culverts, to carry roadways and drainage lines over or under the canal's bed.

In summary then, the Ohio commission's decision to adopt the Erie Canal technology was a decision to build for two-way navigation by towed boats, with the length, lockage, and prism of the line dictating the extent and cost of embankments, reservoirs, and water-flow devices. This technology had all the basic limitations of a water system: ice forming in the channels would close the lines during the winter; damage to any dam or to guard-gates would lead to flooding, overflow of the embankments, and/or damage to locks and other installations; extensive damage to a lock requiring that it be shut down for repair would halt all navigation at its location on the line; and droughts would reduce the water level, forcing boats to travel with less than full loads, or halting navigation altogether. The integrated water-supply system required a delicate balance, and any errors in design or deficiencies in construction might throw the entire system out of order. For all that, canal technology offered a high degree of safety for cargoes. It permitted navigation by heavy vessels built for long working life and designed to carry bulk cargoes; and above all it provided potentially much less expensive transportation than overland wagon hauling. What remained to be learned in 1825 was whether the engineers who had run the Ohio surveys, and those who would design the actual locations and facilities of the lines, could bring sufficient expertise to their task to match New York's success in making a complex system navigable.

Having settled the major technical questions, the canal commission still confronted a delicate political matter—the establishment of construction priorities. The 1825 canal law had not required that the Miami Canal and Ohio Canal lines be built simultaneously; and indeed, in light of the limited labor then available in the state it was practically imperative that the giant Ohio Canal, at least, be constructed in segments. Because funds might not be so easily obtained in future years, moreover, the best strategy was one of building from the projected termini inland, by stages. Thus, in case of forced abandonment or curtailment, at least the partially built canals would be capable of sustaining navigation.[14]

The Miami Canal posed few technical problems since the entire 67-mile line would pass through fairly flat country between Cincinnati and Dayton. (See Table 2.2.) Thus the commission decided to begin with the 44-mile stretch between Cincinnati and Middletown, postponing construction of the remaining link to Dayton. Also postponed were the expensive terminal facilities and

TABLE 2.2
SPECIFICATIONS OF CONSTRUCTION:
OHIO CANAL AND MIAMI CANAL, 1833

CANAL	LENGTH (MILES)	LIFT LOCKS (NO.)	RISE AND FALL (FT.)	AQUE- DUCTS	CUL- VERTS
Ohio Canal trunk line	308	146	1,207.4	14	153
Tuscarawas feeder	3	—	—	—	—
Walhonding feeder	1	—	—	—	—
Granville feeder	6	1	10.0	1	1
Muskingum side cut	3	3	28.8	1	—
Columbus feeder	11	2	13.9	—	1
TOTAL, OHIO CANAL*	333	152	1,260.1	16	155
Miami Canal	66	32	297.0	6	27
Hamilton side cut	1	—	—	—	—
TOTAL, MIAMI CANAL	67	32	297.0	6	27

* Corrected

Source: Canal Commission, *Annual Report,* Jan. 1833 (*Ohio House Journal,* 1833), p. 29. Prism of all canals = 40 ft. top, 26 ft. bottom, 4 ft. depth.

locks within Cincinnati proper. In effect, the commission was concentrating its resources at first on that part of the project which would require the lowest expenditures per mile.

The Ohio Canal presented an altogether different challenge. In the first place, its design was complex. It was to be over 300 miles long, and would involve construction of nearly 150 locks and fourteen aqueducts. (See Table 2.2.) The southern division would pass from an unspecified point on the Ohio River northward up the Scioto Valley to a point south of Columbus. There a navigable feeder 11 miles long would connect the main line with the capital city. At the junction with the Columbus feeder, the canal would turn eastward, climbing some 205 feet by means of thirty locks to the Licking River. At the summit, separating the tributaries of the Scioto from the streams running down to the Muskingum, a reservoir of 2,500 acres would be built to supply water for a "deep cut." Descending from the summit to the Muskingum's headwaters, the canal would there turn northward along the Tuscarawas River. It would cross the junction of the Tuscarawas and Walhonding rivers by way of a long aqueduct, and then follow a northward route to Massillon. There the line would begin a long climb to another major summit, the Portage Summit, and run through a second deep cut to Akron. Entering the Cuyahoga Valley, the canal would descend rapidly to Lake Erie at Cleveland, dropping nearly 400 feet in 38 miles, on a course requiring more than 40 locks.[15]

The magnitude of the Ohio Canal meant that the canal commission could not reasonably undertake construction of the entire line at once; and so the commissioners decided to complete at least one sizable segment before beginning others. But once again there was the highly sensitive question of priorities. Politically, it would be most advantageous to build the southern division (down the Scioto Valley to the Ohio River) before undertaking the remainder of the work. This would have satisfied residents of the Scioto region, a hornet's nest of political activism where the citizenry was already demanding immediate construction. Moreover, because of the large population there, the Scioto division would generate heavy traffic (and revenues) as soon as the line was opened to navigation.

Despite such considerations, the commission decided to concentrate its resources initially upon the northern division of the canal, in the sparsely settled Cuyahoga Valley, and thus to fulfill quickly one of the prime goals of the canal movement: the opening of a route from the interior to Lake Erie and the New York market.[16] The board's other major decision on priorities was based on engineering imperatives, which dictated that work begin early on the Licking Summit. There the heavy excavations for the deep cut would require much more time for completion than any other segment of the canal.

The commission thus prepared to award contracts in 1825: (1) for construction of 36 miles of line between Akron and Cleveland; (2) for initial, limited work on the heaviest facilities on 11 miles of line on the Licking Summit; and (3) for the Miami Canal between Cincinnati and Middletown. With priorities established, the state engineers then laid out the precise location of the canal lines. The projects were subdivided into "sections" or "jobs" (usually one-half mile of level line, or an entire lock or aqueduct) for contract purposes, and cost estimates were prepared for each job. The work in the field was given new impetus by the arrival of many professional contractors from New York, where construction of the Erie Canal was coming to an end. This happy coincidence virtually assured the Ohio commission of heavy competitive bidding for contracts.[17]

The terms of the initial contracts, awarded in June 1825, were hailed as "a triumph over [the] oppositionists," who had said the canals could never be built at the cost predicted by the commission.[18] All contracts for work on the Portage Summit, Licking Summit, and the Miami Canal were at prices below the engineers' estimates. When further contracts were given out during the summer, an average of twenty-three bids was received for each job, again with none of the bids accepted going over the estimates.[19]

Work began at once, and the pace was unexpectedly quick. In Cleveland the local newspaper welcomed the "daily arrival of . . . hardy sons of Erin" who had worked on the Erie Canal. The Irish coming from New York were joined by local farmers and their sons and laborers, eager to work for cash wages. By September more than two thousand laborers were employed on the Ohio Canal, and another thousand on the Miami Canal. Weather was good throughout the year, and the early progress of construction exceeded even the most optimistic predictions of the canal commissioners.[20]

The excellent experience with construction in 1825, together with the success of the initial bond issues, persuaded the legislature to reassess its canal policy. A year earlier, the leading canal promoters—including acting commissioners Kelley and Williams —had feared that Ohio's voters might rebel at the boldness and cost of the canal plan and elect opponents of the project, who would attempt retrenchment. Instead, the legislators who had supported the canal law were nearly all returned in 1825, and this was interpreted as a mandate in favor of the policy. An enthusiastic legislature, advised by the canal commission that construction could readily be accelerated, therefore voted to increase the authorizations for new loans. For 1826, the fund board was permitted to issue one million dollars in bonds, and for 1827 and 1828, 1.2 million dollars each year.[21]

In the first months of 1826, however, there was little chance that the newly authorized 1-million-dollar issue could be marketed on good terms. For, as would often be the case in ensuing years, short-term movements in English and American money markets created temporary difficulties despite a generally favorable business climate. In early 1826 heavy cotton speculation in New York and new issues of joint-stock company securities in London were taking up available funds, depressing the market for low-yield securities. This coincided with an increase in construction activity in Ohio, when the spring thaw permitted heavy work to begin anew; and because the fund board paid contractors monthly for work as it was completed, demands on the canal fund proved heavy. Thus the funds commissioners adopted a new expedient, turning to Ohio banks for $500,000 in short-term loans, to carry them through the period of difficulty in the eastern money market. Only $130,000 was obtained from the Ohio institutions, despite the board's admonition to the banks that "it would be gratifying . . . to manifest to foreigners that we also possess means within our own State."[22]

Pressure in the New York capital market eased in June, and the fund board went east when John Jacob Astor, scion of New York real estate and the western fur trade, expressed an interest in buying Ohio bonds. Finding that New York and Pennsylvania had just succeeded in marketing securities on good terms, the board quickly advertised for bids on its own 1-million-dollar issue. Astor, as expected, offered to take the entire issue. But Rathbone & Lord also bid par value for some of the bonds. Recognizing the importance of cultivating their association with this firm, the fund board decided to sell $180,000 to them, $800,000 to Astor, and $20,000 to another bidder. (See Table 2.1.) All the sales were in 6 per cent securities, the purchasers paying slightly more than par value (a price of nearly 101).[23] Although the effective rate of interest was thus higher than the 5 per cent carried by the 1825 bonds, the competition for capital had become more intensive, with Pennsylvania in the field—having authorized construc

tion of a massive canal-and-railroad system the previous year—
and other states as well planning canals. Considering that some
American government securities were then offering a yield of
7 per cent, the fund board's success in 1826 was no less impressive than its initial effort the year before.[24]

The favorable outcome of bond sales in New York was offset
by some new conditions on the canal lines. In the first place,
Pennsylvania was now vying with Ohio for the services of engineers, laborers, and experienced contractors, as well as competing
for capital. And so the unusual conditions of 1825, when competition for bids among contractors had been intense, were not
to be repeated in 1826. Besides, the low prices on contracts made
in 1825 exposed contractors to financial pressures if increases in
their costs should set in, as occurred when many itinerant laborers
left Ohio seeking higher wages in Pennsylvania. Their departure
drove wages up; contractors began to feel the pinch; and as new
jobs were put under contract, the state had to pay higher average
prices than formerly.[25] Pennsylvania also lured away some of the
Ohio canal commission's engineers, who could not easily be
replaced. As a result, there were delays in preparing specifications
and cost estimates on jobs being readied for contract bidding.[26]
Further compounding the commission's troubles were occasional
outbreaks of typhoid in wet regions, which discouraged farmers
from taking employment as laborers; and seasonal declines in the
work force during periods of planting and harvesting.[27]
At the end of 1826, therefore, none of the lines under construction had yet been completed. This had an adverse effect on
potential investors' interest in Ohio bonds; and the fund board
was told in New York that to sell additional bonds in 1827, it
"must have a part of the line navigable, and be able to tell and
publish in the newspapers a good story of [their] flattering prospects." On receiving this information, the canal commission
decided to concentrate all its available labor and funds on the
northern part of the Ohio Canal line. Elsewhere it would "keep
up appearances . . . but with limited expenditures."[28]
This change in strategy produced the desired effect. On the
line near Akron, where some contractors had been dilatory, the

canal commission took over the jobs and re-let them at high prices, setting a short time limit for completion. The renewed pace of activity on the line evoked "the invigoration and exhilarating impulse" of excitement at Cleveland, where merchants and townspeople prepared to welcome "the hum and bustle of canal boats, vessels, sailors, and bugle."[29] Then on July Fourth, 1827, the 38-mile line between Akron and Cleveland was ready for operation. With gala ceremony, the governor, the canal commissioners, and other dignitaries traveled down the line on a barge built at Akron, so initiating the West's first canal. Before the orchestra at Cleveland had completed its entertainment at a state dinner, a more prosaic but no less significant arrival was reported: a boat laden with flour and whiskey, which came down to Cleveland from the Akron district.[30]

Taking advantage of the enthusiasm and fanfare that marked this occasion, the fund commissioners advertised the 1.2-million-dollar bond issue of 1827 in the East that summer. Their prospects were enhanced by news that by November the Miami Canal would also be opened from Middletown to a point just north of Cincinnati.[31] In late October, therefore, they were able to sell $900,000 in 6 per cent bonds to a syndicate of Philadelphia bankers which paid the surprisingly high price of 107, making the effective interest rate only 5½ per cent. Meanwhile, the fund board marketed an additional $300,000 of 6 per cents in private negotiations at a price of 104, through the New York investment firm of Prime, Ward & King.[32] (See Table 2.1.)

But not all the developments in 1827 were so comforting. For while the fund board was raising additional capital, costs continued to rise on the canal lines. Persistent labor shortages plagued the construction effort, as both the National Road (then being built through central Ohio) and Pennsylvania's public works competed for labor. An "alarm created by the prevalence of fevers" caused a temporary depletion of the labor supply, so serious that a few score inmates from the Ohio Penitentiary (some "known to be of desperate character," a matter of some anxiety among local residents) were put to work on the line near Columbus. Even worse, numerous contractors on Portage Summit and the Miami Canal were abandoning their work without paying laborers, creating morale problems that discouraged local residents from signing on as canal labor. Consequently, the canal commission took over many of the abandoned jobs, completing them with state crews, to assure that construction would go on.[33]

Information of these troubles might have damaged the confidence of investors in the East if it had not been counteracted by three other developments. Ohio bonds had begun to find favor among English investors, and their price was now reported regularly on the London exchange. Also, the fund board could publicize the more favorable news that the Miami Canal would be completed in November 1828. And finally, Congress granted 500,000 acres of Federal land in Ohio to the state, the proceeds from the sale of which would be used for canal expenses. The state set a minimum price of $1.25 per acre, so that the revenue potential of the grant was sizable.[34]

Thus when the fund board went to the New York money market in 1828, it sold the authorized 1.2-million-dollar issue of 6 per cents on good terms. The major purchasers were financiers who had invested heavily (and presumably gained by their resale of bonds in the U. S. and England) in earlier Ohio issues: they were Prime, Ward & King, who took $342,000; and Thomas Biddle and William Woolsey, both members of the 1827 Philadelphia syndicate, who took $278,300 and $65,000 respectively. The remainder was bought by William Bucknor, a New York banker, and the Bank for Savings (New York), which was the city's leading "trustee savings" institution and a heavy purchaser of Erie Canal bonds. The price was 104.[35]

Although the 1828 sales had been advertised as the "final" loans, the fund board was driven into the market later because of unanticipated increases in costs of construction in Ohio. Costs were rising partly because of a sharp upward trend in wages during 1828–30, which increased contractors' expenses and led to higher average bids on new contracts.[36] But no less important was a series of acts by the legislature ordering changes in canal plans. In 1828 the assembly authorized a one-mile lateral canal from the town of Hamilton to the main line of the Miami Canal; later the legislature approved a three-mile lateral from Dresden, the head of navigation on the Muskingum River, to the Ohio

Canal.[37] The most expensive and ill-advised change in canal design was ordered in 1826, when, in response to aggressive demands from residents of Chillicothe, the leading town in the Scioto Valley, the legislature required the state engineers to locate the Ohio Canal line directly through the town. In accord with this mandate, the canal commission planned the canal line to run along the east bank of the Scioto River to a point just north of Chillicothe, where a large aqueduct would carry the line across the river so that it might enter the town, situated on the west shore. South of Chillicothe, the canal was to run down the west bank to the mouth of the Scioto, on the Ohio River, opposite the village of Portsmouth.[38] There the commission planned an elaborate terminal facility designed to carry canal boats across the breadth of the Scioto. The decision to build this expensive (and, as it proved, nearly unnavigable) crossing at Portsmouth was based solely on the town's vested interest as a commercial center, and the board's belief that "this circumstance ought to have much influence."[39]

While the canal commission dealt with "the clamour" in the Scioto Valley, construction went forward on the northern division; and in August 1828 the Ohio Canal was opened south from Akron across Portage Summit to Massillon. Because a smallpox epidemic in 1829 impeded work on the Licking Summit, the section of the canal across the summit to Newark was not completed until July 1830.[40] The full length of the Miami Canal—except for the heavy terminal locks at Cincinnati—was completed in December 1828.[41]

By early 1830, these efforts had exhausted available funds so that once again a new bond issue became necessary. Because the fund board could now boast of two canal lines in actual operation and producing toll revenues of some $100,000 annually, it met with little trouble marketing the additional bonds. Once again former investors dominated the sales, as Prime, Ward & King and William Bucknor paid a price of 118 for $600,000 in 6 per cent securities. This brought the state canal debt to four million dollars, but it provided ample funds for nearly all remaining construction needs. Only one further bond issue proved necessary, for $100,000 in 6 per cents, sold in 1832 to Prime, Ward & King at the unprecedented price of 124—evidence of the extraordinarily high credit standing of Ohio.[42]

With the funds obtained by the 1830 bond issue, construction in the Scioto Valley was accelerated. Anticipating the day when lake-to-river through freight would pay tolls into the state treasury, the commission put pressure on contractors to complete their jobs on schedule. But in 1831 floods caused extensive damage to the recently completed line on the Licking Summit and to the Scioto Valley work then under construction. This forced the commission to divert labor and funds for heavy repairs; but by assigning state crews to jobs abandoned by contractors, the agency opened the line in October as far south as Chillicothe.[43] Traffic from Lake Erie to the Scioto began at once: in November boats laden with New York merchandise were reported as arriving "almost daily" at Chillicothe from Cleveland, a distance of 250 miles on the canal. Moreover, the line opened in 1831 proved to be without defects that impeded traffic, which the commissioners regarded as "truly remarkable, considering its extent."[44]

Completion of the canal to Chillicothe also ended a long period of pressure on the canal commission from that region. For here had been the center of agitation against the commission's plan of construction priorities; and the town's merchants had been remarkably proficient at generating troublesome squabbles over canal questions among themselves and with rival towns—in addition to having coaxed from the legislature the order to locate the Ohio Canal through the town.[45] With arrival of the first boats from Cleveland, however, "the Chillicotheans seemed to have forgotten all their former troubles," Commissioner Williams reported. They staged a "grand *blow out*" to celebrate the occasion, and there was never "a more lively and general display of good feelings."[46]

But only a few months afterward the angry western rivers proved more troublesome than the citizens of Chillicothe at their worst. In February 1832 the Ohio River overflowed its banks in the greatest flood in memory; and all along the river, one witness wrote, was "a scene of destruction and suffering"—urban buildings and homes ruined, crops destroyed, and inhabitants of the valley driven to refuge in the hills.[47] In the lower Scioto Valley, therefore, the 50 miles of canal line between Chillicothe and the Portsmouth terminus became the most difficult segment of the canal to complete. The floods destroyed the partly completed line, and locks and heavy installations at the terminus sustained heavy damage. Another blow was struck when the American cholera epidemic of 1832 spread to the Scioto region in July, killing many canal laborers and driving the rest from the line.[48]

The work was finally completed to Portsmouth in October 1832.[49] Now, almost eight years after enactment of the 1825 canal law, merchandise from New York could reach the Ohio Valley by inland waterways, and farm produce from Ohio's formerly landlocked interior could find markets in either the East or the South. With the long-awaited wedding of lake and river waters, a vision that had captivated a generation was realized.

Ohio's achievement in completing its first canals was partly a matter of successful financing: the board of fund commissioners performed critical tasks for the state, aided by valuable guidance from De Witt Clinton and others in New York and by support from the eastern investment banking community. Moreover, the timing of the first bond issue was propitious: it coincided with an influx of capital from Europe, and in 1825 few other states were seeking long-term capital investment funds in the east. The canal commission's strategy of construction priorities, which led to an early opening of the Cincinnati-Middletown and Akron-Cleveland lines, enhanced the attractiveness of Ohio bonds, not least by proving the state's ability to manage construction well. As construction went on, income-minded small investors and the great Anglo-American banking houses bought Ohio bonds in the open market, and by 1828 they were traded regularly on the London exchange. Their rising reputation was reflected in the excellent prices the state received in the bond sales of 1830 and 1832, and no doubt the original purchasers made high profits in resale of their holdings.[50]

But Ohio's success was also a result of skillful management and engineering on the part of the canal commissioners. They applied well the basic lessons of technology learned from New York, deriving most of their techniques from those developed on the Erie Canal. As with the New York canal, the Ohio waterways were built mainly with the force of human muscle and simple tools: the pick, axe, spade, and wheelbarrow. The contractors employed some heavy equipment, especially animal-drawn plows, to break ground for the initial digging, and heavy scrapers, drawn by teams of oxen, used to grade the line.[51] Then, too, Ohio profited from the availability of experienced contractors, engineers, and laborers who left the Erie Canal in 1825, just as work on the Ohio project began; and the state was able to employ farmers and agricultural laborers who welcomed a chance to earn hard cash by labor on the canals. But not all the techniques, any more than all the labor, were bequests from New York. The Ohio commissioners made a few innovations of their own in construction technology, for example developing a new process for mixing hydraulic lime (used for mortar) of a type commonly found in Ohio; working out a new design for embankments that would resist damage from flooding; and elaborating the techniques of carrying the canal line by aqueducts over rivers and streams, to meet the special needs of topography on the Ohio Canal route.[52]

The canals of Ohio were built to stand. Originally, the commission had planned to build as cheaply as possible, counting on substitution of more durable facilities as the initial installations wore out. But encouraged by the success of the 1825 bond issue, and informed that additional loan capital would be readily forthcoming, the commission changed its design, substituting cut stone for rough on the culverts, locks, and aqueduct piers; and substituting rough stone for wood on smaller installations. Moreover, when weaknesses appeared after contractors' jobs had been accepted, the state spared no effort to remedy them. Partly as the result of such substitutions, the cost of the canals was higher than the original 1825 estimates: the Miami Canal ran to $900,000, or close to the upper range of the original estimate, but the Ohio Canal cost 4.3 million dollars, more than one third above the estimate. (See Table 2.3.) There were other reasons for unanticipated costs than the decision to build durably: natural disasters, such as the cholera epidemic and the floods of 1832; the general increase in wage scales, especially the rapid rise in canal wages during 1828–31; and expansions of the original canal plan

TABLE 2.3
EXPENDITURES FOR CONSTRUCTION
AND SALARIES BY OHIO CANAL
COMMISSION, 1825–1833

YEAR	AMOUNT
1825	$122,296
1826	714,661
1827	807,650
1828	773,858
1829	702,069
1830	944,244
1831	614,530
1832	409,176
1833	181,718

Source: Bogart, *Internal Improvements*, 57.

ordered by the legislature, particularly the costly modifications of design in the Scioto Valley.[53]

The subsequent operating history of the canals revealed certain engineering errors. The Licking Summit design was complex, and its water requirements made navigation uncertain in dry seasons. The small culverts that carried natural streams under the canal lines, or crossed the lines to accommodate the abutting landowners, were built of wood and subject to rapid decay. The most serious error, however, was the selection of Portsmouth as the southern terminus, for the complicated crossing of the Ohio River there proved virtually unnavigable and involved high costs for shippers.[54]

Considering the magnitude of the project and the means available, however, the record of construction was remarkably good. The state had adhered to a rational plan of main-line construction, and it had followed a sound scheme of priorities. In its first major public enterprise, Ohio established a reputation for canal engineering and management which became the envy of her sister states in the west.

NOTES

1. The anxieties of the canal commissioners themselves were expressed in a letter of Micajah Williams to E. A. Brown, Feb. 6, 1825, Ethan Allen Brown Papers, OSL. See also arguments against the canal project in the legislative debates, reported in *Columbus Gazette,* Jan. 29 to Feb. 24, 1825, *passim.*
2. Delaware *Patron,* Feb. 3, March 24, 1825.
3. The fund commissioners received only expenses, and no salaries, for their work on the board; and they were given no office facilities in Columbus, though provided with money to engage a part-time clerk.
4. Clinton to Alfred Kelley, Feb. 7, 1825, De Witt Clinton Papers, Columbia University Library.
5. Circular to Ohio banks, Feb. 7, 1825, Board of Canal Fund Commissioners Letterbooks (BFC Papers), OSA; Ebenezer Buckingham to J. Woodbridge, May 16, 1825, *ibid.,* that an offer by the Bank of Chillicothe for part of the bond issue was rejected because better terms were obtained in New York.
6. Sandusky *Clarion,* March 5, April 2, 1825; Cleveland *Herald,* May 27, 1825; E. Buckingham to Alanson Douglass, March 30, 1825, BFC Papers, that opposition in Ohio was "puffed and blowed" by New York speculators who hoped thereby to depress confidence in Ohio's credit and buy the bonds at bargain-counter prices.
7. Haines to E. A. Brown, Feb. 11, 1825, Brown Papers, OSL. It is instructive that one banking firm (Prime, Ward & King) which became a heavy purchaser of Ohio bonds refused to buy stock in Canada's Welland Canal in 1826 on grounds that "opening of [that] canal would be injurious to them inasmuch as it would divert the course of trade from New York to Montreal." Quoted in Hugh G. J. Aitken, *The Welland Canal Company* (Cambridge, 1954), 82.
8. Nathan Miller, *Enterprise of a Free People* (Ithaca, 1962), 77–114, on Erie Canal finance and the role of individual investors and financial institutions; Ralph W. Hidy, *The House of Baring in American Trade and Finance* (Cambridge, 1949), and Leland H. Jenks, *The Migration of British Capital to 1875*

(New York, 1927), on the general history of British investment in the United States in the 1820's.

9. BFC Report, in Ohio General Assembly, *House Journal*, 1825–26, p. 47. In this report (Dec. 1825) the BFC stated that the entire sum needed to build the canals could have been obtained on favorable terms in New York when the $400,000 issue was sold (*ibid*).

10. New York had paid 6 per cent interest on issuing its first bonds.

11. Entry of Feb. 7, 1825, Canal Commission Minutes (MSS., Board of Public Works, Records Room, Columbus).

12. Entry of May 6, 1825, *ibid*. On February 7, 1825, one of the canal commissioners indicated privately that the board should get "the people of the Cuyahoga Valley and Cleveland to give all they will give," and then announce selection of the Cuyahoga route. (Tappan to Kelley, Feb. 7, 1825, CC Papers.)

13. Entry of May 6, 1825, CC Minutes. The following discussion of cost factors and basic construction technique in canal technology rests upon the annual reports of the canal commissioners and the report by Colonel John Abert in *American Railway Journal*, new series, II (1839), several installments, esp. at pp. 74ff. and 104ff. See also Stanley Lebergott, "United States Transport Advance and Externalities," and discussion by H. N. Scheiber, in *Journal of Economic History*, XXVI (Dec. 1966), 437ff.

14. Williams to Alfred Kelley, Feb. 24, 1825, CC Papers, on rumors in Cincinnati that the Miami Canal would not be commenced till the Ohio Canal was completed. On the importance of construction priorities to the success of the Erie Canal project, see Miller, *Enterprise of a Free People*, 64–65; Ronald Shaw, *Erie Water West* (Syracuse, 1966), 101ff.

15. C. P. McClelland and C. C. Huntington, *History of the Ohio Canals* (Columbus, 1905); Oliver Dale Graham, "History of the Ohio Canal System" (B.C.E. thesis, Ohio State University, 1939); and "Survey of the Miami and Erie Canal, the Ohio Canal, etc.," *House Docs.*, U. S. Congress, 54 Cong., 1 Sess., No. 278 (1896, serial 3425), all contain physical descriptions of the original canals.

16. The canal commission discussed its construction priorities in its 1825 and 1826 reports; in James Kilbourne, ed., *Public Documents Concerning the Ohio Canals* (Columbus, 1832), 176ff., 247ff. Pressure for immediate construction in the Scioto

Valley was expressed through Commissioner Thomas Worthington, who objected vigorously to delay on the southern line. (Worthington to Williams, June 13, 1825, Micajah T. Williams Papers, OSL; Isaac Minor to B. Tappan, Nov. 11, 1825, Benjamin Tappan Papers, OHS.)

17. Kelley to Brown, March 11, 1825, Brown Papers, OSL.
18. Williams to Tappan, June 19, 1825, Tappan Papers; also, Williams to Worthington, June 17, 1825, Thomas Worthington Papers, OSL.
19. Kelley to Williams, Sept. 1, 1825, CC Papers.
20. Cleveland *Herald*, July 22, 1825; also, Williams to Isaac Minor, Sept. 28, 1825, CC Papers; Williams to Clinton, Oct. 14, 1825, Clinton Papers; and on number of workers employed, CC Report for 1825, in Kilbourne, *Public Documents*, 184, 186.
21. The canal commission also argued that wealthy capitalists were "frequently averse to a division of their funds amongst various stocks, in sums comparatively small," and the board anticipated that better terms than in 1825 could be obtained if larger bond issues were authorized. The governor supported this request. (*Senate Journal*, 1825–26, pp. 15, 48–49, 175–76; Canal Commission, *AR*, 1825, pp. 16–17. Also, Williams to Clinton, Jan. 26, 1826, Clinton Papers.) The original authorizations had been for issues of $600,000 in 1826 and 1827. The senate held a roll-call vote on the question, and of only eight negative votes cast, all but one were by representatives of "bypassed" districts of the state. Advertising the one-million-dollar loan in New York in 1827, the fund board declared that the actual cost of the canals would probably be only 3 million dollars, instead of the 3.6 million dollars, originally estimated. (*Acts of the Legislature of Ohio Authorizing Additional Loans for Canal Purposes* [Columbus, 1826], with clippings from eastern newspapers interleaved, copy in OHS.)
22. Buckingham to Chillicothe Bank, Dec. 10, 1825, BFC Papers; also, Clinton to Worthington, Dec. 10, 1825, Worthington Papers, OSL, and J. C. Wright to Brown, Dec. 27, 1825, Charles Rice Collection, OHS, and entries of Jan. 28, Feb. 5, May 12, 1826, BFC Papers, on money-market movements and the decision to seek temporary loans.
23. Brown to Kelley, May 1, 1826, CC Papers; Brown to Buckingham, June 16, 1826, Brown Papers, OSL; entries of July 1826,

BFC Papers; also, Kenneth W. Porter, *John Jacob Astor* (Cambridge, 1931), 1010.

24. Indeed, the canal commission had urged the fund board to agree to 6½ per cent interest if necessary. Micajah Williams declared it essential to obtain at least one million dollars to permit heavy work to be put under contract before the legislature met that winter. (Williams to Brown, May 14, 1826, Brown Papers, OSL.)

25. Cleveland *Herald*, June 16, 1826; Kelley to Brown, May 15, 1826, Brown Papers, OSL, on labor shortages; Williams to Kelley, April 2, 1826, Letters on Canals, CHS, on contractors incurring financial losses.

26. Williams to Worthington, May 22, Nov. 13, 1826, Worthington Papers, OSL.

27. CC Report for 1826, in Kilbourne, *Public Documents*, 247–50; Williams to Brown, June 13, 1826, Brown Papers, OSL; see also Chap. 3, below.

28. Simon Perkins to Kelley, March 23, 1827, CC Papers; Buckingham to Brown, March 7, 1827, Brown Papers, OSL.

29. Cleveland *Herald* copied in Lancaster *Gazette*, May 8, 1827.

30. Kelley to Williams, April 26, 1827, Williams Papers; John Still, "Ethan Allen Brown and Ohio's Canal System," *OHQ*, LXVI (1957), 51–53.

31. Williams to S. Forrer, Oct. 31, 1827, Samuel Forrer Papers, Dayton & Montgomery County Public Library.

32. The official price of private sales through Prime, Ward & King (which the fund board approved as an experiment, to test the method of sales without advertising) was 106½; but this was inflated, probably to keep from depressing prices in the open market, because the state agreed to pay the 3 per cent semi-annual dividend retroactively from January 1827. (Brown to Buckingham, June 27, 1827, Brown Papers, OSL; Buckingham to R. White, June 21, 1827, to Brown, Sept. 7, 1827, BFC Papers. For the $900,000 loan, cf. Buckingham to R. Osborne, Nov. 23, 1827, *ibid.*)

33. Canal Commission, *AR*, 1828, in Kilbourne, *Public Documents*, 266, 286–92; and *House Journal*, 1827–28, pp. 19–20, on convict labor.

34. Ralph W. Hidy, *House of Baring*, 65ff., 151, 206–62; Jenks, *Migration of British Capital*, 70–72, 361; and, on favorable effects of prospect of the land grant, Brown to Kelley, Aug. 7, 1828, CC Papers.

35. See Table 2.1. Also, Appendix I, below. The Bank for Savings invested funds deposited in small sums by tradesmen and other middle class savers, and had done well by its investments in New York bonds. The 1828 bond sales are discussed fully in E. Buckingham to Gov. Trimble, Nov. 12, 1828, BFC Papers, indicating that purchasers gave 10 per cent in cash at sale and 10 per cent monthly for nine months thereafter; on the Bank for Savings and William Bucknor, see Miller, *Enterprise of Free People*, 88–89, 96.

36. See Chap. 3, below.

37. Kilbourne, *Public Documents*, 290–92, 317–18.

38. Canal Commission Minutes, May 28, 1828; *House Journal*, 1825–26, pp. 260–61. The decision to run down the west bank drew an angry reaction from towns on the east shore, where it was regarded as a sellout of their interests. (John C. Parish, *Robert Lucas* [Iowa City, 1907], 91n.) At Chillicothe, a comic opera rivalry among neighborhoods over which part of town the canal should touch ended in a referendum of the citizenry on the "naked and abstract question" of the canal route—all of which signified the extremes to which localism might run. (Scheiber, "Urban Rivalry," *OH*, LXXXI [1962], 230–31.)

39. Canal Commission Minutes, May 28, 1828. See BPW, *9th AR* (1845), 8–9, on the Portsmouth terminus.

40. *Executive Docs.*, 1830–31, pp. 11ff.

41. Kelley to Brown, June 20, 1828, Brown Papers, OSL; Canal Commission, *AR, 1828, passim*.

42. See Table 2.1. Also, *House Journal*, 1830–31, pp. 256–62; *ibid.*, 1832–33, pp. 220–23.

43. *House Journal*, 1831–32, pp. 211–20; Jesse Williams to M. T. Williams, June 22, 1831, Williams Papers, on measures to speed construction in the Scioto; same correspondents, Aug. 6, 1831, *ibid.*, on damage from floods; Williams to Brown, Sept. 25, 1831, Brown Papers, OSL, that as of that date repairs on the Licking Summit line still were not done.

44. Kelley to Williams, Oct. 4, 1831, Williams Papers; Williams to Brown, Nov. 3, 1831, Brown Papers, OSL.

45. See note 38, above.

46. Williams to Brown, Nov. 3, 1831, Brown Papers, OSL; Kelley to Williams, Oct. 4, 1831, Williams Papers.

47. Williams to Kelley, Feb. 19, 1832, CC Papers.

48. W. Price to Williams, Aug. 20, Sept. 17, 1832, Williams Papers;

Duncan McArthur to S. Maccracken, July 5, 1832, Official Governors Papers, OSA; *House Journal*, 1832–33, pp. 296–97.

49. *Ibid.*, 296. The last lock at Portsmouth, which carried the canal down to the river level remained uncompleted in January 1833. However, boats could reach the town of Portsmouth.

50. See Appendix I, below.

51. Data on construction techniques are scattered through Kilbourne, *Public Documents,* and newspaper articles therein; and some information from the contemporary press is systematically given in Ernest M. Teagarden, "Builders of the Ohio Canal," *Inland Seas,* XIX (1963), 94–103. The Cleveland *Herald,* June 16, 1826, reported 300 teams.

52. Williams to Benjamin Tappan, Feb. 10, July 8, 26, 1826, Williams Papers, on development of new method for mortar; Kelley to Williams, March 2, 1828, *ibid.,* on adoption of new embankment design; on aqueducts and other installations, see also Graham, "History of the Ohio Canal System," which is an engineer's analysis, not strictly a history.

53. *House Journal,* 1832–33, p. 299.

54. See Chap. 7, below.

CHAPTER 3

Administration of the Enterprise
1825-1833

SUCCESSFUL canal construction had resulted not only from an infusion of funds from outside Ohio and the availability of a relevant technology: it had also required competent leadership and effective organization. The essential basis of success, Henry Clay had told the canal commission in 1825, must be "good plans well executed."[1] In their organization of an enterprise with components located in remote parts of an extensive territory, as well as in the application of engineering plans which they themselves devised, the Ohio canal commissioners fulfilled the terms of Clay's prescription. This they did in large measure by administrative innovations, without the benefit of precedents in the state's own history. Only mobilization of the militia during the War of 1812 matched the canal enterprise in numbers of men or amounts of money involved. Unlike the military effort, however, the canal project was entirely dependent upon Ohio's own ability to raise funds and—through economical construction—to maintain investors' confidence in the enterprise. Had their performance disappointed the high hopes of 1825, the onus of failure would have been borne solely by the state's own administrative officers.

The seven men named to the Ohio canal commission in 1825 were all prominent in state politics, and nearly all had extensive business interests as well. An unusually high degree of familiarity with the state's geography and resources had been enhanced by the service of Kelley, Williams, Minor, Tappan, Worthington, and Beasley on the old canal commission. The only new member was John Johnston of Piqua, and he had long served as a Federal official in western Ohio. Only two of the commissioners, however, could boast of professional expertise in canal engineering: as the acting commissioners during the pre-1825 surveys, Alfred Kelley and Micajah T. Williams had spent long periods in the field with the Erie Canal engineers used in Ohio. Also, both men had studied construction techniques on the Erie Canal line; and so they probably had acquired as much on-the-job training as most practicing civil engineers of that day.

It was generally assumed that the board would appoint Kelley and Williams to continue as the acting commissioners when construction began. This was done only a few days after the 1825 canal bill became law, when the commissioners met at the capital. As the acting commissioners, Kelley and Williams were expected to give nearly full time to their official duties, for which they would be paid only three dollars a day—a salary prescribed by law—and expenses.[2]

In the same initial meeting at the capital, the board adopted a scheme of organization for its engineering corps, taking the Erie Canal organization as the model.[3] A "principal engineer" was to head the corps and advise the commission on policy-level technical questions as well as supervising work in the field. His salary was set at $2,000 a year plus expenses, or nearly twice what the acting commissioners would receive. As shown in Figure 3.1, "resident engineers" would be appointed as required. They were to be responsible for laying out the actual canal lines, for preparing cost estimates and contract specifications, and for overseeing the work done by contractors. The board set their salary at three dollars a day while in the field. Other ranks in the hierarchy, in descending order of seniority, were to be "senior assistant engineer" with pay of $45 a month, "junior assistant engineer" and "surveyor" at $35 a month, and rod-man, axe-man, and common laborer, all paid lower wages on a *per diem* or hourly basis.[4]

Because completion of the Erie Canal in 1825 had temporarily relieved the national shortage of civil engineers, the Ohio board

FIGURE 3.1
CANAL COMMISSION ORGANIZATION, 1825–33

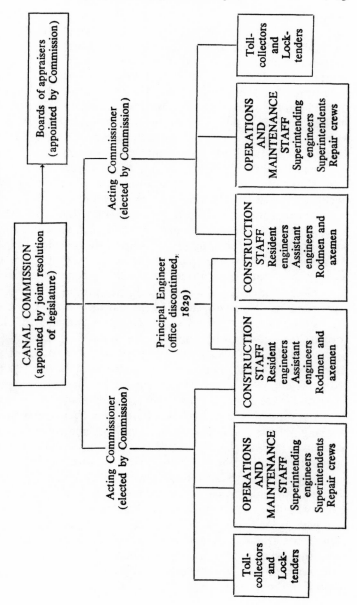

was able to attract to its staff three men with New York experience. David Bates accepted the appointment as principal engineer, while William H. Price, another New Yorker, was named resident engineer. Appointed as well was an Ohio resident, Samuel Forrer, who had been on the Ohio commission's staff before 1825 but also had served on the Erie Canal in 1824 "to perfect his skill in the science."[5] In naming junior resident engineers, the board drew from the surveyors who had been on the Ohio staff during the surveys, and subsequently many of these men rose to senior positions, as they gained additional experience.

Formally, the full board of commissioners retained control over all policies and operations. But as an agency with a line staff as well as a directing board, the canal commission was still of undefined character in 1825. It was in the context of relatively simple political institutions that the commission would have to develop its procedures, its relationships with outside groups, and its responses to pressures from the community. For unlike a mid-twentieth-century state government, Ohio's state organization in the 1820's did not include many agencies with overlapping responsibilities. There was little likelihood of conflict between administrative leadership and staff members because of the latter's professional associations outside the state; and special-interest groups in the community did not enjoy multiple routes of access into government to influence decision-making, as they do today. Nonetheless, some complex problems confronted the canal commission before a canal project of large scale could be undertaken. The question of where in its own bureaucracy particular decision-making powers would be lodged, and assignment of operating functions at different levels, had to be resolved within the commission itself. Decisions of this kind, in turn, would affect the agency's response to outside pressure and its relationship to groups in the community at large. The commission would need to determine what kind of contractual relationships to effect with a small army of private contractors and laborers who would work on actual construction. It would have to treat with staff engineers who enjoyed considerable mobility since demand for their services far exceeded supply, with other states embarking on canal programs and road building. The commission would need to develop procedures for treating with property owners whose lands and other goods might be seized, under eminent domain powers, for purposes of canal construction. And not least, the commission would have to establish a working relationship with the legislature that would give the agency latitude for achieving its own internal goals and yet protect it against erosion of necessary authority and discretionary power. Within a framework set by the commissioners' ambitions for the agency, by constraints of routinizing agency functions, and by the need to meet outside pressures, the canal commission became a working agency of government.

Strictly speaking, the commission was the creature of the legislature, appointed to implement a special measure just as a commission might be named to negotiate with another state over a boundary dispute. But building a multi-million-dollar canal enterprise was not the same as drawing boundaries, and so inevitably the canal commission assumed functions that had not been clearly formulated, if indeed even foreseen, when its "charter" was written in the canal law of 1825.

While the legislature did not give the commission a free hand in all matters, on the whole its controls over the agency limited the commission's powers only marginally. Although removal of commissioners lay within the assembly's authority, it never exercised that authority. In one case, however, the assembly did vote to render ineligible for a commissionership any person who also won election to the legislature itself.[6] Moreover, each year the assembly required the board to submit a report of operations. It also called upon the commission, sometimes on very short notice, for special reports on the merit of proposed new canal projects. In such cases, the board's engineers first reported to the commissioners, usually confining their remarks to the feasibility, probable costs, and (usually vaguely defined) probable benefits of the projects being considered. But in transmitting their engineers' reports to the assembly, the commissioners seldom hesitated to compare a project's merits with the merits of other proposals then before the assembly.[7] Such substantive opinions then became important to promotional groups or their friends in the legislature, who could cite the commission's view as impartial "scientific" evidence for or against a specific project. In this manner, the board assumed a role in the policy-making process more prominent than that of a passive servant of the legislature.

The commission looked with disfavor on new state commitments to canal construction, expressing its opposition in direct correspondence with promoters and politicians as well as in reports to the legislature.[8] Alfred Kelley articulated the board's position when he wrote in 1827 that the state should consider new projects only after the canals under construction were producing revenues from their operation. Until then, the board would view "with concern and regret any attempt to . . . overload the system with new projects, however correct in themselves, but which every dictate of prudence forbids us now to adopt."[9] But beginning in 1828, after the first canal lines had begun operating, the commission became more receptive to new commitments. Several lateral canals were, in fact, approved by the assembly at the commission's request. But the legislature held back when the commission recommended early extension of the Miami Canal northward from Dayton, improvement of the Muskingum River for its entire length, and state construction of a canal from Akron eastward to the Ohio River near Pittsburgh.[10]

The very nature of the board's membership virtually assured that it would become a forum for consideration of new projects and would intrude itself into the policy-making arena. For the assembly had consciously appointed the commissioners with a view to giving representation to each major settled district of the state.[11] In practice, each commissioner spoke for the interests and needs of his region; and naturally each man was receptive to proposals of special importance to his locale. Most of the internal tensions which troubled the board arose from disagreements based on special local interests. For example, during 1825–27 Thomas Worthington of Chillicothe—who as an ex-governor and Congressman was accustomed to respectful attention—unsuccessfully put pressure on the acting commissioners (both of them much junior to him in years) to speed surveys of the line in the Scioto Valley, to change construction priorities to favor the Scioto district, and to locate the line to serve the special town interests of Chillicothe.[12] Similarly, John Johnston of Piqua waged a sustained campaign of persuasion, not only in the board but also in the governor's office and in legislative lobbies, to obtain early construction of the Miami Canal's projected extension north from Dayton.[13] Internal divisions of this sort did not, however, erupt into open conflict which might have damaged the board's prestige. Throughout the period of early construction, no matter how intense their differences with one another, the commissioners maintained a united front in public. This show of unity enhanced their standing as an agency which spoke for the interests of the whole commonwealth in a disinterested manner. Had they aired their internal disputes in public, they might easily have been regarded as merely a political forum for advocacy of special local interests, and thereby undermined their own authority and effectiveness.

The canal commissioners proved no less expert in their relations with the general public than in their dealings with the legislature. The commission's activities were scrutinized closely by the newspapers, and the public demonstrated a lively interest in canal affairs, for the project was seen as a practical test of the predictions made by the promoters of the canal policy in 1825. The progress of construction was watched most carefully in the "by-passed" regions whose interests had not been served by the canal plan. Some political leaders in these areas bore enduring enmity toward the canal commissioners for having "steam-rollered" the canal law through the legislature; others expected the commissioners to do them justice by supporting new projects that would serve their aggrieved constituents. Underlying the skepticism, the hostility, and the disinterested scrutiny of the commission's activities was the painful awareness that the state debt was increasing and that canal taxes were being levied to support the work of construction.[14]

Fortunately for the commisison, it was spared the need to perform alone one of its most sensitive tasks, the seizure of private property for canal purposes. The 1825 canal law had given the agency power to seize, under law of eminent domain, any land required for right-of-way, towpaths, reservoirs, or other facilities;

and in addition, it had empowered the commission to seize timber or stone required for construction purposes. This was in accord with precedents under Ohio law, which had given county road commissioners similar powers; and many property owners willingly surrendered materials or land at prices offered by the commission. But others objected to confiscation, or else they contested the prices offered. In such cases, the canal law provided for binding arbitration by three-man boards of appraisers, appointed by the commission and usually comprised of leading citizens from the locality involved. The decisions of appraisal boards could be appealed only to the legislature.[15]

The constitutionality of the board's power to seize property in this manner was soon tested in the lower courts of the state. The key decision came in a case before the Ohio supreme court in January 1831. At issue was the commission's power to seize for canal purposes a valuable mill site on a stream near Dayton. The court ruled in favor of the commission, asserting that "the power to construct the canal is a high attribute of sovereignty, and in the thousand subordinate operations attending the execution of so vast a work, there is a necessity for the exercise of large discretionary powers." Only if "corruption, malicious intention, or caprice" could be proved against the commissioners would it be proper for the courts to intervene, the decision asserted. In the absence of such evidence, guarantees of the "faithful exercise of this discretion" were to be found "in the individual reputations of the commissioners, . . . in their acting openly on the rights of others, in the face of the people vigilant to watch, and acute to discern, and in their being exposed to the overwhelming force of public opinion."[16]

Not only did the commission settle most of the damage claims under eminent domain proceedings without needing to convene arbitration panels, but it also handled with sensitivity all its relations with a public "vigilant to watch." Even some of the most ardent critics of the 1825 canal policy were won over to support of the commission, often because the commissioners privately expressed sympathy with the aspirations of the neglected regions. For example, when a leading Trumbull County politician was rumored to have sponsored a protest meeting against the canal policy, Alfred Kelley wrote to remind him that "even Trumbull county may at no distant day ask favours from the State [and] aid to make some interesting improvement." The implication that the commission's support for such a project might be invaluable at that "no distant day" was clear enough. But equally important was Kelley's conciliatory tone.[17] After 1828, when the board threw its support to demands from the Mahoning Valley, the Muskingum Valley, and the Miami Valley north of Dayton, to endorse canal projects desired by those districts, its reputation among the citizens of these "neglected" regions improved commensurately.[18]

The commission's record of efficient performance and its sensitive handling of political opposition did much to gain it broad popular support. This trend was epitomized in the statement in 1830 of William Blackburn, a legislator from eastern Ohio who had been a bitter foe of the 1825 canal bill, attesting to "the zeal and judicious arrangement and management" of the board, and to "the good judgement, economy, and vigilance of the Acting Commissioners."[19]

In their day-to-day operations, the commissioners were occupied with more narrowly administrative tasks, especially in their relationships with canal contractors and laborers. When the 1825 canal law was drafted, the legislature assumed that the commission would contract with private parties for construction of the public works. This method had been used successfully on the Erie Canal; and it derived naturally from the eighteenth century tradition of canal building, when the English canal companies engaged master craftsmen on a contract basis to build locks and other facilities. Moreover, none of the arguments which favored financing and operating the canals as a public enterprise—fear of monopoly, the magnitude of the project, the superior ability of the state to raise capital—precluded engaging private enterprisers to do the actual work of construction. This course also comported with the canal commissioners' own belief that the profit motive assured a more efficient performance than could be expected from state crews that would "have no interest in . . . economical prosecution."[20]

Division of the canal lines into "sections" or "jobs" assured that the capital requirements of construction would not exceed the means of small enterprisers, and the commission thereby stimulated competitive bidding.[21] In preparation for soliciting bids, the commission's engineers wrote detailed specifications for each section and estimated its cost. Then the commission advertised for bids and selected the contractor for each job. Once construction began, the resident engineers played an inspectorial role, overseeing the quality of materials used by contractors and of labor performed. Ordinarily the contractors were paid monthly for the estimated value of work completed, with only the acting commissioners authorized to issue warrants for payment. For auditing purposes, the banks which kept the state's deposits and the fund board each retained copies of the resident engineers' valuation of work performed; the canceled checks were kept on file.[22]

The professional canal contractor was an unusual breed of entrepreneur. Characteristically, he migrated from state to state as new projects were begun, carrying with him a small fund of capital, a large store of practical "canalling" knowledge, and a packet of letters of reference from officers on the lines where he had worked. When construction began in Ohio, many professionals moved their seat of operations from the Erie Canal, while others came from the Chesapeake & Delaware Canal, which was also being built at that time.[23] Contractors often formed partnerships, and one man might have different partners for each of several bids on various jobs. Whether he sought contracts individually or in partnership, the professional met competition in Ohio from numerous "active, enterprising citizens, living near the canal and in the neighboring counties," including farmers, merchants, bankers, land dealers, and lawyer-capitalists.[24] When outbid, whether shrewdly or recklessly, by an amateur, the professional often hired himself out as a foreman. Some solicited subcontracts. Indeed the practice of employing experienced "canallers" as foremen was encouraged by a canal commission rule requiring all bidders, "if not expert themselves, [to] hire a superintendent approved by the Acting Commissioner or Principal Engineer."[25] The commissioners also gave preference to professional contractors when local amateurs submitted bids far lower than the more educated bids of professionals; however, when a notably wealthy local capitalist was low bidder, he usually received the contract even if the commissioners knew full well he would lose by it.[26]

Every contract written from 1825 to 1833 contained a clause that no extra payment would be allowed on any work originally specified in the agreement, even if floods or other "foreseeable" accidents should result in damage to work completed.[27] In this way, the commission effectively forced contractors to insure the state against losses from natural disasters during construction.

During the course of construction, however, changes in contracts were often ordered by the resident engineer. Such orders typically required substitution of better materials (for example, cut stone instead of rough stone), or else performance of work not embraced in the original contract. Orders of this kind became the subject of considerable tension between the commission and contractors, as the additional compensation was set unilaterally by the resident engineer after the extra work had been completed. In many cases, the contractors felt cheated by the valuations given to the "extras"; and the commission frequently needed to convene boards of appraisers to arbitrate such disputes. Unable to obtain satisfaction from the appraisers, some contractors went directly to the legislature to obtain special acts granting them compensation.[28]

Probably 12 to 15 per cent of the jobs on the canal lines were abandoned by contractors before they completed their obligations. Some were victims of rising wages and prices. Others suffered because of poor judgment in estimating their probable costs. The commission refused extra payments, even in cases such as that of one Elias Cozad, who surrendered his contract in 1827 when he found himself in debt for $700, having been underpaid (he claimed) for "extras" and squeezed by rising wage costs. To Commissioner Kelley, Cozad addressed a poignant appeal: "I have now (Dear Sir) spent two years and five months of my time labouring faithfully and unceasingly. . . . I have too mutch ambition to bow my neck to the wheel of misfortune and give up and die; before I will do this . . . I will risk life and health and continue canaling as long as their is a canal to make this side of hell." If he could only "git one of those sections" abandoned by other contractors, he concluded, he could salvage his fortunes.[29] In practice, when men such as Cozad did have legitimate grievances, the commissioners sought to appoint them as state agents, who were paid costs plus a percentage, to complete abandoned jobs.

The causes for abandonment of contracts varied, but among the most important was the occasional lack of state funds with which to pay monthly assessments of work already completed. Because the typical contractor had limited cash resources, he ordinarily borrowed from local banks to finance his initial costs.[30] But when the commission failed to pay him on schedule, especially if he were running at a loss anyway, the temptation to give up his job often became irresistible.

Another major cause of abandonment was a general increase in wages and prices. The demand for provisions and materials pushed up prices in local districts where construction was concentrated. And when sections of the canal line were opened to traffic, surplus produce from nearby farmers was exported to eastern markets, so that local prices often increased again twofold or more. Although this was a boon to farmers, contractors were adversely affected.[31] Wages also moved up steadily from 1825 to 1833. Itinerant labor was in short supply except on the Ohio Canal, where Irish laborers had emigrated from New York seeking work. Therefore contractors depended mainly upon local farmers and farm workers for their labor force. But such men were unreliable, tending to drift back to the farms during planting and harvest seasons; and the seasonal peaks of farm employment ordinarily drew off half or more of the laborers from the canal line.[32] During the summer months, moreover, visitations of "the fever and ague" (malaria) deterred farmers from taking on canal work in wet areas. One epidemic virtually suspended construction on the Ohio Canal for two months in 1827; and epidemics of smallpox in 1829 and cholera in 1832 struck down many canal workers, inducing the rest to flee from affected areas.[33]

As the result of such pressures, and the competition for labor from Pennsylvania and elsewhere, wages on the Ohio Canal's central division rose from $5 a month (with board) for common labor in 1825, to a range of $8 to $10 monthly in mid-1827. Skilled workers received higher pay: a blacksmith earned $11 a month in 1827, while in mid-1828 carpenters were paid a $21 monthly wage and men with teams as much as $40. All wages were subject to deductions for days lost because of weather. The contractors put up shanty housing for itinerant workers, usually providing free board and lodging in addition to the cash wages. Some contractors also issued a daily whiskey ration. A few ran company stores, selling straw hats, tobacco, pants, and the like to their workers, no doubt at high prices. Wages rose quickly after 1827, with common labor earning about $10 a month late in the year, $13 in 1828, and $16 in 1829.[34] Contractors in the Scioto Valley were paying wages of $16 to $18 in 1832, when cholera and floods made the work perilous for men on the lines.[35]

The canal commission treated rising wages as its own problem, and not as one that affected only the contractors. To combat labor shortages, the commission planned the pace of construction with a view toward minimizing the strain on available labor supplies— though always balancing this consideration against the goal of completing the canals quickly.[36] Then too, the various resident engineers kept one another informed about local labor needs, referring unemployed workers, especially the skilled masons and lockbuilders, to areas where they were needed.[37]

The commission's most dramatic intervention in labor relations was aimed at contractors who absconded from their jobs without paying workers overdue wages. This usually happened immediately after a contractor had received state money for work already performed; and such incidents not only caused hardships among the man's own laborers, but also set off disquieting rumors in the shanty camps. To allay such unrest, the commissioners announced in 1827 that if any contractor had failed to pay his men in full the previous month, the state would pay wages directly to the laborers, charging the amount against the contractor.[38] At the same time, however, the commission posted a *Notice to Labourers*, drafted by Alfred Kelley and reflecting his own notoriously puritanical ethos. The notice instructed laborers to settle their wage accounts with care each month; and it admonished them "to be industrious and sober and careful to earn the wages that the contractor agrees to pay, remembering that the surest way to get your pay is to earn it first." The commissioners would not interfere with contractors' arrangements to pay workers who were "idle, unfaithful, insolent or disobedient to their employer— Such men do not deserve their wages"![39]

The lesson in personal morality contained in the *Notice to Labourers* was a vivid reminder that the authority governing relations among the state officials, contractors, and laborers who worked and lived together in the raw, dreary shanty camps, was the authority of the acting commissioners, Micajah Williams and Alfred Kelley.

It was a striking feature of the board's operations that the two acting commissioners dominated not only all its technical engineering decisions but also its decisions on large policy questions. It is understandable that the board should have given Kelley and Williams a high degree of autonomy in overseeing technical work and governing relationships with contractors and laborers: for the acting commissioners were the men in the field, and as such were the best informed; and they were also the most highly trained in engineering technology.[40] But how did they gain their influence with other board members in general policy matters as well? Apparently they won the full confidence of the others by virtue of unusual talent, force of personality, intense dedication to the project, and a close working relationship with each other, unmarred by petty frictions or lack of faith.[41]

Their careers and personalities were by no means similar. Williams was a Carolina-born Quaker, who had joined the "Buckeye" migration from the upper South to the Ohio Valley in 1811, when at the age of 19 he became a journalist in Cincinnati. Later he engaged in land speculation and various petty mercantile ventures. A career in local politics carried him into the state legislature, and in 1822 he was speaker of the house.[42] Kelley, on the other hand, came out of the other great strain in Ohio's population, the New England element in the Western Reserve. Three years older than Williams, Kelley was a native of Connecticut who had migrated to Cleveland in 1810. There he was successively a lawyer, county attorney, officer of the town's first bank, and a representative in the legislature. Like Williams, he speculated heavily in real estate; unlike Williams, who dealt mainly in wild lands, Kelley invested in urban property—and unlike Williams, he made a fortune at it. A prototype of the legendary stern New England character, Kelley was renowned for his aloofness and self-discipline. Williams brought southern cordiality to his relations with other men; he was fond of a good joke; and friends said that he went about the business of canal building with all the enthusiasm of a small lad.[43] Superimposed upon these contrasts was a marked difference in political views. Both men had been Jeffersonian Republicans in their early careers, but Williams became a founder of the Ohio Democracy when Andrew Jackson emerged as its leader in the 1820's, while Kelley helped organize the state's Whig party and was a follower of Henry Clay.[44]

None of these differences prevented Kelley and Williams from working together harmoniously in all canal matters. Kelley had charge of the northern and central divisions of the Ohio Canal, and Williams directed its southern division and the Miami Canal line. In their respective jurisdictions, they approved all contract specifications, represented the commission in relations with contractors and laborers, and enjoyed virtually autonomous power to order changes in specifications and repairs on the completed lines. They also had final responsibility for ordering payments to contractors for work done. Despite the large sums of money they handled, never was any evidence of malfeasance uncovered, and there was general agreement among contemporaries that the two men were thoroughly incorruptible.[45]

The acting commissioners also had immediate charge of about twenty men holding the rank of junior engineer or higher in the state engineering corps.[46] One of their important functions was to give the younger scientific personnel technical training. Because of the persistent shortage of engineers, and also because the "principal engineer," David S. Bates, left the state service in 1829 and was not replaced, Kelley and Williams prepared the junior engineers to assume more responsible positions. The commissioners' success in turning out "home made Engineers"— which they regarded as one of their key activities—was evident in the fact that of nine men holding the rank of resident engineer in 1832, at least six had come up through the hierarchy of the Ohio corps.[47]

Although Kelley enjoyed the respect of his junior staff, he seemed nearly incapable of delegating top-level managerial tasks and was impatient with any subordinate whose dedication to the canal was less intense than his own.[48] For example, when in 1831 work in the Scioto Valley was retarded by epidemics among the laborers, floods, and vexing technical problems, Kelley deplored the pessimism of William Price, the engineer in charge, who believed it impossible to complete construction by mid-1832. "There are few things," Kelley wrote, "that cannot be accomplished by *determination* accompanied by *faith*. But a man seldom feels as anxious to *falsify* as to *verify* his own predictions. Therefore I feel it will not be done. I wish Mr. Price felt otherwise—for then I should hope much." Kelley then urged Williams, to whom Price reported, to take over personal responsibility for supervising work in the field.[49]

Williams, on the other hand, recognized the need to develop a bureaucracy capable of functioning without the constant presence of the acting commissioners. Refusing to supervise Price more closely, he urged Kelley to remain away from the canal lines occasionally—as he himself did—asserting: "You have superintending engineers on the line, who are mostly of your own selection. . . . *To these it is proper to commit its charge.* . . . The state will soon be under the necessity of confiding the entire charge and responsibility of the two canals to these very men."[50]

Williams' position in this dialogue reflected his concern to promote systematized procedures and regulations. Upon his initiative the canal commission appointed "superintending engineers" as the completed canal lines were opened to traffic. Each engineer was given full responsibility for maintenance and orderly navigation on his division of the line. Under them were "superintendents," who directed the state crews which performed repairs as needed.[51] Williams insisted, however, that the superintending engineers give full attention to their work and be present near the line. "The object of their employment," he declared, "is, in part, that the line shall have the benefits of their *constant* and *watchful* personal superintendence."[52]

Another important task performed by the two acting commissioners was evaluating applications for appointments to canal posts. As of 1835 the operating canals required five superintending engineers, fifteen division superintendents, and numerous toll collectors, locktenders, and common laborers.[53] What might readily have become a machine for personal or partisan favors was operated instead on a calculus of efficiency: resisting pressures from politicians who sought to influence appointments, the acting commissioners probed closely the personal reputations and business experience of all applicants. Using a remarkably effective intelligence network of informants throughout the state, people they knew from the legislature or their personal business dealings, Kelley and Williams searched diligently to fill the new bureaucracy with capable men.[54]

Aside from their concern with the myriad details of construction and the task of organizing a bureaucracy, Kelley and Williams were alert to larger economic opportunities that the canal enterprise was creating. Unlike the typical merchant-capitalist who then dominated economic life in the West, and who confined himself mainly to traditional, locally oriented enterprises, Kelley and Williams knew intimately the geography and resources of the entire state. Indeed, they viewed the western economy as a totality.[55] When the canal-bond issues produced an infusion of eastern funds, for example, Williams understood that it provided Ohio banks with an opportunity to expand their note issues. Until then, the local banks had issued notes almost exclusively on loans to borrowers in their own communities. But when the funds from bond sales were deposited with them, these institutions could issue notes to contractors in distant areas with little fear that the paper would return quickly for redemption. This in turn permitted the banks to operate on the basis of smaller specie reserves relative to note circulation, effectively increasingly the supply of money in the state's economy.[56] On both the Miami and Ohio canal lines, Williams and Kelley approved payment to contractors in notes of the banks where state funds were deposited—a policy that the commissioners supported over vigorous objections of some contractors, who were forced to accept discounts on the notes when they used the paper locally to buy provisions and supplies.[57] Similarly, the acting commissioners recognized early the vital importance of power sites that the canals would provide; and whenever possible, they obtained for the state land that was adaptable for mill sites.[58]

Kelley and Williams also shared their knowledge of Ohio's resources with capitalists who considered establishing towns, opening mines, or building factories and mills along the canals. The two men kept an eye out for the main chance as well. Kelley speculated heavily in lands at Cleveland and Columbus, both major canal towns; and Williams made numerous small investments in mercantile and mining ventures, also borrowing heavily to buy town lots in Port Lawrence (later Toledo), which he believed was the head of navigation on the Maumee River, then projected as the route for extension of the Miami Canal north and east to Lake Erie.[59]

Their primary concern, however, was the success of the canal project itself, and none of their private investments represented a corrupt use of their offices and powers.[60] Indeed, Kelley and Williams shared a deep involvement in the canal enterprise which can best be termed "proprietary." For though they did not personally bear the financial risks of canal construction, the enterprise could succeed only if the engineering was sound and construction efficient. The financial resources of the state were not inexhaustible; and effective use of those resources was, in the end, the acting commissioners' responsibility.[61] Kelley's dedication was expressed eloquently in a promise to his wife in 1825, just before he accepted an appointment for what became eight years in charge of construction, that one day they might together ride a packet boat "from Lake Erie to the Ohio River, on a canal which your husband had a large share in making." He had already given nearly three years to the project, a period marked by long absences from home, and it would have been easier to resign when the canal bill was enacted, yielding responsibility for construction to others. But Kelley would not "leave so important a work. . . . You know it would be inconsistent with my character for perseverence," he wrote.[62] When Kelley fell seriously ill a year later, his colleagues had to plead with him to rest at home instead of carrying on his canal work in the field, as he had intended. Petitioning Kelley to become a candidate for elective office later that year, a political admirer urged him to respond affirmatively and "not let that second wife of yours (the Canal) answer the question for you."[63]

Even when Kelley lay critically ill at Columbus in the winter of 1832, having apparently contracted pneumonia in the field, he could not put down the reins: he corresponded daily with engineers, contractors, claimants for damages, and minor canal personnel. And when Micajah T. Williams was appointed Surveyor General of the Northwest Territory in 1831, Kelley wrote immediately to implore that "our great project must not be deserted by its friends"; he urged Williams to remain as acting commissioner until they could be sure "that the vacancy will not be filled by some one who will mar our harmony and prove an enemy in disguise."[64]

That Williams fully shared this proprietary attitude was reflected in his decision to remain, without pay, as acting commissioner, as Kelley had requested. Indeed a year earlier, when Kelley's young son had died, Williams put equally strong pressure on him to remain at his post: "Your family, your friends, and your country," he wrote, "have yet a right to expect your energies, and intelligence, to be exerted in their behalf."[65]

As Williams revealed in evoking the expectations of "your country," these men were driven by a pride in the state but no less by a nationalistic vision. In their private correspondence, and also in their public reports, they expressed a faith that "pecuniary advantages are not the only benefits resulting from the opening of these great [canals] through our state: they serve to bind together, by the strong ties of interest, different parts of our state, and of the nation."[66] They shared with De Witt Clinton, with Henry Clay, and with others who were then promoting the cause of transportation improvement by the state and Federal governments, a sense that they were engaged in nation-building.[67] The brand of nationalism that sustained the ardor and dedication of men like Kelley and Williams was well expressed by John C. Calhoun, who wrote of their Ohio canal project: "It seems almost a miracle that a state in its infancy should undertake, and successfully execute so great a work, and it may be cited as one of the strongest proofs of the admirable effects of our political institutions in giving a high degree of intelligence and enter-prize."[68] Kelley and Williams were motivated too by what Kelley said was his concern to prove the merits of the 1825 canal plan "by actual experiment, by real fruition." For as he recognized, the optimistic predictions of the old canal commission as to the feasibility, cost, and probable benefits of the project were "*our* calculations."[69] He and Williams had been responsible, more than any other man except possibly Ethan Allen Brown, for exciting the high expectations that prevailed in the legislature in February 1825. During the ensuing eight years of arduous work in the field, however, credit for the project's successful culmination was more nearly theirs alone.

NOTES

1. Clay to Alfred Kelley, April 9, 1825, CC Papers.
2. Canal Commission Minute Books, Feb. 7, 1825 (MSS., Dept. of Public Works, Records Room, Columbus). The canal law had permitted appointment of three acting commissioners, but the board chose to name only two. For a brief period in 1827 the commission also appointed Worthington to be acting commissioner; but he never played an important role in actually supervising construction, and he died shortly afterward. Williams took over Worthington's projected responsibilities in the Scioto Valley.
3. Daniel Calhoun writes that "the most thorough adoption [by another state] of New York personnel and practices occurred in Ohio," in *The American Civil Engineer* (Cambridge, 1960), 35.
4. John Kilbourne, ed., *Public Documents Concerning the Ohio Canals* (Columbus, 1832), 176ff.; MS. "Abstract of Expenditures, Dec. 1, 1825–March 1, 1826," Micajah T. Williams Papers, OSL.
5. E. Buckingham to T. Worthington, Jan. 3, 1824, Thomas

Worthington Papers, OHS. Also, Kilbourne, *Public Documents,* 176ff.

6. Act of Feb. 8, 1826, *ibid.,* 231.

7. For an example, see *ibid.,* 269–70.

8. CC Papers, for 1827–28, *passim.*

9. Kelley to James B. Gardiner, Jan. 27, 1827, *ibid.* The same view prevailed in the legislature as well. (*House Journal,* 1829–30, pp. 579–80, that "the State ought not to embark her funds on any further Canals of magnitude, until subsequent to the completion of those now in progress.")

10. Kilbourne, *Public Documents,* 297–99, 317–18; *House Journal,* 1830–31, pp. 243–44.

11. The one exception is that the Muskingum Valley was not directly represented. But a leading citizen of that region, Ebenezer Buckingham, was appointed as a member of the board of canal fund commissioners. As such he did not hesitate to press the canal commission to give attention to local interests of his fellow Muskingum residents. (See Buckingham to Isaac Minor, Nov. 21, 1825, CC Papers, pressing for surveys of the line near the headwaters of the Muskingum.)

12. Worthington to Williams, June 13, 1825, Micajah T. Williams Papers, OSL; Minor to Tappan, Nov. 11, 1825, Tappan Papers, OHS. These documents reveal that Worthington was not popular with the other commissioners; he stood nearly alone in dissenting privately from major decisions of the board.

13. See Chap. 4, below, p. 97.

14. James Williams to Kelley, Dec. 27, 1824, M. T. Williams to Kelley, Feb. 24, 1825, CC Papers; M. T. Williams to Clinton, Jan. 22, 1826, De Witt Clinton Papers, Columbia University Library; Kelley to Williams, April 12, 1831, Williams Papers.

15. The work of a board of appraisers may be traced in the papers of a member of one such group, in Vol. 10 of the McBride Papers (MSS.), CHS. Precedents for seizure of property for public roads dated from a territorial law of 1799 (cited in 7 Ohio Rep. 453).

16. Cooper *v.* Williams, 4 Ohio Rep. at 288, 285–86. See also Bates *v.* Cooper, 5 Ohio Rep. 115; McArthur *v.* Kelley, 5 Ohio Rep. 139.

17. Kelley to Simon Perkins, March 13, 1825, Simon Perkins Papers, WRHS.

18. Unfortunately the commissioners sometimes erred by promising

too much. When they encouraged private citizens to donate land or cash to the canal fund, to help finance small changes in the canal plan of importance to localities, they often aroused local expectations that were unreasonable in light of financial realities. (See, for one such case, B. M. Atherton *et al.* to Kelley, Feb. 24, 1825, CC Papers; J. Blickensderfer to Kelley, Jan. 19, 1826, Misc. MS. No. 232, WRHS; for another example, see C. Baker to Kelley, June 8, 1831, CC Papers.)

19. Committee report in which Blackburn joined, *Senate Journal,* 1829–30, pp. 396–99.

20. CC, *12th AR* (1834), 5. The early European employment of master craftsmen is treated in Harold Pollins, "The Swansea Canal," *Journal of Transport History,* I (May 1954), 143.

21. Jobs on the level lines were usually one-half mile in length; in addition, separate contracts were made for heavy facilities such as locks and aqueducts. (Williams to Minor, Sept. 28, 1825, CC Papers; *House Journal,* 1829–30, pp. 227–32.)

22. "Notice to Bidders," broadside dated May 17, 1827, Williams Papers; N. Beasley *et al.* to Minor, Aug. 5, 1825, CC Papers; entries of June 9, 10, 1825, Board of Canal Fund Commissioners Letterbooks, OSA; also, Ernest L. Bogart, *Internal Improvements and State Debt in Ohio* (New York, 1924), 31–32.

23. H. McNamara to Kelley, March 8, 1825, De Witt Clinton to Kelley and Williams, March 30, 1825, CC Papers; *Liberty Hall and Cincinnati Gazette,* June 24, 1825; correspondence with contractors, 1825, *passim,* CC Papers.

24. Kelley to Brown, March 11, 1825, Brown Papers, OSL; see also *Liberty Hall and Cincinnati Gazette,* June 14, 25, 1825; and names in list of Miami Canal contractors, Williams Papers. Local merchants with canal contracts are discussed in *Piqua Gazette,* May–July, 1834, *passim,* indicating that the local entrepreneur continued to play a large role when the Miami Extension Canal was built.

25. "Notice to Bidders," broadside, May 17, 1827, Williams Papers; see also W. R. Dickinson to Kelley, Oct. 24, 1826, CC Papers.

26. For an example, see Jesse Williams to M. T. Williams, Aug. 4, 1829, CC Papers; and Jesse to Micajah Williams, May 13, 1831, Williams Papers. In 1825, when bidding was still highly competitive, Williams wrote: "The great difficulty is in keeping from letting [contracts] too low. It is difficult to know when to stop

while you have bids from good men." (Williams to Minor, Sept. 28, 1825, CC Papers.)

27. "Notice to Bidders," Williams Papers; Kilbourne, *Public Documents,* 188; *House Journal,* 1829–30, pp. 227–30.

28. *Ibid.,* 227–32. The archives of the Canal Commission contain letters of complaint and pressure from contractors for additional payments beginning about November 1826. (Williams to Kelley, Nov. 3, 1826, discusses "run away contractors," as does Perkins to Kelley, Nov. 4, 1826, CC Papers.)

29. E. Cozad to Kelley, Dec. 8, 1827, CC Papers.

30. Perkins to Kelley, Nov. 4, 1826, Wm. Price to Kelley, Nov. 16, 1826, CC Papers.

31. Williams to Kelley, March 29, 1831, R. Howe to Kelley, Dec. 3, 1831, CC Papers; R. Osborne to Williams, July 25, 1829, Williams Papers.

32. Kelley to Allen Trimble, Aug. 15, 1827, Trimble Family Papers, OHS, that "the labourers have been engaged in harvesting and some apprehension of sickness prevents their return in abundance"; Byron Kilbourn to Williams, July 28, 1829, Williams Papers, on the harvest's effect on labor force; Cleveland *Herald,* June 16, 1826, on labor problems in general, and *ibid.,* July 22, 1825, on the Irish.

33. Williams to Tappan, Sept. 8, 1827, Tappan Papers; Kelley to Brown, Oct. 14, 1827, Brown Papers, OSL, that work had been suspended for two months because of sickness; F. Cleveland to Williams, July 27, 1829, on smallpox; Williams to Kelley, Oct. 22, 1832, CC Papers, on cholera.

34. Avery & Whitaker Account Books (MSS.), OHS; J. Dillon to Williams, July 1, 1825, Williams Papers; E. Cozad to Kelley, Dec. 8, 1827, CC Papers, asserting that workers "in the water" (at jobs that required them to wade in the bed of streams) were paid 75 cents to $1.00 per day (or up to $26.00 per month) in 1826. Monthly wages are computed as equivalent to 26 days when only data for daily wage are available. Diggers (common laborers) on the Ohio Canal's northern division were paid $8 to $10 a month plus board and lodging in 1826–27, "but every wet day was counted out," so that it took "all winter to make about two months' time." (W. C. Howells, *Recollections of Life in Ohio* [Cincinnati, 1895], 139.) A British immigrant reported wages on the Ohio Canal's central division in 1830 as $13 a month and board, with quarriers earning $16 to $17 and board,

and highly skilled stone cutters (who were paid by the piece)
clearing $1 a day or more. (H. Rose to John Rose, Feb. 2, 1830,
Scotch Settlement, Ohio, MS. in private possession, copy provided
by Dr. Charlotte Erickson.)

35. F. Cleveland to Williams, April 6, 1832, Jesse Williams to M.
Williams, May 13, 1831, Williams Papers; Williams to Tappan,
May 22, 1832, Tappan Papers; Cleveland *Herald*, Aug. 20,
1829. The great increase in wages in Ohio after 1827 was not
paralleled by wages for repair work (more steady, and lower
paid) on the Erie Canal, where laborers were paid 75 cents per
day throughout 1829–32. However, on other lines of new construction, wages rose apace with those in Ohio; on the Chesapeake & Ohio Canal, in Maryland, common labor was paid
$10–12 per month in 1828, but as high as $20 in 1832. (W. S.
Sanderlin, *The Great National Project* [Baltimore, 1946], 70–71,
71n.; Walter B. Smith, "Wage Rates on the Erie Canal, 1828–
1881," *Journal of Economic History*, XXIII [1963], 303–4.) For
other data on canal wages, see W. A. Sullivan, *The Industrial
Worker in Pennsylvania* (Harrisburg, 1955), 72–73; and Stanley Lebergott, *Manpower in Economic Growth* (New York,
1964), 311–13; and Ralph D. Gray, *The National Waterway: A
History of the Chesapeake and Delaware Canal* (Urbana, 1967),
52.

36. Kelley to Brown, May 15, 1826, Brown Papers, OSL; Jesse Williams to M. Williams, April 13, 1832, Williams Papers.

37. The legislature also permitted the commission to use convict
labor in 1827. (*House Journal*, 1827–28, pp. 19–20; also, Williams to Kelley, Jan. 13, 1826, CC Papers; Kelley to Williams,
April 26, 1827, Williams Papers.

38. Kilbourne, *Public Documents*, 287.

39. Broadside, June 1827, Williams Papers, OSL; also, Williams to
Kelley, June 21, 1827, CC Papers; Kilbourne, *Public Documents*,
247–50.

40. David S. Bates, the principal engineer, was more highly trained,
but he left the state service in 1829 and his position was left
vacant. (*House Journal*, 1829–30, pp. 223–24.)

41. Alexander Bourne, who succeeded Worthington on the board
after the latter's death in 1827, complained that his opinion "had
little or no weight. . . . I suppose the people, also, think that the
services of the commissioners, other than the acting commissioner, are worth nothing, and we might as well stay at home."

(Bourne to Kelley, April 8, 1832, CC Papers.) Aside from some friction with Worthington over the construction priorities set in 1825, and from the testy complaints of Bourne, who was obviously a minority of one, the acting commissioners' relationships with the others were marked by a high degree of mutual confidence and harmony.

42. Scheiber, "Entrepreneurship and Western Development: The Case of Micajah T. Williams," *Business History Review*, XXXVII (Winter 1963), 345ff.

43. Samuel Forrer, ms. sketch of Williams' life and character, Williams Papers; A. L. Cummings, *The Alfred Kelley House* (Columbus, 1953), *passim;* J. L. Bates, *Alfred Kelley* (Columbus, 1888), is the only full biography.

44. Williams' role in the Democracy is treated in Harry Stevens, *The Early Jackson Party in Ohio* (Durham, 1957); Kelley's in the Whig Party, in Francis P. Weisenburger, *Passing of the Frontier* (Columbus, 1941).

45. See reminiscences (Mss.) of contemporaries in the Williams Papers; Walter R. Marvin, "Alfred Kelley," *Museum Echoes*, XXXIII (1960), 11–12; special resolution lauding Kelley and giving him sick leave with pay, *House Journal*, 1831–32, p. 447.

46. *House Journal*, 1829–30, p. 381.

47. Williams to Worthington, May 22, 1826, Worthington Papers, OSL; Williams to Brown, June 13, 1826, Brown Papers, OSL; list of engineers in *House Journal*, 1831–32, pp. 311–12; and Charles Whittlesey, "Pioneer Engineers of Ohio," in Henry Howe, *Historical Collections of Ohio* (2 vols., Cincinnati, 1908), I, 120.

48. Kelley also came into conflict with Principal Engineer Bates over the latter's practice of remaining away from the canal lines for long periods. (Kelley to Williams, Sept. 1, 1825, CC Papers.)

49. Kelley to Williams, Feb. 6, 1832, Williams Papers.

50. Williams to Kelley, Feb. 19, 1832, CC Papers.

51. Canal Commission Minutes, Jan. 30, 1832; *House Journal*, 1830–31, p. 240. Superintending engineers were paid $1200 per year and Superintendents $35 per month. (Tappan to W. T. Rogers, Feb. 5, 1835, CC Papers.)

52. Williams to S. Forrer, April 2, 1831, Williams Papers.

53. Tappan to Rogers, Feb. 5, 1835, CC Papers; see also Williams

to Kelley, April 20, 1830, CC Papers. To my knowledge, there is no accurate estimate of the number of state laborers employed on a *per diem* basis on the operating canals; doubtless the size of the force fluctuated widely.

54. See Kelley to Williams, April 8, 1830, Williams Papers; Williams to Kelley, April 20, 1830, CC Papers. Also, CC Papers, *passim*, 1827–33.

55. In addition to the annual reports of the CC, see, for examples of Kelley's interest in projects of broad importance, Kelley to Brown, Feb. 23, 1824, Brown Papers, OSL; Kelley to Brown, Feb. 23, 1824, Brown Papers, OSL; Kelley to Brown, March 23, 1825, *ibid.*, and to Elisha Whittlesey, Jan. 11, 1825, Elisha Whittlesey Papers, WRHS, on Cleveland harbor improvements; to M. T. Williams and Benjamin Tappan, n.d. (marked Oct. 2, 1826), Alfred Kelley Papers, OHS, on his doing a map "with a view of preserving from loss various items of information . . . collected during the progress of the [canal] surveys"; Kelley to Perkins, Feb. 24, 1833, Perkins Papers, on the Miami Extension project. See also Bates, *Alfred Kelley, passim*. On Williams, cf. my article-length biography, "Entrepreneurship and Western Development," cited n. 42; this and the following paragraph of the text follow that article closely.

56. Ebenezer Buckingham to E. A. Brown, Oct. 18, 1825, Buckingham to W. Welles, Dec. 23, 1825, BFC Papers; Brown to Buckingham, Nov. 5, 1825, Brown Papers, OSL; J. Creed to Williams, Nov. 27, 1825, Williams Papers.

57. "Mr. Kelley and Mr. Williams acted determinedly with contractors [ca. 1825–26] and told them that if they persisted in demanding specie . . . that they would cease to make advances untill the job was compleated." (S. Maccracken to S. Forrer, Apr. 30, 1834, BFC Papers.)

58. R. Anderson to Williams, Apr. 12, 1828, Williams Papers; Williams to Kelley, March 29, 1831, CC Papers.

59. Scheiber, "Entrepreneurship and Western Development," 355; Bates, *Alfred Kelley*.

60. His political enemies in later years accused Kelley of making a fortune on information to which he was privy as canal commissioner. (See the vicious attack in *Western Hemisphere* [Columbus], Oct. 5, 1836.) There was one investigation of Kelley in 1830, but he defended his good name with complete success. (Simon Perkins to Kelley, March 16, 1830, CC Papers.)

61. I have developed at length the argument that both the functions and the psychology of Kelley and Williams were comparable to those associated with innovating private entrepreneurs, in "Entrepreneurship and Western Development," 352ff.
62. Kelley to his wife, Jan. 21, 1825, Kelley Papers.
63. Perkins to Kelley, Aug. 8, 1826, R. Harper to Kelley, Dec. 11, 1826, CC Papers.
64. Kelley to Williams, April 12, 1831, Williams Papers.
65. Williams to Kelley, Sept. 27, 1830, CC Papers.
66. *Senate Journal*, 1832–33, p. 345, report of the CC.
67. Aside from Clinton and Henry Clay, others prominent in the national internal improvements movement who corresponded with Williams and Kelley, and who had met them at one time or another in the course of Ohio canal promotion, were Elkanah Watson, Charles Haines, and Cadwallader Colden, all of New York; Thomas Biddle and Benjamin Chew of Philadelphia; and James Bradford of Virginia. (Correspondence in CC Papers.)
68. Calhoun to Brown, Jan. 28, 1828, Brown Papers, OHS. On nationalism as manifested similarly in the ideas of the Erie Canal promoters, see Ronald Shaw, *Erie Water West* (Syracuse, 1966), 397ff.
69. Kelley to Williams, April 26, 1827, Williams Papers. (Italics added.)

CHAPTER 4

Egalitarian Ideals and Pressure for Expansion
1825-1838

WHEN the canal program of 1825 was undertaken, it was generally agreed in Ohio that the first canals were an experiment in public enterprise. If this venture met with success, then expansion of the public works would follow: the state's patronage would be extended to local districts by-passed by the first canals. Naturally, the "neglected" districts were unwilling to defer for long the fulfillment of their local ambitions; and while the first canals were being built, new projects were planned nearly everywhere in the state. Militating against additional commitments by the legislature, however, were both fiscal constraints and the unyielding opposition of the canal commission.[1] By the early 1830's such restraining influences began to lose their force, and in 1836 they collapsed altogether: the legislature, apparently acting on the maxim "Something for Everyone" authorized between 1836 and 1838 a new program that included construction of three major canals, a costly river-improvement project, and large-scale state aid to private companies engaged in canal, railroad, and turnpike construction.

The legislature's decision for expansion, during 1836–38, was primarily a response to rising local demands for new projects; and these demands no doubt represented above all the quest for concrete economic advantage. Yet something else seems to have conditioned the policy-making process—namely, the influence of an essentially ideological view of state transport policy.

This view, expressed in the rhetoric of men who promoted new projects, held that the benefits of public enterprise must be "equalized" and therefore widely diffused. It was a variant of the egalitarian political ideology that pervaded popular thought in the 1820's and 1830's; and as such, it provided men with a well-developed rationale for expansion of state-financed public works on a comprehensive scale, rather than expansion on a cautious and selective basis.

The Transportation Revolution had captured the imagination of Americans not solely because it was generating vast changes in the material conditions of life, but also because of its democratic implications. This was an era, as one Ohioan declared, "fraught with improvements of the utmost importance to the happiness of the human race: . . . the spirit of Canalling, the progress made in rail roads, and the improvements in Steam."[2] The new technology, which was forging an integrated national economy, also promised to effect a social transformation. The French observer Michel Chevalier expressed a view commonly held by Americans when he wrote in 1835 that transportation innovations would "reduce the distance not only between different places, but between different classes." To improve communications facilities in a society, he declared, "is to establish equality and democracy" because all members of the society would obtain "the power of moving about and using the world which has been given to all as a common patrimony."[3] Similarly, Governor William H. Seward of New York asserted in 1839 that internal improvements, when combined with public education, would produce "the highest attainable equality" in American society. A Virginia promoter praised canals and railroads for bringing "a more general diffusion of wealth and comfort throughout all classes of the community." And Samuel Ruggles, an organizer of the Erie Railroad, declared that "the moment steam entered, aristocracy was doomed and the final enfranchisement of society from artificial distinctions, absolutely and effectively secured."[4]

This view of internal improvements as part of a larger social process was frequently expressed in Ohio, as elsewhere. In 1822, for instance, the old canal commission had predicted that public works would benefit their immediate trade regions, but would also diffuse "wealth, activity, and vigor to the whole" of the state. Later, the public canal officers wrote that "the moral and intellectual condition of a people is improved as commercial facilities are extended."[5]

Unless such declarations are to be dismissed out of hand as empty rhetoric, they signified that there was a reciprocal relationship between the Transportation Revolution and egalitarian ideas in the 1820's and 1830's. The historian Lee Benson has recently commented on one side of this relationship. Rapid innovations in transportation and the dynamic economic expansion that they generated, Benson has written, "acted as powerful stimulants to [reform] movements inspired by the egalitarian ideals of the Declaration of Independence."[6] But egalitarian ideals also worked their effects upon the policy decisions that effected America's Transportation Revolution. For in the United States, in the early nineteenth century, "The people were the state; the state was their 'Common Wealth.' They identified with it and felt that they should share, as of right, in the advantages that it could bring to them as a community."[7] Because egalitarian ideology so thoroughly pervaded American political thought, it easily became a corollary that all members of the community should share *equally* in the benefits that government might provide.

Insofar as ideology became an issue in debates of public transportation policy, therefore, the test of a policy's legitimacy tended to be how well it diffused material benefits, rather than whether it conformed to preconceptions about either *laisser-faire* or interventionism. The popular attitude respecting internal improvements by government seems to have been no less egalitarian than attitudes toward expansion of educational opportunities, extension of the suffrage, and similar reforms. Thus, in Ohio as in other states, egalitarianism converged with the pursuit of local self-interest and the drive for material progress, to condition policy decisions.

Indeed, the very phrase "equalized benefits" became a rallying cry for promoters of new transport projects in Ohio.[8] They demanded state expenditures to benefit "neglected" local districts not as a favor, "but as a right." Although no region of the state was hurt by canals already built, the proper goal was to assure that all regions were "benefited alike." Invoking this doctrine, a group of canal promoters told the legislature in 1842: "We expect [aid], at your hands, as part of your duty, upon the principle of equal rights." Similarly, advocates of a new state canal for northern Ohio professed approval of "the public spirit and liberal policy" embodied in the 1825 canal program; they insisted, however, that "the same enlightened and liberal policy should be extended to all portions of our great and growing State . . . which have not as yet been benefited by the public disbursements which they have contributed to raise."[9]

In this way, Americans elevated their arguments for local advantages to the status of a political principle.[10] Nor was this association between equal rights and "equalized benefits" confined to Ohio. In South Carolina, for example, representatives from the remote undeveloped western region complained in 1827 that building public transportation facilities in all districts of a state "is among the fundamental principles of the social compact—a right without which there would be no equality of benefits." Virginia's board of public works declared in 1837 that a state transport program could not remain confined to only a few regions, any more than "freedom and good government" could legitimately be restricted to "the patriotic band" who had fought the Revolution. In Indiana, a champion of internal improvements similarly asserted that "when public benefits are to be conferred or expected to be so, they ought to be equalized as far as possible. . . ." The same ideas were sometimes expressed in Congress as well: in 1831, for instance, a House committee endorsed Federal aid to internal improvements in the West because only by such action could Congress "equalise the public benefits of the country."[11]

Geared as it was to popular egalitarian ideology, the "equal benefits" doctrine was compelling. Few political leaders dared combat it explicitly with the counter-assertion that expansion of state commitments needed to be kept in balance with fiscal capacity. The typical response was that of the Ohio official who in 1835 declared that the purpose of republican government being "the general good," it must serve "the common interests of the whole people, rather than [giving] to one section, advantages which are withheld from others." Similarly, Governor Joseph Vance asserted in 1838 that, even though the state's finances were being strained by public works expenditures, "every principle of justice" called for enlarging the state program further in order to put every section "on an equality" with those that were benefited by the projects under way.[12]

The doctrine of equal benefits thus dictated that "a course of partial legislation," which aided some but not all, was intolerable.[13] But proponents of new public works did not restrict themselves to this kind of argument. For they were also able to draw upon a fund of rhetoric, bequeathed to them by advocates of the original canal program of 1825, which justified public works expenditures on more narrowly economic grounds. First was the proposition, repeatedly stated in the early canal commission reports, that well-planned transport works would be profitable, self-liquidating enterprises, producing revenues sufficient to amortize any debt incurred to build them. Second was the view that even if toll revenues failed to meet expectations, the indirect benefits—in the form of higher land values, increased tax revenues, and enhanced private income and living standards—would more than justify public transport investment. Third was an argument, based on appeal to the commonwealth tradition, that adequate public transportation was "essential to the honor and prosperity of the state."[14]

All three arguments proved readily adaptable to the purposes of those who advocated expansion. Most convenient of all was the concept of "indirect benefits," which used loosely enough could justify nearly any state expenditure. One spokesman, who favored "extension of Canals to every part of the State" thus maintained that "the State, instead of being impoverished by contracting debts for such a purpose, would be enriched [even] if no tolls were ever collected from them."[15] In the same vein, the Democratic minority caucus of the Ohio legislature declared in 1837 that the state's resources might be said "to increase in proportion to the magnitude of debt incurred."[16] To be sure, such a position was extreme, even a caricature of the indirect returns doctrine. But while most promoters of new transport schemes acknowledged that there were practical limitations upon growth of the state debt, they usually viewed such limits as peculiarly relevant to rival projects, not their own.

Reinforcing the arguments for expansion of the public works was the entrepreneurial spirit of the day. Ohio's electorate seemed to share fully what James Willard Hurst, our leading student of nineteenth-century American law, has identified as a pervasive view of the time: that "the legal order should mobilize the resources of the community to help shape an environment which gave men more liberty by increasing the practical range of choices open to them and minimizing the limiting force of circumstances."[17] Indeed, the belief in maintaining free play for particularistic economic ambitions sometimes became nearly indistinguishable from contemporary definitions of the "common weal" or the "public interest." Thus Ohio's leading Democratic newspaper warned "all wise Legislators" in 1833 that if they ignored pressures for expansion of the public works, they risked "cramping the growing energies of the State" and might "shut her up from progressive improvement." The same spirit was manifest in a petition of merchants who declared in 1838 that the state's canals "were designed to expand our Commerce, and give a free competition to Enterprize, to equallize the profits of Labour." Similarly, the directors of a turnpike corporation demanded public financial aid on grounds that they were "citizens entitled to the fostering care of the State, . . . one of whose great maxims of policy is to advance the interests of the whole by encouraging individual effort and enterprise."[18]

The foregoing analysis of the rhetoric of internal improvements does not, of course, prove that entrepreneurial imperatives or abstract notions of equal rights, equal benefits, or indirect returns were in themselves sufficient to persuade the legislature to approve an enlarged, comprehensive program. But these ideas colored the intellectual milieu in which self-interested schemes for projects of local interest were debated. They contributed to a public mood that is usually described as a "canal mania" in the 1830's, when "the spirit of improvement" was everywhere "animating" the people of Ohio.[19] Political leaders paid lip service, at least, to the abstract concepts that impelled this spirit. Neither the Whigs nor the Jacksonian Democrats in Ohio dared to oppose the principle of state expenditures for public works on ideological *laisser-faire* grounds. When the legislature finally wrote a series of laws in the mid-thirties for expansion of the public works system, the people's representatives may well have read the popular mind and concluded that a bold policy—or even a reckless one—was politically much safer than cautious extension of internal improvements on a system of rational priorities.[20] Few had the courage or insight of the politician who declared in 1838 that "no one can believe a doctrine like this; this system of improvement may be over-done like any other business."[21] It was only when the state treasury approached bankruptcy in the early 1840's that Ohioans were willing to tolerate such heretical views.

THE FORMULATION OF NEW PROJECTS

Although proposals for new public works gained a certain respectability and force because of ideological imperatives, there was no lack of self-interested localism at work in the promotion of new schemes. In every region of the state, local growth obviously depended upon adequate transportation facilities. The struggle to obtain state patronage thus became central to a political situation in which rivalries were marked by intense ambitions, deeply rooted fear of failure, and ingenious employment of the instruments of political leverage by local leaders.

Characteristically, the leading commercial towns spoke in state politics for the trade areas with which they were associated. Yet within each region towns competed vigorously with one another to win hegemony as local market centers. No major project could hope to gain substantial support in its quest for state patronage without first resolving such local differences. The early efforts of transport promoters were usually dedicated to molding an effective coalition of local interests within a region, then to cementing an interregional alliance in favor of their schemes. Even the prospect of new transportation facilities might then disrupt older political alliances, undermining the sense of common interests, or collective consciousness, that formerly bound together the various communities within a given region. Nearly every new project created its own opposition either by challenging vested commercial interests or else by threatening the aspirations of communities that would be bypassed by the proposed new transportation facility.[22]

Ironically, one of the earliest schemes to attract public attention, in a movement that culminated in enlargement of the state's canal system, was a project for railroad construction. This was the Mad River and Lake Erie Railroad, first promoted by a group of businessmen in Sandusky. A lake port town of about six hundred inhabitants, Sandusky enjoyed fine harbor facilities and aspired to be the northern terminus of the Ohio Canal. When Cleveland was selected instead, because of inadequate water to supply a line between Columbus and Sandusky, residents of the village at first responded with attacks upon the canal commission, accusing its members of corruption and self-seeking. But Sandusky's leaders gradually turned to more positive goals. Within a few years, they were developing a plan for a railroad to Dayton, a scheme that made the town feel "big with the fate of empires." Sandusky's representatives in the legislature urged in 1830 that the state build the railway instead of extending the Miami Canal northward from Dayton to Lake Erie, as had been long planned.[23]

The idea of the state's abandoning northward extension of the Miami Canal naturally evoked an outcry from people in the Miami Valley north of Dayton. Opposition from this region, together with widespread skepticism about the feasibility of railroad transportation for heavy freight, proved a formidable barrier in the legislature. And so in 1831 Sandusky instead decided to build its railway as a private work, seeking a charter from the legislature. Even there, however, the project encountered strong local jealousies, emanating from towns with ambitions to be on the route. In order to obtain a charter, the promoters had to agree upon a route between Sandusky and Springfield that followed a meandering course, "not only fixed to pass over the most uneven part of the country" but also crossing the Sandusky River four times![24]

CANALS AND RAILROADS PROPOSED IN OHIO, 1825-1836

—————— Existing canals, 1836
– – – – Proposed railroad
·············· Proposed canals and river improvements
1. Mad River & Lake Erie R.R.
2. Miami Extension Canal
3. Wabash & Erie Canal
4. Muskingum River Improvement
5. Hocking Valley Canal or Improvement
6. Mahoning Canal (Penna. & Ohio Canal)
7. Sandy & Beaver Canal
8. Warren County Canal
9. Whitewater Canal
10. Walhonding River Canal

Map 4-A

Once the charter was obtained, the road's promoters foundered in their effort to obtain capital in the East, and it took until 1835 to raise sufficient investment funds in towns along the designated line to permit construction. But the ground was broken in 1835, as the West's first steam-railway line commenced construction. Progress was tortuously slow, because of lack of funds, and in 1838 only fifteen miles of track had been completed.[25]

Sandusky's railroad scheme generated political effects out of all proportion to its early success, for it posed a direct threat to the Miami Valley country, which looked forward to extension of the Miami Canal northward from Dayton.

If the state were to build the Sandusky railroad—or even if the private company opened such a line—then the Miami Extension Canal might be deemed superfluous and the region stranded without improved transportation. Also at issue was a long-standing matter of political reciprocity. The Miami Valley counties had supported the 1825 canal program only because of an understanding that the canal would be extended northward as soon as finances permitted.[26] Now the towns in the Mad River Valley, including Urbana, Springfield, and Dayton itself, were displaying unashamed enthusiasm for the Sandusky railroad project. Rumors spread that Dayton's merchants opposed extension of the canal because they coveted their "monopoly" position at the head of navigation. "The Canal *must* be extended," a Miami Valley editor wrote, despite "the selfish policy of those, who at a former period, made such professions of friendship to us; but who, since their views have been accomplished, *forget* their obligations."[27]

The canal commission's attitude played a vital role in the ensuing debate. The Miami Valley was represented by Commissioner John Johnston, one of the board's most aggressive members. Johnston himself was a large landowner at Piqua; thus he stood to gain directly if the canal were extended to his town, which was a local market center in the valley north of Dayton. He badgered his colleagues on the commission and other state officials to oppose the Sandusky project and approve immediate construction of the Extension Canal.[28] The other commissioners were early won over to Johnston's view, and they supported extension of the canal as "no more than justice" to residents of the country above Dayton.[29]

To aid construction of the Miami Extension, Congress in 1828 had granted Ohio the public lands in a pattern of alternate sections, five miles on each side of the projected canal line. Residents of the Miami Valley demanded that the lands be placed on the market at once. In December 1831 the legislature responded to rising pressure from the district by voting to place the lands on sale, the proceeds to be set aside as a construction fund for the canal. But the reservations that the assembly attached to the authorization act left the canal's promoters anxious about their prospects. The law set no time for the commencement of actual construction, leaving this question to the discretion of the canal commission and the fund board. Moreover, the act appropriated no general state revenues, making construction entirely dependent upon the revenue from land sales. Finally, a proviso was attached—apparently to appease the Sandusky interests—which specifically disavowed any definite commitment to make future appropriations of state funds for construction of the canal.[30]

This last proviso led to a dispute between the federal government and the state. The General Land Office refused to confirm the land grant, ruling that Congress had donated the lands merely to *aid* construction, and not to finance the canal exclusive of support from the state. For eighteen months, therefore, the lands were sold by the state without approval of Federal officials; and the issue remained a matter of contention until January 1834, when the objectionable proviso was finally repealed by the legislature.[31]

Termination of the dispute with the General Land Office lifted "the shadows, clouds and darkness" that had threatened the project.[32] But in fact it merely rendered legitimate what had already become a commitment by the state to build the Miami Extension Canal. For the canal commission had completed its plans for construction, and when land sales exceeded $70,000 in early 1833, seventeen miles of the line north of Dayton were placed under contract and construction begun.[33] The day when the state would make direct appropriations remained in the future, but Ohio's second river-to-lake canal was under way.

Like the Miami Extension, the Wabash & Erie Canal line was part of the original long-term plan of canal construction envisioned in the commission's 1825 report. The Wabash & Erie was designed to link Lake Erie with the Wabash River in Indiana, via the Maumee River, thereby providing another transport link between the Ohio Valley river system and the lakes. The region of northwestern Ohio where construction was planned was still frontier in 1830, with population density of only 1.4 persons per square mile.[34] This in itself made early construction unlikely. But the project's prospects were further complicated by the fact that the projected canal had to run through two states, Indiana and Ohio. Congress touched the sensitive nerve of state sovereignty when in 1827 it granted to Indiana all lands, on an alternate-section pattern ten miles wide, along the entire route of the canal.[35] State officials therefore opened negotiations to avoid a conflict over Indiana's claim to land situated in Ohio. They agreed that Ohio should construct the canal insofar as the line lay within its borders, in return for which Indiana yielded to Ohio her rights to the land granted by Congress that was situated in Ohio.[36]

The specter of states' rights was thus laid to rest, yet northwest Ohio was still wilderness, and early construction could hardly be expected. But there were important factors working in favor of the Wabash & Erie project. First, the congressional land grant itself was an incentive to build the line, especially since the best-informed estimates were that sale of the federal land grant would finance up to two-thirds of the canal's cost. Secondly, the Indiana legislature approved state construction of its portion of the canal in 1832, making it embarrassing for Ohio to delay any longer its commitment to build the connecting link between the state boundary and the lake.[37] The Ohio legislature therefore passed a resolution in February 1833 that committed the state either to build its portion of the canal with state funds, or else to charter a private company to build the line.[38]

But the most important factor favoring the project was the speculative fever that began to rage in the Maumee Valley in early 1833. Influential Ohio businessmen and politicians, as well as many wealthy eastern speculators, laid out a number of town sites in the lower portion of the valley. Each site was envisioned by its promoters as the canal terminus, and when the legislature convened for its winter session in December 1833, hordes of lobbyists pushed for early state construction of the canal.[39]

Governor Robert Lucas, a Democrat eager to establish for his party a strong record in internal-improvements legislation, was readily persuaded to support the Wabash & Erie project. He argued that the lands should be placed on sale at once, and the proceeds used to build the canal. By construction of the Wabash & Erie, and its ultimate connection with the Miami Extension, he said, "the State would have control of one of the most important avenues in the Western country."[40] His argument that land sales would suffice to pay for the project was politically irresistible. In March 1834 the legislature therefore enacted a law authorizing sale of the land grant, with proceeds to be set aside in a special fund for construction of the canal. Once again, the timing of construction was left to the canal commission's discretion. To avoid another dispute with the General Land Office the law explicitly stated that general revenues might be appropriated for the canal at a future time, "always having in view the object for which the donation [of lands] was made by the United States."[41]

More than two years would elapse before construction actually began. But the legislature was now committed to a second major new canal project, and a vast enlargement of the public works system in western Ohio was taking shape.

At a time when even frontier regions like northwestern Ohio could muster impressive political support for new projects, pressure was all the greater for improvements desired by communities in the older settled regions of the state. One of Ohio's earliest areas of settlement, and one of its most prosperous, was in the Muskingum Valley. There a large farm population produced a surplus of grain, tobacco, linseed oil, and other products that were shipped downriver to the Ohio River and southern markets, mainly by flatboat. Situated at the mouth of the Muskingum was the town of Marietta, a thriving commercial center. Located near the head of navigation farther north, Zanesville was a major milling center and a distribution point for eastern merchandise brought inland from the Ohio River.[42]

Construction of the Ohio Canal and the advent of the steamboat promised to revolutionize trade on the Muskingum. Eager to gain direct access to the Ohio Canal, residents of the valley persuaded the legislature in 1828 to build a side-cut linking the main canal line with the town of Dresden, located 16 miles above Zanesville on the river. The side-cut canal, completed in 1831, gave new commercial importance to Dresden and drew some of the Muskingum region's agricultural produce northward to the Cleveland export outlet. Naturally, this change irritated the merchants at Zanesville, who then won the canal commission's support for further extension of the side-cut canal from Dresden to their town, on grounds that unnavigable river conditions below Dresden lost a heavy potential traffic to the Ohio Canal.[43]

The legislature yielded in 1832 to pressure from Zanesville interests and from the canal commission, voting authorization for extension of the side-cut; and in 1834 the Dresden-Zanesville line was put under contract.[44] But the Muskingum Valley people were not satisfied for long. By the early 1830's, small steamboats were navigating regularly on the river as far upstream as Zanesville; and so merchants at Marietta and farmers in the interior now demanded canalization of the entire river, with locks and dams to regulate water flow and navigation, so that the steamers could establish regular shipping services, even in periods of low water.[45] By 1836 this had become the foremost goal of the valley's representatives in the legislature. And the fact that part of the line, though only a small part, was already built worked in their favor, virtually assuring that a Muskingum improvement would become part of any omnibus expansion program that the legislature considered.

In the Hocking River Valley, located farther west in south-central Ohio, the local citizens were no less alive to the Age of Improvement. And as in the Muskingum region, early construction of a small side-cut canal (in this case by a private corporation) generated demands for a more ambitious project. The headwaters of the Hocking River passed through Lancaster, a scant ten miles south of the Ohio Canal's main line; and from Lancaster the river followed a meandering course seventy miles down to the Ohio River. It was narrow and deep, but its route was treacherous for navigation because of rapids and falls. Between Lancaster and the Ohio River, the principal town in the valley was Athens, where extensive deposits of salt and coal were found. But cheap reliable transport for these bulky commodities was not available.[46]

As soon as the Ohio Canal was approved in 1825, the merchants of Lancaster obtained a charter for a private company, to construct the "Lancaster Lateral Canal" between the main canal and their town. The town's newspaper boosted the project by appealing to the spirit of local rivalry, warning that unless the lateral canal were built, all the town's trade would be diverted to Newark, situated nearby on the main line. Lancaster's own future would then hold only "decay, ruins and desolation."[47] But not until 1831 did private investors (most of them Lancaster merchants and millers) come forward with stock subscriptions sufficient to begin construction. With the aid of short-term loans from the local Lancaster Bank, the lateral canal was built in 1834, at a cost of $37,000.[48]

Lancaster's initiatives merely stimulated new expectations in communities located farther downriver. Led by the salt manufacturers and merchants of Athens, residents of the region demanded extension of the canal or improvement of the river at state expense.[49] And by the mid-thirties, the Hocking Canal project, like the Muskingum improvement, was being urged upon the legislature as a high-priority measure.

Elsewhere in the state, other groups of entrepreneurs formed privately chartered canal companies to pursue local ambitions. The most important of the private projects was the "Mahoning Canal" (formally the Pennsylvania & Ohio Canal), which beginning in 1824 was promoted by merchants and political leaders in the old Western Reserve region of northeast Ohio. This canal was planned to link Akron, on the main line of the Ohio Canal, with the Ohio River by way of the Mahoning Valley. The champions of the project urged that it would open up to exploitation rich coal deposits in the land-locked Mahoning region, would provide a shorter route to the Ohio River than the Cleveland-Portsmouth canal line afforded, and would promote direct trade between Cleveland and Pittsburgh.[50]

The state canal commission was friendly to the plan from the outset, confident that the Mahoning canal would easily produce revenues sufficient to pay costs of construction. But the legislature resisted pressure to authorize the canal as a state project. Instead it granted a private charter in 1827, directing the canal commission to aid the company by conducting surveys and preparing cost estimates.[51] The state engineers soon provided a construction plan for a line about ninety miles in length, running from Akron eastward through Ravenna, Warren, and Youngstown to the Ohio River near Beaver. There it would link with a projected westward extension of the Pennsylvania Mainline canal system from Pittsburgh to the river.[52]

Planning of the Mahoning Canal stimulated formation of a rival enterprise, the Sandy & Beaver Canal, designed to run on a parallel route farther south, between the Ohio Canal port of Bolivar and Beaver. Throughout the early 1830's, the two companies vied with one another for patronage of the legislature, each seeking financial aid and special charter concessions that would help to attract private capital. But the prime objective of the promoters, in each case, was apparently to persuade the legislature to adopt their project as a state enterprise. For each, the private charter was insurance against the chance that the legislature would not comply.[53]

The rivalry reached a climax in 1833, when Philadelphia's wealthy mercantile community awoke to the possibility of direct trade with eastern Ohio. At a convention held in Warren, Philadelphia financiers and commercial men debated the Mahoning and Sandy & Beaver plans, thinking of each as a possible extension of Pennsylvania's Mainline System, recently completed between Philadelphia and Pittsburgh. After reviewing the engineering reports, the Quaker City's representatives threw their support to the Mahoning project. Quickly the Mahoning company's organizers moved to obtain charter concessions from the Ohio legislature. The most important, granted in 1835, freed the company from state regulation of its tolls so long as profits did not exceed 10 per cent on investment. The company had received "assurances from the capitalists of Philadelphia that the stock shall be immediately taken up in the City" if such a concession were obtained.[54] True to their promise (and apparently satisfied with the prospect of a 10 per cent return), the bankers and merchants of Philadelphia subscribed heavily to a million-dollar stock issue opened to sale in 1835. In summer of that year, therefore, contracts were let for the entire line, at a total price of $900,000, and construction began at once.[55]

Their success in obtaining private investment did not cool the Mahoning promoters' enthusiasm for securing financial aid from the state. Nor did it end hopes of the Sandy & Beaver Company for state construction of their line. For the moment, however, it appeared certain at least that the Mahoning line would be built. And the sight of flags waving in celebration at ground-breaking ceremonies on the Mahoning Canal only inspired the Sandy & Beaver people to redouble their lobbying efforts at Columbus.[56]

Another private venture that managed to begin actual construction before the mid-thirties was the Milan Canal Company, organized by promoters at the port town of Milan. Situated near the Lake Erie shore, between Cleveland and Sandusky, Milan had become a major export outlet for grain produced in eighteen counties of north-central Ohio. The project was planned as a three-mile ship canal to carry heavy lake vessels from the town's wharves to the deep water of the Huron River. The legislature granted a charter in 1827, and both private investors and the Milan town government invested in stock. Not for six years, however, were sufficient funds obtained to permit construction. When work began, the actual cost proved four times the original estimate of $6,000 and soon Milan was appealing to the legislature for state aid.[57]

Southwest Ohio produced still another small canal project. In Warren County, the established market town of Lebanon had been by-passed, seventeen miles to the west, by the Miami Canal.

A private company was organized in 1830 to build a branch-line canal from Lebanon to the Miami Canal, but its promoters had difficulty in raising funds. They did make a start on construction, however, and by 1835 the corporation had expended more than $20,000. With the ditch half dug and no further private support forthcoming, the company dismissed its contractors and turned to the state legislature for aid.[58]

As Ohio's largest commercial city, Cincinnati was not likely to be lacking its own plans for internal improvements. Known as a "hotbed of new projects," Cincinnati became interested in the Miami Extension Canal and the Sandusky railroad, and also in the idea of obtaining a direct railroad connection with Charleston, South Carolina. Such a railway, a local editor boasted, "will free us from the dependence on New Orleans and free the South from dependence on New York and New England." But the grandiose Charleston railroad scheme did not gain enough support from men with capital enough to finance it, and Cincinnati's hopes for a railway line to the Atlantic Coast needed to wait more than twenty years to be fulfilled. Far more successful was yet another local project of the mid-thirties, for a canal to be built westward from Cincinnati into the Whitewater Valley of Indiana. Farmers in the Whitewater district were already exporting through Cincinnati, but they had to rely upon poor roads to reach the city. The canal plan became more urgent from the standpoint of Cincinnati interests after 1836, when the State of Indiana began construction of a canal line from the Whitewater River due south to Lawrenceburgh on the Ohio River. For Lawrenceburgh, a town some thirty miles downstream from Cincinnati, aspired to displace the Queen City as entrepôt for the trade of southern Indiana. Cincinnati's merchants organized a company in 1837 to build a lateral canal line that would intersect Indiana's Whitewater Canal midway down its line to Lawrenceburgh, and immediately the promoters sought state aid for the project to assure its successful financing.[59]

Many other private canal companies were chartered in the early 1830's, but the only proposal to gain substantial public support was a scheme for a branch canal line from the Ohio Canal to serve north-central Ohio. This region was a rich wheat-growing district, centered in Coshocton, Holmes, and Knox counties—the very district whose heavy export trade by overland routes to the lake at Milan had led to construction of the Milan Canal. Residents of the region argued that the Walhonding River intersected the Ohio Canal's main line, and thereby provided a perfect route for a branch line northwestward from the canal. Such a canal, they declared, would turn the region's trade away from the lake and carry it instead to the main-line canal, thus producing revenues more than sufficient to offset costs of construction.[60] By the mid-thirties, the Walhonding project had become one of the foremost contenders for patronage of the state.

The agitation for new canals and river improvements did not overshadow completely the more traditional interest in overland transportation. Following the usual American pattern, Ohio had long supplemented a sadly deficient state road program by granting charters to private turnpike corporations.[61] Merchants, farmers, and land speculators situated on turnpike routes often invested in such companies expecting mainly to gain indirect returns, rather than profits from dividends. Because road construction was expensive, however, only the wealthier communities could hope to capitalize turnpike corporations. As a result, the towns and regions where private resources were least abundant applied increasing pressure on the legislature for a generous policy of state aid to private road-building ventures.[62]

On the Lake Shore, interest in road construction centered on an old east-west military route that ran from the Western Reserve along the shore to the Sandusky River. Congress had ceded the right-of-way to the state. But the Ohio legislature had subsequently made only small appropriations for its maintenance, and so it remained little more than a wide path through the forests. By the mid-thirties, legislators from the lake towns had coalesced to demand paving and improvement of the road at state expense. This project too was expected to be pushed hard when bargaining for an expanded public-works program began.[63]

The Ohio debate over internal improvements meanwhile took on a new dimension because of rising interest in railway construction. Reflecting Sandusky's enthusiasm for its railroad, a host of railway promotions was put forward in other towns. One state official complained in 1831 that "the projects for rail roads amount to ten thousand."[64] If his figure was rather inflated, still the statistics of new railroad charters were enough to evoke wonder: Ohio's first charter was granted in 1830, and in the ten years following some seventy-six additional companies obtained charters for railways, thirty-two in 1836 alone.[65] Few of the new companies enjoyed financial resources sufficient to make construction a realistic possibility; and so scores of railway lobbyists soon appeared at Columbus to join the promoters of canals and turnpikes pressing for state aid.

But aside from the Sandusky railroad project, the main thrust of promotional efforts was for new canal construction. Of fifty-four private canal companies proposed for charter by the legislature up to 1837, five were then completed or under construction: the Mahoning, the Lancaster Lateral, the Whitewater, the Milan, and the Warren County.[66] In time, the Sandy & Beaver's promoters would build their line without state aid, whereas the others all obtained public funding. As for the rest—including the Duck Creek Navigation Canal, the Chippewa Canal, the Belleville & Bolivar, and others—they are but names which stand now, alongside those of long-forgotten railroad and turnpike projects, as silent monuments to the Age of Improvement in Ohio.

DECISION FOR THE EXPANDED PROGRAM

As specific projects won popular support in an optimistic atmosphere suffused with egalitarian ideals and entrepreneurial aspirations, barriers to the expansion of the state's public works gradually weakened.

Until 1828 the hostility of the canal commission toward proposals for expanding the public works posed a formidable obstacle to new state commitments. Privately, one of the commissioners condemned as "mean and contemptible" the localism which demanded equal benefits. And during the first three years of canal construction, the commissioners publicly discouraged pressures for new commitments; in fact, they were finding it difficult enough to maintain a satisfactory schedule of construction on the canals already under way. Yet the commission did hold out promises of support for future expansion, asserting that when the first canals had begun to produce adequate revenues, Ohio "will have the means of *extending to almost every part of the State* the benefits of an easy and cheap method of transporting property to market." The legislature itself was occasionally a forum for similar promises. Thus, rejecting a petition for a new state project in 1827, a house committee declared that once the first canals had been completed successfully, "the State must embark in further improvements of a similar character."[67] In this manner moral commitments were made and expectations aroused. In 1828, moreover, the canal commission began to manifest friendliness toward new projects: the Mahoning Canal, the Dresden side-cut, the Miami Extension, and the Wabash & Erie project, all won its support between 1828 and 1833.

As the commission shifted from its earlier position against expansion, the most difficult obstacles remaining were the state's fiscal status and the question of how to allocate priorities among new projects being urged on the legislature. With completion in 1832 of borrowing for the first canals, financial problems began to appear less forbidding. Net earnings from canal tolls, exclusive of interest costs, rose from $35,000 in 1829 to $103,000 in 1832; and in the year 1833 net earnings were nearly $150,000, which proved high enough to provide a surplus of $47,000 even after paying interest to bond-holders.[68] Heavy canal traffic continued to produce high earnings throughout the mid-thirties. At the same time, Congress provided the state treasury with a windfall of 2.7 million dollars, Ohio's share of the Federal surplus distribution that was voted in 1836. Few men could foresee that Federal land sales and customs revenues would fall off rapidly in 1837, quickly ending the flow of national funds to the states; and so the Ohio legislature considered disposal of the surplus revenue—which amounted to half the entire state canal debt—in a spirit of optimism.[69]

The crucial issue still remaining was allocation of priorities among the many projects before the legislature. The usual solution to such problems was simple logrolling—the process of vote-trading that produced "a combination of interests, local in their character, each of which [ideally] ought to stand or fall on its own intrinsic merits," but which might avoid dispassionate evaluation of its merits by inclusion in an omnibus program.[70] If logrolling was a common feature of the American political process, however, so too was the log jam. The Ohio legislature in 1835 was virtually paralyzed by the plethora of transportation projects being promoted in the lobbies. "The strong disposition manifested by people in all sections of the State who have flooded us with petitions for appropriations," one legislator wrote, prevented any easy compromise on logrolling principles.[71]

By 1836, however, a workable compromise had been shaped. If the rhetoric of the legislators and promoters carried any weight at all, the program finally agreed upon in the sessions of 1836 and 1837 was comprehensive and ambitious for reasons other than mere vote-trading: it reflected the egalitarian principles and the irrational public mania for internal improvements of the day. This is why the canal commissioners commented, on passage of the enlarged program, that "the action of the last Legislature . . . is a response to public sentiment. And [the Board] conjecture that nothing short of the extension of canal navigation to every considerable district of the State will satisfy that public will, which justly claims that benefits conferred shall be coextensive with the burthens imposed."[72] Thus the principle that Commissioner Kelley had denounced, a decade earlier, as "mean and contemptible," was now unblushingly proclaimed as state policy.

Even though it probably gained strength from egalitarian ideals, the coalition which finally enacted the new program also reflected effective logrolling. Representatives of the counties which would benefit directly from one or more of the public works approved in 1836 cast altogether only three negative votes in five crucial roll calls.[73] The hard-core opposition came from a group of counties situated on the Ohio River, including Clermont and Brown in southern Ohio, and Trumbull, Columbiana, Jefferson, Belmont, and Monroe in the eastern part of the state.

None of these counties stood to gain directly from the new program; and they cast forty-one of the seventy-six negative votes recorded in the five roll calls.[74]

The enlarged program which the legislature approved in 1836, as regional alliances crystallized sufficiently to break the legislative log jam, called for four new large-scale projects—all to be built mainly at state expense and as public enterprises. They were: (1) The Muskingum River Improvement, which projected the canalization for steamboat navigation of the entire Muskingum River between Dresden and its junction with the Ohio, 91 miles distant at Marietta. (2) The Walhonding Canal, designed to run from the Ohio Canal, where it crossed the Walhonding River, upstream along the river as far as the canal officials deemed desirable. (3) The Hocking Valley Canal, which would incorporate the old Lancaster Lateral Canal, to be purchased by the state, and its extension 56 miles southeast to Athens. (4) Further extension of the Miami Extension Canal, northward from its current terminus at Piqua to a junction with the Wabash & Erie in northern Ohio—this segment to be built with funds borrowed by the state as well as with revenue from land sales.[75]

In addition, the 1836 session of the legislature approved three smaller expenditures: the purchase for $20,000 of the partially built Warren County Canal, and its completion from Lebanon to the main-line Miami Canal; authorization of bond issues to permit a state loan of $200,000 to the Mad River & Lake Erie railroad; and approval of a cash loan from the treasury of $15,000 to permit completion of the Milan Canal Company's short deepwater canal between Milan and the Huron River.[76]

In 1837 the new program was further expanded with enactment of the so-called "Loan Law," under the terms of which the state would lend public funds to private railroad corporations and invest in the capital stock of canal and turnpike companies. This law entitled any Ohio-chartered railroad to qualify for loans, in the form of 6 per cent state faith-and-credit bonds, equal to one-third their authorized capital. The only conditions were that private investors provide two-thirds the estimated capital required for construction, with one-third being actually expended upon construction; and that the railroad be certified by the canal board as likely to yield a 2 per cent annual return on investment. Any chartered turnpike company might obtain a state subscription to half its capital stock, providing that private stockholders had invested half the amount needed to build the road. As for private canal companies, each might obtain a state subscription to one-third the capital stock needed to finance construction when the remainder had been taken by private investors.[77]

The Loan Law was Ohio's first venture in "mixed" public-private enterprise on a general basis, by which any corporation meeting minimum standards was entitled to the aid of the government. It was open-ended, for it set no limit on the total amount of money the state might be required to invest. Modeled on statutes enacted earlier in Virginia and Kentucky, the Loan Law was attractive because it "stretched" state resources by requiring matching funds from private investors.[78] But the law was also regarded in Ohio as a device to aid localities that would be by-passed by the newly authorized public works. As one contemporary enthusiast explained the law's purpose: "Scarcely any settled country is so sparse in population nor poor in property that [it] cannot take *half* the stock in turnpike roads. . . . The *certainty* that the State will take half the stock in any road required by the wants of society, will at once induce the subscription, by individuals, of the other half."[79] Conceived then as a means of extending benefits to all sections of the state, the Loan Law was a paradigm of egalitarianism in public transportation policy.

To finance these new undertakings, the legislature approved the issue of 3.1 million dollars in long-term 6 per cent bonds. Consistent with the precedents established in 1825, the board of canal fund commissioners was authorized to issue the bonds, and the faith and credit of the state was placed behind them.[80] Not content even with the record of 1836–37, the legislature enlarged its program still further in 1838 by approving a $700,-000 bond issue to supplement land-sale revenues in support of the Wabash & Erie Canal's construction, which had begun two years earlier. Appropriations were also made in 1838 for drainage, grading and macadamizing of the Western Reserve & Maumee Road (the former Federal military road), which ran along the Lake Erie shore from a point near Cleveland to the Sandusky River.[81]

The engineers of the canal commission had estimated the cost of the new canal projects as 4 million dollars. Even if such a figure seemed credible, the legislature thus agreed explicitly to double Ohio's state debt in order to build the expanded public works. But in addition, the state committed itself to apparently limitless funding of private transport projects under terms of the Loan Law. The actual cost of the new program proved to be about 15 million dollars, partly because a national business depression during 1839–43 forced the state to borrow funds at large discounts, but partly because the engineers' estimates of costs had been far too optimistic.

Nonetheless, the decision to enlarge the Ohio transportation system should not be condemned out of hand. In the mid-thirties, the state's property tax rested upon an assessed valuation base of more than 85 million dollars; the long-term indebtedness of local governments was nil; and predictions that sizable toll revenues and enormous indirect returns would accrue from the new facilities were not entirely unreasonable. Less defensible, however, was the legislature's failure to set a maximum limit on annual commitment of state funds under the Loan Law. Equally important was its failure to face the issue of construction priorities. Upon authorizing the Miami Extension and the Walhonding, Muskingum, Hocking Valley, and Warren County Canal projects, the legislature did make construction contingent upon approval by the state canal officials: they were required to certify that each work would produce estimated toll revenues sufficient to meet the cost of interest payments and debt retirement. But it was hardly surprising that the canal board quickly certified all five projects; in effect, the legislature had abdicated its own responsibilities under irresistible pressure for an expanded program. Instead, it might better have placed a ceiling on annual expenditures, or at least set out a system of priorities to assure completion of one (or some) of the new projects before others were begun. Whether out of political expediency, misplaced faith in administrative officials, genuine overconfidence about future fiscal strength, or plain short-sightedness, the legislature did not accept this critical responsibility. Because of this failure, the state would be plagued by an initial overcommitment to too many costly projects concurrently, and it would soon come to the edge of bankruptcy in the effort to carry a swiftly expanding debt obligation.

NOTES

1. See pp. 107–108, below.
2. Ira Delano to Jabez Delano, dated Chillicothe, Feb. 8, 1825, Delano Family Papers, Dartmouth College. The relationship between material expansion and American optimism is treated well in Arthur A. Ekirch, *The Idea of Progress in America, 1815–1860* (New York, 1944).
3. Chevalier, *Society, Manners, and Politics in the United States,* ed. John W. Ward (Garden City, 1961), 204.
4. Seward quoted in Lee Benson, *The Concept of Jacksonian De-mocracy* (Princeton, 1960), 14; the Virginia writer, in Wiley E. Hodges, "Pro-Governmentalism in Virginia, 1789–1836," *Journal of Politics,* XXV (May 1963), 343; Ruggles, in James Willard Hurst, *Law and the Conditions of Freedom in the 19th Century United States* (Madison, 1956), 55.
5. Micajah Williams in *Report of the Committee on Canals* (Co-lumbus, 1822), 6; the canal commission's 1833 report, in *Senate Journal, 1832–33,* pp. 340–47.
6. Lee Benson, *The Concept of Jacksonian Democracy* (Prince-ton, 1961), 13, 337.
7. Leonard W. Levy, *The Law of the Commonwealth and Chief Justice Shaw* (Cambridge, 1957), 305.
8. Report of legislative debates, *Ohio Statesman* (Columbus), March 19, 1840. The phrase "equalized benefits" was used by the editor, in the same newspaper, March 16, 1838. Some of the evidence in this chapter is drawn from a slightly later period, but most pertains to the mid-1830's. The rhetoric employed by

new promoters after 1838 was essentially the same, especially in its egalitarian premises, as employed by advocates of expansion prior to adoption of the enlarged program.

9. *Ohio State Journal & Columbus Gazette*, Jan. 12, 1836; legislative debates in *ibid.*, March 3, 1837; petition quoted in *Ohio Statesman*, Feb. 17, 1842.

10. It was in recognition of this fact that Andrew Jackson and many of his supporters attacked the "corrupting influence" of internal improvements as an issue in national politics. Thus, the Jacksonian apologist, James Kirke Paulding, asserted that internal improvements legislation, like banking and tariff laws, "have so directly appealed to the Selfish principle that the Social principle . . . is become too weak to restrain its pampered rival." (R. M. Alderman, ed., *The Letters of James Kirke Paulding* [Madison, 1962], 197.) See also Levy, *Law of the Commonwealth*, Chap. 8.

11. The South Carolina statement is quoted (from an anonymous letter, 1827) in Alfred G. Smith, Jr., *Economic Readjustment of an Old Cotton State: South Carolina, 1820–1860* (Columbia, S. C., 1958), 157; the Virginia board's statement (1839), in Carter Goodrich, "The Virginia System of Mixed Enterprise," *Political Science Quarterly*, LXIV (Sept. 1949), 385; an Indianapolis newspaper (1836), quoted in D. Riker and G. Thornbrough, eds., *Messages and Papers . . . of Noah Noble* (Indianapolis, 1958), 543n.; 21st Cong., 2nd Sess., House, *Report* No. 77 (Feb. 10, 1831), 10–11.

12. Ohio Auditor of State, *Annual Report*, 1835, p. 16; Vance, message of Dec. 1837, in *Ohio Statesman*, Dec. 2, 1837.

13. Debates in legislature, *Ohio Statesman*, Dec. 17, 1839.

14. Columbus *Gazette*, Dec. 2, 1824, Jan. 8, 1825; CC, *Report, Jan. 21, 1824* (Columbus, 1824), 6.

15. Lancaster *Gazette*, Feb. 23, 1830. The editor attributed this view to the canal commissioners.

16. Columbus *Western Hemisphere*, March 6, 1837.

17. Hurst, *Law and the Conditions of Freedom*, 6.

18. Columbus *Western Hemisphere*, Dec. 9, 1833; petition of Jos. Barker and others, Aug. 14, 1838, and petition of Carthage &c. Turnpike Co., Oct. 1, 1838 (MSS.), CC Papers.

19. Editorial in Columbus *Western Hemisphere*, Sept. 16, 1835.

20. See analysis of the roll-call votes, pp. 109–10, below. Harold E. Davis has written that there was little substantive difference between Whig and Democrat views on internal improvements

in the 1830's. (See Davis, "Social and Economic Basis of the Whig Party in Ohio," Ph.D. dissertation, Western Reserve University, 1933, pp. 208, 259.)

21. Legislative debate, in *State Journal and Register* (Columbus), Feb. 13, 1838.

22. See Scheiber, "Urban Rivalry and Internal Improvements in the Old Northwest, 1820–1860," *OH*, LXXI (Oct. 1962), 227ff., for a full exposition.

23. Isaac Mills to Zalmon Wildman, Jan. 19, Feb. 14, 1831, Wildman Family Papers, OHS. Wildman was one of Sandusky's proprietors, and I have based my account of the town's early history on this body of correspondence and on the files of the Sandusky *Clarion*. On the railroad project, see also *Senate Journal*, 1830–31, pp. 364–71. The Sandusky people wished to have the state use the proceeds of the 1828 Congressional land grant in aid of the Miami Canal Extension to support the railroad project instead, and Congress granted permission for such diversion of land-sale revenues.

24. Eleutheros Cooke to Wildman, Jan. 19, 1832, Wildman Papers.

25. H. H. Wilcoxen to Wildman, Jan. 3, 1832; A. Mills to Wildman, Aug. 13, 19, 1832; Joseph Vance to Wildman, April 24, 1835, *ibid.;* L. M. Stewart, "Sandusky," *OAHQ*, LVII (July 1848), 228–29.

26. S. Mason and C. Anthony to Board of Canal Fund Commissioners, broadside, March 1833, in "Miscellaneous Letters," file in State Auditor's Records, Capitol Building, Columbus; *Piqua Gazette*, Feb. 9, 1832, Nov. 2, 1833.

27. *Piqua Gazette*, March 2, 1831; see also Thomas Van Horne to E. Hayward, May 31, 1833, Miami Canal Dossier, Records of the General Land Office (National Archives Record Group 49).

28. Johnston to Kelley, March 18, 23, 1833, CC Papers; Johnston to Lucas, May 27, 1833, Land Office Records and Correspondence, OHS; Johnston to his grandchildren, Jan. 22, 1833, in C. R. Conover, *Concerning the Forefathers* (Dayton, 1902), 363.

29. M. T. Williams to Kelley, Dec. 18, 1831, CC Papers.

30. 30 L. O. (*Laws of Ohio: General*) 14.

31. *Senate Journal*, 1833–34, pp. 163–71; Johnston to Lucas, Sept. 5, 1833, Robert Young to Lucas, April 15, 1833, William Barber to Lucas, Dec. 20, 1833, Official Governors' Papers, OHS.

32. *Piqua Gazette*, Dec. 30, 1833.

33. *Senate Journal*, 1833–34, pp. 13–15.

34. Based on 1830 Census data.

35. Allen Trimble to Messrs. Ruggles and Harrison, Feb. 18, 1828, Official Governors' Papers, OHS; see also James B. Ray, *Messages and Papers*, ed. D. Riker and G. Thornbrough (Indianapolis, 1954), 329–33; and Logan Esarey, *Internal Improvements in Early Indiana* (Indianapolis, 1912), 89.

36. Actually the agreement became final only when the Ohio assembly voted to accept the cession of lands from Indiana by resolution of Feb. 24, 1834 (MS. copy in Wabash & Erie Records, General Land Office, R. G. 49, National Archives). However, it was well understood from 1828 on that Ohio would take responsibility for the canal's construction within the state, and sale of the lands was actually approved by the Ohio legislature prior to February 1834. (See also 4 U. S. Statutes-at-Large 305–6.)

37. Indiana Canal Commission to E. Hayward, March 8, 1833, Wabash and Erie Records, Div. F, Box 91, Records of the General Land Office (National Archives).

38. Resolution dated February 25, 1833, quoted in *ibid.*

39. John Hunt to Lucas, Dec. 16, 1833, Official Governors' Papers, OHS; John W. Weatherford, "The Short Life of Manhattan, Ohio," *OHQ*, LXV (Oct. 1956), 376–98; H. S. Knapp, *History of the Maumee Valley* (Toledo, 1876), 557ff.

40. *Senate Journal*, 1833–34, pp. 11–12.

41. Act of March 3, 1834, copy in General Land Office Records.

42. See Beverley W. Bond, Jr., *The Civilization of the Old Northwest* (New York, 1934); and description of Muskingum Valley farming in *Ohio Statesman*, Jan. 2, 1838.

43. The canal commissioners declared that if Zanesville's export trade (some 1100 tons of flour and oil exported downriver in 1831) could be diverted to the Ohio Canal, the extension would soon pay for itself. *House Journal*, 1831–32, pp. 245–47; see also *ibid.*, 1829–30, p. 227; and Cleveland *Herald*, Aug. 12, 1830.

44. *Senate Journal*, 1831–32, pp. 436–37, 451, *et passim*.

45. Louis C. Hunter, *Steamboats on the Western Rivers* (Cambridge, 1949), 42–43; Thomas W. Lewis, *History of Southeastern Ohio and the Muskingum Valley* (3 vols., Chicago, 1928), I, 120.

46. Lewis, *Southeastern Ohio*, I, 614; Board of Public Works, *5th Annual Report* (1842), 8–9.

47. Lancaster *Gazette,* May 3, 1831; see also *ibid.,* Feb. 2, 1830.

48. Canal Commission, *15th Annual Report* (1839), 12–14; Lancaster Lateral Canal Company, Minute Books (MS., OHS), pp. 5, 15–17, 31–32.

49. *Ohio State Journal and Columbus Gazette,* Feb. 2, 1836.

50. H. Hine to S. Perkins, Dec. 20, 1824, Simon Perkins Papers, WRHS; Harold E. Davis, "The Pennsylvania-Ohio Canal," Hiram (Ohio) Historical Society, *Publications,* No. 1 (1929).

51. Alfred Kelley to E. Whittlesey, Jan. 11, 1825, Elisha Whittlesey Papers, WRHS; Brown to John Sergeant, Oct. 1, 1825, Brown Papers, OSL; John Kilbourne, ed., *Public Documents Concerning the Ohio Canals* (Columbus, 1832), 269–70.

52. Davis, "Pennsylvania-Ohio Canal," not paginated.

53. Simon Perkins to Kelley, Feb. 19, 1835, Letters on Canals, CHS ("I should regret exceedingly to have it [the project] fall into the hands of a Company"); T. Sloane to Kelley, July 30, 1828, CC Papers; L. King to E. Whittlesey, Dec. 8, 1834, Jan. 15, 1835, Whittlesey Papers. On the Sandy project, see R. M. Gard and William Vodrey, *The Sandy and Beaver Canal* (East Liverpool, Ohio, 1952), 12ff.

54. King to Perkins, Feb. 11, 1835, Perkins Papers.

55. Davis, "Pennsylvania-Ohio Canal," *passim;* King to Perkins, Feb. 11, July 31, Aug. 20, 1835, Perkins Papers.

56. E. Whittlesey to Sergeant, Sept. 19, 1835, L. King to Whittlesey, Aug. 18, 1838, Whittlesey Papers; King to Jos. Vance, April 25, 1837, Official Governors' Papers.

57. Charles E. Frohman, "The Milan Canal," *OAHQ,* LVII (July 1948), 237–40; R. C. Downes, *History of Lake Shore Ohio* (3 vols., New York, 1952), I, 131–32.

58. C. P. McClelland and C. C. Huntington, *History of the Ohio Canals* (Columbus, 1905), 39. Discussion of Lebanon based mainly upon Trimble Family Papers, OHS, *passim.*

59. The quotation concerning the Charleston railroad is from the *Western Monthly Magazine,* 1835, cited in W. F. Gephart, *Transportation and Industrial Development of the Middle West* (New York, 1909), 201–2. On the Whitewater canal schemes of Cincinnati and of Indiana, see Esarey, *Internal Improvements,* 99ff.; and Paul Fatout, "Canalling in the Whitewater Valley," *Indiana Mag. of Hist.,* LX (March 1964), 37–78.

60. *Ohio Statesman,* Feb. 6, Dec. 14, 1838; "Extension of the Walhonding Canal" (undated broadside, CC Papers). Public agitation is alluded to in legislative debates of 1836, but surviving

newspaper files of the Walhonding region are sparse and no explicit promotional literature predating 1836 has been found.

61. As a rough index of interest in turnpikes, the legislature chartered 6 private companies in 1833, 4 in 1834, 5 in 1835, 15 in 1836, 23 in 1837, 18 in 1838, and 35 in 1839. (G. H. Evans, *Business Incorporations in the U. S., 1800–1943*, New York, 1948, p. 18, on 1833–35; 1836–39 charters counted directly from Ohio statutes.)

62. W. T. Utter, *Frontier State* (Columbus, 1942), 215; Francis Weisenburger, *Passing of the Frontier* (Columbus, 1941), 106ff. An experienced civil engineer estimated in 1838 the cost of a road 30 feet wide, across flat country, and covered with crushed stone only, as $5,000 per mile. (Report of A. Bourne, Nov. 29, 1838, CC Papers.)

63. R. C. Buley, *The Old Northwest* (2 vols., Bloomington, 1954), I, 450; Ohio Senate, Standing Committee on Retrenchment, *Report*, Feb. 28, 1844, pp. 13–14; M. Kaatz, "The Black Swamp," *Annals of the American Association of Geographers*, XLV (1955), 11–12.

64. Micajah T. Williams to Kelley, Dec. 18, 1831, CC Papers.

65. Number of charters computed from Ohio statutes.

66. Board of Public Works, Minute Books, Vol. II, p. 246 (MSS., Department of Public Works Records, State Office Building, Columbus).

67. Alfred Kelley to James B. Gardiner, Jan. 28, 1827, CC Papers; *House Journal*, 1829–30, pp. 579–80.

68. Huntington and McClelland, *Ohio Canals*, 170; BFC Report, Dec. 1833, *Senate Journal*, 1833–34, pp. 405–7. The excellent financial record of 1833 led the legislature to grant the Sandy & Beaver, the Warren County, and the Lancaster Lateral canal companies full rebates of all tolls collected on the mainline canals on goods entering from their respective works, an important concession. (Canal Commission, *14th AR* [1836], pp. 12–14.)

69. In the spirit of localism, the Democratic majority of Ohio's legislature voted to distribute the state's share of the federal surplus to counties in proportion to population. Although their course accorded with egalitarian doctrine, they might have done better to use the funds for a single major state project. (See Columbus *Western Hemisphere*, March 1, March 6, 1837.)

70. *Lancaster Gazette*, Feb. 23, 1830, quoting opponents of the Miami Extension Canal.

71. Leicester King to Simon Perkins, Feb. 11, 1835, Simon Perkins Papers, WRHS. (King was a state representative.)
72. BPW, *1st AR* (1837), p. 14.
73. These were the votes in the House on the Walhonding, Muskingum, Miami Extension, Warren County, and Hocking Valley projects. Roll calls are in *House Journal*, 1835–36, pp. 619–20, 625–26, 695, 750, 801.
74. *Ibid.* Democrats recorded all but 17 of the 76 negative votes, but this was a function of the fact that the core-opposition counties nearly all had sent Democratic representatives.
75. 34 L. O. 311, 331, 346, 620.
76. 34 L. O. 145, 570.
77. 35 L. O. 76.
78. See Columbus *Journal and Register*, March 3, 1838. On Virginia's law in operation, cf. Hodges, "Pro-Governmentalism," 347ff; and Robert F. Hunter, "The Turnpike Movement in Virginia, 1816–1860," *Virginia Magazine of History and Biography*, LXX (July 1961), 278–89.
79. Columbus *Journal and Register*, March 3, 1838.
80. Authorizations were for $200,000 in 6 per cent bonds to be issued for the Mad River & Lake Erie Railroad; $1.5 million over the period 1836–41 for the Miami Extension, at the rate of $200,000 annually, 1836–38, and $300,000 annually, 1839–41, in 6 per cent bonds payable after 1856; $350,000 in 6 per cents for the Hocking; $400,000 in 5 per cents for the Muskingum Improvement; and $300,000 in 6 per cents for the Walhonding. New authorizations were voted in later years as costs proved to exceed estimates. (37 L. O. 68.) See Chapter 6, below, for post-1836 financial operations.
81. 36 L. O. 78; Canal Commission, *15th AR* (1839), 20–21.

CHAPTER 5

The Public Works and Mixed Enterprise 1836-1845

WHEN the legislature approved the expanded program's first projects in 1836, state canal officials believed that construction would go forward quickly, and with no financial obstacles, for the national economy was in the midst of a boom, and Ohio's public credit stood high in both domestic and foreign money markets. Therefore the only potential hindrance to rapid completion of the program that the canal board foresaw in 1836 was possible inflation of wages and prices in localities where construction would take place.* To minimize this risk, the board planned to limit expenditures to 1 million dollars annually. This, they thought, was the optimal rate for spending; if the state expended more in any one year, it would push up wages and prices, creating difficulties for contractors.[1] Such optimism would have to be tested, and events in fact proved the canal board's view incorrect. For even in 1836 it was obvious that local political pressures were building up that might force costly additions to the construction plans already authorized. And in any event the board's roseate view did not discount the possibility of engineering errors or malfeasance that might further increase expendi-

---

* In this chapter the term "canal board" will refer to the canal commission and its successor agency, the board of public works. Creation of the board of public works in 1836, revival of the canal commission in 1838 (for one year only), and its replacement once again by a board of public works, are treated in the context of partisan pressures and administrative reform proposals in Chapter 7.

tures. Nor did it take account of the possibility that the national economic expansion might slow down and create difficulties in obtaining funds.

Instead of quieting local pressures, the decision to expand the public works system merely changed the focus of rivalry for communities in districts where the new facilities were to be constructed. A bizarre example occurred in the Muskingum Valley. Both Zanesville and Marietta insisted that locks on the river improvement be planned large enough to accommodate heavy steamboats and the largest flatboats.[2] But the citizens of Dresden, located north of Zanesville, recognized that the latter would become the head of navigation if the locks below that city were larger than those already built between Dresden and Zanesville. Their own commerce would then be destroyed. "Commerce to be free requires an open sea, a free competition," declared a Marietta petition favoring the larger locks. "Interprize & adventure must be unshackled," and the small locks would not meet the needs of a new era![3] To this, the Dresden people had no objection, but they also asserted that "the same facts and arguments will apply with equal force, to the improvement above Zanesville."[4] The canal board finally capitulated to demands for locks of the larger design, agreeing to rebuild the Dresden-Zanesville line.[5]

On the Walhonding Canal, a similar squabble occurred when the board decided to build initially only twenty-five miles of canal, delaying its extension farther upriver until a later date. From the upriver towns which had originally favored the canal project now came strong expressions of dissatisfaction. The legislature resisted demands for early extension of the canal, but only because of the financial difficulties that beset the state after 1839.[6]

The most intense warfare between rival towns occurred in the Maumee Valley, where the Wabash & Erie Canal line was planned. The residents and proprietors of the small villages near the mouth of the river—Toledo, Maumee, Perrysburg, and Manhattan—all had favored construction of the canal. But once the time came to specify the exact route, their coalition fell apart, as the towns competed bitterly for designation as the Lake Erie terminus. The board came under such heavy political pressure that it finally agreed to build three termini, with identical terminal locks and basins at Manhattan, Toledo, and Maumee City, thus leaving only Perrysburg unsatisfied. To equalize fully the conditions of rivalry, moreover, the board agreed to complete all three terminals for traffic simultaneously.[7]

Such changes in design markedly increased the expenses of construction and eventually compounded the financial problems of the state. But the pressures of localism alone cannot explain the difference between the board's original cost estimate of four million dollars for the new public works, and the actual cost, which proved to be ten million dollars. A series of errors in engineering and planning contributed in a major way to this difference.

One of the board's most grievous mistakes derived from its early plans for the Hocking Valley works. The original plans called for construction of a river improvement rather than a canal.* The board later stated that there had been "almost universal misapprehension" among civil engineers that improvement of rivers by controlling water flow with dams and locks was a sound, inexpensive alternative to canal construction in river valleys. When more careful surveys proved that the Hocking River could not well be improved for navigation in this manner, the board shifted plans and undertook construction of a canal instead. This was an important element in the difference between the original cost estimate of $347,000 and the final cost of nearly three times that amount.[8]

On the Muskingum River, improvement of the river itself did prove feasible, but the board's decision to enlarge the size of the locks added substantially to its cost. This change may have been justified because of the increasing average size of steamboats and

---

* A so-called *river improvement* involved construction of locks in the bed of the river itself. This type of construction provided "slackwater" navigation for boats; that is, the flow of water would be controlled by the locks and ancillary dams, so that extreme changes in the pressure of currents might be avoided. Wherever necessary, the natural river banks would be shored up to prevent slides. Moreover, where tributary streams emptied into the main river, dams would be constructed to regulate water flow. The river improvement was designed to be navigable for flatboats, rafts, and steamboats, having no towpath on which animals could be driven to tow canal boats. A *canal*, on the other hand, was built so that its main navigational line would be independent of the natural streams. Water from the streams was tapped by feeder lines and aqueducts to provide a flow in the main line. Locks controlled navigation and water flow, and vessels were drawn by mules or horses on a towpath alongside the line.

flatboats. But even the board's most ardent apologists could find no excuse for its engineers' subsequent failure to supervise construction properly. Numerous jobs were accepted from contractors only to be found defective later, so that extensive repairs were necessary before the improvement could be opened to traffic.[9] When the project was finally completed in 1841, moreover, the basic design of locks and dams proved faulty, and more than $200,000 had to be spent on reconstruction. Even then, an additional $250,000 in maintenance work was necessary "to insure any probability of permanency."[10]

Design changes proved costly on the Wabash & Erie Canal as well. The original plans called for a prism design of 40 feet surface width and 4 feet depth, the dimensions used on the Ohio Canal. But immediately before awarding contracts, the canal board decided to substitute a larger design: they adopted prism specifications of 60 feet surface width and 6 feet depth, thereby substantially increasing water requirements as well as initial construction costs. Taken together with the decision to build three termini, this change probably explains half the difference between the original cost estimate of $900,000 and the final price of three million dollars.[11]

The Miami Extension Canal, the largest component of the new public works program, nearly proved to be an engineering disaster. Anticipating heavy traffic volume, the canal board adopted a prism design of 50 feet width at the surface and 5 feet depth.[12] The extension was 125 miles long, with average lockage of 3.6 feet per mile (by comparison with 3.2 feet on the Ohio Canal), and so it required a much larger water supply than did the state canals built previously. To supply the line, the canal board built two reservoirs, said to be the world's largest at the time, but even these could not provide enough water for uninterrupted navigation. In addition, the design of the canal's wooden locks resulted in chaos when the work was opened to traffic in 1845. The locks were built too small for the canal boats then in use on the larger Wabash line, and in two instances locks were destroyed as boats tried to navigate them. The canal therefore had to be closed for extensive repairs and reconstruction only a few weeks after its inauguration.[13]

These engineering errors were costly in themselves. But they had the additional effect of creating heavy new expenses late in the period of construction, when the rate of expenditures normally would have dropped off. Unfortunately, the later part of the construction period coincided with the worst days of the post-1839 business depression. To finance design modifications and repairs, therefore, the state was forced into the money market when funds were available only at high interest rates and heavy discounts.[14]

Ohio began to encounter difficulty in selling its bonds as early as 1837. As a result, the state ended its former practice of paying contractors each month on the basis of work actually completed. "Men who were enterprizing and industrious, but comparatively poor," had taken construction contracts in the expectation of receiving monthly cash payments.[15] The termination of monthly payments caused many contractors to suspend work and discharge employees, disrupting the existing degree of stability in the labor supply. As one engineer explained the problem when the board of public works contemplated suspension of payments in 1837: "The contractors have all their arrangements made for prosecuting the work; tools purchased, teams and shantys built and in fact all their arrangements made. . . . They have spent all their money and can do but little now without money from the State as they had anticipated. What will be the consequences of suspending payment? A total 'break up' and failure with nearly all of them. . . ."[16]

Suspension of monthly payments merely intensified a set of more basic economic problems that threatened the contractors with bankruptcy. The key issue was shortage of labor. The year 1836 witnessed a spectacular proliferation of new public works projects throughout the United States; indeed, the canals undertaken during 1836–38 involved expenditures of more than 72 million dollars.[17] The effect on employment was to absorb a large part of the construction labor force, driving wages upward.

The first portents of a labor crisis in Ohio appeared in 1835, on the short segment of the Miami Extension then under construction north of Dayton. Contracts had been awarded there in 1833, when hands were plentiful and the combined cost of wages and board for laborers was 60 to 65 cents per day. During the next two years, however, general economic expansion increased employment opportunities in industry and agriculture. American-born laborers "found abundance of employment" and German immigrants took their place on the canal line. Meanwhile, local prices rose, indeed by about 50 per cent between 1833 and 1836; and the cost of labor increased to one dollar per day in late 1835. As a result, forty-one of the sixty-four contractors on the line abandoned their jobs in 1836. To meet the crisis, the Ohio legislature broke a long-standing precedent by authorizing the board of public works to amend contract prices upward; but the board resisted this course, instead negotiating new contracts at higher prices or else placing state crews on the abandoned sections.[18]

On the Miami Extension as it was built northward into areas of sparse settlement—and on the Wabash & Erie line as well—contractors could not depend upon use of much local labor drawn from farm families. Instead, they had to attract and hold itinerant workers with high wages. On the Wabash and Erie line, wages rose from $15 a month in 1836 to more than $20 two years later; and contractors' difficulties were intensified by the fear of "fever and ague" which prevailed in the summer, forcing work to a halt between July and October each year.[19] In regions where contractors could rely on casual labor available locally, the problems were nearly as severe: such laborers were regularly employed on farms, and during the planting and harvest seasons were unavailable for canal construction.[20]

In May 1837 a bank panic struck in the United States, and after a brief recovery a serious depression began in 1839. These events bore especially hard upon canal contractors. For in the first place, the state paid them in the notes of Ohio banks; and after 1837 merchants from whom contractors bought provisions and equipment refused to accept such bank paper at its par value. The depreciation of bank paper affected the laborers too, for contractors paid them in the same paper as they received from the state. Second, in isolated areas of Ohio where canal construction was going forward—especially in the Miami Extension and Wabash & Erie region of northwest Ohio—the influx of canal labor and contractors' demand for provisions kept local prices high, even though the level of western prices generally was falling, during the post-1839 depression. This meant that contractors' current operating costs did not decline significantly, closing out the one possible chance of their recouping losses.[21]

And so a vicious cycle vexed the relations between the state and its contractors after 1836. The state encountered difficulty in selling bonds and cut back on payments to contractors. The latter, in turn, were left without cash resources and lost their credit standing "with the capitalist, the farmer, the merchant, and the daily laborer."[22] Faced with rising prices (with no relief during the post-1839 depression) and paid—when the state did have funds—in depreciated bank paper, the contractor often had no alternative but to declare bankruptcy and abandon his contract. A few held on, but most of the work contracted out in 1836 had to be re-contracted by the state at some point before completion. The new contracts called for higher prices to be paid by the state, and this in turn increased the fund board's requirements when it sought loans in the capital markets.[23]

COMPLETION OF THE PUBLIC WORKS

The difficulties that plagued state financial officers and private contractors in Ohio were identical to troubles that drove other states into default or repudiation of their debts in the early 1840's. On the one hand, the failure of sister states to maintain their public works programs under financial pressure raised doubts in investors' minds as to whether Ohio could go on; and loss of confidence meant that Ohio had to pay high interest rates to attract capital. On the other hand, failures elsewhere made it all the more remarkable that Ohio should have succeeded—as it did— in keeping up construction on its public works into 1845, surviving a depression that crippled canal building nearly everywhere in America.

The first segment of the enlarged system to be completed was the Warren County Canal, opened to traffic from the Miami Canal seventeen miles to its terminus at Lebanon in 1840.[24] (See Table

5.1.) It was an empty triumph, for it became apparent at once that the canal would perform no substantial economic function: by 1840, several new turnpike roads offered a more direct and economical route from Lebanon to Cincinnati for all but the heaviest freight. The contribution of the canal to the region's development in subsequent years consisted almost exclusively in its providing water for a few gristmills. Because of turnpike competition, moreover, the board decided to operate the facility free of tolls.[25]

The Walhonding Canal too was ill-starred from the beginning. The board of public works originally planned it as a 25-mile-long initial leg in a system of branch canals that would extend to Mt. Vernon, a market center in Knox County, and to towns on the Mohican and Killbuck rivers. Shortage of funds, however, prevented construction of anything beyond the initial work. First opened in 1841 the Walhonding Canal was a stunted line terminating in sparsely settled country and lacking road connections with the commerical center located farther upriver.[26]

The first of the more important projects to be opened to traffic was the Muskingum Improvement. Construction was delayed by the decision to substitute larger locks after work had been started, and suspensions of payment to contractors further slowed the work. In late 1841, after many of the sections previously accepted had been rebuilt by state crews, the system was prepared for navigation, except for the large lock above Zanesville, which was never built for lack of funds. But faulty engineering forced reconstruction of dams in 1842 and again during 1846 to 1849.[27]

The Hocking Valley Canal involved deepening and enlargement of the old Lancaster Lateral Canal line, which was purchased by the state in 1838, and its extension to Athens.[28] Because of major changes in engineering plans, sickness among laborers, and the bankruptcy of many contractors, the line did not reach the salt and coal region near Athens until 1842. The complete 56-mile line was opened a year later.[29]

The total value of the initial contracts on the Wabash & Erie Canal line, in 1837, was more than twice the original $900,000 estimate, owing to the decision to build with larger dimensions.[30]

TABLE 5.1

ANNUAL DISBURSEMENTS FOR CANAL CONSTRUCTION, 1833–1845
(thousands of dollars)

YEAR	WARREN COUNTY CANAL	MUSKINGUM IMPROV'T	WALHONDING CANAL	HOCKING VALLEY CANAL	WABASH & ERIE CANAL	MIAMI EXTENSION CANAL	TOTAL
1833–37[a]	$ 76.1	$ 169.0	$ 99.1	$ 84.7	$ 108.5	$ 444.4	$ 981.8[a]
1838	61.3	356.7	188.8	165.8	589.2	248.9	1,610.7
1839	26.9	219.5	124.8	225.0	459.9	398.8	1,454.9
1840	38.3	341.1	78.6	146.1	512.1	316.5	1,432.7
1841	—	341.2	62.7	199.5	590.4	415.2	1,609.0
1842	—	26.4	14.2	21.1	487.2	544.5	1,093.4
1843	—	148.8	32.5[b]	105.1	210.9	306.1	803.4
1844	—	25.3	—	27.5	73.1	82.2	208.1
1845	—	34.3	—	—	—	338.5	372.8
Total cost (revised)	$ 217.6	$1,662.1	$ 600.7	$ 975.1	$3,028.3	$3,195.1[c]	$9,678.9 (revised)
1836 estimate of cost	112.0	400.0	250.0	347.0	900.0	2,055.4	4,064.4
Value of original contract	152.0	775.0	387.5	520.0	1,968.5	2,693.7	$6,496.7

[a] 1837 only for Warren, Walhonding, Hocking, Wabash & Erie; 1832–37 for Muskingum; 1833–37 for Miami Extension.

[b] Includes all post-1842 payments.

[c] Exclusive of damage claims outstanding in 1845.

Sources: Annual disbursements as reported in *Annual Reports*, Board of Public Works; revised totals are as given in subsequent reports correcting earlier annual reports. Value of original contracts, from Board of Public Works, Minutes (MS.), Vol. II, p. 322; and *Journal and Register* (Columbus), March 22, 1838. "Disbursements" are checks issued to contractors, whether or not cash was available for immediate payment.

The final cost proved much higher still (Table 5.1) because of contractors' failures and the need to complete many jobs with state crews or by renegotiating contracts. In addition, a shortage of stone impeded work on the western part of the line, located in a remote frontier district without road facilities. Harsh winter weather compounded engineering difficulties, and it proved impossible to set masonry during a five-month period each year. Finally, the board of public works decided to build temporary wooden locks on the western part of the line, planning to substitute more durable materials when the canal was opened.[31]

Because costs on the Wabash line so greatly exceeded estimates, when the canal was finally opened to traffic in 1842 critics of the board charged it with corruption and "almost profligate expenditure of public money" on the line.[32] However, a legislative committee upheld the board's contention that construction costs had been swelled mainly by the prevailing high wages, lack of competition in bidding on re-let contracts, and artificially inflated prices for provisions.[33]

The Miami Extension Canal was built in four divisions. The first, a 32-mile line between Dayton and Piqua, was completed in 1837. Then the second segment, 32 miles north to St. Mary's, was let to contractors. The third consisted of a twelve-mile "deep cut" above St. Mary's, and was begun in 1839. Requiring an elaborate set of culverts, feeders, and heavy locks, the second and third divisions comprised "the most costly piece of canal work of equal distance in Ohio," even though all the major facilities were built of wood.[34] Construction of all except the fourth and northernmost division, a 33-mile line to the junction with the Wabash and Erie, was finally completely in 1843. Because expenditures had greatly exceeded estimates, the legislature hesitated to authorize the final division. But the costs of abandonment appeared to exceed the price of completion; and so, with obvious reluctance, the assembly authorized contracts for construction of the northern division. A proviso was attached to the bill, requiring the board to let the contracts at no more than the engineers' estimated cost ($367,000), to be paid in "domestic bonds" of the state in lieu of cash.[35] Departing from precedent, the board awarded a single contract for the entire line, and the work was completed in 1845. Thus the last project of the expanded public works program came to fruition.[36]

The combined Miami Extension-Wabash & Erie line, some 250 miles in length, gave Cincinnati access to Lake Erie and completed the grand design of 1825, which had contemplated two lake-to-river canals. The era of regional isolation in the Ohio country was now finally ended.

EXPERIMENT IN MIXED ENTERPRISE

The 1837 Loan Law had originally been designed to afford every citizen of the state the benefits of "progressive improvement," but this experiment in mixed enterprise did not prove the undiluted blessing that its advocates had anticipated. The timing was unfortunate, since the law necessitated additional bond issues when the public works were already endangered by a shortage of state funds. In addition, the turnpikes, railroads, and canals built with Loan Law aid competed with the public works for engineering personnel, construction labor, and provisions, thus contributing to the already difficult problems of the state's contractors and the board of public works.

The Loan Law itself was riddled with loopholes that invited abuse. The act was "sweeping in its terms" and vested little discretion in state authorities, as its hapless administrators complained in 1838. By opening the public treasury to all who could provide half or a third of the capital necessary for a new project, the Loan Law fed "the enterprising spirit of individuals in the populous and wealthy districts of the country, so keenly intent upon the advancement of individual wealth."[37]

Cupidity found a willing partner in a law which left power to establish routes of turnpikes or railroads entirely to the private promoters, leaving state officials no voice in the matter. Many companies obtained private capital by promising to build through specific communities or even individual property holdings: for though meandering routes meant higher construction costs, promoters were comforted by the fact that half the difference would be borne by the state.[38]

Under the Loan Law, the state subscribed $1,896,040 to the stock of twenty-six turnpike corporations. All but two of the companies aided were located in the southwest quarter of the state, and half the total capitalization involved was in roads in the region directly tributary to Cincinnati. To be sure, a total of 692 miles of turnpike road were built in Ohio with Loan Law aid. But expectations that the Loan Law would "equalize benefits" of improved transport were confounded. The main effect of the turnpikes so built was to enhance the trade of the state's wealthiest city. As far as its impact in poorer districts outside southwest Ohio was concerned, the law might never have been enacted.[39]

The record with regard to aid for canal construction was much brighter. Two canal companies received stock subscriptions under the terms of the Loan Law. Some $450,000 of state funds played a critical role in bringing the Mahoning Canal to completion in 1840, opening direct water travel between Cleveland and Pittsburgh and providing an alternate route between Lake Erie and the Ohio River. The Cincinnati and Whitewater Canal Company received a $150,000 state subscription, which helped to overcome severe construction problems caused by labor shortages and high prices. Alert to the power of the printing press, the company also issued promissory notes in small denominations to its contractors, a spurious currency which circulated widely in the Cincinnati area. By this expedient, and with the aid of a $400,000 stock subscription by the Cincinnati city government, the Whitewater Canal was completed in 1843.[40]

Under the Loan Law, more than $500,000 was lent to railroads. This amount was largely wasted, in terms of either contributing to actual construction or obtaining returns on the public funds involved. Six companies received loans in the following amounts:

Painesville & Fairport R. R.	$ 6,182
Ashland & Vermilion R. R.	44,000
Ohio Railroad	249,000
Mansfield & Sandusky R. R.	33,333
Mad River & Lake Erie R. R.	270,000*
Little Miami R. R.	115,000

* Includes special loan under 1836 Act.

Only the Little Miami repaid its debt in full. The Painesville and the Ashland roads failed altogether, with a total loss of the loans made to them.[41]

The fanciful Ohio Railroad, designed to be built on piles, was a colossal fraud from its inception. Chartered in 1836, the company planned a line to run 177 miles parallel to the Lake Erie shore, from Pennsylvania to the Maumee River. When the promoters applied for a state loan in 1838, not a penny had been disbursed for construction or equipment. Subscribers to its stock had conditionally deeded land in lieu of cash, and Alfred Kelley and others familiar with the project denounced the application for public aid as "an unhallowed attempt to filch money from the state."[42] In the 1838–39 session of the legislature, critics attempted to amend the Loan Law to require cash payment of private stock subscriptions in any company applying for state aid. This effort failed, and the board of fund commissioners interpreted the legislature's inaction as tacit approval of the Ohio Railroad and its financing. The board proceeded to authorize a succession of loans amounting to nearly a quarter million dollars. This was nearly all the cash the company ever commanded, and the inevitable bankruptcy occurred in 1845, before the line had been built. Meanwhile, all the other assets had drifted back into the hands of the private subscribers. Through court action, the state government finally recovered "one set of small car-wheels and axles, one locomotive steam pile-driver, and one steam saw mill," the entire return on its investment.[43]

The Mad River & Lake Erie received total loans of $270,000 under the special act of 1836 and the Loan Law. In 1843 the company obtained permission to discharge its debt to the state in common and preferred stock, which the state sold in 1866 for a total of $36,075. The Mansfield & Sandusky Railroad also was permitted to pay its debt by deeding stock to the state. This was later sold for $583, at a loss of nearly $33,000 to the public treasury.

Only the Little Miami Railroad loan, amounting to $115,000, proved a sound investment. This line was planned to run from Cincinnati to Springfield, where it would eventually connect with the Mad River & Lake Erie to provide a through line between the Ohio River and Sandusky. The company was formally organized in 1837, and despite the unsettled character of the money market raised sufficient funds—including a $200,000 subscription from the City of Cincinnati and $50,000 from Greene County's government—to build fourteen miles of its line by 1841. It went into receivership in 1843, but Boston investors refinanced the company, and the line to Springfield was completed three years later.[44] Once again, the state accepted common stock in payment of its loan, and this was sold in 1862 for $256,000.[45]

The railroads constructed with state aid included the Little Miami's 14-mile line, 56 miles completed by the Mansfield & Sandusky in 1846, and 134 miles of jerry-built road completed by the Mad River & Lake Erie between Sandusky and Springfield in 1848. None of these were more than small links in what would later become integrated systems. Moreover, only the Little Miami corporation maintained itself on a relatively sound fiscal basis, and even it went to the wall in the depression of the early forties.[46]

The blatant political influence exerted to obtain loans, the concentration of the state's turnpike investment in one relatively wealthy district, and the rising crisis in state finances, all combined to produce public hostility toward the Loan Law. By 1839 both Whig and Democratic leaders were beginning to speak out in favor of retrenchment, and there was general agreement that a cutback in state aid to private firms was preferable to curtailment of the public works. In March 1840, therefore, the legislature enacted a bill forbidding new commitments of aid under the Loan Law. Two years later, the law itself was repealed outright, closing a dismal chapter in the history of state economic policy in Ohio.[47]

THE ENLARGED PROGRAM

Completion of the public works program in 1845, together with construction by companies aided under the Loan Law, provided Ohio with the major canal and road facilities shown in Table 5.2.[48]

TABLE 5.2
PRINCIPAL OHIO TRANSPORTATION LINES, 1845

STATE-OWNED CANALS	MILES	OTHER CANALS	MILES	ROADS	MILES
Miami Canal and		Mahoning		Western	
minor branches	86	(in Ohio)a	86	Reserve	
Miami Extension	125	Whitewater		& Maumee	
Wabash & Erie	89	(in Ohio)	25	Road	31
Ohio Canal and		Milan		Turnpikes	
minor branches	333	(deepwater)	3	aided by	
Muskingum Imp.	90			Loan Law	692
Walhonding	24				
Hocking Valley	56				
Total	803	Total	114	Total	723

a The Mahoning Canal was formally incorporated as the Pennsylvania & Ohio Canal Company. The state subscribed to stock of the Mahoning and of Whitewater canal companies, and aided the Milan Canal Company.

The major objectives of the 1836–38 program had been achieved. There was now a direct water route between Ohio's foremost commercial city, Cincinnati, and the waters of Lake Erie. The Wabash & Erie Canal had been completed, giving both Toledo and Cincinnati access to the developing farm regions of central Indiana and western Ohio. The Wabash canal also promised, as Indiana progressed with her own portion of the line, still another canal route between the Great Lakes and the Ohio Valley. The new program had expanded the Ohio Canal trade system, enhancing the commercial position of cities and farm areas in the eastern part of the state. The Muskingum Improvement, for all its engineering difficulties, had made the river navigable for steamboat transportation for its entire length; and the Mahoning Canal linked the trade areas of Cleveland and Pittsburgh, two of the most important commercial entrepôts of the West. Both the Mahoning Canal and the Muskingum line offered to Cleveland merchants and to producers in the interior of Ohio alternate routes to the Ohio River market—indeed, routes much more reliable and on the whole less expensive than the old Portsmouth outlet on the main-line canal. The Walhonding Canal, to be sure, remained a stunted line and never was extended to the commercial cities of north-central Ohio. But the Hocking Valley Canal assumed importance to the state's trade soon after its completion. As expected, it opened the coal and salt deposits near Athens to markets in central Ohio, and it also provided a route for both merchandise and farm products in interregional trade. Even the Loan Law provided some important benefits, despite its poor administration and the heavy financial losses incurred for the state: for with the aid it gave to private companies, Cincinnati obtained her branch line to the Whitewater Valley Canal, the Mahoning Canal was completed, and three railroads that would later become major transportation arteries (the Little Miami, the Mad River, and the Sandusky & Mansfield) all made a start on construction, while southwestern Ohio acquired an impressive network of turnpike roads.

By 1845, then, Ohio was one of the best-endowed states of the Union in transport facilities. Even the men who had argued for "equalized benefits" a decade earlier might have been satisfied with the record of construction—except that egalitarianism had given way to disillusionment with canal technology, and there was increasing disrespect in Ohio for public enterprise itself. For though the new public works provided many of the economic benefits that had been promised by their promoters, in the short run their cost had exceeded all expectations. They nearly forced Ohio to default on its state debt, or to repudiate outright, as many states did in the early 1840's. The record of their financing, and the manner in which state finance became wrapped up with other issues, notably banking policy, made the public works an increasingly sensitive political issue after 1836 and finally contributed to the growing popular disillusionment with the active state.

NOTES

1. Board of Public Works, *1st Annual Report* (1837), 14. Board of Public Works *Annual Reports* hereafter abbreviated BPW, *AR*.

2. Petition of Joseph Barker and others, Aug. 14, 1838, in BPW Papers, Ohio State Archives. The 1836 law authorizing the Muskingum Improvement (34 L. O. 346) directed the board to build locks large enough to accommodate steamboats of the size most common on the upper Ohio River.

3. Petition of Joseph Barker and others, Aug. 14, 1838, BPW Papers.

4. Dresden petition dated July 31, 1838, *ibid.*

5. Canal Commission, *15th AR* (1839), 18; BPW, *5th AR* (1842), 9.

6. *Ohio Statesman* (Columbus), Feb. 6, 1838; BPW, *5th AR* (1842).

7. Micajah T. Williams to L. Ransom, Aug. 1, 1840, Micajah T. Williams Papers, OSL; Williams to E. A. Brown, Sept. 2, 1836, Ethan Allen Brown Papers, OSL; H. S. Knapp, *History of the Maumee Valley* (Toledo, 1866), 557–58.

8. Canal Commission, *15th AR* (1839), 17–19.

9. BPW, *3rd AR* (1839), 17–18.

10. BPW, *9th AR* (1845), 10–11. See also BPW, *5th AR* (1842), 9–12.

11. For specifications of the prism design, see BPW, Minute Books, II, p. 10 (ms., Department of Public Works Records, State Office Building, Columbus).

12. U. S. Congress, 54th Cong., 1st Sess., *House Doc.*, No. 277 (ser. 3425), 7, 12; Oliver D. Graham, "History of the Ohio Canal System," B. C. E. thesis, Ohio State University, 1939, pp. 25–31.

13. BPW, *9th AR* (1845), 16–19; see also John J. George, Jr., "The Miami Canal," Ohio Arch. and Hist. Soc., *Publications*, XXXVI (1927), 92–115; and Arthur Hirsch, "Construction of the Miami and Erie Canal," Mississippi Valley Historical Assoc., *Proceedings*, X (1918–21), 349–62.

14. See Auditor of State, *Annual Report, 1843,* p. 38.
15. BPW, *4th AR* (1841). On financing, see Chapter 6, below.
16. Leander Ransom to Simon Perkins, June 5, 1837, Simon Perkins Papers, WRHS.
17. Harvey H. Segal, in *Canals and American Economic Development,* ed. Carter Goodrich (New York, 1962), 171ff., 189ff. On rising canal wages outside Ohio, cf. Walter S. Sanderlin, *The Great National Project* (Baltimore, 1946), 57, 126. (See also note 23, below.)
18. The quotation regarding native-born workers' departure from the canal is from the Piqua (Ohio) *Western Courier,* Jan. 9, 1836. See also BPW, *1st AR* (1837), 9; BPW Minutes, I, p. 336; Canal Commission, *14th AR* (1836), 8–9; and BPW, *4th AR* (1841), 19–20.
19. BPW, *3rd AR* (1840), 11–14; *4th AR* (1841), 14–16; *Maumee Express* (Maumee City), Aug. 18, 1838; and, on wages, Francis P. Weisenburger, ed., "Memoirs of Edwin Phelps," *Northwest Ohio Quarterly,* XVIII (1945), 94.
20. Canal Commission, *15th AR* (1839), 12–14; BPW, *2nd AR* (1838), 11.
21. *Maumee Express,* April 7, 1838; BPW, *6th AR* (1843), 15–20; and Thomas S. Berry, *Western Prices before 1861* (Cambridge, 1943), 424–25, on behavior of regional prices. See also Canal Commission, *14th AR* (1836), 8; and BPW, *3rd AR* (1839), 7, 14, on rising prices near canal lines.
22. BPW, *3rd AR* (1839), 12.
23. On depreciation of paper paid contractors, cf. Weisenburger, ed., "Memoirs of Edwin Phelps," 103–4; and *Executive Docs.,* 1843, No. 25, p. 3. In Pennsylvania, too, from 1837 to 1840 despite hard times the prevailing canal-labor wage remained inflexible, at one dollar per diem. (William A. Sullivan, *The Industrial Worker in Pennsylvania* [Harrisburg, 1955], 73.)
24. BPW, *2nd AR* (1838), 9–10; C. P. McClelland and C. C. Huntington, *The Ohio Canals* (Columbus, 1905), 39.
25. BPW, *4th AR* (1841), 11; and *8th AR* (1844), 19.
26. *6th AR* (1843), 7–8.
27. BPW, *3rd AR* (1839), 17–18; *5th AR* (1842), 9–12; *9th AR* (1845), 10–11; *Executive Docs.,* 1860–61, I, 497.
28. Canal Commission, *15th AR* (1839), 12–14; Lancaster Lateral Canal Co., Minute Books (OHS), p. 35.
29. BPW, *6th AR* (1843), 8–9; *7th AR* (1844), 11.

30. BPW, *2nd AR* (1838), 7.

31. There was little competitive bidding for re-let contracts because regular monthly payments could not be promised, thereby excluding men of limited means. (*Executive Docs.*, 1842–43, No. 42, pp. 2–3.) See also BPW, *4th AR* (1841), 14–16; and Hirsch, "Construction of the Miami and Erie Canal," 358.

32. Auditor of State, *Annual Report*, 1843, p. 48.

33. BPW, *7th AR* (1844), 27–29; Ohio Senate, *Report of the Standing Committee on Retrenchment . . . Feb. 28, 1844*, pp. 5, 15–17.

34. Hirsch, "Construction of the Miami and Erie Canal," 361; also, BPW, *5th AR* (1842), 14–15.

35. 41 L. O. 43 (Feb. 23, 1843). Domestic bonds provided for payment of interest and principal in Ohio rather than eastern or specie funds. The contract was awarded to P. W. Taylor & Co. of Granville, who in turn gave out sub-contracts for the work. (See BPW, *7th AR* [1844], 18–22.)

36. Charges of favoritism and corruption were made against engineers directing the Miami Extension Canal construction work. Subsequent investigation proved that resident engineers had given the legislature unwarrantedly optimistic reports on progress of the work, had awarded contracts at unpropitious times, and had made unduly large discretionary allowances to contractors. All told, administration of work on this line was undoubtedly the worst in the history of the state. (See *Report of the Standing Committee on Retrenchment . . . Feb. 28, 1844*, pp. 4–13; Auditor of State, *Annual Report*, 1843, 48.)

37. BPW, *2nd AR* (1838), 15–16.

38. Canal Commission, *15th AR* (1839), 25–26. The experience with mixed enterprise under a Virginia law permitting state investment was comparable to Ohio's, in terms of both administrative problems and accrual of benefits to the wealthier districts. (Wiley E. Hodges, "Pro-Governmentalism in Virginia, 1789–1836," *Journal of Politics*, XXV [May 1963], 347–48.)

39. *Executive Docs.*, 1845–46, Pt. II, pp. 603ff.; this report on administration of the Loan Law is the basis for all factual data in following paragraphs.

40. On the Whitewater Canal, see Waldo C. Moore, "Early Ohio Internal Improvements," *The Numismatist*, XXXI (1918), 372–74; and discussion of labor problems and issue of paper by the directors in Joseph Gest to Erasmus Gest, July 5, 1840, Erasmus Gest Papers, OHS.

41. *Executive Docs.*, 1845–46, Pt. II, pp. 606ff.; Ernest L. Bogart, *Financial History of Ohio* (Urbana, 1912), 305ff.

42. Kelley to Perkins, Feb. 4, 1838, Simon Perkins Papers, WRHS; see also C. P. Leland, "The Ohio Railroad," Western Reserve Historical Society, *Tracts*, No. 81 (1891), 265–84.

43. BPW, *9th AR* (1845), 33; on the attack in the legislature, cf. *Journal and Register* (Columbus), March 2, 1838, and Kelley to Perkins, Feb. 4, 1838, Perkins Papers, WRHS.

44. Commissioner of Railroads, *Annual Report*, 1870, Vol. I, pp. 277–78; Robert L. Black, *The Little Miami Railroad* (Cincinnati, n. d. but 1941), 13–31.

45. Black, *Little Miami*, 44–45; Bogart, *Financial History*, 309; *Executive Docs.*, 1845–46, Pt. II, pp. 613–14.

46. The Painesville & Fairport opened its four-mile line in 1838, but went into bankruptcy and closed in 1845. (L. Klein, "Railroads in the United States," *Journal of the Franklin Institute*, n. s., XXVI [1840], 100.) Ohio's railroads in 1850 are shown in Frederic L. Paxson, "Railways of the 'Old Northwest' before the Civil War," Wisconsin Academy of Sciences, Arts and Letters, *Transactions*, XVII, Oct. 1912, Pt. I, p. 253 (map). See also Map 11–A, below.

47. Whig sentiment for retrenchment in public works spending may be found in *Journal and Register* (Columbus), March 21, 1838; Democratic sentiment, in *Ohio Statesman* (Columbus), Oct. 20, 1839. Representatives of the northern counties fought outright repeal of the Loan Law, seeking instead to restrict new loans to companies projecting facilities in counties not served by the enlarged public works system. (*Ohio Statesman*, Jan. 22, 1840.)

48. Broadside in Williams Papers, OSL; *Executive Docs.*, 1848, No. 28, pp. 502–3; McClelland and Huntington, *Ohio Canals*, 30ff.

CHAPTER 6

Financing Expansion
1836-1845

To say that financing Ohio's internal improvements after 1836 was something of a miracle does not exaggerate much. For during 1836–45 the state built new canal lines costing ten million dollars, spent another three million dollars on aid to private companies, and yet managed to maintain without interruption its interest payments (which by 1842 were $800,000 a year) to current bondholders—all of this despite a panic in 1837 and a severe business depression lasting from 1839 to 1843. Many other states which had then undertaken public works programs of equivalent magnitude were forced to abandon construction; some, including the proud Commonwealth of Pennsylvania, defaulted on interest payments or else repudiated their debts during the early forties.[1]

In normal times the Ohio fund board would have sold bonds, as it had during 1825–32, by seeking bids at par value or higher from the large Anglo-American bankers and investment houses in the Atlantic Coast cities. In turn, the bankers would have resold the bonds at a profit to income-minded investors content to earn an annual return of 5 to 6 per cent, or less.[2] But these were not fated to be normal times. In the first phase of financing the expanded program, from 1836 to 1840, the fund board did in fact make regular sales of long-term bonds at par value prices or higher. But in the second phase, 1841–42, depression conditions reached a low point, forcing the board to accept short-term loans at extremely high cost to the state, in order to maintain construction schedules in Ohio and to keep up semiannual interest payments. The third phase, 1843–44, was marked by a revival of business conditions that permitted Ohio once again to issue bonds on good terms, this time for the purpose of retiring the short-term loans and of paying contractors on the public works their long-overdue claims.

Administrative responsibility for finance continued to be vested, in this period, in the board of canal fund commissioners. Of its three members, only Simon Perkins, the land agent and banker, remained from the early days of canal construction. The new members were Samuel Maccracken, a merchant and banker from Lancaster; and Daniel Kilgore, a Cadiz land speculator, merchant, and banker, who also served as a member of Congress from 1834 to 1838. All three commissioners shared common interests as bankers, especially since they were all directors of the Ohio Life Insurance & Trust Company of Cincinnati, one of Ohio's largest banking firms and after 1836 a major supplier of long-term capital to the fund board. Though actively engaged in private business, each board member gave much of his time to state finance; yet the office carried no salary, and the board was not even provided with official quarters or a staff.[3]

During 1832–36, when no bond issues were required, the board's duties had been routine. Twice annually, in January and in July, it arranged to pay interest on the state debt by transferring to New York the surplus canal revenues and money appropriated by the legislature from taxes. The commissioners also administered the special funds earmarked for the Miami Extension and Wabash & Erie canals, accruing from the proceeds of land sales.[4] When the expanded program was undertaken, however, the board's tasks became far more complex. During the period beginning in 1836, its members traveled frequently to New York and sometimes to London, in the effort to obtain investment capital. Moreover, Ohio's increasing dependence upon the state's own banks would bring the board into a close working relationship with local bankers, eventually drawing them into the vortex of partisan politics.

Conditions in the money market during 1836 were unsettled because of pressure on American banks from the Federal Treasury Department and because of rising demand for specie from England. Under these pressures, the fund board made only one small bond sale in 1836, for $20,000; immediate requirements were met by "borrowing" from school reserves and general funds.[5] When in May 1837 the board learned that no large bond issue was possible on favorable terms, it decided on a temporary suspension of payments to contractors on all the public works except the Wabash & Erie.[6] The initial reaction to the suspension was shock, for only a few months had passed since the gala ground-breaking ceremonies inaugurating the expanded program. The fund board's unexpected action did produce one salutary effect, however: it induced banks at Zanesville and Marietta to purchase $100,000 of bonds at par value, though on condition that the money be expended on the Muskingum Improvement. These special terms were unprecedented, and probably illegal, but the board accepted the arrangement willingly, being fearful that otherwise contractors might sue the state for damages.[7]

Amidst these difficulties, the Panic of May 1837 struck, bringing suspension of specie payments by nearly all American banks. This event posed a critical question for the fund board: the interest due to bondholders in July was payable "in New York funds," which in normal times were equivalent to specie value. But after the panic, New York bank paper circulated at a discount of 10 per cent or more. Risking charges of exceeding their legal authority, the fund commissioners chose to pay bondholders the full specie value of their interest. The board justified this action on grounds that they had "a moral obligation to pay in specie"; but it also proved a shrewd move, for it bolstered public confidence in Ohio's fiscal position.[8]

The decision to pay interest at specie value received favorable notice, in particular from Prime, Ward & King, the New York investment firm which had bought a large portion of Ohio bonds issued during 1825–32. In July 1837 a syndicate of bankers led by this firm purchased $500,000 in 6 per cent bonds from the fund board, paying a price of 112.6 (that is, a premium of 12.6 cents on each dollar of face value).[9] This sale in turn helped persuade bankers in Ohio that they might safely invest in bonds of their own state government. Two Ohio banks took a total of

$200,000 in bonds during the year, paying a premium for the securities and bringing total sales for the year to $700,000.[10]

TABLE 6.1

ORIGINAL PURCHASERS OF OHIO BONDS, 1836–1839

YEAR	AMOUNT	PURCHASER
A. *Eastern purchasers*		
1837	$ 500,000	Prime, Ward & King syndicate, N.Y.
1838	700,000	Prime, Ward & King (own account), N.Y.
1839	1,030,000	North American Bank & Trust Co., N.Y.
	26,123	Bank of Manhattan Co., N.Y.
	10,000	Chelsea Bank, N.Y.
	$2,266,123	SUB-TOTAL, NEW YORK PURCHASES
B. *Ohio purchasers*		
1837	$ 150,000	Bank of Marietta
	50,000	Bank of Muskingum (Zanesville)
1838	1,000,000	Ohio Life Ins. & Trust Co. (Cincinnati)
	100,000	Urbana Banking Co.
	100,000	Commercial Bank of Lake Erie (Cleveland)
	100,000	Lancaster Bank
	10,000	Gustavus Swan
1839	665,000	Ohio Life Ins. & Trust Co.
	210,000	Lancaster Bank
	100,000	Urbana Banking Co.
	85,000	Gustavus Swan, Simon Perkins, and others
	80,000	Bank of Wooster
	25,000	Commercial Bank of Lake Erie
	200,000	Columbus Insurance Co.
	$2,875,000	SUB-TOTAL, OHIO PURCHASES
C. *Residence Unknown*		
1836	$ 20,000	David Crouse.
D. TOTAL		
1836–39	$5,161,123	

Source: Bond-sale records, Auditor's Records, Ohio State Archives; *Executive Docs.*, 1845–46, Pt. II, 650–59. (N.B. $309,515 of bonds were issued also to railroads, 1836–39, of which $100,000 was sold to the U. S. Treasury in 1837, to credit of the Mad River & Lake Erie Railroad. The remainder was issued directly to companies receiving aid.)

In 1838 heavy obligations fell due to the public-works contractors, who had resumed construction and were demanding
payment on completed jobs. The fund board had paid the January 1838 interest to bondholders in specie funds, thereby helping
to sustain investor confidence; but even more important to new
bond sales was a brief general business revival beginning in
April. Prime, Ward & King again came forward to support the
financing effort, this time purchasing $700,000 in bonds at a
price of 106.[11] But before the year had ended, the fund board
marketed another $1,300,000 of securities to Ohio banks—a
most important development, since from 1825 through 1837
all but $300,000 of the five million dollars of bonds issued by
Ohio had been sold outside the state. Appropriately enough, the
largest Ohio purchaser in 1838, taking one million dollars of
the total, was the Ohio Life Insurance & Trust Company, then
probably the state's most heavily capitalized corporation engaged
in banking.[12] If the emergence of Ohio banks as a source of long-
term capital in 1838 was significant in itself, the Trust Company's
large purchase had special implications, both financial and political. For since its founding four years earlier, the company had
been a prime object of political attack by radical antibank Democrats who viewed it as a giant and dangerous monopoly. Any
association between the Trust Company and the fund board
would thus be closely scrutinized by the bank's enemies, especially considering that all three fund commissioners were directors
of the firm. Moreover, the sale to the Trust Company enlarged
the role in Ohio finance of Baring Brothers of London, one of
the world's largest merchant banking houses. Having long sold
Ohio bonds on consignment from Prime, Ward & King, and
having purchased some on their own account, the Barings opened
a new line of credit to the Ohio Life & Trust in 1838, taking as
collateral the state bonds that firm had just purchased.[13] In this
way, the 1838 bond sales cemented a complex of interdependent
interests that would affect profoundly Ohio's financial operations
in ensuing years.

In 1839 the fund board again enjoyed excellent success in
marketing long-term bonds. More than $2,400,000 were issued,

some at par but most at prices slightly above face value. Ohio banks continued to play the major role, purchasing $1,365,000 of the 1839 issues; and again the Ohio Life & Trust was the largest single purchaser among the state's own institutions, taking $665,000 of the bonds.[14]

The fund board's effort to sell bonds to Ohio banks might well have been hindered by the effects of a bank-reform bill enacted in early 1839. The state legislature was then dominated by the Democratic party, which reflected the rising influence of a hard-money, antibank faction—radicals who stood for a specie currency and favored strict control of banking operations.[15] The 1839 law required Ohio's banks to maintain fractional specie reserves on note issues and forbade suspension of specie payments by any bank for more than thirty days a year. But for all its apparent stringency, the law in operation proved most ineffective, as Ohio banks circulated out-of-state notes and issued non-interest-bearing promissory notes (termed "post notes") in order to evade specie-reserve requirements. Furthermore, the fund board blatantly encouraged banks that purchased bonds to deal in this spurious currency.[16] For when an Ohio bank bought state bonds, the board allowed the bank to pay out the amount in small sums to contractors on the public works. Needless to say, the paper that the banks disbursed, although credited by the fund board at face value, was often badly depreciated currency. Thus the contractors were forced to accept "promiscuous" notes or else go without any payment whatever.[17]

In its operations in the East in 1839, the fund board adopted another expedient: the sale of bonds on credit, especially to the North American Trust & Banking Company, an aggressive New York firm that was then dealing heavily in state securities.[18] North American bought for cash $500,000 in bonds in June; but the next month it took another $300,000 and committed itself to pay in three installments between then and mid-December. With $200,000 still due in November, the firm revealed that it could not pay. To salvage the debt, the fund board "sold" North American an additional $230,000 in bonds; North American put up New York real-estate mortgages as security, paying no cash. The fund board then sent the bonds to the Barings of London with instructions to sell at any price, the proceeds to be credited to North American, which would be liable for any difference between sale price and par value.[19]

Although the debt owed by North American was later settled at only a slight loss to the state, in the last months of 1839 it created a temporary crisis. Bondholders had to be paid their interest in January 1840, and the board depended on North American's installment payment to provide it with cash for the interest. By two expedients, the board finally managed to distribute interest on schedule. First, it used a temporary loan of $133,000 from Baring Brothers of London, obtained in mid-1839 when the board in return agreed to name the Barings as its exclusive agent for direct bond sales in Europe; and second, the board drew upon general tax revenues being held at Columbus in a special fund earmarked for debt retirement, treating the draft as a "temporary loan" from the treasury.[20]

By these means, the board realized cash receipts of less than $2,000,000 on its total bond sales of $2,400,000 face value in 1839; it maintained construction on the public works at home; and it kept up interest payments to bondholders on schedule. But it had meanwhile extended a large credit to a near-bankrupt firm; and deepening depression conditions in the national economy made prospects for additional bond issues in 1840 dim indeed.

The difficulties that had been encountered in late 1839 were symptomatic of more basic problems, not least of which was that the original purchasers of Ohio bonds recently issued—notably the Ohio Life & Trust and Prime, Ward & King—had not yet resold in the open market many of the securities already on hand.[21] This made it unlikely at best that they would be interested in purchasing still more, especially since the Ohio legislature had as yet not permitted the fund board to issue bonds at less than par value—and the open-market price in New York was only 90.[22] To be sure, two major gains had been registered in 1839. First, Ohio banks had continued to buy bonds despite the effects of regulatory banking legislation. And second, the Barings had given tangible recognition to their stake in Ohio canal finances by extending a cash loan of $133,000—a gesture that the fund board hoped was a harbinger of further aid from the powerful London firm. But offsetting these gains was the general deterioration of economic conditions and the unprecedented weakness of prices for state bonds in the English and American markets.

When the legislature met for its winter session in December 1839, it faced the need to adjust policy to these mounting difficulties. None of the major public works under construction had yet been completed, despite increase of the state debt to ten million dollars. Some three million dollars' worth of contracts were committed, contractors were already owed nearly $400,000, and some $1,245,000 had been "borrowed" for canal purposes from school-fund, debt-retirement, and other reserves. Abandonment of the half-built public works was one possible course, but the state engineers advised that this would result in at least $500,000 worth of damage to the contract jobs already accepted.[23]

As a first step toward retrenchment, the legislature voted to bar any new commitments of state aid under the Loan Law, and also to prohibit new contracts on the Miami Extension Canal, where work was progressing slowly and costs were astonishing in light of original estimates. Second, the assembly decided to move ahead with the other public works under construction, authorizing new bond issues, all to be sold at par, for the various projects—and also a special "unrestricted" bond issue of $400,-000 which the fund board might issue at any price or any rate of interest.[24] Designed to give the board additional flexibility, the unrestricted issue was expected to be sold at a discount, well below par value.

In a separate action, the assembly required Ohio banks buying state bonds to pay "legal currency" directly into the state treasury at the time of purchase, instead of issuing small sums to contractors.[25] Moreover, the definition of "legal currency" was narrowed significantly by terms of a new bank-reform law, which like the 1839 law was the work of the radical hard-money Democrats. The 1840 law prohibited the issue by banks of post notes or notes of small denomination.[26]

These reform measures were aimed at the fund board as much as at the banks; for the radical Democrats were accusing the fund

board of "dark doings behind the curtain," and they attributed
the crisis in state finances to the board's having aided in bankers'
evasion of the 1839 banking act.[27] These attacks culminated in
a new requirement that board members (who were still paid no
salaries by the state!) put up individual bonds of $250,000 to
secure the state against losses from malfeasance; and they led
promptly to resignations of two of the commissioners, Perkins
and Kilgore. The third member, Joseph Lake (who had succeeded Samuel Maccracken as commissioner in 1837), remained
on the board at the urging of banker friends who feared appointment of a radical "demagogue" in his stead.[28] But though the

TABLE 6.2
PURCHASERS OF OHIO BONDS, 1840

MONTH OF SALE	AMOUNT SOLD	PURCHASER
April–July	$ 405,000	Various Ohio banks
July	400,000	Baring Brothers (London)
August	50,000	Wooster Bank of Ohio
	50,000	Bank of Chillicothe, Ohio
	25,000	Bank of Dayton, Ohio
	25,000	Bank of Xenia, Ohio
	100,000	Commercial Bank of Cincinnati, Ohio
October	20,000	Kilgore, Taylor & Co. (Ohio)
	50,000	Wooster Bank of Ohio
	10,000	Wooster Bank of Ohio
	100,000	Urbana Banking Co., Ohio
November	50,000	R. H. Winslow (New York)
	50,000	Alexandrian Society of Granville, Ohio
December	50,000	R. H. Winslow (New York)
	50,000	Lafayette Bank, Cincinnati, Ohio
	25,000	Wooster Bank of Ohio
TOTAL	$1,460,000	

Source: Executive Docs., 1840–41, No. 52; ibid., 1845–46, Pt. II, 450–59.

bankers feared the worst, the Democratic governor, Wilson Shannon, did not intend to appoint radicals to take charge of state

financing. To the relief of the opposition, he chose two conservative Democrats, both bankers.[29]

Despite the new restrictive banking legislation and adverse conditions in the money market, the new board sold a total of $1,460,000 of bonds during 1840, shown in Table 6.2. The most important sale was to the Barings of London, who in July agreed to buy the entire $400,000 unrestricted issue at a price of 95. "We could probably have got one or two per cent more," one of the fund commissioners asserted, but the board had accepted the Barings' offer in hopes that the house would hold the bonds for high prices and thus protect the open-market price.[30]

Nearly all the remainder of the bonds sold in 1840 were purchased by Ohio banks. It is surprising that they should have been so willing to lend to the state, in view of the harsh 1840 banking law and the new requirement that they pay for their bond purchases directly to the treasury with "legal currency." The key to the puzzle rested in the state treasurer's willingness to permit unblushing evasion of the law: he accepted post notes and depreciated Indiana bank notes from one Cincinnati bank that purchased bonds, and from the Ohio Life & Trust he took "Indiana trash" and other depreciated paper.[31] Only by this unsavory expedient, together with long delays in meeting obligations to many contractors, did the state keep up its construction program and pay bondholders' interest on schedule in 1840.[32]

The legislature that met at Columbus in the winter of 1840–1841 set the stage for a new phase of state canal finance, in which short-term loans rather than bond sales would become the mainstay of fiscal policy. Indeed, during 1841 the fund board would sell only about $300,000 in long-term bonds (all marketed in January), and for the remainder of its current needs would rely on special loans from banks.[33]

When the legislature first convened in December 1840, the fund commissioners estimated total needs during 1841 to be $2,500,000. With contractors pressing for payments due, "the powers of Midas" were needed "to keep things going," one commissioner wrote.[34] But lacking such magical powers, the commissioners determined that they must depend upon Ohio's banks for funds; bond sales in the East or in Europe appeared impossible. This posed a serious dilemma, for bankers in Ohio felt "as if the state had treated them like aliens and enemies," by dint of the recent legislation that curtailed banking powers.[35] Since the elections had brought to power a Whig governor and a Whig majority in the house of representatives, the fund board saw now an opportunity to obtain revision of the "evidently suicidal" banking law.[36] It requested of the legislature (1) that banks extending loans to the state should be permitted to issue post notes, which would be made receivable for payment of state taxes; and (2) that the fund board be empowered to negotiate three-year loans at whatever rate of interest proved necessary, to see the public works through to completion. Although the board admitted that post notes were not desirable, it saw no alternative to making this concession if loans were to be obtained from banks.[37]

But even the pro-bank Whigs in the legislature found the sanctioning of post notes too strong for their taste, and the entire question of banking reform was sidestepped.[38] However, the lawmakers found more appealing the idea of three-year loans. In March 1841, therefore, the assembly voted to empower the board to issue $2,300,000 in new bonds, either as long-term securities or as three-year obligations. Of this amount, $581,000 could be issued without restrictions as to price of sale or rate of interest.[39]

On this authority, the fund board in 1841 borrowed $581,000 from the Chillicothe Bank at 6 per cent interest, with the state agreeing to repay the loan in installments between May 1842 and May 1843. This money was used to pay debts to contractors, and the bank was given state bonds as security. From the Franklin Bank of Columbus the board obtained a $500,000 loan on similar terms. In each case, the bank paid the loans in Ohio bank paper, but the fund board agreed to repay in New York funds, which then were worth 6 to 14 per cent more than the Ohio paper. The commissioners regarded these terms as so harsh that "any amount of funds" could be procured on a similar basis; but they viewed acceptance of the loans as "decidedly preferable to suspending or checking at this stage any of the leading public works of the State."[40]

Still another $200,000 short-term loan was taken from the Wooster Bank, of which Fund Commissioner Joseph Lake was an officer. In a clearly illegal deal, the board accepted post notes and small bills (outlawed under the 1840 banking act), with the bank agreeing to accept comparable funds when the principal was repaid. Once again, state bonds were turned over as security.[41]

Having raised $1,281,000 by taking the three-year loans, in addition to the $300,000 of bonds sold in January, the fund board still lacked cash sufficient to pay bondholders their interest at the year's close. To avoid default, the board decided to exceed its statutory authority: it issued to the Ohio Life & Trust $300,-000 in state bonds as security on a $200,000 loan, to be repaid within ninety days out of tax funds then being collected at Columbus. In addition, the commissioners signed individual, personal notes to guarantee the loan against possible repudiation by the legislature.[42] Thus only by risking their own fortunes and by enlisting aid of the Trust Company in an illegal operation did the board save the state's credit.

As the result of the 1841 elections, the legislature which convened in December of that year was dominated in both houses by Democratic majorities hostile to the fund board, and it debated for three months before giving retroactive approval in March to the illegal $200,000 loan.[43] At the same time, the assembly decided to authorize still further bond issues to permit completion of the expanded public works system—the Muskingum Improvement and the Hocking Canal already having been substantially finished.[44] In one action, the legislature authorized $1,300,000 in "domestic" bonds, which—unlike all securities previously issued—would pay interest and principal in Ohio rather than New York. Of this amount, $500,000 was designed for direct payment to contractors in the form of scrip receivable on the lands granted by Congress to Ohio. In a second measure, the assembly approved issue of whatever amount of 6 per cent bonds, redeemable in 1870, was necessary to meet $500,000 due in 1842 on the three-year temporary loans from Ohio banks. Finally, the assembly barred new contracts for further extension of any project under way except the Wabash & Erie Canal; and it repealed outright the 1837 Loan Law, which already had cost the state three million dollars.[45]

The long duration of the debate at Columbus over the illegal loan made the state's creditors justifiably uneasy. Unfortunately, false rumors reached New York that the legislature had indeed repudiated the agreement. Acting on this information, the New York agent of the Ohio Life & Trust held an auction sale of bonds he held as security for the loan. With buyers and sellers alike under the impression that the state had repudiated, prices at the auction ranged from only 50 to 55 per cent of face value. The fund board despaired that "a fatal stab" had been administered, deploring the auction as "wanton, unnecessary, and unprovoked."[46] But even when correct information of the legislature's decision reached the East, Ohio's credit continued to be held in low esteem; for when the board sold $150,000 in 6 per cents later in the year, it obtained prices ranging only from 68 to 71.[47]

Meanwhile, the Wooster Bank, which held $200,000 in bonds as security for its three-year loan to the state, found itself nearly insolvent and similarly threw its bonds on the open market at forced sales. The average price realized was only 58.[48]

During the remainder of 1842, the fund board sustained installment payments on the three-year loans by issuing bonds to Ohio banks at prices of 70 to 75. In this manner, nearly $700,000 of bonds were sold for cash payments of only $500,000.[49] Even these sales might have been impossible had the Barings not once again come to the aid of the board: for in late May, the Barings purchased $400,000 of bonds at the distressingly low price of 60. A sale at 60 per cent of face value was hardly an expression of unbounded confidence, and yet any sale whatever of American securities was astonishing news in the London money market of 1842. Not least important, the Barings' purchase enabled the fund board to pay the July 1842 interest to bondholders as scheduled.[50]

Total sales of bonds in 1842 were, then, $1,477,200 in par value, with the state actually receiving only $950,000 because of low prices. In addition, $350,000 in scrip had been paid out to contractors.[51] In order to pay the January 1843 interest, the fund board once again needed to adopt extraordinary measures.

Rebuffed by the state auditor when it sought to draw upon tax funds not yet appropriated by the legislature, as had been done a year earlier, the board transferred to New York every penny of toll revenues then in the possession of canal collectors. In addition, the board once again obtained temporary loans in the East, on the co-endorsement of the Ohio Life & Trust.[52] Desperate expedients had again been pursued, but Ohio's credit was preserved and the interest was paid.

The situation that the state government faced in December 1842 was one of mixed prospects. On the one hand, the public works had been carried close to completion—except for the Miami Extension Canal, whose northernmost division remained to be built. On the other hand, contractors were owed nearly $1.400,000 in arrears. The market for Ohio bonds in England and the East remained depressed, and even state scrip issued to contractors the previous year was being discounted up to 50 per cent by local banks and merchants.[53]

After a lengthy debate, the legislature determined to marshal all the state's remaining public resources to avoid default. The assembly authorized a new issue of $1,500,000 in 7 per cent bonds, redeemable in 1851 with interest and principal payable in New York, to be offered first for sale at par value or above in New York. If sales there failed, then the fund board might borrow the same sum in Ohio by issuing 7 per cent "domestic" bonds at par. To back the new issues, the legislature pledged Ohio's portion of the Federal surplus funds that had been distributed in 1837—some two million dollars, which had been loaned to the state's county governments. Also pledged were the canal lands not otherwise committed; and if domestic bonds needed to be issued, then such securities would be receivable for state property such as school lands and salt lands.[54] Finally, the legislature authorized construction of the northernmost portion of the Miami Extension Canal, but only if it could be done at the $367,000 estimated price or less, and only if the contractors agreed to accept domestic bonds in payment.[55]

In the same session, the assembly rejected a bill to recharter thirteen Ohio banks whose corporate privileges had expired in 1842.[56] This left only ten banks in the state, all subject to harsh regulatory legislation, and it ended with utter finality any prospect of future bond sales to banks. If funds were to be raised without resorting to the issue of domestic securities to contractors, it would have to be in the East.

While the assembly debated these measures, a group of Wall Street speculators reportedly "bandied about" Ohio securities in bogus sales on the New York market. "Capitalists have not been slow to conceive that a large amount of the 7 per cent loan is coming upon the market," one fund commissioner reported, "and the warfare of the speculators . . . has therefore the additional motive of keeping them depressed in order to depreciate the 7's when they come to sale."[57]

This was the inauspicious setting in which the fund board prepared to sell bonds in New York in early 1843. At this point, however, the financial institutions with the largest stake in Ohio's credit again came to its aid. A syndicate was organized by the New York cashier of the Ohio Life & Trust. Nearly all its members (notably the Ohio Life itself and Prime, Ward & King) were already large holders of Ohio bonds. Encouraged now by the imminent completion of canal construction in Ohio, and no doubt by reports of large toll revenues on the public works (especially the newly opened Wabash & Erie), the syndicate agreed to purchase $600,000 of the 7 per cent bonds at par value in May 1843. At the same time, it took an option to buy in September the remaining $900,000 of the 7 per cent issue.[58]

This was a spectacular move, and nearly overnight the open-market price of Ohio bonds rose from 67 to nearly 100. In Ohio the fund board sold its 6 per cent securities at par, whereas earlier in the year it had settled its three-year debts to Ohio banks by turning over bonds at heavy discounts. Then, in September, the New York syndicate decided to exercise its option on the remaining $900,000 of 7 per cents at par. Total sales for the year included also some $900,000 of 6 per cents sold at varying discounts.[59]

And so order began to emerge from the chaos of improvisation that had so long marked Ohio finance. An additional bond issue of $210,000 was sold in 1844, enough to pay the last debts in arrears to contractors, and meanwhile the canal board awarded the final Miami Extension Canal contract at the prescribed price of $367,000, with the contractor agreeing to accept "domestic" bonds at par in payment.[60]

From 1844 on, Ohio's state debt for internal improvements remained stable. As principal fell due, the state encountered no difficulty in refunding its debt with new loans. But the 1844 bonds were the last to be sold to finance new construction. For though local and county governments would be permitted to aid railroad corporations by issuing their own bonds, the era of debt-financed state canal construction and mixed enterprise had come to an end. Cured of excessive optimism, the Ohio legislature resisted all popular pressure for new borrowing to finance additional transport improvements; and in 1851 a new state constitution prohibited outright any enlargement of the state debt.[61]

A review of the state canal debt in 1845 revealed total funded indebtedness of about $19.5 million. A more comprehensive accounting made in 1850, when the debt was still close to its peak level, is shown in Table 6.3.

TABLE 6.3
OHIO CANAL DEBT, 1850

(1) "Foreign debt" (interest and principal payable in New York)		
5% bonds, redeemable 1850	$	400,000
5% bonds, redeemable 1860		150,000
6% bonds, redeemable 1850		4,018,659
6% bonds, redeemable 1856		3,365,779
6% bonds, redeemable 1860		6,862,781
6% bonds, redeemable 1870		667,064
7% bonds, redeemable 1851		1,500,000
(2) "Domestic debt" (interest and principal payable in Ohio)		
Transferred state school reserves	$	1,425,093
Domestic scrip outstanding		29,342
Domestic bonds		728,680
Federal surplus revenue loaned by county governments		141,925
(3) Total (adjusted)		$19,389,412

Source: *Executive Documents*, 1845–46, Part II, 593–594; *ibid.*, 1850, No. 26.

In addition to sums obtained by borrowing, the fund board had drawn from the treasury between 1825 and 1845 some seven million dollars in canal-toll revenues, tax moneys, revenue from canal-land sales, and general funds, for a total of over $26,-000,000. Construction of the public works and Loan Law aid amounted to $18,804,000.[62] The difference was accounted for by discounts on bond sales, interest payments to bondholders, and disbursements for repairs, salaries and other expenses on the public works.

Standing nearly alone among the states that undertook major internal-improvement programs in 1836–37, Ohio had completed nearly all its projects and avoided either repudiation or default. The state's success at a time when other states, equally wealthy, failed may be attributed to several factors. Of prime importance was the timing of construction in Ohio. When the state encountered its most desperate difficulties in raising funds, the public works were already about half completed. Unlike the situation in Indiana, Michigan, and some of the other defaulting states, in Ohio by 1841 the cost of abandonment clearly outweighed the prospective cost of accepting heavy discounts on new bond issues and paying harsh terms for temporary loans.[63] Closely related to this factor was the political situation. In many defaulting states, the programs under construction in the early forties were still the objects of strong local hostility, which readily became a base of political support for abandonment or for repudiation of debt.[64] In Ohio there was no such hostility, for the expanded program affected nearly every settled region of the state not already aided by the 1825 canal program. Indeed, abandonment of any of the projects under construction no doubt would have brought local vengeance upon the political party that approved such a policy.

Narrower financial considerations were equally important. Unlike Illinois and the other western states, Ohio already had an operating canal system which produced net revenues of $200,000 to $300,000 annually, even during the worst depression years.[65] Also, Ohio was nearly unique among American states in providing for direct taxation to support its debt for public works.

The original 1825 canal law had given the state auditor discretionary power to levy canal taxes, at an annual level sufficient to cover interest on the state debt. The auditor had not increased taxes commensurately with need in the mid-thirties, but in the early 1840's he did levy progressively higher canal taxes each year. Well might the agent of Indiana's foreign creditors, who faced the spectre of imminent repudiation, point to "the brilliant example of Ohio" when recommending direct taxation to the Hoosier legislature during the depression crisis.[66]

No less important, Ohio enjoyed the benefit of strong financial alliances. In the earlier period of canal financing, from 1825 to 1832, the state had marketed its bonds at high prices and many investors had reaped large returns from appreciation of the bonds' market value in the late twenties. After 1836 the Ohio Life & Trust, the Barings of London, Prime, Ward & King and other major firms again invested heavily in Ohio securities, and they still held large sums in the bonds in 1840.[67] Their existing investments gave them a direct interest in maintaining the state's credit standing and successful completion of her public works. Even after reform legislation had severely curbed the role of Ohio banks as a source of capital, therefore, the Ohio Life & Trust and its eastern and foreign connections, including the Barings, provided timely support. It was no coincidence that the eleventh-hour loans in 1842 and 1843 were obtained with the aid of these banks, nor that the crucial $400,000 bond issue of 1842 was purchased by the Barings.

In the last analysis, however, the decision against repudiation was made in the legislative halls at Columbus. Even with all the foregoing considerations favoring the state's effort to remain solvent, expediential financing had to be sanctioned by the Ohio general assembly. The fact that only a small group among the radical Democrats viewed repudiation or default as a respectable course thus assumed great significance. These radicals portrayed the fund board's negotiation of loans with Ohio banks and foreign investment houses as "coon [Whig] financiering. This is the way they take money out of the pockets of the people of Ohio . . . and put it in the hands of their friends, the British lords and capitalists." So charged a leading radical Democratic newspaper.[68] But this view was held by only a minority of the state's political leadership. Neither the more conservative Democrats nor the Whigs were willing, "as a party, to encounter the odium of a sacrifice of the credit and character of the state," one insider wrote.[69] On the contrary, the two parties vied with one another to take exclusive credit for the expanded program of internal improvements: the Democrats as defenders of the public works against predatory Whig financiers, the Whigs as defenders of the state's credit in alliance with the bankers and investors who were providing the capital necessary for bond sales. In its own way, each party thus posed as the champion of fiscal responsibility.[70]

And so the counsels of prudence and party discipline prevailed. Despite bitter partisan wrangling over methods of finance and over banking regulation, first one expedient and then another was accepted in order to tide the state through the depression. Both the Whigs and the Democrats, even the hard-money radicals, compromised with principle to avoid the abandonment of works half built. With the support—essential to success—of the Anglo-American bankers, the Ohio banks, and a web of interdependent financial interests in Ohio and the East, party leaders on both sides countenanced pragmatic solutions to the trying problems of depression finance.

NOTES

1. See Reginald C. McGrane, *Foreign Bondholders and American State Debts* (New York, 1935); and Leland Jenks, *The Migration of British Capital to 1875* (New York, 1927) on financing of American state internal improvements in the 1830's and 1840's. Ernest L. Bogart, *Internal Improvements and State Debt in Ohio* (New York, 1924) examines post-1836 finance, but contains inconsistencies and some major errors. More accurate is Bogart's *Financial History of Ohio* (Urbana, 1912). Harvey H. Segal, "Canal Cycles: Public Construction Experience in

New York, Pennsylvania, and Ohio" (Ph.D. diss., Columbia University, 1956) is fuller and more analytical, but is based only upon published contemporary sources. These were sometimes misleading because of the fund board's confidential operations involving the Ohio Life & Trust and other financial institutions, operations treated fully in the present chapter.

2. The best source for an understanding of the Anglo-American money market is Ralph W. Hidy, *The House of Baring in American Trade and Finance* (Cambridge, 1949); also valuable is Nathan Miller, *Enterprise of a Free People* (Ithaca, 1962).

3. A review of the board's administrative routine is in *Executive Docs.*, 1845–46, Pt. II, 606ff. Biographical data based upon Simon Perkins Papers, WRHS; and Daniel Kilgore Papers, OHS.

4. A detailed study of the board is in my unpublished dissertation, "Internal Improvements and Economic Change in Ohio" (Cornell University, 1962), Chap. 10.

5. Entries of July 1836, *passim*, Board of Canal Fund Commissioners Letterbooks (MSS., Ohio State Archives), hereafter cited BFC Letters. Also, *Executive Docs.*, 1836–37, No. 26, p. 2.

6. Samuel Maccracken to Perkins, Sept. 5, 1836, to T. Bates, May 13, 1837, to L. Ranson, May 15, 1837, BFC Papers.

7. Maccracken to Perkins, May 24, 1837, Perkins Papers, WRHS. The banks (the Bank of Marietta and the Muskingum Bank) had made large loans to contractors and so had a direct interest in continuation of construction.

8. Kilgore to Perkins, June 30, 1837, Perkins Papers. On pressures of 1836–37, see H. Scheiber, "The Pet Banks in Jacksonian Politics and Finance," *Journal of Economic History*, XXIII (1963), 196–211; and R. C. McGrane, *The Panic of 1837* (Chicago, 1924), *passim*.

9. The premium paid made the bond-purchase funds equivalent to specie value. (*Executive Docs.*, 1837–38, No. 20, pp. 4–5; Maccracken to Bates, July 19, 1837.) Payments to contractors had been suspended from May until August, while the loan was being negotiated, in order to protect funds needed for July interest and for repairs on the operating lines of canal.

10. See Table 6.1. The sales to Ohio banks are detailed in Maccracken to Kilgore, Sept. 25, 1837, BFC Papers.

11. *Executive Docs.*, 1838–39, No. 39, pp. 3–5. The Barings of

London, one of England's largest banking firms, had shipped four million dollars in specie to Prime, Ward & King in the spring of 1838 to help New York banks resume specie payments and give new force to the business revival. Receipt of these funds no doubt enabled Prime, Ward & King to take Ohio bonds. (See Miller, *Enterprise of Free People*, 234–53; and on the sale in New York, Maccracken to L. Ransom, April 23, 1838, Board of Public Works Papers, OSA.)

12. See Table 6.1. The Ohio banks paid prices ranging from 108 to 112.5. (*Executive Docs.*, 1838–39, No. 39, pp. 3–5.)

13. Scheiber, "Entrepreneurship and Western Development," *Business History Review*, XXXVII (1963), 355–67, on the Trust Company; and Hidy, *House of Baring*, 264–66, 273–74.

14. See Table 6.1.

15. C. C. Huntington, *History of Banking and Currency in Ohio* (Columbus, 1915), 392; Francis P. Weisenburger, *Passing of the Frontier* (Columbus, 1941), 340ff. The rising capitalization of Ohio banks was both a basis for their new ability to provide the state with long-term capital and a cause of concern to reform-minded Democratic radicals who attributed the depression to bank corruption. Some six million dollars in 1835, bank capital in the state was eleven million dollars by 1837.

16. This practice was first revealed in a house investigation of 1837, in *House Journal* (Ohio General Assembly), 1837, pp. 649–56.

17. *Ohio Statesman* (Columbus), Dec. 6, 1839, on depreciated paper paid to contractors by the Ohio Life & Trust; also, T. P. Handy to J. Whitehill, Oct. 8, 1839, (Correspondence of the Treasurer of State, OSA.

18. See Joseph Dorfman, "A Note on the Interpenetration of Anglo-American Finance, 1837–1841," *Journal of Economic History*, XI (1951), 140–47; the company's elaborate dealings in Arkansas bonds may be traced in Packet D-131, Papers of Frederick Huth & Company, Business Archives Council, London.

19. *Executive Docs.*, 1845–46, Pt. II, 596ff., 710–11; *ibid.*, 1839–40, No. 74, pp. 3–5.

20. On the Barings' advance, *Executive Docs.*, 1841–42, No. 77, Appendix B; and *ibid.*, 1839–40, No. 63, pp. 3–4; and on interest payment, *ibid.*, 1839–40, No. 77, p. 8. The debt-retirement fund had long been a fiction, as the fund board drew upon it constantly from 1837 forward.

21. See Appendix I, below. Fully half the total of bonds issued

during 1838–39 were still owned by large institutions, including many of the original purchasers (over two million dollars was still held by the Ohio Life & Trust alone).

22. J. N. Perkins to M. T. Williams, Jan. 20, 1840, Micajah T. Williams Papers, OSL. Evidence that the Barings were having difficulty marketing their Ohio bonds at good prices is in Hidy, *House of Baring,* 274.

23. Board of Public Works, *3rd AR,* 1839, pp. 23–24.

24. 38 L. O. 81 (March 23, 1840). See *Ohio Statesman,* Dec. 3, 1839, on the issue of cost of abandoning works under construction.

25. Bogart, *Internal Improvements and State Debt in Ohio,* 62.

26. Huntington, *Banking and Currency,* 395; Williams to J. N. Perkins, March 27, 1840, Williams Papers.

27. *Ohio Statesman,* Jan. 20, 1840.

28. Williams to Lake, April 7, 1840, Swayne to Williams, April 6, April 11, 1840, Williams Papers; Maccracken to John Brough, March 28, 1840, BFC Papers. That the legislature's attack on the fund board was not wholly unwarranted is clear. The board had indeed cooperated hand in glove with the bankers, besides which the agency's accounts were found to be "in a singular and lamentable state of confusion." (Swayne to Williams, June 10, 1840, Williams Papers.)

29. They were Gustavus Swan and Noah H. Swayne. Swan was a Columbus banker, and Swayne was a member of the Ohio Life & Trust directorate as well as a lawyer of wide reputation.

30. On the loan, see Lake to Barings, July 29, 1840, BFC Papers.

31. See Table 6.2. The Commercial Bank of Cincinnati paid Indiana and Illinois bank notes, notes of insolvent Ohio banks, and even (it seems) its own post notes. (James Hall to Whitehill, July 14, 1840, Lake to Swan, Aug. 12, 1840, M. T. Williams to Whitehill, Aug. 6, 1840, Correspondence of the Treasurer of State.)

32. In August 1840 the board had ceased issuing funds to turnpike companies under the Loan Law. "Turnpike gentlemen . . . must expect nothing more from the State until after the next session of the Legislature," one commissioner wrote. (Swayne to Lake, Aug. 27, 1840, BFC Papers.)

33. The purchasers were the Ohio Life & Trust, $50,000; the Urbana Banking Company, $50,000; Samuel F. Maccracken (presumably as an official of the Lancaster Bank), $108,500; R. H.

Winslow, $59,000; and J. N. Perkins (presumably as cashier of the Ohio Life & Trust), $41,000. (*Executive Docs.*, 1840–41, No. 52, pp. 3–4; *ibid.*, 1845–46, Pt. II, pp. 650–59.)

34. Swan to Lake, Nov. 20, 1840, BFC Papers.
35. Swan to Lake, Nov. 2, 1840, to Forrer, Nov. 15, 1840, BFC Papers.
36. Swan to Forrer, Nov. 15, 1840, *ibid.; Executive Docs.*, 1840–41, No. 30, pp. 6ff.
37. *Executive Docs.*, 1840–41, No. 66, pp. 4, 6. The board recommended in effect that the banks' post notes be guaranteed by the state, with sanctions to be levied against other banks that might refuse to accept the post notes in settlement of debts.
38. Swayne to Williams, March 17, 1841, Williams Papers.
39. In addition, Alfred Kelley, former canal commissioner and now a Whig leader and critic of the Loan Law, was appointed to succeed Gustavus Swan as fund commissioner. The 1841 legislation is summarized, *Executive Docs.*, 1841–42, No. 49.
40. Swayne to Kelley, Aug. 3, 1841, BFC Papers.
41. *Executive Docs.*, 1845–46, Pt. II, 625–26; Kelley to Maccracken, Oct. 12, 1841, BFC Papers.
42. BFC to Baring Brothers, Nov. 9, 1841, BFC Papers; *Executive Docs.*, 1841–42, No. 77, Appendix B; *ibid.*, 1845–46, Pt. II, p. 770.
43. See Weisenburger, *Passing of Frontier*, 406–7; *Executive Docs.*, 1842, No. 29, p. 11.
44. Or so it was thought, until later the Muskingum line was found to be so poorly engineered that much of it needed to be rebuilt.
45. *Executive Docs.*, 1842, No. 29, p. 10. See also Bogart, *Internal Improvements*, 66–68.
46. Swayne to Williams, March 14, 1842, Williams Papers; Kelley to J. N. Perkins, March 17, 1842, BFC Papers.
47. Prices given in St. Mary's (Ohio) *Sentinel*, Sept. 27, 1843.
48. *Ibid.*, Feb. 28, 1844; *Executive Docs.*, 1845–46, Pt. II, p. 626.
49. Swan to Kelley, April 30, 1842, BFC Papers; *Executive Docs.*, 1842, No. 29, pp. 11ff. Prices of individual sales given in St. Mary's *Sentinel*, Sept. 27, 1843.
50. Swayne to Baring, July 22, 1842, BFC Papers; Hidy, *House of Baring*, 291–92.
51. St. Mary's *Sentinel*, Sept. 27, 1843; *Executive Docs.*, 1842, No. 29.
52. *Ibid.*, p. 11; Auditor J. Brough to BFC, Nov. 2, 1842 (MS.,

State Auditor's Office Records Room); entries of Nov. 9, 10, 28, BFC Papers.

53. Auditor of State, *AR*, 1842, p. 32.

54. 41 L. O. 80.

55. 41 L. O. 43. Also the BFC was reorganized (41 L. O. 54), the board to comprise two regular state officers and a full-time paid commissioner.

56. Huntington, *Banking and Currency*, 408–9.

57. E. Hubbard and J. Brough to J. M. Espy, April 12, 1843, BFC Papers.

58. *Executive Docs.*, 1843, No. 25.

59. Computed from *ibid.*, 1850, No. 26, to which is added $316,000 in bonds turned over to the Franklin Bank at rated value of $250,044 (*ibid.*, 1843, No. 25).

60. Bogart, *Internal Improvements*, 177.

61. Eugene Roseboom, *The Civil War Era* (Columbus, 1944), 132.

62. *Exec. Docs.*, 1845–46, Pt. II, *passim*.

63. Thus the fund board had consistently given high priority to the Wabash & Erie when cash funds were short, since that line was expected to pay high revenues. See also *Executive Docs.*, 1840–41, No. 30, pp. 6–7.

64. In Illinois, for example, the Illinois & Michigan Canal was still regarded in 1845 as "a northern measure, and being considered by the south [as] local fails to secure many friends in that region; and there is an evident reluctance among the population to assess any tax." (Report of John Davis to Barings, March 20, 1845, quoted in McGrane, *Foreign Bondholders*, 123.)

65. C. P. McClelland and C. C. Huntington, *History of the Ohio Canals* (Columbus, 1905), 170.

66. Charles Butler quoted in McGrane, *Foreign Bondholders*, 137; also, Carter Goodrich, *Government Promotion of American Canals and Railroads* (New York, 1960), 274, 276.

67. See Appendix I, below.

68. St. Mary's *Sentinel*, Sept. 27, 1843. See also the attack on the "foolish and extravagant" measures of the fund board, in *Ohio Statesman*, Feb. 20, 1840.

69. Micajah T. Williams to S. Jaudon, March 6, 1843, Williams Papers.

70. Lima (Ohio) *Reporter*, April 15, 1846; BFC to John Brough, Oct. 28, 1842, BFC Papers: Bogart, *Internal Improvements*, 179–80.

CHAPTER 7

Administration: Change and Adjustment 1833–1850

MICHEL CHEVALIER, the perceptive French student of the American scene, traveling in the west in the 1830's, regarded the Ohio canal enterprise as one of the chief wonders of the New World. To the European mind, he wrote, it was inconceivable that the government of a new western state, "with its population of farmers, which has not a single engineer within its limits, and none of whose citizens had ever seen any other canal than those of New York," should have undertaken a $4,500,000 canal program. The Ohio Canal alone was longer, and in some respects presented more difficult engineering problems, than any canal in France. Yet the "farmers and lawyers" who comprised the 1825 canal commission had "set themselves about making canals, naturally, easily, and without even a suspicion that in Europe no one dares undertake such a work without long preparation and scientific study." They were aided, Chevalier wrote, only by "some second-rate engineers" borrowed from New York.[1]

This eminent critic underestimated the engineering skills of those "farmers and lawyers" of the canal commission and the quality of their "borrowed" scientific personnel. But he was also too ready to portray the canal commissioners as naive rustics, charmingly innocent of the real complexities of their task. For in fact these quasi-amateurs, who had built successfully in a situation where Europeans might have refused to take risks, were deeply concerned that future canal administration in Ohio should be made more genuinely professional. Thus in their 1832 report the commissioners expressed dissatisfaction with the hybrid political-administrative character of their agency. The responsibilities of the board, they declared, required a high degree of technical competence. To replace the seven-man board—of which only two members, the acting commissioners, could give full time to their duties—they recommended a commission to consist only of three full-time, paid civil engineers. Such professional administrators, the board asserted, could "devote the necessary time and attention—make themselves fully acquainted with all the details of the business, and . . . feel the responsibility of the important trust committed to their direction."[2]

The legislature responded unsympathetically to this proposal. For in fact the lawmakers preferred the existing structure, with members appointed from different regions of the state and expected to represent local interests in the policy-making process.[3] Therefore, when the initial canal project was completed, the legislature merely reduced the number of commissioners from seven to five; otherwise, the board was continued on the old basis. There had already been some movement, however, toward *de facto* professionalization. For as resignations occurred, trained civil engineers were appointed—though in each case the assembly selected men active in partisan politics. When Micajah Williams resigned in 1833, Samuel Forrer of Dayton, who had been a high-ranking engineer on the board's technical staff, was named to succeed him. And when Alfred Kelley resigned as acting commissioner the same year, though remaining on the board, his successor was Leander Ransom, another staff engineer. The two new acting commissioners carried full responsibility for the direction of traffic on the completed canals and for construction of new projects. But broad administrative powers, including regulation of toll rates and appointment of personnel, remained under the aegis of the full board.[4]

The multitude of new transport projects advocated in Ohio during the early thirties drew the commission deeply into political controversy. This was inevitable because of the board's role in the consideration of new proposals being studied by the legislature. The assembly customarily ordered the commission to run surveys and to estimate the engineering feasibility, the costs, and the probable fiscal returns and indirect benefits of each project. In effect, then, the commissioners needed to say "yea" to this project and "nay" to that one—and in asserting such views, to tread over dangerous political ground. For when the board reported unfavorably upon a proposal, the reaction from its local champions was often directed against the commission rather than against the legislature. Consequently, sentiment began to build up in the legislature for the reorganization of the canal commission—but not for the purpose of making the agency more independent of local pressures. Instead, there was evidence, as one staff member of the commission said in 1836, that "friends of local canals . . . want commissioners of their own."[5]

In addition, the structure of the commission, with its membership appointed for indeterminate periods of tenure, was becoming increasingly anachronistic as measured by the prevailing Jacksonian political ethos. For by the mid-thirties, in Ohio as elsewhere in America, patronage was being employed as a weapon in political warfare and the rotation-in-office idea was gaining currency. Covetous eyes were cast, therefore, upon the small host of collectorships, engineering posts, and common-labor jobs controlled by the canal board.[6]

Sentiment for "reforming" administration of the canals on a spoils basis crystallized in 1836, when the legislature approved the first major expansion of the public works. The Democrats had won large majorities in each house of the legislature; and the Jacksonian governor, Robert Lucas, proposed replacing the commission with a "board of internal improvement," which would have responsibility for long-range planning as well as for performing the older administrative functions. The Democrats in the legislature supported the proposed reorganization. But they insisted that commissioners be appointed on a district-representation system, to bring the board (in the standard Jacksonian rhetoric) "nearer the people." Although the Democrats pretended that the measure was not politically motivated, the party's official newspaper regularly attacked Whig members of the existing commission. Its abuse was lavished especially upon Alfred Kelley, now a leader of the Ohio Whig Party, who "was in the Legislature when the Canal law [of 1822] passed, got himself elected Canal Commissioner, . . . took the Canal to Cleveland, and . . . became immensely rich."[7]

The reform move came to fruition in March 1836, when the legislature voted to replace the canal commission with a "board of public works," consisting of six members appointed by joint resolution of the assembly. Two were to be acting commissioners, at a salary of $1500 per year, and the other four were designated "advisory commissioners," paid on a *per diem* basis only while attending board meetings. The other provisions of the reorganization act reflected Jacksonian principles. Rotation in office was introduced, with each member to serve for two years, three to be appointed annually. The board was brought closer to the people by making the principle of geographic representation explicit rather than, as formerly, only tacit. The state was divided into four districts of approximately equal area, and one advisory commissioner was to be named from each district. All the powers of the old commission were vested in the board. In addition, it was given control over improvement and operation of the National Road, which had been ceded to the state by Congress in 1831 and had since been administered by a special superintendent. Finally, the board was instructed explicitly to present for the legislature's consideration "such objects of internal improvement as the public interest may require."[8]

Whatever the motives for the reorganization, the new board was given important discretionary powers by the various laws of 1836 that authorized construction of four major new canals. Each act made construction contingent upon the board's certification that the new works would pay interest and principal upon the debts incurred to build them.[9]

The reorganization bill's preamble asserted its purpose to be the "promoting and maintaining [of] a *general system* of internal improvements within this State, and . . . uniting all its branches under the same supervision." Whig party spokesmen scoffed at such pretensions, asserting that the law would give the Jacksonians "the exclusive control of the state improvements, and secure the appointments of engineers, collectors, superintendents, lock-tenders, and even contractors, from among the faithful adherents of Van Buren."[10] In sum, the effects of the 1836 reorganization and the authorization acts for new projects were to enlarge the board's discretionary power in approving construction of new works; to introduce explicitly the system of geographic representation; and, not least, to inject party politics into administration of the public works on a scale previously unknown in Ohio.[11]

To no one's surprise, the new board members appointed by the legislature were all Democrats.[12] Perhaps no more surprising, the board's first official act was to certify that all the new canals authorized in 1836 would indeed produce sufficient revenues to justify their construction. The board did qualify this view by stating that the new works would not produce revenues large enough to pay interest on the debt until ten years after their completion.[13] But at that time such ambivalence did not trouble the legislature; only later was the board's excessive optimism to be cited as evidence of alleged incompetence.

The rising destabilizing effect of politics in canal administration was made clear in 1837, when the Whig party captured control of the legislature. The Whigs charged the Democratic board members with "incompetency and negligence," and they proposed still another administrative "reform," ostensibly to eliminate the district representation system because it "fostered favoritism and operated unfairly upon the judgments of the commissioners."[14] The Democrats, on the other hand, defended the district system on well-tested egalitarian grounds, as one which "equalized the benefits of State improvements." The partisan struggle ended in March 1838, when the legislature voted to disestablish the board of public works and create a new agency with the old name "canal commission." The new commission was to be comprised of four full-time administrative officers, each of whom would have responsibilities in the field; and the men appointed (three were Whigs and one a Democrat) were all engineers with long records of state service. If this appeared to be a victory for those who sought to professionalize the board, the Whigs nevertheless adhered *de facto* to the old principle of geographic representation by appointing men who were residents of different regions of the state.[15]

A year later, the Democrats regained control of the legislature, and immediately they legislated the new canal commissioners out of office by re-establishing the board of public works, with five members. All five commissioners were made full-time officers, and the district representation system was not revived. In 1840 the legislature reduced the board to four members, and in 1842 to three. The only major overturn in its membership occurred in 1845, when a six-year period of Democratic ascendency was ended and Whig control restored. In 1850, the Democrats once again recaptured control of the board.[16]

Apparently the successive reorganizations and reforms did not have much impact on the engineers and minor canal officials, at least not until the 1840's. "When the Board is Whig," one editor asserted in 1839, "it always happens that the subordinates are Locofocos, and when the latter form the Board the Whigs step down into snug offices a grade lower, so that both parties continue office holders."[17] This probably was accurate so far as engineers were concerned; for until 1845, when the expanded program was completed, engineers were in short supply and the board could ill afford to discharge technical personnel for mere political reasons. Some of the most experienced staff engineers did leave the state service, however, as the result of salary cuts ordered by a Whig legislature in 1841 for reasons of economy.[18] Scanning the roster of the board's engineers in 1842, a former canal commission officer remarked that there remained "but one or two of the *old stock*": "Ohio's tried and faithful servants are set aside to make way for some upstart who is willing to spend his time for a few dollars less salary."[19]

Reduced salaries did not, however, deter political hacks from applying for vacant posts, and throughout the 1840's party patronage was increasingly the touchstone in selection of staff personnel. Hence a Democratic board member admitted privately in 1842 that his first concern was the appointment of qualified men; but the board would, he said, "as a matter of course prefer one of their own school." Although the Whigs tried to label their political opponents as the spoilsmen *par excellence,* they were no less adept at finding office-seekers of the right persuasion for canal posts, even instituting political meetings "for the special benefit of the Irish canal hands."[20]

By the late forties, the public works had been absorbed fully into the apparatus of party patronage. A political overturn at the top level was reflected immediately in removals and new appointments in subordinate posts. Not even a sharp Buckeye sense of humor could save the Whig collector, faced with removal by a new Democratic board in 1850, who stated: "Now I believe in rotation in office just as much as any of you—yet I should not like to be rotated out quite so soon. I might perhaps have no objection to be rotated in the most usual way, from one office to a better."[21] By this time, officials of the wrong political school could expect rotation only into private life. Unfortunately for the public works, the successive reorganizations and salary reductions, and the ascendency of spoils ethics, demoralized the engineering corps while the 1836–45 construction program was still in progress. Thus one informed insider attributed "Tom-fool engineering," which had produced costly errors, to the inexperience or incompetence of newly appointed personnel.[22]

No doubt, corruption and incompetence did raise the costs of the 1836–45 program. An expert French engineer, for example, believed engineering errors in Ohio to have resulted in unnecessary expenditures of two million dollars.[23] In any case, accusations were freely made that "an inordinate and almost profligate expenditure of public money" had characterized construction of the expanded program.[24] The poor administrative record of the 1836–45 period, combined with the flagrant partisanship of public works personnel policies, contributed greatly to the later decline of popular confidence in the efficacy of state enterprise.

Although the board of public works passed through several reorganizations, the various commissioners who headed the agency made few modifications of basic staff organization, and they failed to adjust either their administrative routine or their hierarchical arrangements to new requirements.[25] The functions of the board itself after 1836 may be classified broadly as (1) long-range planning, (2) administration of construction, and (3) management of the public works already completed and in operation.

In the realm of planning, the board enjoyed little formal autonomy, for the assembly made all key decisions in authorizing new projects. The only case on record in which the board exercised real authority in this area had occurred in 1836, when construction of the newly authorized canals was made contingent upon the board's certification that the canals would repay the cost of their construction. Occasionally the commissioners did attempt to influence basic state policy, as when they denounced the "suicidal" policy of granting charters to railroads that were obviously planned to compete with the state's canals.[26] In some instances, too, the board declined to build certain minor works that the legislature had authorized but not required. More often, however, the board recommended new projects which the assembly refused to approve.[27]

But some ostensibly administrative decisions did have major ramifications for larger policy. The awarding of contracts, for instance, was in theory a purely administrative matter. Yet when the board let out contracts for the Miami Extension and Wabash & Erie Canals, it specified construction on larger prism dimensions than the legislature had originally contemplated. These decisions respecting capacity of the canals were directly responsible for a great increase in construction costs, which in turn had profound effects on the subsequent requirements for capital. In addition, the canal board chose not to establish a system of priorities when it commenced construction of the new works authorized during 1836–38. Instead, it placed all the new projects under contract at once; and by the time the 1837 panic struck, large sums had already been paid to contractors for numerous partially completed canals. So large was the investment already committed that by 1839 the point of no return had been reached— abandonment having become less economical than continuing construction amidst great financial difficulties. Had the board instead put new work under construction by stages, giving priority to the projects most likely to produce large revenues from toll collections, this predicament might never have troubled state finances.[28]

Canal construction after 1836 included numerous projects

located at remote distances from one another throughout the state. Adjusting to this situation, the canal board assigned each commissioner responsibility for one or more specific projects; but the board adopted no system for auditing commissioners' accounts or inspecting their performance. "There seems to be no sufficient check," a legislative committee found in 1844, "upon any of the officers, either those under the employ of the Board, or the Board themselves."[29]

Similar decentralization of responsibiltiy and failure to exercise checks prevailed in the supervision of the canals already in operation. Although the full board met occasionally to appoint collectors and other officials, and also to set canal tolls, there was no inspection of financial accounts for maintenance work. Consequently many abuses occurred in the awarding of repair contracts, which were not subject to competitive bidding.[30]

It seems incontestable that the expanded program was not administered, after 1836, in the spirit that Alfred Kelley and Micajah Williams had brought to their work in 1825. Strikingly absent in the intra-agency correspondence after 1836 are the kinds of letters to be found in the archives of earlier years: warnings from one commissioner to another about the need to train a competent bureaucracy, admonitions to be alert against bids judged too high or too low, or expressions of fear that administrative failures might invite political criticism and jeopardize the whole canal policy. In sum, the later commissioners displayed little of that "proprietary" sense which had marked the attitudes of Kelley and Williams. There was also a hardening of routine procedures: "a strong disposition [on the part of board members and their staffs] to tread in each other's footsteps, and a singular reluctance to depart from what may have been, in some degree, a sort of usage."[31] There is ample evidence that the declining public confidence in the integrity and competence of the board, manifest in the 1840's, was well justified.

The board's administration of the Loan Law of 1837 was still another source of criticism. The law had offered the board a signal opportunity to play a significant role in planning the development of transportation in Ohio. Before any private company could obtain aid under terms of the law, it was required to submit its construction plan to the board. The board was then responsible for ascertaining that cost estimates were reasonable and for checking the accuracy of claims as to construction already completed. In the case of railroads, the board had even greater power: for to qualify for state loans a railway had to obtain the board's certification that "the road would be of public utility, and would, within two years after . . . completion, yield a net profit of at least 2 per cent per annum on the money invested."[32]

The commissioners accepted this authority most reluctantly, complaining that they had "but little discretion . . . to enable them to distinguish between such works as are of decided utility, and those which are of less value."[33] For all its protestations, the board made little effort to investigate the claims of companies applying for aid. In some cases not even a nominal inquiry was conducted. In other instances, individual commissioners behaved more as spokesmen for projects of special interest to them than as disinterested public administrators.[34]

In 1840 the board declared that the Loan Law had invoked an "unnatural alliance" between the state and private enterprise. But in complaining that the law created temptations "too powerful to be resisted," the commissioners described all too accurately their own response to the statute.[35] By the mid-1840's, the Loan Law was popularly known in Ohio as the "Plunder Law," and in public opinion the plundering class included the men who had administered the law. Malfeasance and outright abdication of responsibilities in this area of the board's operations did much to tarnish the reputation of the active state in Ohio.[36]

Mounting public criticism of the board impelled the legislative branch of government to reassert its jurisdiction in certain areas of canal administration. In 1844 the assembly attacked the obvious abuses in expenditure of canal funds by subjecting board members' financial accounts to review by the state auditor.[37] It also curbed the board's autonomy in supervision of construction when in 1841 it suspended appropriations for the Miami Extension Canal, and when in 1843 it required the board to let new contracts at prices no higher than the engineers' cost estimates.[38]

In addition, the assembly frequently ordered the board to make special reports on its operations and personnel policies. On two occasions in the mid-forties the assembly conducted full-scale inquiries to assess specific charges of corruption. Both investigations resulted in reports generally critical of the board.[39]

Not all legislative interference had good effects, especially when the assembly exerted its authority in personnel matters. A law of 1839 required the board to reduce the size of the engineering corps. Two years later, salaries of engineers were reduced, and in 1844 the assembly slashed by one-third the pay of all other employees on the public works. Although the legislature later restored the board's discretionary power to establish the salaries of toll collectors (the offices most consistently awarded as political patronage), the assembly still retained control over engineers' pay. As late as 1851, the board's highest ranking engineers were paid only $800 per year. This situation led to an exodus of the best trained men from state service to employment with private railroad corporations.[40]

No less ill-advised was the legislature's course of action in dealing with claimants for damages, including aggrieved contractors who sought retroactive increases in contract prices. Several times the assembly authorized the board of public works to pay additional compensation on construction contracts when such "unavoidable causes" as increased prices had caused contractors to suffer.[41] But the board refused to employ this power, asserting that such action would inevitably lead to fraudulent claims.[42] Contractors seeking additional payments thereafter swamped the state courts with damage suits and sent lobbyists to Columbus to seek private appropriations bills. In every court suit or legislative hearing, the board of public works and its engineers were required to present reports, appear as witnesses, and reply to charges against them. This proved a constant burden in terms of both time and personnel, especially since claims often went unsettled for a decade or more.[43]

Occasionally, complaints about the operation or construction of specific canal facilities prompted the legislature to take remedial action. One controversial case involved the giant Mercer County Reservoir, built to supply the northern part of the Miami Extension Canal. Construction of the reservoir required the flooding of a considerable extent of woodland. Fearful that it would produce a health hazard, local residents persuaded the legislature to require the canal board to remove all timber from the area to be flooded. The board ignored the assembly's directive, finding a loophole in the resolution, and a mob of outraged local citizenry breached the reservoir's banks and drained it in 1844. While a grand jury quickly cleared the defendants in the resultant criminal action, the legislature acted once again, ordering the board to remove all timber before putting the reservoir back in operation.[44]

A more common type of popular complaint related to navigational hazards in the canals. The Portsmouth terminus on the Ohio River was never made safe for canal boat navigation, and its condition was the subject of repeated investigations by the legislature. When the board of public works failed to improve the Portsmouth facilities, the assembly finally chartered a private corporation to build docks and navigational improvements.[45] Nor were the newly built canals free from hazards or interruptions. On the Licking Summit and the Portage Summit sections of the Ohio Canal, low water and sediment made the line impassable for fully loaded boats during seasons of little rainfall. The locks on the Miami Extension proved to be faulty, and traffic was disrupted for a full season while they were rebuilt. On the Muskingum Improvement, shippers complained of "the continual deposit of mud" which impeded traffic. The Walhonding Canal was closed frequently for repairs, and its junction with the Ohio Canal was said to be impassable in 1851. The Warren County branch line, once an object of powerful local interest, had been allowed to fall into complete disrepair in the 1840's, and farmers whose lands suffered from resultant flooding demanded abandonment of "this abominable nuisance of a canal."[46]

Besieged with petitions for better maintenance of the public works, the legislature occasionally made special appropriations for heavy reconstruction work or for building additional locks and dams.[47] The board of public works, reluctant to make large expenditures for repairs without prior approval, often sought legislation authorizing heavy repairs.[48] For regular maintenance and light repairs, however, the board relied upon its discretionary authority and drew upon general canal funds. The costs of maintenance varied considerably from year to year, influenced greatly by weather conditions and the occurrence of natural disasters. Ordinarily a new canal would require high maintenance expenditures for a few years, until the weaknesses were corrected and necessary minor alterations made.[49] The record of the Ohio Canal conformed to this pattern: its combined maintenance and superintendence costs averaged $511 per mile annually during 1835–39, and then fell to $349 during 1840–44, $322 during 1845–49, and $316 during 1850–55. But the major engineering errors made during initial construction of the later canals, notably the Miami Extension and the Muskingum Improvement, required costly repairs in ensuing years. Moreover, the practice of building temporary wooden locks, later replaced with works of stone, produced an erratic pattern of repair costs. Hence, on the combined Miami Extension-Wabash and Erie, repairs and superintendence cost $321 per mile annually during 1845–49 but rose to $732 during 1850–55. Maintenance costs on the Muskingum Improvement went as high as $1,200 per mile in the year 1848.[50] Average maintenance costs on all the state canals during 1844–49, however, were only $344 per mile, or only half the average expenditures on the New York canals.[51] Although the comparison with New York was cited by Ohio canal officials as evidence of their own efficiency, in fact it reflected the Ohio board's laxity in correcting navigational deficiencies.

Many of the navigational problems of the Ohio canals were attributable simply to the nature of canal technology, which required an entire halt of traffic while major repairs were made. Canals were subject as well to swift and extensive damage from heavy rains or deterioration of dirt embankments during dry seasons. But the poor administrative record of the canal board after 1836, and numerous instances of malfeasance and negligence, compounded the normal problems of maintenance. This led to loss of public confidence in the integrity of canal administration—and this in turn was but a step short of disillusionment with public enterprise itself. By the early 1850's, therefore, it was safe for elected officials to declare, as a truism, that any major project built by the state would involve excessive costs and would be staffed with political hacks.[52]

It was universally acknowledged, too, that the board of public works had become a tool of partisan politics. Consistent with the progressive changes since 1836, the new state constitution adopted in 1851 provided for the annual popular election of board members. This marked the final step in absorption of public works administration into party politics and into the mechanism of political patronage.[53]

The decline of public confidence and the deteriorating quality of canal administration occurred during a crucial period in the history of Ohio's public works—the years of new construction. Although not widely recognized at the time, these years of the early forties had also brought Ohio to the dawn of the railroad era, when the canal trade would be dangerously challenged. For all the failures of public administration which marked the 1840's, however, the public works of Ohio did provide many of the indirect benefits that had been so buoyantly predicted when they were first planned in 1825 and when their expansion was promoted a decade later. It was in the stimulus they gave to economic growth in Ohio that the canals made their enduring contribution to the state's history and the nation's.

NOTES

1. Michel Chevalier, *Society, Manners, and Politics in the United States*, ed. J. W. Ward (New York, 1961), 234–35.
2. Canal Commission report in *Senate Journal*, 1832–33, pp. 345–47. See also *House Journal*, 1831–32, pp. 308–9.
3. See I. A. Lapham to Darius Lapham, Feb. 18, 1836 (copy), Increase Lapham Papers, OHS.
4. As of December 1835, the commissioners were Benjamin Tappan, John Johnston, and Kelley, all of whom had served since 1825; and acting commissioners Forrer and Ransom.

5. I. A. Lapham to Darius Lapham, Feb. 18, 1836, Lapham Papers, OHS.

6. *Ibid;* Daniel Kilgore to S. Perkins (n.d. but 1836), Simon Perkins Papers, WRHS; S. Perkins to E. Whittlesey, Feb. 8, 1836, Elisha Whittlesey Papers, WRHS. On the Jacksonian spoils doctrine and its implications for public administration, cf., Paul P. Van Riper, *History of the United States Civil Service* (Evanston, Ill., 1958), Chap. 3.

7. Columbus *Western Hemisphere,* Oct. 5, 1836; also *ibid.,* Sept. 16, 1835. See reply to earlier attack upon Kelley, *ibid.,* March 5, 1836. On Lucas's support, see "Internal Improvements Meeting," broadside, Jan. 23, 1830, Canal Commission Papers, Ohio State Archives.

8. Act of March 14, 1836, copy in *ibid.*

9. 34 L. O. (*Laws of Ohio: General*), 311, 346, 331, 620. In the case of the Muskingum Improvement, the board was further required to certify that the project would not tend to reduce Ohio Canal revenues.

10. Columbus *Journal and Register,* Feb. 13, 1838. The district representation system was common in other western states.

11. Cf. Daniel H. Calhoun, *The American Civil Engineer: Origins and Conflict* (Cambridge, 1960), 61ff. on commission organization and the role of professional engineers in canal administration.

12. The acting commissioners were Ransom and William Wall; the advisory commissioners were Alexander McConnell, Timothy G. Bates, Rudolphus Dickinson and John Harris. All except McConnell and Harris were engineers.

13. Board of Public Works Minute Books, II, 93ff. (mss., Dept. of Public Works Records Room, State Office Building, Columbus).

14. Editorial in Columbus *Journal and Register,* Feb. 13, 1838; John H. James quoted in Columbus *Ohio Statesman,* March 9, 1838.

15. *Ohio Statesman,* March 9, March 16, 1838, on equalized benefits. The Democrats chided the Whigs for capitulating and accepting *de facto* district representation. (*Ibid.,* March 20, 1838.) The Commissioners appointed were Benjamin Forrer, Leander Ransom, Sebried Dodge, and William H. Price.

16. Personnel appointed in recurrent reorganizations are listed conveniently in Hasse's index to Ohio state documents, under "Board of Public Works." See also 1850 Constitutional Con-

vention, *Official Reports of the Debates and Proceedings,* ed.
J. V. Smith (Columbus, 1851), 176; BPW, *6th Annual Report*
(1843), 3.

17. *Maumee City Express,* Feb. 23, 1839. The Cincinnati *Gazette*
made the same complaint (see clipping in *Ohio Statesman,* July
13, 1838.) Under a Democratic board in 1838, of 24 engineers
appointed, 18 were said to be Whigs; of 15 toll collectors, seven
were Whigs. (*Ohio Statesman,* Feb. 23, 1838.)

18. *Ibid.,* March 29, 1841.

19. I. A. Lapham to Darius Lapham (copy), Feb. 18, 1842, Lapham Papers, OHS.

20. John Patton to Board of Public Works, Aug. 13, 1845, Leander Ransom to Nelson Franklin, Jan. 19, 1842, Board of Public
Works Papers, Ohio State Archives (hereafter cited BPW
Papers); G. Sanderson to P. B. Ewing, Oct. 3, 1842, Ewing
Family Papers, OHS. See also Randolph C. Downes, *History
of Lake Shore Ohio* (3 vol., New York, 1952), I, 360.

21. J. Cradlebaugh to Manypenny, July 8, 1850, Daniel Skinner to
E. S. Hamline, Dec. 31, 1850, BPW Papers.

22. Oran Follett to S. Forrer, Oct. 24, 1845, Samuel Forrer Papers,
Dayton-Montgomery County (Ohio) Public Library. On engineering errors, cf. Chapter 5, *supra.*

23. Henri Stucklé, *Voies de Communication aux Etats-Unis* (Paris,
1847), 441.

24. Auditor of State, *AR, 1843,* pp. 38–39, 48.

25. Cf. *ibid.,* 38.

26. BPW report quoted in *Ohio Statesman,* Jan. 26, 1838.

27. See *Executive Docs.,* 1843–44, No. 25.

28. Ohio House of Representatives, *Special Report of the Board
of Public Works . . . Feb. 20, 1840* (n.p., n.d.); Ohio Senate,
*Report of the Standing Committee on Retrenchment . . . Feb.
28, 1844* (n.p., n.d.), 8.

29. *Ibid.,* 3. On the lack of inspectorial systems in prevailing public
administration of the period, see Leonard D. White, *The Jacksonians* (New York, 1954), 540–43.

30. *Report . . . on Retrenchment,* Feb. 28, 1844, p. 7.

31. *Ibid.,* 6. See also M. T. Williams to Elisha Whittlesey, Dec.
21, 1840, Whittlesey Papers, WRHS. The foregoing analysis is
based mainly on the author's observations as to what does *not*
appear in the intra-agency correspondence of the BPW, and its
admittedly impressionistic nature must be emphasized.

32. *Executive Docs.,* 1845–46, Pt. II, p. 609.

33. BPW, 2nd AR (1838), 15–16.
34. *Executive Docs.*, 1845–46, Pt. II, 606ff. For an example of how an investigation might conclude with a special plea for recognition of local interests, see T. G. Bates to McConnell, Dec. 17, 1837, Letters on Canals, CHS.
35. Quoted in *Ohio Statesman*, Jan. 22, 1840.
36. 1850 Constitutional Convention, *Debates and Proceedings*, 954; *Journal and Register* (Columbus), March 2, 1838.
37. 42 L.O. 74.
38. Acts of March 7, 1842, and Feb. 28, 1843.
39. *Report on* . . . *Retrenchment* (1844); *Executive Docs.*, 1845–46, Pt. II, *passim*.
40. BPW, *4th AR* (1841), 12; 42 L. O. 22; BPW, *14th AR* in *Executive Docs.*, 1850–51, No. 34, pp. 673–74.
41. An act of March 1836 (34 L. O. 525) granted 25 per cent of contract price to every contractor on the Miami Canal north of Dayton, for work done subsequent to May 20, 1835. It also permitted the commission to grant 15 per cent on contract price at its discretion, for work done before that date. A year later (35 L. O. 104) the legislature authorized the board to pay generally extra allowances on contracts.
42. The board took the position that "the indiscreet, the improvident, and the inefficient contractors will be the first and largest claimants." (BPW Minutes, I, 337.)
43. BPW, *4th AR* (1841), 12–20. For two examples of longstanding cases where consideration by the assembly required depositions from engineers and board members who had long since departed from the public service, see Ohio Senate, reports on claims of Thomas White and F. H. Bryan, dated, respectively, Feb. 5, 1842 and Feb. 8, 1841.
44. BPW, *7th AR* (1844), 19–20; Ohio Senate, *Special Report of the Board of Public Works* . . . *Feb. 8, 1844* (n.p., n.d.); James F. Winter, *A History of Northwest Ohio* (New York, 1917), 377–78.
45. D. Gross to J. Blickensderfer, Jan. 12, 1847, John Robinson to BPW, Jan. 5, 1847, BPW Papers, on the Ohio Canal. The corporation chartered to build facilities at Portsmouth had difficulty raising funds and by 1856 was selling the lands it had acquired at the terminus. (Portsmouth Dry Dock and Steam-Boat Basin Company, *Report of the President* [New York, 1856].) For interruptions of navigation on the Scioto Valley

line of the Ohio Canal see petition dated June 7, 1851, BPW Papers.

46. A. Nye to Blickensderfer, Dec. 23, 1846, BPW Papers, on the Muskingum Improvement; and John Mulford to J. Woods, Jan. 30, 1851, John Woods Papers, CHS, on the Warren County Canal. See also BPW, *9th AR* (1845), on the Miami Extension; and A. Medbury to G. W. Manypenny, July 26, 1850, C. Bassett to BPW, July 26, 1850, BPW Papers, on the Walhonding.

47. See, for example, Ohio Senate, *Special Report of the Board of Public Works . . . Feb. 17, 1841* (n.p., n.d.); *idem, Special Report of the Board of Public Works . . . Feb. 24, 1851* (n.p., n.d.).

48. Cf. BPW, *9th AR* (1845), 24.

49. *Report of the Joint Committee of the General Assembly on the Public Works of Ohio* (Columbus, 1857), 41.

50. *Ibid.*, 41–42; BPW, *13th AR* (1850), 12.

51. BPW, *13th AR* (1850), 13, 20.

52. *Report of the Joint Committee*, cited n. 49, p. 32; 1850 Constitutional Convention, *Debates and Proceedings*, 349.

53. *Ibid.*, 176. The general assembly had already provided by statute in 1849 for annual election of BPW members.

PART II

THE COURSE OF ECONOMIC CHANGE

1820-1851

THE promoters of the 1825 canal policy and of expansion in the 1830's had predicted momentous economic effects from the construction of new transportation facilities. Within Ohio, they believed, land values would rise as new settlement was attracted and agricultural prices were boosted by giving farmers access to profitable markets; the increase in farm income would provide a vigorous local market for manufacturing industries; and new cities would grow up to serve a thriving agricultural hinterland. Moreover, lake-to-river canals would turn the trade of the Ohio Valley away from New Orleans: a more direct, less expensive, and safer route to the New York market would be provided, and Ohio's revenues would swell as the state—by dint of canal tolls—levied tribute on the entire commerce of the West. As a concomitant of local growth and of a rising canal trade, the state might finance virtually continuous expansion of the public works program, to benefit every region of the state.

This was the promoters' vision. But to what extent were the early hopes realized, once the public works were actually built? In the three chapters that follow, the expectations of the 1820's and 1830's will be compared with the actual record of economic change in Ohio during the canal era. First, the effects of planning and construction, before the period of opening to traffic, will be examined. Second, the commerce of each major canal will be considered: what commodities were carried, the direction of trade, the pattern of marketing, and the like. Throughout the discussion the data of canal traffic, together with population statistics and other evidence, will be assessed with a view toward identifying significant differentials in local development. Finally, in Chapter 10, the impact of canal operation on the structure of transport rates will be considered, to illuminate an often neglected feature of state policy in the canal period: the conscious allocation of markets through the manipulation of tolls by public officials.

Paradoxically, though the early canal promoters postulated that dynamic growth would occur within the state once the public works were built, they did not recognize that proliferation of new transport routes in the national economy could exact costs as well as generate benefits for their own state. In fact, the larger Transportation Revolution in the United States—to which the Ohio state enterprises contributed significantly—would render some of the canal promoters' premises obsolete, even while it helped fulfill many of their hopes in full measure.

CHAPTER 8

The Canals in the Economy
1820–1840

THE first impact of the canals upon the Ohio economy occurred even before construction had begun. In districts that
expected to benefit from the new waterways, a climate of optimism took hold, while in localities that would be by-passed there
was jealousy and considerable gloom. Developments in the land
market were indicative of the manner in which canal planning
colored investment decisions and stimulated expectations. Immediately after enactment of the 1825 canal bill, the state's newspapers were filled with advertisements offering land for sale in
districts through which the canals would pass. A new edition of
the standard emigrants' guide for Ohio was published, showing
the projected canal routes—information now deemed essential
for every prospective settler or speculator. In localities where
the canals were planned but where precise locations of the lines
were still undetermined, promoters urged the canal commission
to complete the routing quickly: otherwise it would be "impossible . . . to retain strangers with Capital who are examining
all along the line in search of a place to settle."[1] Townsite promoters besieged the canal board with letters seeking information;
indeed, one enterprising landowner offered to sell the state an
interest in his real estate, "thinking it reasonable that the State
should derive some of the benefits"! In any event, it was widely
assumed that those "located in the immediate vicinity of these
canals will reap a rich harvest."[2]

While some investors were interested in land, others looked
to new opportunities in manufacturing, banking, or commerce.

Along the Miami Canal line, for example, several towns were founded in the 1820's exclusively as industrial centers and located where waterpower was to be made available by the canal. Only a few weeks after the 1825 canal law was enacted, the merchants of Lancaster organized a private company to build a side-cut canal to the main line, hoping thereby to assure the growth of their town as a commercial center. At New Philadelphia a similar company was formed; and when the Ohio Canal reached the Granville region in central Ohio, local capitalists raised money to help finance construction of a canal line to connect with the main route. Some Boston investors put money into a new bank at Cleveland, to service the town's canal trade; similarly, a group of New York promoters incorporated a company to build a canal basis and steamboat dry-dock facilities at Portsmouth, the Ohio Canal's southern terminus.[3]

Plans for expansion of the canal program a few years later led to much the same pattern of speculative activity and new enterprise. For example, many farmers in western Ohio put money into petty land speculations along the line of the projected canal when the Miami Extension bill became law in 1831. During the mid-thirties, they were joined by scores of wealthy large-scale speculators, who snatched up much of the best land in western and northwest Ohio near the planned canal lines.[4] Approval of the Wabash & Erie Canal by the legislature in 1834 produced the most frenzied episode of land speculation in the state's history. "Wild land and wild cities" were bought and sold at prices that spiraled upward; and a full year before construction of the city's canal actually began, town lots in Toledo were selling for $22 per foot frontage, a price comparable to what downtown Cincinnati real estate then commanded.[5] And all along the northern division of the projected Miami Extension, speculators traded in leases for waterpower sites on the canal line in what became an active and profitable market. The promoters of little hamlets in the Wabash Valley planned grandiose railroad ventures to link their sites with towns in the interior, and capital flowed into the canal region, where banking, commerce, and forwarding offered promising fields for new investment.[6]

But the prospect of canal construction was not an unmixed blessing. The interests of individuals often suffered, as when lands or building materials were seized under eminent-domain proceedings. No doubt the prospect of construction also blunted the edge of new enterprise in regions distant from the projected canal lines. Thus a newspaper reporter at New Lisbon claimed in 1825 that local land values in southeast Ohio fell "nearly 100 per cent" when the canal law was enacted.[7] Although the canal commission attempted to locate the canals through existing urban centers, some well-established market towns inevitably had to be by-passed. A case in point was Miltonville, which until 1835 was Wood County's leading retail and wholesale center. When the Wabash & Erie Canal was built on the opposite bank of the Wabash River, however, the local farmers took their business instead to a rival town, located farther downstream on the canal line. Eventually Miltonville was abandoned altogether, and today only an historical marker remains at the site.[8] In this manner the "canal frontier," no less than the miner's or cattleman's frontiers, produced not only boom towns but also ghost towns, symbols of social dislocation in an expanding economy.

Once the actual work of canal construction began, a new set of economic forces was set in motion. First there was the stimulus that construction gave to the development of a cash economy, which supplanted the primitive barter system that still prevailed in many rural districts of Ohio in 1825. The transition to cash exchange was made possible by an influx of eastern capital, which the state obtained by means of its canal-bond sales in New York. The state deposited its newly borrowed capital in selected Ohio banks. Until then the state's banks had made loans, and issued their notes (the main source of currency in the state economy), almost exclusively to local merchants. As depositories of state canal funds, they now found it possible to issue their paper —in the form of disbursements to contractors, as the latter were paid for construction work—in distant places. This meant that they could expand their note circulation relative to specie reserves, since note issues at a distance involved less chance that the paper would return quickly for redemption in specie; but it also meant that the reserves of the Ohio banks were much larger, since the successive bond issues by the state provided the banks with eastern bank credit, the equivalent of specie funds.[9]

Payment of cash wages induced local farmers and farm workers in many regions to take seasonal canal employment, and in the 1820's local casual labor provided most of the construction labor force. But the impact on the labor market was more far-reaching, for opportunities in canal construction soon attracted a considerable migration of unskilled laborers into the state. In northeastern Ohio, on the northern line of the Ohio Canal, "the hardy sons of Erin" came from New York State seeking employment, and many stayed on as permanent settlers in Akron, Cleveland, and other cities in the region.[10] After 1834, moreover, German immigrants to the Cincinnati-Miami Valley area provided most of the labor on the Miami Extension; and in regions of sparse settlement, such as the Wabash & Erie area in the late 1830's, contractors advertised throughout the country for labor, offering to pay emigrants' passage to Toledo in the form of advances on wages. In the more isolated areas, especially along the Wabash & Erie line, the predominance of itinerant laborers and immigrants (mainly Irish) introduced a raw, unvarnished type of camp life. Despite the hostility of the early settlers in the northwest region toward the newcomers, many Irish and German laborers later settled permanently in the area.[11]

Construction generated demand for farm products and manufactures as well as for labor. Throughout the building period, the canal commission advertised for picks, shovels, and other construction tools; stone, lumber, mortar, and other building materials were required; and local retailers found an active market for straw hats, boots, whiskey, and the other essentials with which laborers supplied themselves. The effects of such expenditures on overall local demand are difficult to measure, but the prevailing canal technology involved little equipment that needed to be purchased outside the state; and the contractors' heavy reliance upon local labor meant that most of the secondary and tertiary expenditures were made in Ohio. Bearing testimony to this was the experience, repeated in all the regions where canal construction took place, that both local wages and local prices for farm produce rose as soon as the work began.[12]

The stimulus to the economy afforded by construction itself was, of course, only transitory. The major long-term impact of the canals derived rather from their actual operations as going concerns—working lines of transport carrying trade within Ohio and between the interior and outside markets. From their first year of operation in 1827 until about 1840, the canals functioned in a different economic context from that which would prevail afterward. For much of the region served by the Ohio Canal during 1827–40 enjoyed no alternative routes of transport to the East; by virtue of its otherwise landlocked position, it depended exclusively upon the canal for both imports and exports, and, indeed, the region was not heavily settled until the canal was built. Moreover, the Ohio Canal was the only water-transport link between the Ohio River and Lake Erie in this period. As such, it held a virtual monopoly position for long-haul freight between the two major market areas of the West. The Miami Canal differed in two important respects: first, it had only one trade outlet (at Cincinnati, on the river); and second, it was built into an already settled area which had long enjoyed a steady export trade. Even so, the Miami Canal too was free of significant competition from other routes as compared with what its situation would be after 1840.

THE OHIO CANAL TRADE

Consider first the case of the Ohio Canal during 1827–40, while it held its peculiar monopoly position. In its contribution to population growth and economic development in the region it served, the canal was a spectacular success. As the opportunities for exporting to cash markets became more attractive, settlers began to come into the Ohio Canal region, their migration expedited by the ease with which the packet boats carried them, their families, and their baggage into the interior. "Many families moving, foreigners as well as eastern emigrants, take passage of the Canal," one of the commissioners reported in 1828.[13] Potential emigrants from New York State and Pennsylvania found it a simple matter to take passage on the packets to scout the country for promising land. And they were attracted by what they found: Congressional lands available at $1.25 per acre; good stands of hardwood; "corn planted, which was from ten to fourteen feet high, and so close together," one such traveler wrote, "that a man would be out of sight in it one rod from the edge" of the field.[14] Hence population in the counties through which the canal ran in northern and central Ohio gained by 70,000 in the 1820's. It increased by another 100,000 in the next decade, far exceeding the rate of gain in older settled sections of the state in the thirties.[15]

Immediately after the Ohio Canal was opened to traffic in 1827, farmers in its newly populated northern region moved into commercial production of wheat for the first time. Although statistics of crop output were not recorded, it was well known, as a prominent contemporary economist asserted, that "immediately after completion of the canal . . . not only greater attention but a greater breadth of land was devoted to wheat" in the counties that bordered the canal. Until the canal went into operation, the price of wheat near Akron had been 20 to 30 cents a bushel. But by 1833 the price was 75 cents; no longer was the farmer without cash markets, "the produce of his farm . . . literally rotting in his yards."[16] When the canal was extended southward, it had a similar effect in central Ohio, where producers were situated too far from the Ohio River or its tributaries to ship their farm surplus to the New Orleans market. At Newark, which in 1831 was the southernmost point of navigation, wheat prices were then 56 cents a bushel "and higher as you advance toward the lake," a state official reported. "At Massillon [it] is 75 to 80 cents and these prices [have] brought in an immense quantity all along the line of the Canal. . . . This doubling in value of wheat . . . seems to infuse new energy into our Farmers," he wrote, "and it would not be surprising if the quantity raised should be more than doubled in three years."[17]

Except for years when the crops failed because of natural disasters, Cleveland's grain trade increased steadily until the early 1850's, when railroad competition began. Receipts of wheat by canal at Cleveland, shown in Table 8.1, were about 300,000 bushels in 1832, but increased to more than two million bushels in 1840; arrivals of flour by canal were 54,000 barrels in 1832, rising to more than half a million in 1840. The warehouses and the busy lake wharves at Cleveland symbolized the realization of

TABLE 8.1

PRINCIPAL COMMODITIES IN OHIO CANAL TRADE AT CLEVELAND 1832–51

| YEAR | ARRIVED VIA THE CANAL | | | | | CLEARED | |
	WHEAT BUSHELS	CORN BUSHELS	COAL BUSHELS	FLOUR BARRELS	PORK BARRELS	SALT BARRELS	MERCHANDISE POUNDS
1832	288,722	n.a.	12,900	54,404	13,801	29,329	5,260,535
1833	386,760	74,913	49,131	98,302	22,758	28,447	9,896,444
1834	333,868	2,653	95,634	105,326	33,884	36,803	10,127,613
1835	387,232	53,373	50,473	132,319	19,814	46,139	14,839,095
1836	464,756	392,281	84,924	167,539	13,496	22,334	13,394,081
1837	549,141	280,234	183,484	203,691	42,057	62,977	8,776,154
1838	1,229,012	107,514	73,292	287,465	39,055	63,465	18,875,286
1839	1,515,320	65,272	134,881	264,887	30,717	109,916	19,125,852
1840	2,155,407	72,569	172,206	505,461	23,017	77,254	10,783,514
1841	1,564,421	245,018	478,370	441,425	29,704	59,773	15,164,747
1842	1,311,665	218,756	466,844	492,711	53,272	49,456	10,091,803
1843	813,536	227,694	387,834	577,369	13,177	44,310	13,250,758
1844	976,551	263,508	540,305	494,099	36,561	73,325	11,552,460
1845	229,105	146,272	878,785	378,182	18,722	54,918	10,801,868
1846	1,597,597	557,872	850,931	342,210	43,134	58,864	8,243,412
1847	2,195,581	1,382,219	1,212,887	656,999½	16,313½	35,904	10,774,407
1848	1,573,427	615,094	1,959,210	413,437½	26,262½	72,734	10,728,746
1849	862,810	527,464	1,827,040	375,680	21,114½	73,888	10,395,235
1850	1,192,559	831,704	2,347,844	367,737	18,859	61,468	9,711,472
1851	2,529,699	998,059	2,992,342	645,730	12,011	57,864	10,847,118

Source: Canal Commission and Board of Public Works data, in McClelland and Huntington, *History of the Ohio Canals*, Appendices. (Checked for accuracy against original CC and BPW reports.)

earlier expectations that the Ohio Canal would make the state a vast granary serving the growing urban population of New York and the Atlantic Coast. Whiskey became another important export commodity from the grain region of northern and central Ohio, with Cleveland receipts increasing seven-fold in the decade after 1832.[18]

This burgeoning trade made Cleveland the principal primary market for grain on the Great Lakes, and in the 1830's nearly all the wheat and flour received at Buffalo for shipment to New York originated from Cleveland. The degree of Cleveland's dependence on the Ohio Canal was evident from the statistics of her grain trade. In 1841 the canal delivered 441,000 barrels of flour to the city, compared with 461,000 barrels shipped to outside markets from Cleveland that year. An even larger proportion of Cleveland's wheat exports—all but 30,000 bushels out of a total of 1,593,000—reached the city by way of the canal.[19] Because of the Ohio Canal's transport services, then, northern and central Ohio had become part of an emergent western Wheat Belt by 1840, with Cleveland as the hub of the export trade.

Although the northward-flowing trade to Cleveland dominated the Ohio Canal's commerce, Portsmouth—the southern terminus —also attracted surplus produce from the interior. Exports destined for Portsmouth came mainly from the Scioto Valley counties on the canal's southern line. Farmers in the Scioto region shipped their wheat and flour north to the lake, but their pork and bacon (especially in bulk form, processed on the farm) they sent to the South, where dietary preferences sustained demand for such meat. Moreover, the southern river route was free of ice earlier than Lake Erie, an important advantage in the meat trade.[20] Bulk pork and bacon thus comprised Portsmouth's principal export, with 200,000 to 700,000 pounds arriving there by canal each year in the late 1830's.[21]

The Ohio Canal also played a major economic role as a channel for importation from the East of such items as hardware, textiles, clothing, farm implements and other machinery, processed foods, and miscellaneous finished goods loosely classified, in the parlance of the period, as "merchandise." As population

TABLE 8.2

PRINCIPAL COMMODITIES IN OHIO CANAL TRADE AT PORTSMOUTH 1833–51

YEAR	CORN BUSHELS	WHEAT BUSHELS	FLOUR BARRELS (ARRIVED VIA THE CANAL)	BULK PORK AND BACON POUNDS	OATS BUSHELS	PORK BARRELS	CLEARED MERCHANDISE POUNDS
1836	43,117	3,399	32,629		31,043		7,220,003
1837	3,197	735	13,546	287,940			3,487,271
1838	8,768	2,368	13,898	276,843		12,463	3,763,398
1839	6,444	1,100	6,932	706,533		11,968	7,085,735
1840	30,530		34,134	228,469	125	7,827	6,747,565
1841	128,191		62,447	1,312,929	185	25,144	5,773,929
1842	56,748		18,688	1,533,047		18,755	5,111,112
1843	28,758	605	28,736	2,950,569	8	30,284	5,851,843
1844	100,388	487	35,338	1,657,807	25	62,006	5,176,823
1845	146,438	635	29,716	1,096,985	320	22,965	5,897,918
1846	134,032	8,004	38,742	2,770,873	1,308	35,136	2,795,682
1847	348,155	8,782	71,047	2,561,515	41,723	46,575	2,754,243
1848	106,206	4,002	21,491	5,921,783	3,254	33,455½	3,247,849
1849	197,875	1,834	29,688	6,486,693	52	69,298	3,023,522
1850	476,482	16,372½	32,613	5,246,572	2,411	32,411½	2,847,526
1851	403,094	70,430	49,802½	4,679,759	2,924	13,524	2,604,084

Source: Canal Commission and Board of Public Works data, in McClelland and Huntington, *History of the Ohio Canals*, Appendices.

increased and farm income rose in the canal region, demand for such merchandise imports also increased. (Table 8.1.) For communities situated on the northern and central divisions of the Ohio Canal, there was but one economical route for importing such commodities—the Cleveland entryway. As a result, Cleveland's merchandise shipments by canal to the interior rose from ten million pounds in 1833 to about twenty million in 1839. Only one-fifth to one-fourth of this amount was sent through to Portsmouth for sale in the Ohio Valley market.[22] The remainder was sold at way points on the canal. The promoters' earlier hope, that the canal would displace the New Orleans route for shipping eastern goods through to the Ohio Valley, was frustrated by two unforeseen developments of the 1830's: (1) continuing improvement of steamer service on the southern rivers drove rates down and injected new vigor into the New Orleans upriver trade; and (2) additional competition for the Ohio Canal came from Pittsburgh, which, with the opening of the Pennsylvania Mainline in 1834, became an important entrepôt for eastern merchandise bound for the Ohio Valley.[23]

While the unanticipated competition for the Ohio Valley market hurt Cleveland's position, it benefited the merchandise trade of Portsmouth, the Ohio Canal southern terminus. Commission merchants at Portsmouth brought goods from New Orleans, Cincinnati, and Pittsburgh to their wharves by river steamers, and then shipped by canal northward into the interior. By the late 1830's, merchandise shipments from the Portsmouth terminus up to the Scioto Valley towns—which earlier in the decade had imported merchandise by way of Cleveland—ranged from 3.4 to 7 million pounds annually, or about a third the volume of Cleveland's comparable canal trade in 1839.[24]

After merchandise, the second largest import item on the Ohio Canal was salt, a basic dietary item and a necessity for meat-packing. Until the canal was built, salt had been in short supply in northern Ohio, the nearest salt springs being in the Muskingum Valley, too far south to permit economical overland shipment to the area between Columbus and the lake. As soon as the canal was opened, the market situation changed radically. Now it was possible to bring New York salt from Buffalo via Cleveland to

TABLE 8.3

PRINCIPAL COMMODITIES IN MUSKINGUM IMPROVEMENT TRADE
AT HARMAR (MARIETTA) 1841–51

| YEAR | ARRIVED VIA THE IMP'VT | | CLEARED |
	WHEAT & FLOUR[a] BUSHELS	DOMESTIC[b] SALT BARRELS	MERCHANDISE POUNDS
1841	31,955	n.a.	n.a.
1842	76,405	n.a.	117,148
1843	227,002	3,300	629,773
1844	195,545	n.a.	2,274,873
1845	205,265	2,532	3,415,647
1846	264,750	2,239	1,746,391
1847	653,535	n.a.	n.a.
1848	368,673	n.a.	n.a.
1849	570,178	n.a.	n.a.
1850	620,638	3,800	3,665,800
1851	677,000	3,900	3,291,000

[a] Flour rated as equivalent, 1 bbl. = 5 bu. wheat
[b] Ohio-produced (no doubt all Muskingum Valley salt)
Sources: Ohio Board of Agriculture, *14th AR* (1860), 497; Board of Public Works, *AR, 1852*, Tables; *id., 8th AR*, 14–15; U. S. Commissioner of Patents, *AR, 1847*, p. 638.

the interior—or even to Portsmouth and the Ohio Valley, where it competed with Ohio salt and the products of western Virginia's mines. The advent of canal navigation thus wrought a fundamental change in the price structure for this precious import commodity—as was manifest in the rise in Cleveland's salt clearances by canal to the interior, from 28,000 barrels in 1833 to more than 100,000 barrels in 1839.[25]

The farmers who outfitted their households with merchandise brought inland by canal, and who cured their meats with salt carried to them by the same route, also relied upon the canal for imports of gypsum, which was used both for fertilizer and for construction purposes.[26] The canal was the mainstay of a busy lumber trade as well. In the early stages of settlement, when land was being cleared, lumber and crude wood products were shipped out to Cleveland as an export product, providing a source of cash income for farmers while they were getting their land into production. But by 1840 the growth of towns on the canal lines and new rural construction had outstripped local lumber supplies. The trade therefore reversed direction, with Cleveland importing shingles, staves, and board lumber from western Ohio and Michigan, and shipping large quantities to the interior by the canal.[27]

Although the Ohio Canal disappointed hopes that it would capture the Ohio Valley trade, it did play an impressive role in the development of central Ohio and the northern canal region. Together with the surge in population came the anticipated increase of land values, reflecting both agriculture's new profitability and the rising total acreage of land in cultivation. But perhaps the most striking features of development were the growth of cities and the prominence of commerce and industry in the central and northern canal regions. In the six counties on the canal's northern division, for example, urban property valuations rose 360 per cent, or nearly two million dollars, during the brief period 1832–40.[28] This rapid rate of urban growth was also reflected in the occupations by which the people earned their livelihood. In the regions where urbanization was taking hold, along the central and northern portions of the canal, the proportion of all nonprofessional workers engaged in manufacturing, trades, and commerce was 22 percent—as compared to less than 15 per cent in Ohio counties lacking canal facilities. Indeed, four counties on the Ohio Canal line reported between 23 and 29 per cent of nonprofessional labor force engaged in these urban-based occupations.[29] This degree of diversification in the local economies of the northern and central regions was all the more remarkable considering the near-frontier status of most of those areas two decades earlier. Apparently the model of development postulated by the early canal advocates had been realized: rising farm income and population brought new business to the commercial towns, and also a larger "home market" for local goods produced in shops and factories which had the advantage of canal transport for raw materials. A diversified economic structure produced an interaction between agricultural growth and urban-based commerce and industry that pushed the canal counties ahead in the race for economic development.

Not everywhere on the Ohio Canal line, however, did this kind of development take place. In fact, the Scioto Valley counties, on the southern part of the canal, lagged in nearly all respects. The Scioto was not a poor region, for the per capita property valuation there was higher than in the central and northern districts. But by all indications, the rate of growth was slower.[30] And the Scioto's labor force composition was still predominantly agricultural in 1840 with only 11 per cent engaged in urban-based activities—half the proportion elsewhere in the canal's trade area.

The lag in growth of the Scioto canal counties was apparently attributable to factors other than transportation. One reason for local retardation was the landownership pattern. The land had been taken up early, for this region lay in the old Virginia Military District, reserved to the Old Dominion by Congress to honor the land-bounty scrip issued to Virginia's soldiers during the Revolution. The dream of settling impoverished veterans on small farms had been shattered when a coterie of wealthy Army officers managed to acquire most of the scrip issued to enlisted men. As a result, some 70 per cent of the Military District lands became the property of one hundred men. Enjoying the lives of lords of the manor or absentee landlords, they rented their land instead of selling freeholds.[31] And because the typical western settler harbored "an inherent love of being independent," as one local citizen wrote, migrants by-passed the Scioto—and the dreary prospect of becoming tenants—to buy government land in the equally attractive Miami country, or else along the canal lines in northern and central Ohio.[32] Such land-management practices may well help explain why the four Scioto Valley counties on the canal line gained altogether only 22,000 in population during 1820–40, while other regions near the canal were filling up quickly.

But the Scioto was disadvantaged in still another way: the canal did not provide it with waterpower comparable to the amount it afforded on the northern and central divisions of the line. Mill sites were no small benefit of canal construction in this era, before the widespread adoption of steam, when manufacturing industries were still mainly dependent upon water. Where a canal ran through a region of ample natural water supply and steep gradients, its water could be passed through mill-races alongside the main line or feeders without impeding navigation. Such artificial power sites provided more reliable and readily controlled water than did the natural streams.[33] On the Ohio Canal, the conditions for building mill-races were best on the central and northern divisions, and were least favorable in the Scioto Valley. Hence Muskingum County alone had twelve mills operated by canal water, producing power sufficient to run the equivalent of 11,000 cotton spindles—more power than on all the canal mill sites in all four counties of the Scioto Valley line. In 1839 the Ohio Canal was providing power for more than eighty factories, of which only eight were located in the Scioto counties. Plentiful power, combined with the lower transfer costs for raw materials by canal, proved a potent force for industrial development. Thus we find that the distribution of waterpower sites on the canal conformed to the other indicators of industrial growth: the heaviest concentrations of urban-based employment in 1840 were in the counties that enjoyed the greatest advantages of waterpower from the canal.[34]

In sum, the early predictions of increases in population, land-value increments, stimulation of manufacturing, and commercialization of farming were all fulfilled prior to 1840 in the Ohio Canal region, with the significant exception of the Scioto district, which lagged for special reasons.

THE MIAMI CANAL TRADE

Whereas the Ohio Canal was built through a vast area of undeveloped country, the Miami Canal serviced an already settled region between Cincinnati and Dayton. Because it had only one terminus facing on outside markets, moreover, the Miami line did not offer shippers the option of using any entrepôt except Cincinnati, which by 1831 was already known as the "Queen City." The canal therefore reinforced the existing orientation of the Miami Valley's trade toward the southern river markets, and it strengthened Cincinnati's pivotal position in that trade.[35]

Opening of the Miami Canal did, however, give further impetus to commercialized farm production, especially in the area around Dayton, which from 1831 to 1837 was the line's northern terminus. "The country, particularly the farmers," a Dayton merchant reported in 1829, "already feel the advantage [of the canal] in an increased price for their articles and a regular market, as what is not consumed here is now boated to Cincinnati."[36] As far north as Piqua, for instance, farmers could reach Dayton after 1831 by way of local roads—a dramatic change from a decade earlier, when surplus crops from Piqua had been sent by keelboat, on narrow and treacherous northward-flowing streams, to markets as far away as Fort Wayne or Fort Meigs. During peak periods of the canal season, wagon trains from Darke, Miami, Champaign, Clark, and Greene counties crowded Dayton's streets, hauling the surplus of the countryside down to the canal boats.[37]

The nature of the trade that flowed down the canal to Cincinnati reflected the continuing reliance of the Miami region on two main staples, wheat and corn. The mainstays of the commerce (shown in Table 8.4) were flour, whiskey, barreled pork, and bulk pork and bacon, with shipments to Cincinnati maintaining a fairly steady level in the 1830's. The canal's import trade, by which Cincinnati supplied country retail stores and farm households with eastern merchandise, was also fairly steady in the thirties at about six million pounds shipped inland from the Queen City annually—about one-half the volume of Cleveland's comparable trade. (See Table 8.4.) Here again, trade relationships that antedated construction of the canal continued to prevail: Cincinnati relied mainly upon New Orleans as its merchandise source, though Philadelphia became increasingly important after 1833.[38]

The picture changed drastically in 1837. For the Miami Canal was then extended northward up the Miami Valley to Piqua, which succeeded Dayton as the northern terminus. Settlement near Piqua had been much sparser than farther south, and settlers cleared new farmland in response to marketing opportunities offered by the canal. Thus, despite a panic in 1837, new production led to a doubling of Cincinnati's flour receipts by canal

TABLE 8.4

PRINCIPAL COMMODITIES IN MIAMI CANAL TRADE AT CINCINNATI 1833–51

| YEAR | ARRIVED VIA THE CANAL | | | | | CLEARED |
	WHEAT BUSHELS	CORN BUSHELS	FLOUR BARRELS	PORK BARRELS	WHISKEY BARRELS	MERCHANDISE POUNDS
1833		4,101	137,633	21,880	53,620	6,128,562
1834		24,628	118,855	24,581	47,686	5,902,800
1835			66,000			
1836		24,210	50,969	16,345	54,721	6,658,144
1837		89,492	74,563	22,776	53,853	6,020,287
1838			127,637	23,502	53,952	
1839		18,000	138,120	26,921	43,228	8,664,640
1840	97,200	41,600	165,762	20,835	74,026	5,566,282
1841		90,737	118,577	22,106	69,893	4,359,433
1842	5,283	84,523	74,204	29,584	48,853	2,842,861
1843	5,983	80,802	127,093	18,890	58,798	3,867,819
1844	13,272	82,863	133,544	33,118	68,933	4,112,291
1845	6,404	45,950	121,723	26,099	69,312	4,388,873
1846	14,896	112,195	117,671	35,263	60,434	9,438,548
1847	105,605	547,903	209,166	15,501	40,789	4,738,691
1848	22,451	290,486	91,631	23,544	58,490	4,164,096
1849	22,203	239,530	104,705	14,397	52,201	4,100,444
1850	81,331	615,864	110,603	21,614	83,624	
1851	130,292	270,147	317,107	8,176	67,394	6,322,645

Source: McClelland and Huntington, *History of Ohio Canals*, Appendices.

between 1837 and 1839, and whiskey receipts also increased rapidly. Merchandise shipped to the interior from Cincinnati also rose in volume for a time, and larger quantities of lumber and such crude lumber products as shingles were sent down to the river port from the newly opened district.[39]

Cincinnati traded with a much larger region than the Miami Valley in the late 1830's, when new roads had made the city accessible to an extensive farm region of Indiana and Kentucky as well as southern Ohio. But still, the Miami country remained Cincinnati's principal supplier and customer, and the canal was crucial to the trade. Of 200,000 barrels of flour shipped to the Queen City in 1840 from the Miami region, the canal brought 166,000; of 80,000 barrels of whiskey, the canal brought 74,000; of meat products (pork, lard, and beef) valued at $1,400,000, the canal brought $400,000; and all of this was in addition to lumber products and corn.[40]

Although construction of the Miami Canal and its first extension to Piqua merely strengthened Cincinnati's hold on the Miami region's trade, the canal did initiate a transformation in the location of manufacturing industries. At all the canal-port towns, manufacturing plants began to cluster along the canal lines: Middletown, Dayton, Troy, Hamilton, and Piqua were the principal industrial towns of the interior, where distillers, and flour, paper, malt, and flaxseed-oil mills were located.[41] Before the canal era, farmers had brought their flour to small custom mills located on streams dispersed throughout the countryside. But when the canal was built, it afforded mill sites with sufficient water to permit construction of much larger, more efficient mills than were common elsewhere in the district. Hence the old country mills underwent a relative decline in importance, and the pattern of dispersion gave way to one of heavier concentration at cities on the canal. Dayton benefited most from this shift: provided with many new power sites by the canal, the town became the dominant milling center of the region, and in 1840 half of Cincinnati's arrivals of flour by canal came from Dayton. Distilleries also were built near the canal line, and until the 1840's the canal brought in nearly all the whiskey arriving at Cincinnati for consumption there or re-export to outside markets.[42]

TABLE 8.5

PRINCIPAL COMMODITIES IN WABASH & ERIE CANAL TRADE AT TOLEDO 1841–51

| YEAR | FLOUR BARRELS | WHEAT BUSHELS | ARRIVED VIA THE CANAL | | | CLEARED |
			OATS BUSHELS	CORN BUSHELS	PORK BARRELS	MERCHANDISE POUNDS
1842	1,678	12,976	774			81,033
1843	21,709	98,220	23,388	116,143	1,873	3,811,768
1844	26,122	211,698	4,649	32,659	17,415	4,599,801
1845	86,382	565,711	9,741	30,037	7,859	9,818,737
1846	126,715	664,314	105,402	1,105,909	18,219	8,947,092
1847	116,730	962,170	17,018	1,275,410	18,861	11,670,754
1848	171,872	1,121,491	96,762	1,309,911	33,209	10,890,414
1849	142,452	714,703	15,985	2,052,071	37,593	10,843,045
1850	106,901	935,936	3,409	1,581,130	40,600	12,882,736
1851	196,839	1,250,355	40,176	2,562,961	32,410	13,327,527

Source: McClelland and Huntington, History of Ohio Canals, Appendices.

The development of urban centers in the Miami Valley was no less profoundly affected by construction of the canal. Middletown, which was the northern terminus from 1827 until the canal was completed to Dayton, doubled in population during the first year of navigation, while both Hamilton and Dayton were experiencing rapid population growth and new construction. In Cincinnati real-estate values rose 20 to 25 per cent in the three years after the canal was first opened, and population increased rapidly. The value of Cincinnati's export trade, estimated at one million dollars in 1826, had increased fourfold by 1832, and to about six million dollars by the mid-thirties.[43] Throughout the Miami Valley region, as Sherry O. Hessler's careful research reveals, the canal towns increased their population during 1820–40 far more rapidly than did urban centers lacking canal facilities.[44] In the six counties on the Miami Canal, urban property valuations rose from 4.7 million dollars in 1832 to 6.8 million dollars in 1840; and in 1840, the Miami counties had a higher proportion of labor force engaged in trades, commerce, and manufactures than any other region of the state, with fully 40 per cent of workers in these occupations. In Hamilton County, which embraced Cincinnati, more than 60 per cent of labor force was so engaged; the second-ranking county in the state was Montgomery (including Dayton), with nearly 30 per cent.[45]

The largest single manufacturing interest in the region was Cincinnati's meat-packing industry, and it must be said that the canal contributed only marginally to its growth. Of the city's seventeen million dollars of industrial output in 1841, meat-packing accounted for more than five million dollars. Unlike distilling or flour-milling, the packing industry was not dispersed at country towns on the canal outside the main urban center: Cincinnati dominated the region, and indeed the entire West, earning its sobriquet "Porkopolis." It was well provided with roads to the rich corn-and-hog farm country surrounding it, and farmers obtained their best prices by driving hogs into the city to the slaughter-house markets. Moreover, the city's packers were aggressive and imaginative, and from the early 1830's they maximized the profits of packing by developing such by-products as soap, tallow, candles, glue, leather, and lard-oil.[46] These innovations permitted them to bid higher prices on livestock than smaller-scale producers in the interior generally could offer. The number of hogs packed at the Queen City rose sharply, from 85,000 in 1833 to nearly 200,000 at the decade's end. But carrying livestock by canal boat to the city was not common. In the early forties only 5,000 to 7,000 hogs arrived at Cincinnati annually by the canal, mainly from the Dayton region—only a small part of the city's total pack.[47]

Although the Miami Canal had a major developmental impact on Cincinnati and the Miami Valley, then, it did not change the orientation of the import or export commerce of its trade region, as did the Ohio Canal in central and northern Ohio. For whereas Cleveland opened a newly settled area to trade with New York, Cincinnati continued to face southward. All its basic exports—flour, whiskey, and pork—were marketed mainly in the new cotton plantation region of the Southwest, at towns on the southern rivers, or else in foreign and Atlantic Coast markets which were reached by way of New Orleans. Not until well into the 1840's would Cincinnati begin to shift its trade focus, gradually abandoning the river route that had handled its exports since the turn of the century.[48]

NOTES

1. Jacob Blickensderfer to Alfred Kelley, Jan. 19, 1826, Misc. MSS., WRHS; also, advertisements of lands and a new edition of Kilbourn's gazetteer, in *Columbus Gazette*, Apr. 28, May 12, 1825.

2. George Canfield to Kelley, July 3, 1826, CC Papers, OSA; Delaware *Patron*, Feb. 3, 1825; also, Sandusky *Clarion*, Feb. 26, 1825. The phenomenon described here is comparable to what Leland H. Jenks has identified as the initial economic effects of railroad planning. Once a new project for railroads was conceived and plans elaborated, Jenks writes, "other innovating ideas" clustered around the project. For the localities to be affected, "the characteristics of the prospective future are altered; they assume an aspect more favorable to men and firms with new plans. . . . Thus early railway projects were at-

tended by a retinue of satellite innovations." (Jenks, "Railroads as an Economic Force in American Development," *Journal of Economic History*, IV [1944], 1–20, esp. 1–3.)

3. Sherry O. Hessler, "Patterns of Transport and Urban Growth" (M.A. thesis, Johns Hopkins, 1961), 151–54, 157; Cincinnati Federal Writers' Project, *They Built a City* (Cincinnati, 1938), 79; on the Portsmouth venture, James Bradford to Kelley, Sept. 12, Nov. 18, 1831, CC Papers; on the projects for branch line canals, Chap. 4, *supra;* on the Boston investment, H. Scheiber, "The Commercial Bank of Lake Erie," *Business History Review*, XL (Spring 1966), 47ff.

4. H. N. Scheiber, "State Policy and the Public Domain," *Journal of Economic History*, XXV (March 1965), 96ff.

5. Quotation from C. N. Glaab, "Jesup W. Scott and a West of Cities," Ohio History, LXIII (Winter 1964), 4; also, H. E. Davis, "Elisha Whittlesey and Maumee Land Speculation," *Northwest Ohio Quarterly*, XV (1943), 139–58; Z. Wildman to F. Wildman, Oct. 4, 1835, Wildman Papers, OHS, on Toledo land prices.

6. A. F. Hinsch to T. G. Gates, Feb. 12, 1842, BPW Papers, on water sites; Platt Card to Richard Sears, July 6, 1835, Jacob Barker Papers, OHS, on railroad promotion at Manhattan City; also, J. W. Weatherford, "The Short Life of Manhattan, Ohio," *OHQ*, LXV (Oct. 1946), 376. Printed promotional literature of the Portage Canal and Manufacturing Company, 1837, in the New York Public Library, also reflects the importance of newly provided water sites.

7. New Lisbon *Ohio Patriot* clipped in Sandusky *Clarion*, Apr. 23, 1825; also, *Liberty Hall*, Sept. 20, 1825.

8. William Fowler and others to BPW, Dec. 26, 1836, BPW Papers; Anthony Wayne Parkway Commission marker (1959) at Miltonville site.

9. Governor Lucas recognized the importance of "five millions of dollars . . . thrown into circulation" during the period of state borrowing, in his annual message, Dec., 1833, *Senate Journal*, 1833–34, pp. 9–10. A tenant on a British-owned farm reported in 1826 that he must pay his rent in corn, which the landlord's agent had agreed to accept, unless he decided to work for cash wages at canal construction. (John Rochester to George Courtauld, dated Englishtown, Ohio, Aug. 24, 1826, in *The Courtauld Family Papers* [8 vols., Cambridge, Eng., 1916], III, 1482.)

10. Cleveland *Herald,* July 22, 1825, on "sons of Erin"; see also Chaps. 2–3, *supra,* on opportunities for canal labor. William Cooper Howells recalled that canal construction afforded farmers a chance to get cash wages, needed for payment of their taxes. (*Recollections of Life in Ohio* [Cincinnati, 1895], 139.)

11. Irish and German names appear among those who entered lands with state scrip, entry books of Wabash & Erie Lands, 1842, Lima Land Office, State Auditor's Office, Records Room, Columbus. See also Harlan Hatcher, *The Western Reserve* (Indianapolis, 1949), 201, on Irish settlers in Akron; and *Maumee Express,* Aug. 25, 1838, on camp life. Wages are discussed in Chapters 3 and 5, *supra.*

12. CC Minutes, Vol. I, p. 336, MS., Dept. of Public Works, Records Room, Columbus; William T. Utter, *Granville* (Denison, 1956), 110; Lee Newcomer, "Construction of the Wabash & Erie Canal," *OHQ,* XLVI (1937), 199–207.

13. Kelley to Brown, June 20, 1828, Brown Papers, OSL.

14. Diary of Moses Quinby, 1831 (MS.), Cornell University Library.

15. The northern and central Ohio Canal counties were those on the line between Franklin and Cuyahoga. Their population was 93,000 in 1820, 161,000 in 1830, and 264,000 in 1840 (1820–40 gain, 184 per cent). The Ohio River counties, excluding three on canal lines (Washington, Scioto, Hamilton), reported 86,000 in 1820, 125,000 in 1830, and 161,000 in 1840 (1820–40 gain, 87 per cent). (From U. S. Census data.)

16. John Klippart in Ohio Board of Agriculture, *14th AR* (1859), 496–97; and CC *AR* in *Senate Journal,* 1832–33, pp. 340–47.

17. Ebenezer Buckingham (Canal Fund Commissioner) to Brown, Feb. 17, 1831, Brown Papers, OSL.

18. Cleveland whiskey receipts, 1843–14,600 bbls.

19. *Ibid.;* Cleveland *Herald,* Jan. 5, 1842. There was some Cleveland export trade as well to Canada's Welland Canal for shipment *via* Oswego and the New York canals to the seaboard, or else for export through Montreal. See Donald Creighton, *Empire of the St. Lawrence* (Toronto, 1956), 251–52.

20. To what extent the grain and meats of the Old Northwest, shipped southward on the rivers, were consumed in the southern urban and plantation market is a matter of considerable dispute among historians. For an important recent statement, see Albert Fishlow, *American Railroads and the Transformation of the Antebellum Economy* (Cambridge, 1965), 262ff., arguing

that little was so consumed; also, Eugene Genovese, "Significance of the Slave Plantation for Southern Economic Development," *Journal of Southern History*, XXVIII (Nov. 1962), 442–37. For a contrary view, see also John G. Clark's persuasive discussion in *The Grain Trade in the Old Northwest* (Urbana, 1966), 47–48, 130–31.

21. See Table 8.2. See also column for pork in barrels.

22. BPW, *8th AR* (1844), p. 5, on proportion of merchandise shipped from Cleveland through to Portsmouth.

23. C. M. Giddings to Kelley, July 30, 1834, Letters on Canals, CHS; CC, *14th AR* (1836), 7. The late 1830's marked a high point in the Mainline's competitive position in the westbound merchandise trade. See Roger L. Ransom, "Interregional Canals and Economic Specialization in the Antebellum United States," *Explorations in Entrepreneurial History/2nd Series*, V (Fall 1967), 15, 30.

24. Table 8.2. The decline in rates on the rivers, documented in Thomas S. Berry, *Western Prices before 1861* (Cambridge, 1943), 79ff., also benefited the Muskingum River traders, who imported and exported via Pittsburgh and the downriver cities. See Norris F. Schneider, *Y-Bridge City* (Cleveland, 1950), Chap. 12, on the Muskingum's commerce.

25. Table 8.1. On the salt trade, see Chap. 10, *infra*, and L. C. Hunter, *Studies in the Economic History of the Ohio Valley* (Northhampton, Mass., 1933–34), 53, 68–69; BPW, *4th AR* (1841), 6–8; *6th AR* (1843), 8–9.

26. Cleveland's gypsum shipments inland, reported by the CC, ranged from 1.6 million to 2 million pounds annually.

27. For instance, in 1833 Cleveland received by canal some 88 tons of ashes and 808,345 feet of lumber, clearing for the interior 280,970 feet of lumber and 615,000 shingles. Receipts of lumber products declined steadily in the late 1830's, except for staves and headings (for cooperage).

28. From State Auditor's annual reports. There was an increase of 83 per cent in urban valuations for all canal counties in Ohio. Farmland and buildings rose in the Ohio Canal's northern division counties by 40.3 per cent, 1832–40, and by 31.2 per cent in the central division counties, less than the rise (41.4 per cent) in all canal counties; yet tax-valuation figures are a crude measure at best and give only a sense of rough magnitudes. Contemporary students of the economy regarded only post-1846 tax data in Ohio as meaningful for accurate com-

parative estimates. There is abundant testimony in the population data, however, for asserting a dramatic rise in rural and urban values. See especially James S. Matthews, *Expressions of Urbanism in the Sequent Occupation of Northeastern Ohio* (Chicago, 1949); and Francis P. Weisenburger, *Passing of the Frontier* (Columbus, 1941), *passim*.

29. 1840 U. S. Census. The four counties were Muskingum (29 per cent), Stark (28 per cent), Summit (28 per cent), and Cuyahoga (23 per cent).

30. Rural property valuation rose only $600,000 (14 per cent) during 1832–40 and urban valuation $600,000 (73 per cent). Compare data for northern and central Ohio at n. 28 above.

31. William T. Hutchinson, "The Bounty Lands of the American Revolution in Ohio" (Ph.D. diss., University of Chicago, 1927), 157.

32. Samuel Williams to John Williams, July 29, 1818, Samuel Williams Papers, OHS.

33. A. H. Fenichel estimates that in 1838 all but 1.1% of power used in manufacturing in the West-north-central states was waterpower. (NBER, "Output, Employment, and Productivity," *Studies in Income and Wealth*, XXX [New York, 1966], 456.)

34. The mills included 59 flour mills, 17 saw mills, 6 textiles mills, and miscellaneous, given in CC, *15th AR* (1839), 9–10. Correlation of 1840 labor force composition with mill sites, from 1840 Census and data on mills in BPW, *Special Report . . . in relation to Sales of Waterpower* (Jan. 29, 1844), tables.

35. See Frank P. Goodwin, "Building a Commercial System," *OHQ*, XVI (April 1907), 316–39; and Richard C. Wade, *The Urban Frontier* (Cambridge, 1959), 54–59.

36. George Houston to Williams, May 9, 1829, Micajah T. Williams Papers, OSL.

37. Ada Cook, "The Growth of Industry in Dayton" (M.A. thesis, Miami University, 1940), 15; on keelboating from Piqua, see advertisement in Piqua *Gazette,* June 6, 1822.

38. On Cincinnati's general commercial growth, see Berry, *Western Prices, passim*.

39. Some 474,000 board-feet of lumber were received, 1839.

40. James Hall, *The West: Its Commerce and Navigation* (Cincinnati, 1848), 289.

41. Cook, "Growth of Industry," 18–19; R. Standafer, "History of the Miami Canal" (Miami University Library), 100 *et passim*.

42. M. T. Williams to Kelley, March 29, 1831, CC Papers; Hessler, "Patterns of Transport," 146ff.; Berry, *Western Prices,* 165; Hall, *The West,* 289, on whiskey trade. There were 41 flour and flax mills, 6 saw mills, 6 textiles factories, 2 machine shops and foundries, and 1 distillery (surprisingly low, if accurate) on the Miami Canal in 1839. (CC, *15th AR,* 9–10.) Possibly the number of distilleries increased very rapidly in the early 1840's, on which cf. Berry, *Western Prices,* 202.

43. Hall, *The West,* 266; M. T. Williams to Brown, Sept. 25, 1831, Brown Papers, OSL; Standafer, "The Miami Canal," 173.

44. Hessler, "Patterns of Transport," 38–48.

45. Auditor of State reports; also, 1840 Census data. In the 1820 Census, comparable percentages of workers in manufacturing alone ranged from 11 to 25 per cent in the Miami Valley counties. Frank Goodwin, "Manufactures in the Miami Country," *American Hist. Rev.,* XII (July 1907), 774.

46. Hall, *The West,* 284. The canal was important as a route for shipping finished barrels and staves and headings from the Miami Valley down to Cincinnati.

47. *They Built a City,* Chap. 5, on diversification; Isaac Lippincott, *A History of Manufactures in the Ohio Valley* (New York, 1914), 112, 177–78; and C. T. Leavitt, "Some Economic Aspects of the Western Meat-packing Industry," *Journal of Business,* IV (Jan. 1931), 68ff., on the Cincinnati industry generally.

48. On the southern market for Ohio exports on the river, see n. 20, above. On the Old Northwest's trade, more generally, the major sources are Berry, *Western Prices;* Thomas D. Odle, "The American Grain Trade of the Great Lakes, 1825–1873," *Inland Seas,* VII–VIII (1951–52); and A. L. Kohlmeier, *The Old Northwest* (Bloomington, 1938). See also Stuart Bruchey, ed., *Cotton and the Growth of the American Economy* (New York, 1967).

CHAPTER 9

The Transportation
Revolution: Second Phase
1840-1851

THE 1840's marked a distinct second phase in America's
Transportation Revolution—that series of technological innovations and waves of transport investment which forged an
integrated national economy prior to 1860. The first phase began
when steamboats were introduced in river commerce after 1815
and New York's Erie Canal was opened, substituting water
facilities for overland hauling in the east-west trade. The 1830's
and 1840's, according to the standard view, represented an extension of this initial phase: additional canals were built, while
navigational conditions were improved on the western lakes and
rivers. The second phase, it is usually asserted, occurred only in
the 1850's, when long-line railroads were built between the
Atlantic Coast and the West, changing the basic conditions of
commerce.[1] But this standard interpretation overlooks, I think,
the fundamental character of two changes that occurred in the
decade of the forties, prior to the advent of railroad competition
with interregional canals: first, the proliferation, with unprecedented swiftness, of new canal routes in the West, occurring simultaneously with great additions to shipping tonnage on the rivers
and lakes; and second, a sharp decline in freight rates on all the
major waterways, both old and new. It is in this twofold context
of change, then, that one must interpret transport development
and patterns of local growth within Ohio in the 1840's, and also
the shifting relationship between Ohio's economy and the nation's.

Within Ohio, the completion of the public works made the

Ohio Canal the trunk line of a larger transport system, with two
new improved routes (by way of the Mahoning Canal and the
Muskingum Improvement) between Cleveland and the Ohio
River. The Miami Canal also became but one component of a
larger system of waterways, reaching into Indiana and giving
western Ohio access to both the Ohio River and Lake Erie. And
in addition to the completion of new state canals, the Mad River
& Lake Erie Railroad route was completed in 1848 between
Sandusky and Cincinnati, marking the West's first all-rail connection between the Great Lakes and the Ohio Valley.[2]

The pace of proliferation within Ohio was more than matched
in the larger system of interregional trade routes: in 1845 Pennsylvania extended her canal system with completion of a line from
Pittsburgh north to the lake port of Erie; in 1848 Indiana completed extension of her Wabash & Erie Canal as far as Terre
Haute; and, also in 1848, Illinois completed its state-financed
Illinois & Michigan Canal, opening still another major water
route between the Great Lakes and the Ohio-Mississippi basin.[3]
Each of these new routes was competitive with the Ohio canals,
so far as commerce between lake and river was concerned; and
each increased the range of feasible transportation for large areas
of the West, which could now trade with either New York or the
South.

But while new lines were being built, the older river system
that served New Orleans showed renewed vigor as well. There
was a great expansion of steamboat capacity on the western
rivers; but surprisingly enough the flatboat trade also continued
to flourish. The flatboats competed with the steamers, the steamers
with one another, the river route with the new waterways that
linked East and West. And as competition became more intensive,
the structure of freight rates buckled.[4]

The decline in rates, although difficult to measure precisely because of commodity-by-commodity differences and seasonal fluctuations, was nonetheless general. For instance, upriver steamer
charges from Cincinnati to Pittsburgh fell from 25 cents a barrel
in 1841 to 15 cents in the late forties; downstream rates from
Cincinnati to New Orleans fell from 50 cents a hundred pounds
to 20–28 cents in the same period.[5] As rates on the river routes
declined, officials operating the state canals of New York,

Indiana, Pennsylvania, and Ohio reacted by cutting their tolls, often drastically, to avoid losses of trade to New Orleans. The forwarders who operated boats on the canal lines followed suit, and rates fell on all the major canals.[6] The canal officials' efforts to protect the eastward-moving trade against renewed competition from the rivers were aided by a considerable expansion of shipping capacity on the Great Lakes, from 47,000 tons to 184,-000 tons during 1840–50. Together with increased cargo capacity came more intensive competition among ships in the trade, and average freight charges on the lakes apparently fell sharply during the forties.[7]

Taken as a whole, the construction of new lines of transportation thus meant that many local areas of the West, formerly accessible to only one market outlet such as New Orleans, gained multiple outlets by way of improved routes. But the flow of trade from each region did not shift—automatically, as it were—from one market outlet to another merely because new routes were opened, even if they might be shorter and more direct than older transport lines. Rather, trade shifted direction because of changes in the structure of rates on competing routes—and transport rates altered swiftly during the 1840's. The record of actual rate changes in the forties is hardly consistent with the concept of a neatly demarcated "canal period," as often defined by historians: a period that allegedly commenced in the 1820's, when construction of new waterways brought "average" rates down to a level that presumably was maintained until 1851, when railroad competition began in the interregional commerce of the country.[8] Indeed, the very concept of "average rates" obscures the reality, that in the 1840's competition among all-water routes drove freight rates down dramatically. The interregional rate decline of the forties was greater, in fact, than any further decrease that occurred when east-west railroads challenged the water lines in the 1850's.

THE OHIO CANAL AND ITS BRANCHES

The economic role of Ohio's canals shifted apace with changes in the physical transportation network. The canals built in the

1840's gave farmers and merchants in many regions of the state increased flexibility in choice of markets: no longer were they typically confined to trade with only one coastal center, be it New Orleans, Philadelphia, or New York. Once shippers and consumers gained access to multiple outside markets, the structure of transport rates on competing routes became crucial to them. As rates permitted, they could select different routes for the different commodities in which they dealt—for instance, merchants could ship corn to New Orleans and grain to New York, buying sugar from the South and dry goods directly from the Atlantic Coast.

The traffic of the canals reflected these new conditions. During the 1840's, there was an overall increase in the volume of canal commerce, especially after the 1839–43 business depression had ended. Not only were new commodities introduced into the canal trades, but there was a shift, as between lake and river, in the direction in which certain commodities were shipped.

In northeastern Ohio, the Mahoning Canal was instrumental in bringing three major commodities into prominence in the canal trade: coal, dairy products, and wool. The Mahoning line passed through the Brier Hill district of the Mahoning Valley, near Youngstown, where coal resources had long been identified but to little economic purpose. Remoteness from outside markets had restricted production to what was needed in the locality. When the canal opened, the mines took on new importance in the local economy, their output rising from 300,000 bushels in 1840, the first year the canal operated, to about two million bushels in 1848. Responsible for only one-tenth of Ohio's coal output in 1840, the Brier Hill mines produced one-third of Ohio coal eight years later.[9] Until the Mahoning Canal began operating, Cleveland had brought coal down the canal from the Tuscarawas Valley of central Ohio. Her trade was not inconsiderable even in 1840, when 172,000 bushels arrived by canal—a thirteen-fold increase from 1832 receipts. But then the Mahoning Canal began to tell. By 1845 Cleveland was receiving half a million bushels annually, and in 1851 the receipts were three million bushels.[10] The new source of supply enabled Cleveland to become a major fueling port for steamboats on Lake Erie; and by 1851 it was also (after Erie, Pennsylvania) the second largest port on the lakes for coal export.[11] The rise of local iron milling and ironware manufacture at Cleveland would be rapid in the 1850's, but even in the forties accessibility to Brier Hill coal gave Cleveland industries a significant advantage.

The Mahoning Canal also stimulated dairy production in its trade region, and it carried large quantities of cheese and butter bound for Cleveland and for the Ohio River market. The Mahoning Valley intersected the old Western Reserve, where a Yankee migration out of Connecticut had already established a specialty in dairy farming. But until the canal was built, farmers in the area had to carry their cheese by wagon eastward to the river or westward to Akron on the main-line canal. The Mahoning Canal, then, ushered in "a golden age for the Western Reserve dairymen" by reducing the costs of transportation to both market's. Construction of the canal coincided with a rise in demand for Ohio cheese in New York, in Upper Canada, and (after 1849) even in distant California; meanwhile, Cincinnati and other river towns also consumed increasing quantities of the Reserve's dairy products.[12] Thus the Mahoning Canal was responsible for doubling Cleveland's canal trade in butter, and the volume of cheese transported on the Mahoning line increased six-fold between 1841 and 1850.[13]

Along with cheese production, the Western Reserve's farms also specialized in sheep raising, and the canal stimulated this branch of agriculture as well. During the 1840's, sheep raising became steadily more prominent as a specialty of Ohio farms, and by 1850 the state stood first in the Union in wool output. A phenomenal increase of wool exports from Cleveland (see Tables 9.3, 9.4) reflected the fact that the Western Reserve led within Ohio itself, the Ohio Canal carrying more than one-third the volume of Cleveland wool exports in 1843, two-thirds in 1851.[14]

While augmenting Cleveland's export commerce in these three trades, the Mahoning Canal was in other respects a threat to Cleveland. For it opened an alternate route to the interior from eastern markets, enabling northeast and central Ohio to import merchandise by way of the Ohio River, the Mahoning, and the Ohio Canal. No longer did Cleveland enjoy unquestioned hegemony as the entry for manufactured goods, to be carried inland by the main-line canal.[15] As a competitor in this trade, the

Mahoning was especially effective because it linked Pittsburgh—
the West's leading manufacturing center and the western terminus
of the Pennsylvania Mainline—directly with Ohio's interior. The
canal carried four million pounds of ironware in its first year of
navigation, and within five years iron shipments had risen to more
than twelve million pounds, reflecting the growing trade in farm
implements, hardware, and machinery from Pittsburgh factories.
No doubt this rising trade contributed to the relative decline in
Cleveland's standing as a merchandise-import point: the volume
of Cleveland's canal clearances of merchandise to the interior
remained stable throughout the 1840's.[16]

Still another threat to Cleveland was the Muskingum Improvement, which in 1843 opened an additional improved route between the Ohio River and central Ohio. Like the Mahoning
Canal, it carried manufactured goods from Pittsburgh and New
Orleans into the interior; and by 1850 the volume of its north-
bound merchandise traffic was one-third the amount that cleared
southward from Cleveland.[17]

Such were the major changes in the Ohio Canal trade in the
1840's. Underlying these shifts in the composition and direction
of traffic, however, was one major factor that bespoke stability:
wheat and flour remained the largest component of the canal's
export commerce, with Cleveland holding its place as the major
outlet for grain. There were, nonetheless, striking year-by-year
fluctuations in Ohio's production of wheat and in the volume of
grain carried on the canal. During 1835–39, the state's wheat
output had probably doubled: her production of 16.5 million
bushels in 1839 gave her first place among the American states.
This pattern of sustained increase did not continue in the forties,
for output rose as high as 25 million bushels in 1843 but fell to
less than 15 million in 1849.[18] The fluctuations in output were
reflected in Cleveland's canal receipts, as shown in Table 9.1.
Cleveland's trade in grain reached its peak in 1846–48, when
European crop failures led to unusual overseas demand for
American flour and wheat, and the high prices of those years
stimulated output in Ohio.

But even after 1848 the volume of Cleveland's exports held
close to the peak. The continued strength of the wheat and flour
trade after 1848 was the result of two factors. First, the Wal-

TABLE 9.1

AVERAGE ANNUAL CLEVELAND WHEAT AND FLOUR
RECEIPTS, OHIO CANAL, THREE-YEAR
PERIODS 1837–51

YEARS	WHEAT (000 BU.)	FLOUR (000 BBL.)
1837–39	1098	252
1840–42	1797	179
1845–45	740	213
1846–48	1789	852
1849–51	1528	786

Source: Table 8.1.

honding and the Muskingum Improvement were both contributing grain to the canal trade from farm regions that concentrated
heavily on wheat. (See Table 8.3.) Their shipments in the late
1840's were equivalent to 10 per cent or more of Cleveland
receipts.[19] Secondly, the farm region bordering the northern and
central portions of the Ohio Canal was becoming more and more
specialized in wheat production, so that by 1849 the canal counties were among the leaders in Ohio's wheat belt. Access by canal
to the Cleveland outlet was itself an important incentive to wheat
production. For Cleveland served both the Canadian and the
New York markets; the New York City port was well served by
coastwise and foreign shipping (and also by warehouse facilities),
giving shippers of grain to that point considerable flexibility as to
choice of ultimate market; and at the major Erie Canal cities,
large-scale mills were looking to the West for supplies of unprocessed grain. Climate too was an incentive: the lake route
was relatively cool during the shipping season, diminishing the
risk of spoilage and rot.[20] On the Ohio Canal line in the Scioto
Valley—the southern third of the canal region—farmers did not
find these incentives so compelling; indeed they reduced their
production of wheat just when the canal counties farther north
were producing more. For in the Scioto Valley, the structure of
economic incentives pushed farmers increasingly into a corn-

and-livestock specialization. In neighboring counties to the west, they could buy cheap stock cattle that had been fed on open grass ranges. They fattened the cattle on their corn, and then drove the stock eastward through the mountains for sale at the Atlantic Coast cities. But no less important, they fed their corn to hogs, then packed pork and bacon on their farms and shipped the meat south on the canal to Portsmouth for re-export to New Orleans or other points in the lower Mississippi Valley. The Scioto Valley farmers responded readily to the demand of the southern market for pork, especially after their wheat crops failed in 1842, in 1843, and again in 1845. Three years of trouble with wheat proved enough for many Scioto farmers, especially when attractive alternatives were available to them.[21]

The grain trade of the Ohio Canal reflected the Scioto region's move into a corn-and-livestock pattern of production. The canal ports of southern Ohio had shipped half the wheat and flour carried on the canal in 1835 and 1837, but their share fell to only one-third in 1844 and about one-fifth in 1847.[22] Meanwhile the meat trade to Portsmouth showed an increase. Pork and bacon receipts by canal remained stable at Cleveland throughout the 1840's, but at Portsmouth arrivals of pork and bacon rose from 16 million pounds in 1839 to 70 million (more than twice Cleveland's trade) in 1844.[23] In the meat trade, climate favored the southern river route: for pork was packed during the winter, and the southern route was clear of ice earlier in the spring than the lake route.[24] Hoping to maintain Cleveland's strength in the meat trade (and to obtain the higher revenues that could be derived from long-haul shipment, from the Scioto Valley northward), Ohio canal officials reduced the tolls on meat in 1843. But these efforts failed, as is evident from Table 9.2. For as the commissioners explained it, reductions in freight rates on both the rivers and the coastwise routes from New Orleans to the East, linked with "the advantages resulting from an early shipment," which reduced risks of spoilage, "outweighed every inducement" they could offer.[25]

THE CANALS OF WESTERN OHIO

In western Ohio, the canals built after 1840 had much the same kind of influence on local economic development as the Ohio Canal had exerted two decades earlier: a large area of sparse settlement in northwest Ohio was given improved transportation for the first time, immigration into the region was given a new impetus, and the commercialization of agriculture was made possible. But there were other major changes as well in western Ohio's economy during the 1840's: manufacturing industries at Cincinnati profited from their access to the newly opened farm regions along the canal lines, Toledo emerged as a major entrepôt for interregional trade with the east, and (after 1845) the combined Wabash & Erie-Miami Extension system served as a channel for trade between the Ohio Valley and the lakes.

When the Wabash & Erie first opened in 1842, much of the region in northwest Ohio through which it passed was still nearly wilderness. What settlements there were had been planted close to the Maumee and Auglaize rivers, but elsewhere in the district travelers could pass for miles along trails and crude roads without seeing cultivated land. The advent of canal transportation stimulated commercial farm production on the pattern common in northern frontier areas—a heavy concentration on grain crops, year after year. (Indeed, while Ohio's statewide output of wheat in 1849 was smaller than in 1839, wheat production tripled in a few northwestern counties.) The canal board commented in 1848 that the former "wilderness district" on the northern part of the Miami Extension—where three years earlier "not a single barrel of flour, or a single bushel of grain, found a market beyond the immediate neighborhood"—had increased its exports of grain products to more than $400,000 annually, through the Toledo outlet. Moreover, the new canals had provided ample watersites for the first time, and both lumber and flour mills were constructed on the lines.[26]

Apart from sparking the process of development in a wilderness country, the new canals improved the terms of trade along the southern half of the Miami Extension Canal, which until 1845 had carried export products only southward to Cincinnati.[27]

Prior to the linking of the Extension Canal with the Wabash line, Cincinnati merchants had made a practice of riding express into the country when prices took a sudden upward turn at their own market to buy up grain quietly before the farmers understood what had happened. But once Toledo was made accessible, all of western Ohio's canal region could boast of competition "alive, and actively at work," between the lake and river markets, "between the various lines of public works, . . . between the different towns and cities on the same lines of public works, and finally, between the various dealers to the same towns and cities—until the Ohio farmer is obtaining for his produce the highest price the market will possibly justify."[28]

Cincinnati's canal commerce in exports did not gain much by this turn of events. Piqua (situated 100 miles on the canal above Cincinnati) and ports south of Piqua did continue to export their farm surplus to Cincinnati; but above Piqua, the newly opened region of northwestern Ohio shipped its surplus mainly northward to the Lake Erie outlet at Toledo. Thus while the tonnage of Cincinnati's canal trade had been augmented significantly in 1837, when the canal was first extended to Piqua, the subsequent extensions northward profited Toledo and did little to enhance the Queen City's role as an entrepôt of the export trade.[29]

On the other hand, Cincinnati's canal commerce in the products shipped inland did change radically in the 1840's. Thousands of new farms were built in northwestern Ohio, where the population increased by 80 per cent between 1840 and 1850. New farms created rising demand for stoves, agricultural implements and other machinery, household utensils, clothing, and finished wooden products; and as Cincinnati's manufacturers responded to this opportunity, industrial output in the Queen City rose from 18 million dollars in value to 54 million dollars during the 1840's. Iron and ironware made at Cincinnati rose fourfold in value of output, between 1841 and 1851, increasing to a value of 7 million dollars.[30] Because the city's iron products were finding a market in western Ohio and in the farm region along Indiana's Wabash Canal, the volume of the canal trade in iron goods increased rapidly during this period.[31]

At other canal towns as well, industrial production reflected the stimulus of an expanded local market. At Dayton, seed-oil mills processed about 150,000 bushels of flax seed each year in the late forties, with the oil sent to Cincinnati by canal.[32] Lumber mills and shops in Cincinnati produced shingles and furniture for the inland market. But the meat, whiskey, and flour packed at the Queen City were exported in barrels produced on farms or in cooperage shops at Piqua and other canal towns. At Dayton, Middletown, and Hamilton, paper mills exploited the multiple advantages of waterpower provided by the canals, cheap transportation, and access by canal to nearby forest areas to the north, then being cleared of timber for farming. Cincinnati provided a steady market for their product, as the city's publishing industry thrived in the 1840's.[33]

Cincinnati was also the hub of the Ohio Valley's salt and coal imports, and the canals served the city in both trades. Coal came to the Queen City from mines near Pittsburgh, from the Brier Hill district, and from the Pomeroy mines of Meigs County, on the Ohio River. Although most of the coal brought down the river to Cincinnati was used locally for household heat or steampower, each year an increasing amount was reshipped northward by canal.[34] For her salt, Cincinnati relied upon New Orleans, western Virginia, and other parts of Ohio. During 1839–44 her merchants shipped more than 20,000 bushels inland each year by canal, but it was a two-way trade: the canal also brought salt to the city. Some came from the Hocking Valley, where salt was sent overland on the National Road, and then transshipped by canal to Cincinnati. After 1845, moreover, New York salt could reach Cincinnati through Lake Erie and Toledo; and during 1846–50 the canal receipts comprised fully one-fifth of Cincinnati's salt imports for domestic use and for meatpacking.[35]

The construction of new canals also revolutionized western Ohio's trade in sugar, molasses, and coffee—"southern groceries," in commercial parlance of the day. Until 1845, from Buffalo westward to Chicago the Lake Shore region had obtained its groceries mainly by way of New York and the Erie Canal. The Ohio Valley, however, had relied mainly upon the New Orleans entryway, with some groceries reaching the upper valley through Pittsburgh. When the canal line between Cincinnati and Toledo opened, Ohio state officials perceived a valuable trade opportunity, and they determined to break down the barrier that separated Lake Shore and river markets. They cut tolls drastically on southern groceries from Cincinnati to the lake, from $4 a ton in 1845 to only $1.50 in 1850.[36] By the late forties, Toledo annually received more than a million pounds of sugar and another 600,000 pounds of molasses from Cincinnati, while the Queen City sent half again as much into central Indiana via the Wabash line. Southern groceries were high-value commodities, and it was a profitable trade: during the 1840's it became increasingly prominent in Cincinnati's total commerce.[37]

Although Cincinnati dominated the trade of western Ohio in southern groceries, coal, and her own manufactures, she met formidable competition from Toledo as an entryway for the traditional "import" commerce in eastern merchandise. After 1845 a strong rivalry emerged between the two terminal cities on the western-Ohio canal system. Moreover, the dramatic canal toll reductions after 1845 lent additional force to that rivalry. Toledo's merchandise shipments by canal increased from 4 million pounds in 1843 to 11 million in 1848 and 13 million in 1850. By the decade's end, Toledo's canal trade in merchandise exceeded Cincinnati's and even rivaled Cleveland's.[38] In valuation of total imports (shown in Table 9.5), Toledo was by 1851 the leading Ohio lake port.

THE COURSE OF URBANIZATION

Nothing revealed the commercial changes of the forties so clearly as the swift expansion of Toledo's trade. In 1840 the town was still only one of a group of hamlets huddled on the lower Maumee River. Much of its real estate was still in the hands of the original proprietors; and though the canal to Indiana's Wabash region was under construction, two other terminal basins were planned nearby, at Manhattan and Maumee City. Whether Toledo could capture the canal trade was therefore still questionable; and the national business depression cast a gloomy aspect over the whole town-building project in any event, dulling the proprietors' earlier optimism. A decade later, there was no longer any doubt that Toledo was to be the "great meeting-place and mart" for the commerce of northwest Ohio and northern Indiana.

It had become one of America's leading primary markets for grain, and the combined value of its imports and exports already was half Cincinnati's and about the same as Cleveland's.[39]

The city had outstripped itself by the speed of its growth. For most of the transformation had come in a four-year period, between 1847, when Toledo's trade was barely 8 million dollars, and 1851, when it reached 31 million dollars.[40] Toledo's population in 1850 was still only about 4,000, as compared to Cincinnati's 115,000. But in contrast with the mature urban culture of Cincinnati, with its fine architecture and fashionable social life, Toledo remained a raw boom town, with muddy streets and jerry-built hotels, "filled up with a hard set of people, money makers, speculators, loafers, and blacklegs."[41] Toledo had grown as a city in the wilderness. Unlike Cincinnati, whose commerce was based mainly on trade with a region of a hundred miles' radius, much of it densely settled for a quarter century, Toledo's immediate trade region had few settlers despite an influx of population in the 1840's. The town's commerce expanded rather because its canals had "pierced the forests and brought . . . from afar the richest harvests of the West."[42] Now came a flood of flour and wheat, corn and pork, from western Ohio—and from the Wabash Valley of Indiana, where prior to the mid-forties farmers had shipped their surplus to New Orleans by flatboat. As early as 1843 Toledo's flour exports were a third as large as Cincinnati's. In addition, Toledo shipped large quantities of unprocessed corn and wheat, which Cincinnati did not export in significant measure. Eight years later, in 1851, Toledo forwarded three times as much corn as any other port in the state, on either river or lake. It had become the largest export point for Ohio lumber, and its grain trade stood a close second, behind Cleveland's.[43]

Cincinnati's export trade did not languish as Toledo's grew. But the rate of increase was much slower, and the canal played a much smaller role. Imports of flour at Cincinnati were about 200,000 barrels in 1841, and during 1846–50 averaged 300,000 barrels annually. Of this amount, the Miami Canal brought 40 per cent; the rest came by wagon roads or by the Whitewater Canal from southern Indiana. In addition, the Queen City imported

460,000 bushels of wheat, on the average, during 1846–50; but of this amount, only about 10 per cent came by the Miami Canal route.[44] The city's local milling industry was not yet dominant in the flour export trade to the South and New Orleans, most of the flour that Cincinnati exported coming from the hinterland. The same was true of whiskey, for some 80 per cent of the whiskey exported from Cincinnati during 1846–50 was distilled outside the city; and of total whiskey imports to Cincinnati, the canal carried about one-third.[45]

But Cincinnati was still Porkopolis: its principal export commodities were meat and such by-products of meat-packing as candles, soap, and lard-oil. In the city's trade in these commodities, however, the canal played only a small part. The number of hogs slaughtered at Cincinnati increased from 190,000 in 1839 to a pre-Civil War peak of 475,000 in 1848.[46] Afterward, the annual hog pack declined, averaging less than 380,000 in 1849–51. The drop was attributed to completion of the Mad River & Lake Erie railroad route and its Cincinnati connection: farmers in southwestern Ohio now sent many of their hogs live to Sandusky for re-export via Buffalo and direct-line railroads to Boston. But even before the railroad began to cut into the trade, the canal had been of little significance: in 1850 Miami Canal receipts of pork and bacon were equivalent to less than 3 per cent of Cincinnati's pork-bacon exports.[47]

Despite the availability of both the railroad and the canal route to the lake, most of Cincinnati's export trade remained southern in orientation. As late as 1850 fully 90 per cent of Cincinnati flour exports and 85 per cent of whiskey were shipped to the South or New Orleans.[48] In summary, then, western Ohio's canals had made Toledo prominent in the grain trade, altered the pattern of commerce in southern groceries and in merchandise, and stimulated manufacturing at Cincinnati.[49] The export commerce of the Queen City itself, however, continued to look southward in 1850. Declining freight rates on the rivers and on coastwise routes from New Orleans to the east, linked with expanding demand for foodstuffs in the plantation country of the lower Mississippi Valley, meant that the southern third of Ohio—including the Miami Valley south of Piqua as well as the Scioto

TABLE 9.2

SELECTED OHIO EXPORTS FROM LAKE ERIE AND OHIO RIVER PORTS; PERCENTAGE CARRIED FROM INTERIOR BY CANAL 1843, 1851

| COMMODITY (UNIT) | EXPORTS | | | | CANAL RECEIPTS (AS PERCENTAGE OF EXPORTS) | | | |
| | 1843 | | 1851 | | 1843 | | 1851 | |
	RIVER	LAKE	RIVER	LAKE	RIVER	LAKE	RIVER	LAKE
Flour (000 bbl.)	278	705	597	1,051	72%	86%	72%	80%
Wheat (000 bu.)	6	2,121	76	6,308	(a)	46	(a)	59
Corn (000 bu.)	41	417	543	4,880	(a)	92	(a)	75
Whiskey (000 bbl.)	94	19	288	78	67	84	35	79
Live hogs (000)	negl.	negl.	0	176	(a)	0	0	0
Pork (000 bbl.)	160	43	153	60	31	37	14	73
Bulk pork and bacon (million lb.)	16	2	54	10	19	100	16	100
Wool (000 lb.)	n.a.	489	684	6,875	—	80	n.a.	33

[a] Canal receipts at river ports exceeded 100% of exports because of large consumption of corn and wheat, for domestic use and for processing, at Cincinnati. Several thousand live hogs received by canal, for slaughter at the Cincinnati plants.

Sources: Underlying data for exports by River and Lake ports in Tables 9.3, 9.4. Data for canal receipts from Board of Public Works, Annual Reports.

country—simply did not seek or need that "liberation" from the southern market which the early canal advocates had postulated as essential to growth.

CANALS IN THE EXPORT TRADE

The proportion of Ohio's exports that the canals carried to lake or river cities indicated the extent of their importance. In 1843 and 1851, as shown in Table 9.2, the canals played a greater role in the Lake Erie trade than they did in the commerce of the river cities. Indeed, of the Lake Erie exports of flour, corn, whiskey, and bulk pork, more than three-fourths arrived from the interior by canal in both 1843 and 1851. Barrel-packed pork exports by the lake did not indicate as great a reliance on canals in 1843, since exports from Sandusky were then a large part of the total. But the rise of Toledo had changed the balance by 1851, when canal receipts were equivalent to 73 per cent of pork exports by Lake Erie.

Sandusky and Milan were major export cities for wheat, and so only 46 per cent of lake exports in 1843 and 59 per cent in 1851 came by canal. Sandusky was served by the Mad River & Lake Erie Railroad, but Milan built its strength in the wheat trade without benefit of either a railroad or a long-line canal to the interior. Milan did, however, have excellent wagon roads running into the highly productive farm region of Richland and Knox counties; and its mile-long deepwater ship canal (navigable by the largest and most efficient lake vessels) also benefited the city's trade.[50] In the wool trade of Lake Erie, Cleveland was dominant. The commerce in wool expanded more swiftly than any other on the lake during 1843–51, but the proportion of exports brought to the lake by canal declined to only 33 per cent by the end of the period; even so, there was a considerable absolute increase in the tonnage of wool carried by canal.

The Ohio River trade relied less overall upon the canals than did the lake trade, principally because Cincinnati exports loomed so large in the total by the river: the city had a great volume of "autonomous" exports (the meat and other products processed

TABLE 9.3

SELECTED OHIO EXPORTS FROM LAKE ERIE AND OHIO RIVER OUTLETS, BY INDIVIDUAL PORT 1843

COMMODITY (UNIT)	OHIO RIVER PORTS			LAKE ERIE PORTS			
	CINCI	PTSMTH	HARMAR	TOLEDO	CLEVE	SANDY	HURON-MILAN
Flour (000 bbl.)	205	29	44	72	577	32	24
Wheat (000 bu.)	—	—	6	279	814	442	586
Corn (000 bu.)	8	29	4	158	228	19	12
Pork (000 bbl.)	130	30	—	9	13	13	8
Whiskey (000 bbl.)	90	4	—	1	15	2	1
Bulk bacon and pork (million lb.)	14	2	—	1	1	—	—
Wool (000 lb.)	n.a.	—	—	—	391	58	40

Sources: Exports of Cleveland, Portsmouth and Harmar treated as equivalent to canal receipts in 1843. Data from 1843 *AR* of Board of Public Works.
Exports of Cincinnati for commercial year ending Aug. 31, 1844; in *DeBow's Review*, V (1848), p. 376.
Exports of Sandusky and Milan from *Hunt's Merchants' Magazine*, IX, p. 484.
Exports of Toledo estimated as equal to Toledo and Maumee City canal receipts for 1843 plus 1841 exports, given in *Hunt's*, VI, p. 342 (the assumption being that exports of 1841, consisting of products brought mainly from Michigan, by road and railway, held constant to 1843).

TABLE 9.4

SELECTED OHIO EXPORTS FROM LAKE ERIE AND OHIO RIVER OUTLETS, BY INDIVIDUAL PORT 1851

COMMODITY (UNIT)	OHIO RIVER PORTS			LAKE ERIE PORTS			
	CINCI	PTSMTH	HARMAR	TOLEDO	CLEVE	SANDY	HURON-MILAN
Flour (ooo bbl.)	487	50	60	243	656	148	4
Wheat (ooo bu.)	—	70	6	1,640	2,142	1,922	604
Corn (ooo bu.)	102	403	38	2,775	905	712	486
Whiskey (ooo bbl.)	276	12	—	22	39	14	3
Live hogs (ooo)	—	—	—	24	80	72	(a)
Pork (ooo bbl.)	139	14	—	39	14	6	I
Bulk pork and bacon (million lb.)	49	5	—	9	I	—	—
Wool (ooo lb.)	684	—	—	596	3,939	2,340	(a)

(a) Included in Sandusky total.

Sources: Exports of Cincinnati for commercial year ending Aug. 31, 1852; in *Railroad Record*, I, 81 (Apr. 7, 1853), except bulk pork and bacon exports computed from Cincinnati Chamber of Commerce, *Annual Report*, 1882, p. 222, and flour exports from Berry, *Western Prices*, p. 168.

Exports of lake ports from U.S. Cong., Senate, *Ex. Doc.*, 32nd Cong., 1st Sess. (1852), No. 112 ("Andrews Report"), serial 622, pp. 166ff., with Toledo wool exports computed on basis of $76 per bale, consistent with standard valuation for other ports; except bulk pork and bacon exports treated as equivalent to receipts by canal.

Exports of Harmar and Portsmouth treated as equivalent to 1851 canal receipts.

locally), and it brought a large part of its farm produce from the interior by wagon road or turnpike. Even so, the canals and the Muskingum Improvement had carried out from the interior most of the flour exported by the river cities in both 1843 and 1851. But the relative importance of the canals in the pork, bulk pork and bacon, and whiskey trades declined between 1843 and 1851.[51] Moreover, Table 9.2 does not reveal the full importance of canal receipts of corn and wheat. Canal receipts far *exceeded* the volume of Ohio River exports of both wheat and corn in 1843 and 1851, because Cincinnati purchased large quantities of grain to consume locally or to process at city mills and distilleries.

Between 1843 and 1851, statewide exports of all products increased impressively: flour, 60 per cent; wheat, 333 per cent; corn, 845 per cent; whiskey, 292 per cent; barreled pork, 10 per cent; and bulk pork and bacon, 281 per cent. Wool exports rose perhaps tenfold, while shipments of live hogs rose from almost none in 1843 to 176,000 animals eight years later. But not all the aggregate increase represented higher output by Ohio's own farms. A large portion of the corn and wheat shipped from Toledo—probably two-thirds or more—was from Indiana, while Cincinnati's meat packers purchased their hogs from a wide area of Kentucky and Indiana.

The export commerce that flowed to the Lake Erie ports reflected the emergence of a specialty Wheat Belt in the northern and central trade regions of the Ohio Canal, exporting through Cleveland; in the north-central region, exporting through Sandusky and Milan; and, to a lesser extent, in the newly settled region of northwest Ohio, exporting through Toledo. By contrast, the Scioto and Miami valley regions were dedicated heavily to corn and livestock production—though the corn belt overlapped with the wheat belt in the relatively diversified Miami country— so that meat was of greater significance in the Ohio River export trade than in the Lake Erie trade.[52] About three-fourths of Ohio's wheat and flour in 1851 sought an eastern market by way of the Lake Erie ports, whereas pork and bacon flowed mainly southward to the Ohio River ports.[53] Of the river ports, only Cincinnati was a major export outlet for flour, for in the 1840's wheat yields had remained high in the Miami country; there had not been a massive shift away from wheat there, as occurred in the Scioto region. On the other hand, corn went mainly to the lake outlets, bound for the east; the south was principally a market for meat, not for unprocessed grains, and of the river towns only Portsmouth boasted any considerable trade in corn as of 1851.

There were some other products, not shown in Table 9.2, which Ohio exported in large amounts in 1851 but which were not dependent on the canal trade.[54] Foremost among these were exports of live horses, mules, and cattle. Some 50,000 to 60,000 head of cattle were driven in herds each year from farms in the Scioto Valley and west-central Ohio, to Philadelphia and other East Coast markets. Mules and horses were sold in Kentucky and other states of the South.[55] Other important export products not carried by canals were Cincinnati's beef, soap, candles, and lard, all of which were sent mainly to the New Orleans market. Like the city's meat trade, however, Cincinnati's commerce in these products was based ultimately on the corn-livestock specialty of the Miami Valley, whose attraction to settlers and overall growth had been enhanced for a quarter century by the presence of canal facilities.

POPULATION GROWTH

If the early canal promoters' dreams of liberating the Ohio Valley from dependence on the South had been shattered by basic market changes in the national economy, the overall impact of Ohio's investment in public works nevertheless remained impressive. During 1830–50 nearly every section of the state that was "improved" by canal or railway facilities shared in a pattern of vigorous population growth. Together, they grew far more quickly than the nonimproved areas. As Map 9.A indicates, nearly all the Ohio counties that increased population by 10,000 or more during 1830–50 were located within the trade regions of canals and railroads operating in 1850. Increases of 10,000 or greater were registered by every county on the Ohio Canal between Cleveland and Columbus, all the Mahoning Canal counties, and all the Muskingum Valley counties—many increasing by 20,000 or more. Similar gains were reported in all counties but one on the Miami Canal as far north as Allen County—that is, to a point about sixty miles north of Piqua, which had been the northern terminus

TABLE 9.5

VALUE OF TRADE AT MAJOR OHIO PORTS 1832–1852, SELECTED YEARS

(thousands of dollars)

YEAR	CINCINNATI		TOLEDO		CLEVELAND		SANDUSKY		MILAN-HURON	
	IMPORT	EXPORT	IMPORT	EXPORT	IMPORT	EXPORT	IMPORT	EXPORT	IMPORT	EXPORT
1832	n.a.	4,000	—	—	—	—	—	—	1,071	173
1835	n.a.	6,000	1,692	210	—	—	—	—	1,035	437
1838	—	n.a.	1,679	217	—	—	930	302	1,534	467
1840	9,142	—	1,861	341	—	4,000	1,179	694	1,520	727
1841	—	—	2,232	409	n.a.	—	1,170	970	—	—
1845	—	—	—	—	5,148	4,402	n.a.	814[a]	635[a]	825[a]
1847	51,630	55,790	4,034	4,035	4,519	9,728	7,147	—	—	—
1848	62,780	64,190	—	—	7,003	6,713	—	3,599	—	2,200
1851	—	—	23,021	7,914	22,164	12,310	16,258	6,559	1,567	1,017
1852	41,260	33,230	—	—	—	—	—	—	—	—
1853	51,230	36,270	—	—	54,971	32,707	—	—	—	—

[a] 1844 data.

Sources: (1) Cincinnati, 1832–40: Hall, *The West,* 264–90; 1847–53: White, "Wholesale Prices," 83–84.

(2) Toledo, 1835–40: 28th Cong. 1st Sess., *House Ex. Doc. No. 2* (1843), 158ff.; 1847, 1851: *Andrews Report,* 185–86.

(3) Cleveland, 1841: *Hunt's,* VI (1842), 190, and Cincinnati price multiples from Hall, *The West,* 289; 1847–51: *Andrews Report,* 169; 1845: Rose, *Cleveland,* 206; 1853: *Hunt's,* XXX (1854), 619.

(4) Sandusky, 1835–41: *House Ex. Doc., No. 2* (1843), 158ff.; 1844 (shown as 1845): *Hunt's,* XII (1844), 192; 1847: Cleveland & Pittsburgh R. R. Co., *Report . . . 1849* (Cleveland, 1850), 12; 1851: *Andrews Report,* 166ff.

(5) Milan-Huron, 1835–41, 1844, 1851: same as Sandusky; 1847: Clark, *Grain Trade,* 67.

of the canal until the mid-1840's. Lucas County, which embraced Toledo, also gained by more than 10,000. On the Hocking Valley branch of the Ohio Canal as well, only one county failed to share in this pattern.

The only two major areas well provided with canal facilities that failed to register population growth of 10,000 or more per county were the Scioto Valley, whose lag has already been explained, and the northwestern quarter of the state.[56] In the northwest region, development was already well under way, with an 80 per cent increase in population during the 1840's. But even this rate was only half that of counties with comparable resources, situated on the Wabash & Erie Canal in Indiana. The relative lag in northwest Ohio was caused mainly by the short-sighted land policies of both state and Federal governments. Congress had granted most of the land near the canal lines, on both the Miami Extension and the Wabash & Erie, to Ohio in 1828. Instead of adopting a policy to encourage actual settlement, the Ohio legislature had modeled its program on the national government's, setting no upper limit on the amount of land any individual or company might acquire. As a result, the region's best land fell into the hands of a small group of speculators in the mid-1830's, most of it at the minimum legal price of $1.25 an acre. These speculators held the land for high prices, some until well after 1850. Meanwhile, the state held the poorest land at $1.25 an acre, and the Federal lands near the canal were $2.50 an acre minimum. New settlement thus by-passed northwest Ohio, and as late as 1860 the region would still be badly under-developed.[57]

Two smaller regions, ostensibly "improved" as shown in Map 9.A, also failed to register major population gains during 1830–50. One was Columbiana County on the Sandy & Beaver Canal in eastern Ohio. A private company opened this canal for its length only in 1850, and neither then nor later did available water supply permit regular navigation. Hence it was of little importance as a transport facility.[58] The second region was on the southern part of the Mad River & Lake Erie railroad line. Although this area would undergo rapid growth in the fifties, as of 1850 the railway had been open for only two years, and its impact on settlement had not yet been felt.

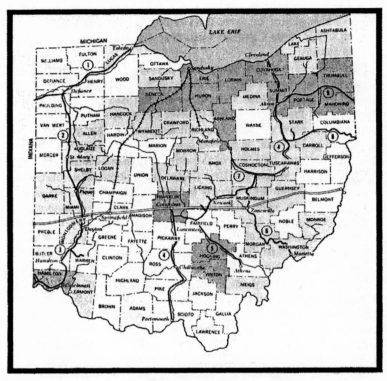

MAJOR LINES OF TRANSPORTATION OPERATING IN
OHIO, 1850; AND POPULATION GROWTH, 1830-1850

LEGEND

+++++ Railroads completed before Jan. 1, 1850

——— Canals completed before Jan. 1, 1850

=== The National Road

Counties reporting population increase of 10,000 to 19,999 during
1830-1850

Counties reporting population increase of 20,000 or more during
1830-1850

1. Wabash & Erie Canal.
2. Miami Extension Canal.
3. Miami Canal.
4. Ohio Canal.
5. Hocking Valley Canal.
6. Muskingum Improvement
7. Walhonding Canal.
8. Sandy & Beaver Canal.
9. Mahoning Canal (Pennsylvania
& Ohio Canal).

Sources: Base map from Roderick Peattie, Geography of Ohio (Geological
Survey of Ohio, Fourth Series, Bulletin 27, Columbus, 1923), p. 24.
Population data from Twelfth Census of the United States:
Population (Washington, 1901), Part I, pp. 34-35.

Map 9-A

On the Canal Lines: Navigation and Travel

The technology of canal navigation and transportation of passengers changed very little in the 1840's. Ungainly wooden freight vessels, usually about 75 feet long and 14 feet wide (close to the maximum that the Ohio canal locks would admit) and of 30 to 60 tons' capacity, passed up and down the lines, towed by horses or mules in teams of two or more. They traveled at about three miles per hour. Because their cargoes were usually in relatively small containers—sacks, boxes, barrels, or bushel baskets—rather than in bulk form, loading and unloading took considerable time. The crew typically numbered a captain and two or three deck hands, with perhaps a small boy to tend the animals that walked the towpath ahead. Horses and mules were stabled at way stations, and the boatmen changed teams every ten or fifteen miles.[59] On the Ohio Canal, no attendants were stationed to operate the locks until the late thirties, and the boat crews often battled for the right to pass through first. The men must have welcomed such excitement, for theirs was a prosaic life—as was suggested, in a sense, by their efforts to assert the more romantic, maritime aspects of their work. Some of the boats were given the names of Lake Erie schooners, such as "American Eagle" and "Bunker Hill," which dated from the earliest days of lake commerce. And a song sung on board or in the grog shops expressed the crews' identification with the traditions of seamanship: "Full o'er the waters our bonny boat glides/Nor wait we for fair winds nor stay we for tides. . . ."[60]

Not all the vessels that plied canal waters carried the produce of farms and the goods of merchants' warehouses, for there was also an active passenger traffic. Tourists usually preferred the canal to the alternative of a swaying stagecoach on rutted or muddy roads, even though overland travel was considerably faster. Emigrants carrying heavy loads of furniture and baggage, and in areas where roads were poor even local travelers, found the canals indispensable. The Ohio Canal attracted a heavy passenger traffic from the first, and was for many years the principal passenger route between Lake Erie and the Ohio Valley.[61] Many travelers transferred from the canal at Dresden, boarding the Muskingum River steamboats that ran down to Harmar or Marietta on the Ohio River. Some freight boats were built to sleep and feed as many as twenty persons, but in 1837 a packet line was established on the Ohio Canal, running boats designed exclusively for passenger service. When the Miami Extension linked with the Wabash canal to Toledo, several packet lines were opened on that route as well. In the late forties, packets ran between Cincinnati and Toledo, some 250 miles, in four days. Making no long stops to handle freight, the packet boats maintained average speeds of about four miles an hour. Some luxury packets accommodated up to sixty passengers, and boasted staterooms, dining facilities, and parlors convertible to dormitories. Fares on these vessels were about three cents per mile, including meals.[62]

The curtained windows, games of whist in the parlor, and sometimes lavish dining did not tell the whole story of travel by canal. On the boats that carried light commercial freight in their baggage holds, for instance, passengers were afforded a glimpse of the seamier side of canal life. State inspectors weighed the cargo when the boat left a terminal port, and as one canal traveler described it: "At first everything was carefully brought to the scales, but whenever the Inspector turned away, much was shoved back in the hold, and the Captain had to pay tolls on less than half the goods."[63] Breaks in the line or damage to locks often meant long delays, so that state engineers sometimes recruited passengers to help shovel or haul with the repair crews. On board, there were other annoyances. "The heat was so great that I did not sleep until near midnight," a complaining passenger recalled, "and then [I] had slept not more than an hour, when the bedbugs, by which the lower berths were infested, became so ravenous that I was compelled to get up . . . and sit on a stool the remainder of the night." When the line passed through farm country, passengers often walked along the towpath, and purchased apples and other food (or helped themselves) at farms on the way. But when the boats passed through more built-up areas, as in the region between Piqua and Dayton, "Very frequently we were annoyed," wrote the same complaining fellow, "by the stench from *distilleries & pig styes* along the canal, at some of which several hundred hogs were in pens, fattening for market, on 'pig slops.' "[64]

Passenger traffic on the Ohio Canal reached its height in 1843, when more than 20,000 people arrived by packet at Portsmouth.[65] On the Miami and Wabash & Erie canals, however, some 20,000 passengers traveled on packets as late as 1850. The Mad River & Lake Erie railroad route was already in competition with the western canals for passenger traffic in 1850, and even then the railway carried nearly twice as many people as the canals. Within a few years other railway lines deprived the waterways of all that remained of the passenger trade. By the late 1850's, the railroads of Ohio were carrying more than 2 million passengers annually, which dwarfed the volume of passenger travel by canal even at its peak.[66]

On the eve of the railroad era, then, the canals had not shattered the Ohio Valley trade's dependence upon New Orleans and the southern market. But the canals had been instrumental in attracting settlement to Ohio, had opened multiple market outlets, and had played a crucial role in the export trade of the state. At Cincinnati, which by 1850 was one of America's leading industrial cities, local manufacturing gained important advantages by virtue of canal transportation to western Ohio and Indiana. Elsewhere in the state, the canals had provided mill-sites and cheap transport of raw materials, thereby influencing the locational distribution of manufacturing activity. The new canals of the 1840's had opened up mineral resources previously little exploited, especially in the coal region of northeastern Ohio. And throughout their trade regions, the canals carried merchandise and southern groceries inland from lake and river ports, improving the terms of trade for consumers.[67]

Canal revenues failed to keep pace with the increases in traffic because the tolls charged by the state were forced down in the 1840's. Therefore, despite a doubling of the state canals' mileage, from 400 miles in 1834 to more than 800 in 1845, and a great rise in tonnage carried, net earnings on operation lagged: they averaged $221,000 during 1835–40, $295,000 during 1841–45, and $395,000 during 1846–50—less than half the annual interest on the state canal debt. After 1851, moreover, earnings were fated to decline steadily under the impact of railroad competition.[68]

Whether or not external benefits (that is, "social returns"—transport-rate savings and indirect effects enhancing private income in the canal regions) exceeded the cost of construction (plus debt-service costs beyond what toll revenues covered), is a much more complex issue.[69] Taking into account the sizable decline in rates during the 1840's, a decline that generated private savings for shippers and consumers, and also the increase in traffic volume, it appears to be a reasonable estimate that the canals did generate social savings before 1851 that exceeded amortization costs. Of course, had construction been more efficient in 1836–45 and had post-1838 bond sales been effected at full (par) prices, higher social savings would have accrued from the canal investment. With benefit of hindsight, one may postulate, too, that it would have been better to await the advent of railroads instead of undertaking so massive an expanded canal program in those years. But as a matter of historical fact, the men of that era chose to build canals; and their great error—measured in abstract terms of investment costs and economic effects—may have been to permit unbridled private railroad development in the ensuing period.

What costs and gains might have been, and indeed whether railroad investment would have been attracted so quickly if the canals had been lacking, are speculative questions difficult to treat with any certainty. One must perhaps rest content with noting the irony that the record of canal traffic, and also local developmental patterns, indicate that from 1825 to 1851 the canals aided growth in Ohio sufficiently to justify the enormous railway investment that poured into the state in the fifties.[70]

NOTES

1. See George Rogers Taylor, *The Transportation Revolution, 1815–1860* (New York, 1951), 102 *et passim,* for the standard

interpretation, stressing the importance of the two changes, from overland to water transportation, and then from water to railroad in the fifties. An important caveat to the notion that genuine integration of national transport had occurred even by 1860 is provided by Albert Fishlow, *American Railroads and the Transformation of the Antebellum Economy* (Cambridge, 1965), 287–98. In their excellent discussion of transport in the western economy, 1830–1850, in *Boston Capitalists and Western Railroads* (Cambridge, 1967), 63–80, Arthur M. Johnson and Barry E. Supple periodize transport change in terms of waves of promotion and construction, but do not distinguish the 1840's on the basis proposed in this chapter.

2. On the Mad River & Lake Erie and its connection with the Little Miami to link Sandusky with Cincinnati in 1848, see Chap. 11, below.

3. Carter Goodrich, *Government Promotion of American Canals and Railroads* (New York, 1960), 138ff.

4. Some 600 vessels of 200,000 tons were built during 1836–42 on the western rivers—equal in tonnage to all the steamers built in the west prior to 1836. And during seven years beginning in 1844, new steamboat construction in the west amounted to at least 20,000 tons each year. (Thomas S. Berry, *Western Prices before 1861* [Cambridge, 1843], 557). I treat the vigor of flatboat commerce in the 1840's, in "The Ohio-Mississippi Flatboat Trade: Some Reconsiderations," to appear in a Cornell University Press *festschrift* volume for Paul W. Gates. Remarks on the general rate decline of the 1840's are in *Hunt's Merchants' Magazine*, XI (1844), 77, 172.

5. Rates are for the April–June season. (Berry, *Western Prices*, 58–59, 559–61.)

6. Thus on the Erie Canal, Buffalo-to-Albany rates on flour fell from $1.00 in 1832 to 71¢ in 1841, to 60¢ in 1844 and 56¢ in 1849. On Pennsylvania's Mainline System, Philadelphia-to-Pittsburgh charges on merchandise declined from 6.5¢ per ton-mile in 1833, to 4.5¢ in 1849. Hardware charges fell from 10.5¢ in 1837 to 3.5¢ in 1849. Eastbound flour paid 3.8¢ per ton-mile in 1837 and 1.8¢ in 1849. Computations for Erie Canal from U. S. Secretary of the Treasury, *Statistics of the Foreign and Domestic Commerce of the U. S.* (Washington, 1864), 179; and (on 1832 only) John G. Clark, *Grain Trade in the Old Northwest* (Urbana, 1966), 66. Pennsylvania rates are from Pittsburgh Transportation line charges, 1838, MS., Charles

Ellet Papers, University of Michigan Transportation Library; and Clarence D. Stephenson, *Pennsylvania Canal: Indiana and Westmoreland Counties* (Marion Center, Pa., 1961), 18, 46. On Ohio rates, see Chap. 10, below. On the Welland Canal toll cuts, cf. *Toledo Blade*, June 1, 1846.

7. Isaac Lippincott, "Internal Trade of the United States, 1700–1860," *Washington University Studies*, IV (Oct. 1916), 184. Buffalo-Toledo merchandise charges were 44¢ per hundred pounds by steamer in 1838 and 15¢ in 1845. (Buffalo list of forwarders' rates, 1838, Ellet Papers; Palmer, Brown & Co. to Board of Public Works, June 28, 1845, BPW Papers.)

8. See, for instance, Harvey H. Segal in *Canals and American Economic Development*, ed. Carter Goodrich (New York, 1962), 243.

9. J. B. D. DeBow, *Industrial Resources and Statistics of Southern and Western States* (New Orleans, 1852–53), 348. By the late 1840's, moreover, four blast furnaces were in operation in the Mahoning region, the beginning of the Youngstown iron and steel industry. (Francis P. Weisenburger, *Passing of the Frontier* [Columbus, 1941], 79.)

10. Annual data on coal receipts given in Table 8.1, above.

11. Cleveland coal exports in 1851 were 82,000 tons, a tenfold increase from 1847.

12. Robert L. Jones, "The Dairy Industry in Ohio," *OHQ*, LVI (Jan. 1947), 51–52.

13. Cleveland butter arrivals were between 500,000 and 700,000 pounds in the late 1830's, but during 1841–46 receipts were 1,200,000 pounds or more each year. Cheese shipments on the Mahoning Canal were 9 million pounds in 1851. (Cleveland data from BPW, *Annual Reports*, and Mahoning Canal data from Pennsylvania & Ohio Canal Co., *Annual Reports*, published each year in Ohio's state *Executive Documents*.)

14. The Ohio sheep industry is treated in Weisenburger, *Passing of Frontier*, 71; distribution of sheep in map, *ibid.*, 72. See also Steven L. Stover, "Early Sheep Husbandry in Ohio," *Agricultural History*, XXXVI (1962), 101–7.

15. To say "unquestioned" may be something of an exaggeration, since a state road operating between Wellsville and Massillon carried heavy quantities of merchandise from the Ohio River to Massillon (three million pounds in 1847) and Canton (four million pounds in 1847). How great the volume of overland trade from the river eastward may have been prior to 1847 is

a matter of speculation; but probably until the state road was opened in 1845 there was relatively little. (Data from Dwight James to BPW, MS. report dated Feb. 17, 1848, BPW Papers.)

16. See Appendix 3, on Cleveland; also Catherine E. Reiser, *Pittsburgh's Commercial Development, 1800–1850* (Harrisburg, 1951), 48, 115–22, on the Mahoning Canal. Pittsburgh's competitive position as a wholesale supplier of eastern and imported goods was improved by the option its merchants enjoyed in shipping from the east either *via* New Orleans or *via* the Pennsylvania Mainline. See Richard Lowitt, *A Merchant Prince of the 19th Century: William E. Dodge* (New York, 1954), 38–39. For the impact of Sandusky's first railroads on its position in the Ohio import trade, see Table 9.5.

17. Merchandise imports on the Improvement rose from 0.7 million pounds in 1843 to over 3 million in 1850. (Data from BPW, *AR*, 1843, 1850.) Cleveland's import trade in salt was also vitally affected by construction of the Hocking Canal and the Muskingum Improvement, discussed below in Chap. 10.

18. U. S. Patent Office, *AR*, 1843; Clark, *Grain Trade*, 30; *8th Census of the U. S.: Agriculture* (1860), xxxi *et seq.*

19. About half the wheat and flour shipped on the Muskingum Improvement was sent southward to the Harmar outlet for re-export via the river, some going to Pittsburgh. (BPW, *AR*, 1841–51.) On the fluctuations in foreign demand for grain, see Clark, *Grain Trade*, 172ff.

20. Thomas D. Odle, "Grain Trade of the Great Lakes," *Inland Seas*, XI–XII (1951, 1952), *passim*. New York's role in the western trade is discussed more generally in Robert G. Albion, *The Rise of New York Port* (New York, 1939).

21. BPW, *10th AR*, in *Executive Docs.*, 1847, No. 31, pp. 390–91; *7th AR* (1844), 7; Clark, *Grain Trade*, 132–33.

22. Computed from data in BPW, *7th AR* (1844); Table 9.5; and Clark, *Grain Trade*, 133 n. 21.

23. BPW, *7th AR*. Includes bulk meats.

24. See Chap. 8, n. 20, *supra*, regarding a controversy as to the perpetuation of southern demand. As late as 1860 Census officials stated that two thirds of Cincinnati's downriver exports were sold at ports above New Orleans. (*8th Census of U. S.: Agriculture*, clviii.)

25. BPW, *7th AR* (1844), 7–8. See also A. L. Kohlmeier, *The Old Northwest* (Bloomington, 1938), 35, 51ff.

26. *Executive Docs.*, 1848, No. 19, p. 106; *ibid.*, 1849, No. 11,

pp. 142–43. Output of wheat in an eleven-county area of north-west Ohio was 264,000 bushels in 1839 and 668,000 in 1849. (U. S. Census data, for Allen, Auglaize, Defiance, Fulton, Henry, Mercer, Paulding, Putnam, Van Wert, Williams, and Lucas counties.)

27. The National Road carried an unknown quantity of farm products, probably mainly flour and whiskey—enough to force the BPW to raise tolls to protect the canal trade in 1844. Because National Road traffic was charged by vehicle capacity and not actual cargo, these data are shadowy at best. (See BPW, *8th AR* [1845], 19.)

28. Lima (Ohio) *Reporter*, June 22, 1847. The telegraph lines built in the late 1840's would have ended the Cincinnati merchants' "quiet buying" in any event.

29. See Tables 8.4, 8.5, *supra*. Piqua as a dividing line is discussed in Kohlmeier, *The Old Northwest*, 88, 93.

30. Charles Cist, *Sketches and Statistics of Cincinnati in 1859* (n.p., 1859), 341–44; Berry, *Western Prices*, 254.

31. By the mid-1840's iron goods were third in volume among commodities carried inland by the Miami Canal. Between 1843 and 1850, the tonnage of iron and ironware shipped by canal from Cincinnati rose nearly fivefold; it was nearly seven million pounds in 1851. (BPW, *AR*, 1841–1851; see also Berry, *Western Prices*, 252ff.)

32. U. S. Patent Office, *AR*, 1847, p. 164; Sherry O. Hessler, "Patterns of Transport and Urban Growth in the Miami Valley, Ohio" (M.A. thesis, Johns Hopkins, 1961), 147.

33. Based on statistics of the trade in annual reports of BPW. Publishing output in 1851 was $1.3 million, given in Cist, *Cincinnati in 1859*, 341–44; see also Weisenburger, *Passing of the Frontier*, 82; and Isaac Lippincott, *A History of Manufactures in the Ohio Valley* (New York, 1914), 121.

34. Forty thousand bushels annually in the mid-forties, and 170,000 bushels in 1850. *Annual Statement of the Trade and Commerce of Cincinnati*, 1859 (Cincinnati, 1859), 17 (hereafter cited *ASTC*); Charles H. Ambler, *History of Transportation in the Ohio Valley* (Glendale, 1932), 299.

35. CC, *15th AR* (1839), 9; BPW, *8th AR* (1844), 17. Average annual arrivals by canal were about 20,000 barrels during 1846–50. (See also Berry, *Western Prices*, 296, 320.)

36. From 1840 to 1845, the Mahoning Canal also carried southern

groceries inland from Pittsburgh to northern Ohio. But rates
on the Ohio Canal main line were such that little penetrated
the market past the Mahoning's junction at Akron. By contrast,
the state controlled rates on the entire canal line between Cincinnati and Akron, and the prospect of a 250-mile-long haul,
with the revenues it produced for the state, was an inducement to cut tolls. Toll charges are from BPW Minutes. Vol.
IV–A, pp. 9ff., 415ff. The groceries trade is discussed in Berry,
Western Prices, 335ff.; U. S. Cong., Senate, 32nd Cong., 1st
Sess., *Exec. Doc.* No. 112 (*"Andrews Report"*), 705–6; BPW,
13th AR (1850), 16–17; also D. Webb to E. S. Hamlin, March
25, 1850, BPW Papers; and petition, Cincinnati chamber of commerce June 20, 1845, *ibid.*

37. By 1850 the Mahoning Canal too was carrying 2 million pounds
of sugar and molasses inland from the river; the Muskingum
Improvement brought 2.5 million pounds. (See *Andrews Report*, 706; and P. & O. Canal Co., *AR* for 1851.)

38. Trade data from BPW, *AR*, 1843, 1850; on declining freight
rates, cf. text, *supra*, at n. 6. Toledo's imports from the lake
in 1851 were valued at 23 million dollars; Cleveland's at 22
million dollars; Cincinnati's 41 million dollars. (*Andrews Report*, 166ff., *ASTC*, 1856, p. 4.)

39. The quotation is from *Andrews Report*, 85. Data on export
values from *ibid.*, 166ff.; *ASTC*, 1856, p. 4.

40. *Ibid.* In 1840 Toledo's trade was about 2 million dollars, consisting almost entirely of commerce with southern Michigan.
(28th Cong., 1st Sess., *House Ex. Doc.* No. 2 [1843], 158ff.)

41. "Diary of Charles Peabody," *Bulletin of the HPSO*, XI (Oct.
1953), 275. Also, cf. Tables 9.3, 9.4. On Cincinnati, see Weisenburger, *Passing of Frontier*, 29–30.

42. *Toledo Blade*, quoted by Odle, "American Grain Trade," *Inland Seas*, VIII, 24–25.

43. See Chap. 10, *infra*, on 1846 toll reductions and their impact;
also Tables 9.3, 9.4.

44. Berry, *Western Prices*, 165–66; Appendix 3, Table 3; BPW
data on canal trade from *Annual Reports*, taken as percentage
of imports given in Berry; 1841 flour trade from James Hall,
The West, Its Commerce and Navigation (Cincinnati, 1848),
289; see also Charles B. Kuhlmann, *Development of the Flour-
Milling Industry* (Boston, 1929), 81–83. There may have been
some truth, too, in the *Toledo Blade's* claim that much of the

flour that went south on the canal to Cincinnati, instead of seeking an outlet at Toledo, was of inferior quality, marketable in the South or New Orleans but not good enough "to sell well at this place or any Eastern market." (*Blade*, Aug. 22, 1845.)

45. Canal trade from BPW reports; exports from Berry, *Western Prices*, 91, 166; and *ASTC*, 1855, p. 29.

46. Ohio Bd. of Agriculture, *13th AR* (1858), p. 645. Data therein suggests that in 1848 Cincinnati probably packed 80 per cent of all hogs slaughtered in urban centers in the West.

47. Canal receipts were 9 million pounds, whereas total exports were over 380 million. (Computed from data in BPW reports and in *ASTC*.) See also the excellent discussion in Charles T. Leavitt, "Some Economic Aspects of the Western Meat-packing Industry," *Journal of Business*, IV (Jan. 1931), 68ff. On livestock shipped to Cincinnati, see Sherry O. Hessler, "The Great Disturbing Cause and the Decline of the Queen City," *Bulletin of the HPSO*, XX (July 1962), 183.

48. On the flour trade, see Berry, *Western Prices*, 168; William Switzler, *Commerce of the Mississippi and Ohio Rivers* (Washington, 1888), 286; and BPW trade data. On whiskey, Berry, *Western Prices*, 166; *ASTC*, 1855, 29, and BPW trade data. The Mad River & Lake Erie Railroad carried only 7,226 barrels of pork north to Sandusky in 1849, and its pork trade fell steadily until 1853. (From annual reports of the Company.)

49. Cincinnati shipments comprised nearly one-fifth of westbound merchandise freight carried on the Wabash & Erie line into Indiana in 1851. (W. J. Benton, *The Wabash Trade Route* Baltimore, [1903], 106n.)

50. See *Andrews Report*, 175–76, on Milan; and Chaps. 4–5, *supra*, on the Milan deepwater canal and the state's aid in its construction.

51. In some years Cincinnati shipped flour and meat northward by canal to Toledo for re-export; probably 4–10 per cent of flour exports in 1846–50, at most the same proportion of barreled meat, and perhaps as much as 15 per cent of bulk-meat products. (Berry, *Western Prices*, 90–91; *Andrews Report*, 711; on frequent repairs, impeding commerce between the termini, on the Cincinnati-Toledo line, see BPW report in *Executive Docs.*, 1847, No. 31, pp. 398–400.)

52. The emergence of the Ohio wheat and corn belts is analyzed in Clark, *Grain Trade*, 131ff.; see also J. E. Spencer and R. J.

Horvath, "How Does an Agricultural Region Originate?" *Annals of the American Association of Geographers*, LIII (March 1963), 78ff.; and Weisenburger, *Passing of Frontier*, 58–64 and maps.

53. *Andrews Report*, 708; Tables 9.1, 9.3.

54. Israel D. Andrews (*ibid.*, 709) estimated the produce exported from Ohio as follows: flour and wheat (flour equivalent), 3 million barrels; corn, 5 million bushels; wool, 7 million pounds; pork, 300,000 barrels (equivalent); lard, 100,000 barrels; beef, 50,000 barrels (of which Cincinnati exported about half); cheese, 10 million pounds; butter, 8 million pounds; candles, 1.5 million pounds; soap, 300,000 pounds; and whiskey, 300,000 barrels.

55. Number of cattle based on drives for 1852, reported by *Railroad Record*, I (1853), 82. On exports of Ohio horses (perhaps 16,000 head in 1852) and mules (no export statistics available), see Robert L. Jones, "The Horse and Mule Industry in Ohio to 1865," *Mississippi Valley Hist. Rev.*, XXXIII (June 1946), 74, 86–87.

56. On the Scioto Valley's retardation, see Chap. 8, *supra*.

57. H. Scheiber, "State Policy and the Public Domain: the Ohio Canal Lands," *Journal of Economic History*, XXV (March 1965), 86–113, treats the intersecting effects of transport improvement and land-disposal problems in northwest Ohio.

58. The dismal record of a canal project that failed is chronicled in R. Max Gard and W. Vodrey, Jr., *The Sandy and Beaver Canal* (East Liverpool, Ohio, 1952).

59. In 1831, the Ohio Canal had 45 boats running; in 1850, the Miami Canal had 400, with probably at least as many on the Ohio Canal. (Cleveland *Herald*, Oct. 13, 1831; Sherry O. Hessler, "Patterns of Transportation and Urban Growth in the Miami Valley," pp. 53–54.) In 1878, when an active canal trade in coal and other heavy commodities made the canals' commerce roughly comparable to the late fifties, there were 300 boats on the Ohio Canal; 66 on the Hocking Canal; and 149 on the Miami-Wabash line, employing more than two thousand hands in all. Some 800 horses and mules were maintained, for 170 boats, on the northern line of the Ohio Canal. (Commissioner of Statistics, *AR, 1878*, 206–7.) Excellent introductions to canal technology and passenger transportation in Ohio are in Randolph C. Downes, *The History of Lake Shore*

Ohio (3 vols., New York, 1952), Vol. I; and *The Wabash-Erie Canal* (Ft. Wayne, Ind., Public Library, n. d.).

60. Canal song printed in W. C. Moore, "Early Ohio Internal Improvements," *The Numismatist*, XXXI (1918), 340. Boat names in reports of arrivals, Cleveland *Herald*, 1842, *passim*.

61. In 1842 the Ohio Canal reported nearly 50,000 passenger arrivals and 3,782,424 miles traveled; on the Miami Canal between Cincinnati and Dayton, 10,708 passengers traveled 431,181 miles; on the Muskingum Improvement, 6,799 passengers traveled 197,144 miles; and on the Wabash & Erie, 1,046 passengers traveled 30,123 miles. (BPW, *7th AR* [1844].)

62. The Cleveland-Portsmouth line discontinued service in 1844. (BPW, *7th AR*, p. 8; also, on its founding, Cleveland *Herald*, March 2, 1837.) The Miami-Wabash canal packets are fully described in *The Wabash-Erie Canal*, not pag.

63. "Swiss Emigrants Seek Home in America," ed. Leo G. Titus, *Bulletin of the HPSO*, XIV (July 1956), 172.

64. MS. diary of Samuel Williams, Vol. IV, pp. 856–57. Vol. V, pp. 1021–22 (1846, 1849), OHS; on recruiting travelers to repair a line, see MS. diary (1832) of Moses Quinby, Cornell University Library. The vicissitudes of canal travel are well described in Doris M. Reed, ed., "Journal of James D. Maxwell," *Indiana Mag. of Hist.*, XLVI (March 1950), 75–76; and "The Canal Journey of Malvina Badeau," Allen County (Ohio) Historical Society, *Reporter*, XV (June 1959), 15–19.

65. Of Ohio Canal ports, only Harmar, on the Muskingum Improvement, where regular steamer service attracted passengers to the line, reported an increase after 1843.

66. Mad River & Lake Erie R.R. Co., *AR, 1851* (Sandusky, 1851); Ohio Commissioner of Statistics, *4th AR* (1860), 33.

67. For price indices and terms of trade at Cincinnati, cf. Berry, *Western Prices*, 120.

68. Computed from H. P. McClelland and C. C. Huntington, *The Ohio Canals* (Columbus, 1905), Appendix F.

69. The problem of computing indirect returns is discussed more fully in Appendix 4, below.

70. See Albert Fishlow, *American Railroads and the Transformation of the Ante-bellum Economy* (Cambridge, 1965), 171ff.

CHAPTER 10

State Rate-Making and Market Allocation

1827-1851

THE early canal advocates had been thoroughgoing mercantilists both in their objectives and in their advocacy of an active
role for the state in the economy. They had sought to persuade
the legislature and the public that Ohio was a commonwealth
whose *collective* growth and prosperity would ultimately benefit
all social classes and all regions, even though the canals would
initially yield special benefits to the localities in their trade region.
If they did not exactly regard their commonwealth as one pursuing its destiny in a universe of hostile states (as the eighteenth-
century mercantilists had viewed their nations), they did believe
that if Ohio failed to construct canals, then other western states
would do so; thereby rival states would capture investment and
new settlement that might otherwise be attracted to Ohio.[1]

In light of their mercantilist persuasion, it was ironic that the
early promoters failed to foresee—or at least, failed to discuss
explicitly—the full extent of new powers that the canals would
give the state government for regulating private economic activity.
For as events of the post-construction period proved, the canals
permitted the state to exercise the crucial rate-making power, by
which it could manipulate the terms of trade in many of the
regions served by the new waterways. Because the canals enjoyed
an effective transport monopoly in many regions of Ohio, the
government did not terminate its interventionist economic role
after it had built new lines of transport: control of canal tolls

permitted state officials to engage in day-to-day control of the market, with important ramifications for local patterns of economic development. At least in theory, for instance, they might permit all goods to move on the canals free of toll charges, thereby maximizing the volume of commerce. Alternatively, they might discriminate in favor of one kind of producer (say flour millers) over another (wheat growers); or one region over another; or one trade outlet (for example, the lake ports or else the river cities) over the other.

Of course, there were practical constraints on the exercise of such options. The need to obtain revenues was foremost, for the interest and principal on the canal debt had to be paid and exclusive reliance on general taxation for this purpose was politically unacceptable. Moreover, no important regional or functional interest group would suffer passively any discrimination against itself. Nor were ideological precepts irrelevant, for arbitrary use of the rate-making power to discriminate against a sizable interest group would have been hard to square with the egalitarian doctrine of the day. Nonetheless the canal officials enjoyed wide discretion under the 1825 canal law and subsequent statutes, which empowered them to set rates according to virtually any criteria they chose—subject always to reversal by juridical decrees, legislative mandate, or pressure-group action as part of the informal political process.[2] And throughout the canal period, the canal commission and its successor agencies did in fact exercise their rate-making power to manipulate prices and markets in the state.

The canal officials understood full well that their rate-making power was "a subject of much delicacy and responsibility," requiring a careful balance of conflicting purposes and interests. In one of their early public reports, they explained that they set toll schedules "with a view to encouraging exportation; to develop the various resources of the country; to encourage a transsit through our canals; to equalize, as far as practicable, the benefits of navigation between various portions of our State; to raise a revenue for defraying the interest on the capital invested; and at the same time not to discourage the transportation of articles of great weight and small value [nor] to drive property from the canals [into] other channels."[3] These objectives characterized the rate-making decisions of the Ohio canal board through the period 1827–51. But at various times one or another of these goals took precedence. The subordination of one goal to another at particular times was the result of two factors: first, the changing economic context in which the canals operated, especially the prevailing price levels and the intensity of competition for the canals' trade; and second, the differing policy views of the board's changing membership.

From the time the first toll schedule was established in 1827, the canal authorities consistently discriminated in favor of long-haul shipments. The 1827 schedule provided for one rate on freight carried up to 100 miles, and a lower rate for each mile in excess of 100.[4] When the Ohio Canal was opened for its full length, the board introduced still another incentive for long-haul shipment: it concluded an interstate agreement with New York canal authorities giving a 25 per cent toll rebate on all through freight shipped on the Erie and Ohio canals from Albany to Portsmouth. The forwarding companies attempted to capture the additional profit for themselves, however, by increasing their freight charges by an amount almost equivalent to the toll reduction. The Ohio canal board responded with an even bolder use of the rate-making power by imposing a schedule of maximum allowable rate charges, including tolls and commissions. Any forwarder who exceeded such charges would be required to pay double canal tolls as penalty.[5] The forwarders, outraged by this, accused the board of "dictatorial" tactics. To avoid the penalty, moreover, many of them issued false bills of lading that conformed to the prescribed charges and then collected a premium in cash upon delivery. But the Ohio commissioners stood firm, asserting their intent to enforce their regulations. Whether because of the commission's intransigence, or because the Erie Canal was beginning to meet stiff competition in the Ohio Valley market from Philadelphia and Baltimore merchants who used the newly opened Pennsylvania Mainline route to the West, the New York forwarders finally capitulated and reduced their charges to the prescribed levels.[6] In ensuing years, long-haul discrimination remained a constant feature of tolls on nearly all commodities in the canal trade.

While long-haul preferences were maintained, both general toll levels and tolls on specific commodities shifted significantly from year to year, as the canal board attempted to maximize revenues and the volume of traffic. To encourage the trade in iron, southern groceries, and tobacco, for instance, the commissioners reduced tolls on these items in 1832. But in 1837 they increased tolls on all products, across the board, by 20 per cent, in response to rising prices in the national market during a boom period. A year later, after the 1837 panic had broken the upward price trend, the board rescinded the increase on merchandise entering the state via Cleveland and on southern groceries and cotton entering the state via Portsmouth.[7]

More thoroughgoing adjustments of tolls proved necessary after 1840, when the Transportation Revolution's second phase altered the competitive conditions under which the canals operated. The first major change was on the Ohio Canal, whose merchandise import trade from Cleveland to Portsmouth was adversely affected by lower river-steamboat rates and resultant competition from the New Orleans entryway. The board cut tolls radically in 1841 on Cleveland merchandise shipped to Portsmouth, from the old maximum of $9.16 per ton to $6.88. Because farmers in the interior were finding it attractive to ship southward to the river, for re-export to either New Orleans or Pittsburgh, the board also instituted reduced tolls for pork, flour, and whiskey, charging a maximum of $3.12 per ton for any distance—reduced from an effective $4.30 maximum under the former schedules.[8] Also pertinent in the decision to reduce tolls was the need to adjust to the sharp decline of agricultural prices during the 1839 depression. Rather than disadvantage Ohio farmers in eastern markets by charging high tolls, the board reduced its charges.[9]

The competitive situation on the Ohio Canal was further complicated by completion of the Mahoning line in 1840. Traffic from this branch canal greatly augmented the trade (and the revenues) of the main line by carrying coal, dairy products, and Pittsburgh manufactures to Akron for reshipment to Cleveland. But in 1845 this entire trade was threatened by construction of the Erie Extension Canal between the Mahoning's line near the Ohio River and Erie, Pennsylvania. The Erie Extension was a private company, and its principal stockholders were merchants at the City of Erie who were less concerned with direct profits from the canal than with building up their port's trade. These men were also steamboat owners, and they were interested as well in obtaining cheap coal for the vessels they operated on Lake Erie. Therefore the Erie Extension adopted tolls much lower than those on the Mahoning Canal, threatening to capture a large part of the Mahoning's traffic to the lake.[10] In order to compete, the officials of the Mahoning line cut their tolls by one-third to one-half. To cooperate with them and protect the Cleveland trade, Ohio's state authorities then reduced Ohio Canal tolls on goods carried on the Mahoning line destined for Cleveland.[11]

Because both the Mahoning Canal and the Erie Extension offered direct and low-cost transportation between Lake Erie and the Ohio Valley, the volume of eastern merchandise shipped through from Cleveland to Portsmouth dwindled in the mid-forties, "until there was scarcely any thing transported on this canal, except the products of the State, or merchandise designed for home consumption."[12] But completion of the new canal route between Cincinnati and Toledo in 1845 offered the state a fresh opportunity to capture the lake-to-river trade. The new route was more than fifty miles shorter than the Cleveland-Portsmouth line; unlike the Cleveland-Muskingum Improvement or the Mahoning routes, it required no transshipment between the lakes market and Cincinnati; and, by way of the Wabash & Erie, it offered a direct entryway to the Indiana market as well. And so the Ohio canal board cut tolls once again in 1845, reducing the charge on through merchandise between Toledo and Cincinnati to $6 per ton, and cutting the maximum toll on flour, wheat, and pork to $2 per ton for any distance. In 1846 tolls on flour, corn, and pork from the Wabash region of Indiana, bound for Toledo, were also reduced sharply.[13]

A continuing decline in Ohio River steamer charges, the completion of the Illinois & Michigan Canal in 1848, and toll reductions on the Pennsylvania State Mainline designed to attract

southern Ohio's exports to Pittsburgh and Philadelphia, all forced
the Ohio canal board to reconsider rates of toll once again. In
1850 the board therefore reduced its charges on flour to $1.50
per ton maximum on the Miami-Wabash line and $2.50 on the
Ohio Canal system; pork, to $1.50 on the western canals and
$2.50 on the Ohio Canal; and wheat, to $2 on the western
lines and $2.50 on the Ohio Canal.[14] These drastic reductions
did not signify that the Ohio canal board had subordinated revenue considerations. Rather, the reductions were selective: on
routes where the canals still enjoyed a near monopoly position,
the canal board maintained high rates of toll. The 1850 toll cuts
were a pragmatic response to new competition, and nothing
more.[15]

More generally, the canal board's various decisions to adjust
tolls were not merely responses to new competition based upon
a cold economic calculus for maximizing traffic or revenues: for
during this period special interest groups in the state pressed the
board for toll changes that would benefit them, often at the
expense of other groups. Among the most articulate were the
merchants and forwarders, who consistently demanded lower
tolls. The forwarders were the men engaged in the transportation
business only, including small-scale operators of one or two
boats as well as the owners of large fleets, maintaining regular
through-freight arrangements with Erie Canal, Pennsylvania
Mainline, and river boat lines. The merchants were the men
who performed the critical middleman functions in Ohio's far-
flung trade with the East and overseas markets: they owned
warehouse facilities, extended credit to millers and farmers, and
—through arrangements with "correspondent" houses in the
coastal cities—arranged for the sale of Ohio produce, and for
the purchase and shipment of merchandise from the seaboard to
Ohio retail stores. The pressure from these groups was for competitive toll schedules that would maximize the volume of trade
and thereby increase their business volume and profits. In a
sense, they spoke not only for farmers who sought low rates to
the East and South, but also for Ohio consumers who relied on
outside sources for manufactured goods.[16]

The Ohio merchant's dominant role in local and state politics in the 1830's and 1840's made him a powerful spokesman: the merchants were the wealthiest men in the cities; and even in rural regions they took the lead in representing local or regional interests in the state political arena. The canal board explicitly recognized their influence, asserting in 1850 that "Forwarders and consumers are always interested in low tolls, and are ever anxious for their reduction. For this reason it is difficult to raise the tolls, and they should therefore be reduced with caution."[17] When all the leading commission merchants of Toledo petitioned for lower canal tolls in 1848 and declaimed against the Mad River & Lake Erie Railroad, then threatening to capture for Sandusky all their merchandise trade with Cincinnati, and when they reminded the canal board "of the superior advantages possessed by wealthy corporations in efforts of this kind over the desultory attempts of individual enterprise," their voices commanded attention. Nor was their interest always antagonistic to the state's. Taking a position for reduced tolls not only bespoke the prospect of lower consumer prices and higher commercial profits; it also expressed a "fear that the Canal which was completed at so great cost to the State [might] become a 'desolate waste.' "[18] The Cincinnati Chamber of Commerce did not exaggerate when it petitioned that "a liberal reduction, one that will at all times hold out inducement to the shipper to avail himself of the Ohio routes, will be attended with the happiest results, not alone to the carrier and merchant, but to the state as a wise revenue measure."[19] For in the mid-forties Cincinnati found itself burdened with serious disadvantages, as the Miami Canal system met new competition in the merchandise trade from the Pennsylvania Mainline, the Erie Extension, and the Mahoning Canal routes. And as subsequent events proved, the Miami Extension Canal did indeed produce larger revenues for the state after toll charges between Cincinnati and Toledo were brought down to a competitive level.

The merchant class of the state was not a monolithic group with a single interest. As the Cincinnati chamber's position revealed, each local center struggled for an advantage over its rivals by demanding lower tolls on the canal that served it. But the net effect of rival pressures was to intensify the demand for

reduced charges on all routes. When one local interest did ex-
tract concessions from the board, it merely strengthened the
hand of its rivals elsewhere, who demanded "that the policy of
Ohio should place [them] in fair competition with other important points."[20] So long as the canals remained the principal channels of import and export, as they did until the railroad period,
the state government continued to enjoy the power to determine
what rate structure assured "fair competition."

Not all the interest-group pressure was for lower tolls. From
another quarter, there were demands for discriminatory toll
policies that would *increase* consumer prices and effectively shut
off certain avenues of trade. Such demands originated principally
with Ohio's manufacturers: these men advocated the manipulation of tolls so that their "domestic" (Ohio) products would be
charged less than competing out-of-state manufactures. The canal
board had asserted that one of its prime objectives was "to develop the various resources of the country," and encouraging
local manufacturing became an important element of this policy.
In the 1829 toll schedule, the board charged 1½ and 2 cents per
ton-mile on Ohio-made paper, glass, processed tobacco, iron
castings, nails, cordage, woolens, and cottons. On identical goods
manufactured in other states and seeking a market in Ohio, the
charges were twice as high. Gradually the discriminatory list was
extended. By 1848 it included preferential tolls for Ohio manufactures of crockery, cooperage, glassware, hops, lard-oil, paper,
powder, salt, starch, and woodware.[21] Ohio manufacturers of
these products, if situated near Lake Erie or the Ohio River, still
met the competition of out-of-state producers in their local market; but their goods could be shipped into the interior farther
than products of their competitors, if local prices were about
equal. The protectionist effect was still greater for Ohio manufacturers located in the interior regions, especially on bulky
low-value products such as salt, for only by canal could out-of-
state competitors reach their local market.[22]

The policy of setting discriminatory tolls to protect local manufacturers was common to all the major canal states. "Each State
finds a justification on the score of interest," the Ohio board
declared, "in furnishing to its own citizens the cheapest transpor-

tation of the surplus products of its industry to a market; while, as a rule of compensation and revenue, the importations are burdened with as heavy a tax as their value will bear."[23] Protectionism was a producer-oriented policy. As such, it divided the business community, setting the interests of manufacturers against those of the merchants—as did the protective tariffs of the national government. Thus a Hocking Valley salt works owner wrote in 1845 that New York was "just like the British or any foreign government competing for our domestic markets." New York was remitting Erie Canal tolls on salt and paying cash bounties to her producers, he declared; then "If it is politic for N. York to enlarge the business of her people, it is equally important to Ohio to do the same thing."[24] The salt manufacturers in the Muskingum and Hocking districts called upon the canal board "to awaken enterprise and insure a permanent and abundant supply" of salt from local producers, so that "the New York monopolists" might not "gain an easy triumph" over Ohio's own salt works.[25] But in regions of the state where New York salt had been imported, the Ohio commission merchants and their commercial allies complained: "How far it is consistent with modern ideas of right, to tax us [by protective tolls] for the direct benefit of Muskingum salt manufacturers, is beyond our ability to divine."[26] When the mercantile interests finally persuaded the state legislature to order a reduction in all salt tolls in 1848, the Ohio salt works owners treated it as "a triumph gained by the Com-[mission] Merchant, over the poor manufacturers of his own State."[27]

The farmers of Ohio also articulated a set of demands regarding tolls. In 1845, for example, the board ordered higher tolls on wheat than on processed flour—a measure designed to favor Ohio millers by discouraging export of grain for milling at Buffalo or Rochester. This action brought forth a strong protest against "fostering a few Millers and Coopers at the expense of ware house men and the Farmers." Invoking the traditional rhetoric of the national tariff policy controversies, one petitioner declared: "We in this county go for a Protective Tariff, but no such an unequal rate of duty as is on Wheat and Flour."[28] Millers at Toledo complained that the flour-wheat differentials discouraged the shipment of unprocessed grain to their city from the Indiana region of the Wabash canal. They noted that Indiana had been setting tolls on exactly this basis, to aid its own millers. "But why Ohio should assist Indiana in its endeavours to monopolise the manufacture of flour," one Toledoan wrote, "I confess, I cannot comprehend." In the face of such pressures, the Ohio canal board yielded and reduced the toll on wheat.[29]

The manipulation of canal tolls swept the state government into a political maelstrom. For just as contending regional and functional interest groups would struggle over rate-making policies when the state later entered the field of railroad regulation, so—during the canal period—did such interests seek to influence the state's toll policies for their own purposes. Moreover, the protectionist features of tolls in all the canal states indicated that a considerable residue of real power over interstate commerce rested with the state governments, despite the strictures of the Constitution and of John Marshall's Supreme Court.

The controversy over rate-making would have signified little if canal tolls had comprised only a small part of transportation charges or of total commodity prices in the local Ohio markets. But in fact tolls were of major economic significance, and the ardor with which special interest groups responded to every move of the canal board was well justified.

The tolls on salt, mentioned above, were a prime case in point. Until construction of the Ohio Canal, the principal sources of salt in the state were the Onondaga works near Syracuse, New York, which supplied the Lake Erie shore; and the Kanawha works of western Virginia, which supplied the Ohio River district. In Ohio's interior region, some salt was produced at mines in the Muskingum Valley and in the Hocking Valley, but high transport costs limited their markets severely. When the Ohio Canal opened in 1827, salt immediately became one of the most important commodities in the import trade by way of Cleveland. Each year thousands of bushels of New York salt were brought inland by the canal to markets in northern and central Ohio; but only in 1839 and 1840 was any significant quantity shipped over the canal's entire line to Portsmouth and the Ohio Valley market.[30] The unusual volume of salt shipments from Cleveland to Portsmouth in 1839–40 resulted directly from the canal board's toll policy: for the board had instituted in 1839 a rebate of 20 cents per barrel on all through shipments from Cleveland to the southern terminus, as a means of maximizing long-haul trade and the revenues of the canal. The rebate made it more costly to ship salt to central Ohio than to ship a greater distance to Portsmouth; and so the practical (and indeed intended) effect was to protect "domestic" Muskingum and Hocking Valley producers from the competition of New York salt in the interior region. The rebate policy was abandoned after 1840, however, following completion of the Hocking Valley Canal and the Muskingum Improvement. Again, the purpose was protection of domestic producers, who could now reach the Ohio River market because of their newly built canal facilities. To implement further their protectionist aims, the canal commissioners increased discriminatory tolls against Onondaga salt three times between 1845 and 1847, each time magnifying the transfer-cost advantages of domestic salt.[31] Pursuing its own protective policy with equal ingenuity, New York responded each time by increasing its state-cash bounty to Onondaga producers, or else rebating Erie Canal tolls on salt bound for the Ohio market.[32]

In this manner, the two state governments struggled for control of the Ohio salt market in the mid-forties. But by manipulating tolls, the Ohio canal board permitted sale of New York salt along the Ohio Canal only between Cleveland and Roscoe, in central Ohio. On the Muskingum Improvement, high discriminatory tolls excluded Virginia's Kanawha salt. In central Ohio, west and south of Roscoe, the board thereby effectively allocated local markets to the "domestic" salt producers of the Muskingum and Hocking districts. The state was powerless to affect the Ohio Valley market by canal tolls, except that New York salt was excluded by raising the Cleveland-Portsmouth toll to a prohibitive level; otherwise, the Ohio Valley was left largely to the Kanawha producers, with some of the Virginia salt being carried up the canal from Portsmouth to the Scioto region. The result was a subsidized market in central Ohio; a decline in the salt imports via Cleveland, from 109,000 barrels shipped in 1839 to 36,000 in 1847; and reduced competition that caused salt prices to rise throughout the central portion of the state. Cleveland's merchants, and the other interests that were affected adversely, immediately protested this policy. Under pressure from them, the legislature intervened directly, and in 1848 ordered the canal board to reduce all salt tolls. The Cleveland trade responded to the stimulus of the more favorable toll structure, and the city's canal shipments of salt to the interior doubled between 1847 and 1848. The Hocking and Muskingum manufacturers, on the other hand, suffered sharply reduced prices.[33]

The Wabash & Erie Canal's commerce provided equally vivid testimony that toll policy could be the crucial determinant of marketing patterns. From the opening of the canal until 1845 its exports of corn, flour, and meat products remained relatively small. Extension of the Miami Canal to a junction with the Wabash resulted in a marked increase in trade volume in 1845. But in 1846, there was an even greater surge in trade: flour shipments to Toledo by canal rose from 86,000 barrels in 1845 to 126,000 the next year, pork from 8,000 to 18,000 barrels, and corn from 30,000 bushels to more than 1.1 million. The aggregate weight of lard, pork, and bacon in all forms received at Toledo rose to 12.8 million pounds—an increase in lard shipments alone of over three million pounds, in one year.[34] Nor was the unusual increase of 1845–46 merely temporary; for in 1846 the canal officials of New York, Ohio, and Indiana acted in concert to reduce the costs of shipping grain, meat, and other farm produce from central Indiana and western Ohio to the New York market. Until then, nearly all Indiana's surplus had gone south to the Ohio River. In one year the direction of that trade was shifted—thereafter the Wabash region exported to New York by way of Toledo. To accomplish this far-reaching trade revolution, New York cut Erie Canal tolls while Ohio and Indiana state authorities cooperated to slash tolls on the Wabash & Erie. To retain that trade when new competition threatened later, New York once again reduced tolls, by one-third on corn in 1849, and by one-fourth on corn, lard, pork, bacon and whiskey in 1850.[35] Lacking such toll cuts, it is doubtful that Toledo's trade would have grown to even half the level it had reached by

1851, when its exports were valued at eight million dollars—or two-thirds the value of Cleveland's export trade.[36]

The political struggles that centered on canal toll policy concerned real economic issues, not merely issues of symbolic importance. For the structure of tolls in Ohio was a crucial element in the relative market advantages of local and functional interest groups. The changing rates for transportation of merchandise on the Ohio Canal will illustrate the point. In 1834 it cost $12.40 per ton to ship merchandise from Cleveland to Newark, a distance of 176 miles. Seventeen years later the cost had declined to $6.60 per ton. But while the private forwarding companies' charges had dropped from 3.5 cents per ton-mile in 1834 to 1 cent in 1851, the tolls charged by the state had declined much less, only from 3.6 cents to 2.8 cents. Thus the private interests involved had made a greater effort than the state to keep the Ohio Canal route competitive; and it is readily understandable that merchants and forwarders in the Ohio Canal area should have pressed with such urgency for more drastic toll reductions.[37]

What an aggressive policy could accomplish when the state officials did reduce tolls—under pressure from mercantile groups or when market conditions required it—was manifest in the canal trade of western Ohio. When completion of the Miami Extension in 1845 linked Toledo and Cincinnati, it cost $12 per ton to ship heavy merchandise from one terminus to the other. This included a toll charge of $7, or more than half the total cost. In July 1845 the state reduced tolls to $6, and again in 1850 to $3. Assuming forwarders' charges to have remained the same (at $5 per ton), the successive toll reductions brought Toledo-Cincinnati charges down from 4.8 cents per ton-mile, when the canal first opened, to 4.4 cents in July 1845, and to 3.2 cents in 1850. Three years later, in 1853, when railroad competition became severe, tolls were reduced further, so that the total charge (forwarders' rate and tolls) on merchandise was only 2.6 cents.[38]

The toll reductions in Ohio were part of a larger movement by American state canal authorities to meet new competition by cutting toll charges. It was largely attributable to Ohio's toll adjustments and a 50 per cent reduction on the Erie Canal in 1851, for instance, that the cost of shipping light merchandise from New York to Cincinnati via Toledo fell from $28.60 per ton in mid-1845 to about $19 in the early 1850's.[39] This was less than half the cost of transporting merchandise from New York to Portsmouth via the Ohio Canal in 1835, when $40 or more had been the prevailing rate. The New York and Ohio toll policies had the same effect on transfer rates for exports from the West to the seaboard. Thus to ship flour from Cincinnati to New York, via Toledo, cost $1.40 per barrel in 1845, but by 1850 reduced tolls and middlemen's charges had brought the rate down to about $1.10.[40]

That the state's exercise of the rate-making power was critical in establishing cost advantages for competing routes was evident from the structure of prevailing charges in 1850. This is illustrated in Table 10.1, which shows transportation costs on the Ohio Canal between Newark and Cleveland, a distance of 176 miles. For every commodity listed, tolls comprised more than half the total charge.

TABLE 10.1
OHIO CANAL CHARGES IN THE NEWARK-CLEVELAND TRADE 1850

COMMODITY	PER TON	TOTAL RATE PER TON-MILE[a]	TOLL ALONE PER TON-MILE
Merchandise (lowest charge)	$6.60	3.8¢	2.8¢
Merchandise (highest charge)	9.00	5.1	3.6
Salt	4.33	2.5	1.8
Wheat	4.33	2.5	1.4
Flour	3.70	2.1	1.3
Lard, pork	4.33	2.5	1.3
Whiskey	3.80	2.2	1.5

a Toll and forwarder's charge.

Source: Collector J. M. Byers, Newark, to G. W. Manypenny, Jan. 21, 1851, BPW Papers. The distance from Cleveland to Newark, 176 miles.

The Ohio Canal charges for 1850 also manifested a wide range of freight rates, from 2.1 to 5.1 cents per ton-mile, according to commodity. Forwarders' charges alone, exclusive of tolls, ranged from 0.7 cents on salt to nearly twice that rate on lard and pork. Many factors entered into rate decisions by the private boat operators and forwarding companies: the magnitude of their fixed costs, the level of demand for various commodities, the intensity of competition between the canal and alternative transportation routes, and the amount of handling and space that a specific type of commodity required.[41] It is therefore misleading to suppose, as is commonly done, that an "average" ton-mile freight charge can be cited to reflect the structure of transportation charges in the canal era: not only did canal rates decline rapidly in the 1840's and early 1850's, but differentials persisted between one commodity and another. In any case, it is unacceptable to treat the "average" rate on the Ohio Canal as 1 cent per ton-mile, as scholars have recently done.[42] For in 1851 the main items in the Ohio Canal trade were carried at a minimum of 2.1 cents; and even in the mid-1850's, when railroad competition had forced further rate reductions on the canal, only charges on coal fell as low as 1.4 cents per ton-mile.[43] Because of the toll structure, moreover, the shortest and most direct route was not always the least expensive; and so inefficient and curious trade patterns were often forced on merchants and shippers.[44]

Anomalies of this kind provoked frequent attacks on Ohio canal-tolls policy, generating protests against "the steady persecution of our State authorities" whenever discriminatory tolls damaged any self-conscious interest group.[45] Such assaults on the canal board's policies, whatever their merit in individual instances, indicated the importance that men of that day attached to the rate-making powers of the state. For so long as the state's canals monopolized trade between outside markets and Ohio's interior, the policy of canal tolls comprised an important dimension of state policy.

Indeed, the canal authorities' aggressive pursuit of mercantilistic goals—together with their efforts to maximize canal revenues, to meet new competition, and to capture new trade—critically affected the course of the Transportation Revolution. The mere construction of canal lines did not change the patterns of trade between the seaboard and the West. It was rather the shifting structure of rates. These rates were subject to manipulation for special purposes, and there was nothing automatic about changing commercial patterns—witness the case of the Wabash & Erie Canal, which was operating from Toledo into central Indiana in 1843 but which did not attract the valley's surplus produce to the Lake Erie route until 1846, when the canal tolls in three states were reduced sufficiently to accomplish the reversal of trade. Nor did construction of the new western canals alone assure that eastern manufacturers and wholesalers could penetrate the interior by way of the northern canal-and-lake route: for the extent of their market depended upon the willingness of state canal officials to give them *entrée*. If the interests of the Ohio "commonwealth" (or political expediency) appeared to require exclusion of eastern products, this too was possible, as in the case of salt.

Whether the Ohio canal board's rate-making policies in fact promoted optimal economic development in the state is another question. Possibly inefficient manufacturing firms were aided by protective tolls, only to be wiped out when the railroads penetrated the state a decade later. Possibly Ohio might have done better to sacrifice, say, its domestic salt mining interests and to depend instead upon imports from New York. Consumers would thereby have benefited, and investment capital might have been released for other purposes. But speculations of this kind were not, and could not be, predicated on a model consisting of free market forces alone. For all of Ohio's neighboring states were pursuing their own mercantilistic goals, and they too maintained rigidities and barriers that reduced the free movement of goods in interstate commerce.

In the 1850's the state rate-making power would erode under the impact of private railway operations; and as the railroads destroyed canal monopolies, they also stripped the state of this crucial instrument for the exercise of economic controls. Ironies inhere in the railroad story: for as we examine Ohio's public policies toward railroads, it will become manifest that the state might have retained far more control over railway development than it did. Indeed, the state government might even have continued to allocate markets. But the commonwealth idea, as expressed earlier in canal promotion and in rate-making policies, was to be shattered; and there would be a sweeping redefinition of legitimate state power and its proper uses.

Viewed in light of rate-making during the canal period, the Granger Law agitation of the 1870's may be interpreted as an effort to restore effective state authority over transport rates, rather than as a movement to vest unprecedented regulatory powers in American state government. But Grangerism was as yet two decades in the future. In the interim, in Ohio as in the other major canal states, railroads would be given ample inducements to build and overbuild. As canals declined in commercial importance, the rate-making policies that had once provoked intense controversy became less and less relevant to popular discussion of how state policy might best promote economic growth and the public interest.

NOTES

1. Despite the early promoters' undoubted nationalism, expressed in their belief that the Ohio canals would help integrate the American nation both politically and commercially, they were solidly provincial in their main concerns and policy objectives: inducing immigration to Ohio, enhancing farm land values and state revenues, building up a home market for Ohio manufacturing, and so on.
2. The power to set tolls and rules and regulations of navigation was vested in the canal commission by the law of February 4, 1825, and was transferred to the board of public works by the act of March 14, 1836, sec. 2.
3. CC, *11th AR* (1833), in *Senate Journal*, 1832–33, p. 346. For purposes of convenience, both the canal commission and the board of public works are referred to in this chapter as "the canal board."

4. See Appendix 2, below.
5. CC, *12th AR* (1834), pp. 2–3. The schedule called for maximum rates, for instance, from New York to Akron of $1.27 per hundred pounds (heavy merchandise) and $1.41 (light); New York to points between Chillicothe and Portsmouth of $1.86 (heavy) and $2.00 (light). (CC Minute Books, MS., Vol. I, pp. 257–58, in Board of Public Works, Records Room, State Office Building, Columbus.)
6. C. M. Gidings to A. Kelley, July 30, 1834, W. G. Oatman to Kelley, Feb. 1, 1835, on Canals, CHS; R. Putnam to Kelley, Aug. 9, 1834, CC Papers; CC, *13th AR* (1835), 12–13.
7. BPW, *2nd AR* (1838), pp. 4–5; CC, *15th AR* (1839), pp. 5–6; BPW, *7th AR* (1844), p. 6; CC, Minutes, Vol. II–A, pp. 11–13. See also Cleveland *Herald & Gazette,* May 8, Sept. 2, 1837, for an editor's criticism of the 1837 toll increase and objections that "the Ohio Canal has always been trammelled with high rates of toll . . . coupled with excessively strict regulations."
8. See Appendix 2, Table A, on 1841 tolls; the previous maximum charge on Merchandise of $9.16 per ton computed on basis of 309 miles on Ohio Canal, charged at 1830 schedule of 4¢ first 100 miles, 3¢ second 100, 2¢ thereafter. (CC Minutes, Vol. I, pp. 201–3.) Pre-1841 maximum charges on pork, flour, and whiskey based upon 1827 tolls and surcharge of 20 per cent ordered in 1837.
9. CC, *15th AR* (1839), pp. 5–6; BPW, *3rd AR* (1839), pp. 5–6.
10. Leicester King to BPW, April 4, 1845, S. Dodge to BPW, March 28, 1845, BPW Papers, requesting Ohio Canal toll reduction on Mahoning Canal shipments to Akron bound for Cleveland; Dodge wrote (*ibid.*) that the Reed family of Erie was the principal stockholder in the Extension Canal "and controlls most of the Steam Boats on the Lakes." The BPW order is published in Cleveland *Herald,* March 25, 1845.
11. Even after Ohio Canal tolls were adjusted, the Extension Canal route from Pittsburgh to the lake involved charges of $3 per ton on iron and nails (including $1.15 tolls) as compared to $4 (including $2.30 tolls) on the Mahoning Canal-Akron-Cleveland route. (W. A. Otis to O. Follett, Aug. 4, 1845, BPW Papers.) The Cleveland *Herald,* Jan. 31, April 21, 1845, complained that the Erie Extension's tolls were only one-third to one-half those on the Ohio Canal route.
12. BPW, *9th AR* (1845), p. 3.

13. Appendix 2, Table B; BPW, *10th AR* (1847), *Exec. Docs.*, 1847, No. 31, pp. 404–5; Toledo *Blade*, July 4, July 25, 1845.
14. Appendix 2, Table B. In the mid-forties the canal board also acted to protect the canals from intensified competition from the newly built turnpikes, by (1) obtaining agreement on a new, uniform schedule of (higher) turnpike tolls, and (2) instituting, unilaterally, higher tolls on the National Road, on which traffic volume had increased in competition with the canals. (BPW, *8th AR* [1844], pp. 28–34.)
15. See Appendix 2, Table C. The canal board's principle that "It is always good policy to reduce the rate of tolls upon such articles as find their way to market by some other routes than our canals," in the context of a more embracing apologia, is in BPW, *13th AR* (1850), p. 15. To indicate the board's pragmatism: on the Miami Extension Canal, it charged a toll of $1.50 a ton on through shipments of "southern groceries" between Toledo and Cincinnati (250 miles), but $2 a ton for the same commodities carried between either Cincinnati or Toledo and a way point on the canal. Similarly, operation of the Mad River & Lake Erie Railroad line between Cincinnati and Sandusky (on the lake) forced down merchandise tolls between Cincinnati and Toledo to $3 a ton (250 miles). On the Ohio Canal between Columbus and Cleveland (200 miles), where no competition threatened, the toll was $5 a ton.
16. On the merchants and the forwarders, as they functioned in the grain trade, see the important studies by Thomas D. Odle, "The American Grain Trade of the Great Lakes, 1825–1873," *Inland Seas*, VII–VIII (1951, 1952), numerous installments; and Odle, "Entrepreneurial Cooperation on the Great Lakes: The Origin of the Methods of Grain Marketing," *Business History Review*, XXXVIII (Winter 1964), 439–55. The mechanism whereby eastern goods were distributed by wholesale and retail in the West is treated in Fred M. Jones, *Middlemen in the Domestic Trade of the United States, 1800–1860* (Urbana, Ill., 1937); Harry A. Mitchell, "The Development of New Orleans as a Wholesale Trading Center," *Louisiana Hist. Quar.*, XXVII (Oct. 1944), 933–63; and Lewis Atherton, *The Pioneer Merchant in Mid-America* (Columbus, Missouri, 1939).
17. BPW, *13th AR* (1850), p. 15. On merchants in western urban society and politics up to 1830, cf. Richard C. Wade, *The Urban Frontier* (Cambridge, 1959).

18. Field & King, Collins Brown & Co., *et al.* to BPW, Jan. 1, 1848, BPW Papers.
19. Petition of Cincinnati Chamber of Commerce, June 20, 1845, *ibid.*
20. The rivalry among cities was present despite the disclaimer of the Cincinnati chamber that it sought no "exclusive advantage," but only a chance to realize "the full benefits of [the city's] position." *Ibid.*
21. The 1829 tolls are in CC Minutes, Vol. I, pp. 76–77; glassware, hops, paper, and stationery were added to the list in 1832 (*ibid.*, pp. 201–3); the 1848 discriminatory list is given in BPW, *Special Report . . . relative to the Toll Charged on Salt* (Columbus, January 29, 1848), p. 5.
22. On the other hand, the manufacturers also pressed for low tolls, or none, on the raw materials they used. In the 1850 schedule, coal used in Ohio salt works for fuel was exempt from tolls. See Appendix 2.
23. *Special Report* (Jan. 29, 1848), p. 5.
24. Samuel Vinton to Thomas Ewing, April 5, 1845, BPW Papers.
25. Petition of Athens salt manufacturers, Feb. 8, 1847, *ibid.*
26. Report of the P. & O. Canal Co. (Mahoning Canal), *Exec. Docs.*, 1851, No. 48, Vol. I, p. 847.
27. Fuller & Walker to Follett, March 20, 1848, BPW Papers.
28. F. W. McCanley to BPW, May 14, 1845, David Chalfant to BPW, May 14, 1845, BPW Papers.
29. H. Reed to Follett, May 29, 1845, *ibid.*; also J. Blickensderfer to O. Follett, Oct. 17, 1845, *ibid.*, on restoration of equal tolls. In light of the oft-cited view that the Whig party was closely associated with the mercantile interests in this period, it is worth noting that at various times both Democratic- and Whig-dominated canal boards manipulated tolls for protective purposes.
30. Cleveland clearances were 63,000 barrels of salt in 1837 and 1838; but in neither year did even 1,000 barrels reach Portsmouth. In 1839 Cleveland cleared 110,000, with 17,000 to Portsmouth; in 1840 she cleared 77,000, with 12,000 to Portsmouth. (BPW, *8th AR* [1844], 6–7; BPW, *Special Report in Relation to the Tolls on Salt*, Feb. 5, 1842, p. 6.) On the Ohio Valley salt trade, see Thomas S. Berry, *Western Prices before 1861* (Cambridge, 1943), pp. 286–317; and on Ohio production, Francis P. Weisenburger, *Passing of the Frontier* (Columbus, 1941), 74. There is a large correspondence with Ohio salt

manufacturers, giving details of their production and trade, in BPW Papers.

31. BPW, *Special Report* (Jan. 29, 1848), *passim;* New York, Superintendent of the Onondaga Salt Springs, *AR, 1849* (Albany, 1850), 13.

32. *Ibid.;* Fuller & Walker to BPW, Jan. 22, 1847, BPW Papers.

33. Trade data from BPW, annual reports for 1840's. Fuller & Walker to Follett, March 20, 1848, BPW Papers, discusses the political struggle over salt tolls; BPW, *7th AR* (1844), p. 8, outlines the allocation of markets for salt in the state. In 1843, the Hocking Valley Canal carried 10,000 barrels of Ohio salt into central Ohio; the Muskingum Improvement, another 6.000 barrels into central Ohio and 3,300 southward to the Ohio River; Cleveland shipments of New York salt were 44.300 barrels, none reaching ports south of Roscoe; and Portsmouth shipments to the interior were 11,300 barrels. (BPW, *7th AR*.) By 1847, the Sandusky railroad to Mansfield was also carrying New York salt to the interior region. (Petition dated Jan. 1847, BPW Papers.)

34. BPW, *10th AR* (1847), *Exec. Doc.*, 1847, No. 3, p. 405.

35. Thomas Richmond to Follett, Dec. 11, 1845, BPW Papers, on trade of the Wabash in 1845 and the need for toll reductions; BPW, *10th AR, loc. cit.*, pp. 404–5, on toll reductions instituted Sept. 10, 1846; BPW, *13th AR* (1850), 16–17, and New York Canal Commission, *AR, 1852,* 11–32, on Erie Canal toll cuts. Also, J. W. Scott to Follett, Jan. 21, 1846, H. P. Thayer to J. D. Walbridge, Nov. 26, 1845, BPW Papers, on Ohio officials' negotiations with New York on joint toll cuts. See also Toledo *Blade*, Aug. 29, 1845.

36. U. S., 32nd Cong., 1st Sess., *Senate Exec. Doc.* No. 112 (serial 112), "Report of Israel D. Andrews . . ." (1853), pp. 168, 185.

37. The 1850 data are given in detail in the Newark collectors' letter to the canal board, J. M. Byers to Manypenny, Jan. 21, 1851, BPW Papers. The 1834 rates are computed from the canal board's prescribed charges from New York to Newark per ton (including tolls and other charges), given in CC Minutes, Vol. I, pp. 257–58; I have deducted New York-Cleveland charge, $20.60, given in W. G. Oatman to Kelley, Feb. 1, 1835, Letters on Canals, CHS. State tolls are given in tables accompanying text.

38. For tolls, see tables in Appendix 2. Private forwarders' charge

of $5 per ton on heavy freight is given in Palmer, Brown & Co. to BPW, June 28, 1845, BPW Papers. Private forwarders' charges varied seasonally and annually, and the $5 figure is probably the maximum.

39. Based on toll reductions given in BPW Minutes, Vol. V, pp. 355ff. (1853 tolls); and Erie Canal tolls, in New York Canal Commissioners, *AR, 1852* (Albany, 1853), pp. 11–32.

40. Berry cites Cincinnati-New York flour rates, via Toledo, of $1.40 per barrel in 1845, $1.10–1.15 in 1848, $1.10 in 1849, and $1.05 in 1853 (*Western Prices*, 90, 92). James Barton, *Lake Commerce* (4th edition, Buffalo, 1846), 17, reported 1846 Cincinnati-New York rates as $1.33 per barrel. The Switzler Report (U. S. Dept. of Treasury, *Commerce and Navigation*, Pt. II, Washington, 1888), p. 211, gave the 1847 rate as $1.53 per barrel.

41. In 1845, for instance, a sudden increase in the volume of foodstuffs that flowed east through the Lake Erie outlets taxed existing canal and lake boat capacity. As a result, flour charges from Cincinnati to New York, via Toledo and the lake route, rose from $1.15 to a high of $2 per barrel in the autumn, driving Miami Valley flour southward for export by way of New Orleans. (BPW, *9th AR* [1845], pp. 23–24.)

42. Harvey Segal in *Canals and American Economic Development*, ed. Carter Goodrich (New York, 1962), 286 n.

43. The low 1.4 cent rate was on coal in 1855, reported in Cleveland & Mahoning Railroad Company, *Exhibit, Oct. 1, 1853* (New York, 1853), 10.

44. For instance, to send railroad iron from Cincinnati to Detroit in 1845 the most direct route was *via* the Miami Extension to Toledo and then by lake to Detroit. Charges on this route would be $6.90, including tolls alone of $4. But it was cheaper to ship upstream by steamer on the Ohio River to the Erie Extension Canal, on which the toll was $1, and then by lake to Detroit. The total charge on this roundabout route would be only $4.62 per ton. (Thomas Richmond to S. Forrer, Jan. 9, 1845, BPW Papers.)

45. Fuller & Walker to Follett, Feb. 24, 1848, *ibid.*

PART III

BEGINNING OF THE RAILROAD AGE: TO
1861

CANAL-DIGGING had scarcely begun in Ohio when the first agitation for railroads commenced. Experiments in Great Britain had aroused a lively interest on this side of the Atlantic in the railroad as an alternative to canals, and by the early 1830's several cities in the East—notably Baltimore and Charleston—were actively developing major railroad projects. Even so, when Ohio moved to expand its public works in the mid-thirties, the state once again restricted its outright public enterprise to canals; and though the 1837 Loan Law permitted investment of state funds in railroad companies, the construction of railways was left to the private sector. Why policy-makers in Ohio eschewed a policy of public railroad construction, and why they encouraged private railroad construction even when it threatened the commerce and revenues of the state canals, comprise an important theme in the following pages.

To understand how Ohio had by 1860 acquired more railroad mileage within its borders than any other American state, it is essential to recognize at the outset one feature of the process: while there were, to be sure, shifts of initiative (from the public to private sectors) and of technology (from canals to steam railroads), there was basic continuity in some of the political forces that shaped state policy. In Ohio there was a society infused with the spirit of the expectant capitalist, impatient with restraints and obstacles that stood in the way of rapid economic growth; and it was a society whose political life, when it came to settling matters of public economic policy, was organized largely around localistic interests. In the 1820's and 1830's, the people had adduced commonwealth principles and egalitarian ideals to justify state government investments in transportation. In later years the popular conception of "commonwealth" would be modified severely under pressure from localistic and entrepreneurial ambitions; and the active state as it had functioned earlier would fall into disrepute. But although the state's public policy toward railroad enterprise was largely permissive and gave free play to private investment as the means of pursuing localistic aims, appeals were still made to commonwealth interests. Not only did promoters demand public financial aid for their railways, but they argued for liberal charters and general laws in order to attract to Ohio investment which, they claimed, would otherwise go to other states; and they justified special immunities and privileges on the grounds that such concessions were in the interest of the commonwealth.

Indeed, the entire development of railroads in Ohio reflected the effects of public policy. When a group of promoters—with or without sufficient capital to back up its dreams—planned a railroad, its first task was to obtain a charter from the legislature. Once a charter was in hand, the costs that the company would incur in obtaining a right-of-way, the taxes it must pay (or be exempt from paying), and a wide range of other factors affecting the profitability of the investment were greatly influenced by the structure of law. And if the company was at all typical, it sought by every means possible to obtain financial aid from public authorities—aid that often meant the difference between success and failure in building the line.

Once railroads were built, the wider economic effects were similar to the impact of the canals in an earlier period. Above all, the railroads significantly changed the position of Ohio's agricultural and industrial producers in the national market, subjecting some to damaging dislocation and opening for others a wider and more profitable market. In some regions of the state they fostered growth; elsewhere, they seriously injured existing local interests. As had been true of the canals, some of the early dreams of the promoters were realized in full measure, while others proved illusory.

Part of the price exacted by the shift from public canals to private railroads was loss of trade on the public works. The manner in which railroad competition with canals developed, and the response of the state legislature and Ohio's administrative agencies to the threat of railway competition, provide evidence vital to an understanding of changing conceptions of the state's legitimate role in the economy.

Competition and Response: The Ohio Railroads, 1826-1861

THE debate over railroad policy in Ohio began in early 1826, only a few months after initiation of the first canal program.[1] The first public call for railroad construction was sounded by James Kilbourne, a prominent politician and engineer who formerly had been the leading champion of a state-built canal between Portsmouth and Sandusky, a route that passed through his extensive landholdings in north-central Ohio. Now Kilbourne proposed a railroad on the same route. Such a railway, bisecting the state on a north-south axis, could readily be expanded, Kilbourne argued, by construction of lateral branches to all the state's major towns. He denounced the recently adopted canal policy, and urged the state to put its funds instead into his proposed railroad, asserting that recent experiments in England had proved the superiority of railways over canals for transportation of both freight and passengers.[2]

However foresighted Kilbourne's proposal, it smacked of self-interest. Above all, however, it was premature. Few civil engineers were prepared to shift so abruptly as Kilbourne, from advocating canals to boosting railroads. They did not regard the British experiments as conclusive, and most believed that heavy freight could not be carried as economically by rail as by water. There was, too, an abiding popular prejudice against railroads as naturally "monopolistic," since the individual capitalist probably could not put his own vehicles on the track as he might put boats on a canal. Moreover, because Ohio had just embarked on its canal program after three years of ardent and absorbing public debate, it was only natural that men should look skeptically on a plan to abandon canal construction at that juncture, especially for so novel an alternative.[3]

Nevertheless, the consensus in favor of canal construction could not forestall all plans for railroad enterprises. Interest in railroad schemes ran highest, as might be expected, in those regions of the state that had been by-passed by the 1825 canal plan.[4] Residents of these "neglected" districts argued in egalitarian terms for government-built railroads in the late 1820's and early 1830's, urging that railway lines ancillary to the canal system might "restore an equilibrium of the unequal benefits derived from [the] canals."[5] But in the canal-port towns, too, there was some agitation for railroads in the early thirties. Although most of the schemes involved only "little local works," there was some pressure for an integrated state railroad system.[6] Some of the largest railroad plans were formulated as responses to projects for rail lines from the eastern seaboard to the Ohio River, as Ohio promoters grasped the importance of gaining direct connections with such railroads as Charleston's line to the interior and the Baltimore & Ohio project.[7] Motivated by these widely varied aims, local projectors of railroads besieged the Ohio legislature with requests for charters and state aid, while local jealousies resulted in still further proliferation of railway schemes by exciting fears and rivalries.

The legislature responded by opening the field wide to private railroad enterprise. Nineteen railroad corporations were chartered during 1830–33, and a total of 77 received charters up to 1840.[8] Nearly all the railroads built in Ohio prior to the Civil War were organized and operated under these pre-1840 charters. Therefore, despite the enactment of a general railroad law in 1848, the immunities, privileges, and obligations written into the early charters had precedent standing: as a practical matter, they collectively comprised public policy toward railroad development in the antebellum period.

This policy was on the whole extremely permissive, for the various powers allocated by special charter to railroad companies were far more solicitous of private investors' interests than of commonwealth goals. But the legislature did not surrender altogether its role as planner of basic transport facilities. By means of specific charter provisions, the state reserved to itself certain regulatory powers designed to assure protection of the public interest; in fact, however, charter terms found onerous by the private companies were often soon revoked or amended. In a broader sense, the legislature's willingness to design and grant charters one by one, and to permit railroad policy to unfold piecemeal, as it were, reflected a changing conception of how "commonwealth interests" should be defined and nurtured.

The most important special privilege granted to private railroad companies was incorporation, which carried with it the principle of limited stockholder liability. The 1802 state constitution had contained a provision permitting corporate charters for charitable, educational, and "other" purposes.[9] Under this vague mandate, the legislature and the courts until 1851 held railroad investors liable only for the amount they had subscribed in stock. A crucial advantage for railway promoters seeking investment capital, limited liability reflected the notion, deeply rooted in American law, that corporate privileges were bestowed for a public purpose—and that such a purpose was best served by granting valuable incentives to investors.[10]

Another vital power granted to railroads, in every Ohio charter prior to 1851, was the right to exercise eminent domain for seizure of privately owned land, stone, and timber needed to lay out the right-of-way and construct the line. The eminent domain power permitted railroad companies to take land from stubborn property owners who might otherwise have blocked the construction of the line on the route adopted; and it freed the companies from the need to haul construction materials, at great expense, from distant locations. Although grants of eminent domain power to corporations were as old as railroad law itself in America, Ohio went further than many sister states: for in the charters her legislature awarded, there was no requirement that railroad companies pay property owners prior to seizure of their land or goods. Still more important, Ohio provided that in cases of dispute over the value of property seized, court-appointed appraisers should set awards by (1) estimating the damages according to fair market value, and then (2) subtracting from damages the "offsetting benefits" that allegedly accrued to property owners as the result of the railroad's construction.[11] In practice, the railroad promoters used their political influence to assure that the courts appointed friendly appraisers. Thereby they obtained rights-of-way and materials at nominal prices, as offsetting benefits were overvalued— and this amounted to a major subsidy for the railroad corporations.[12] The legislature further encouraged railroad promotion by permitting all such special charter privileges to become effective when only a small amount of the authorized capital was paid in. In this manner, one company, with only $10,000 actually subscribed, could legally seize private land and materials.[13]

Railroads were also subsidized more directly through grants of tax exemption. Many of the early charters included no provision for taxation. A few companies were made subject to taxes, but only if profits exceeded a specified return of capital, and even then only eight or ten years following their incorporation.[14] Not until 1848 did Ohio place a general tax on railroad property, but the law did not apply uniformly to companies chartered prior to its enactment.[15]

The state courts of Ohio extended a blanket of judicial approval over these various grants of special power and immunities. As early as 1836, the Ohio supreme court had upheld grants of the power of eminent domain to private corporations. Private turnpike, canal, and bridge companies were chartered, the court declared, "because the public have an interest in them." Hence it was consistent to force private property rights to yield, in order to expedite their construction.[16] In subsequent years, the courts upheld application of the same sweeping doctrine in cases affecting the railroads. "It is our duty to foster and promote such enterprises," one judge asserted. "We cannot and ought not to be indifferent to the imperative demand made by the rapid progress of the age."[17] When aggrieved property owners challenged the constitutionality of vesting eminent-domain privileges in railroad firms, the courts upheld such procedures as an indispensable instrument of the active state seeking "to develop its resources and add to its strength and security." The state might pursue developmental goals by outright public enterprise, and no less properly by granting extraordinary powers to private firms chartered in the public interest. "Theorists may have assigned to government a more restricted sphere of action," the state supreme court declared; but it was too late in the day to translate such theoretical constructs into public policy.[18]

The privileges thus approved by the courts represented only the beneficent side of Ohio railroad policy. For there was a corollary to the judiciary's view that railroads were chartered in the public interest, namely that they might for the same reason be made subject to public regulation. As one of the lower courts phrased it, a railroad "must be a public work for all purposes, not solely for that of appropriating the citizen's land."[19] Among the regulations that the legislature therefore built into railroad charters were a myriad of painstakingly detailed procedures for the issuing of stock-subscription notices, for conduct of directors' and stockholders' meetings, for transfer of stock, and so on. But potentially far more important were provisions concerning the route on which the company might build its line. Most of the charters issued in the 1830's named the two terminal points, and many also specified one or more locations as way stations, through which the line must run.[20] By the early forties, however, the legislature was giving most newly chartered railroad companies much greater freedom in selection of a precise route—even of termini—in response to the movement for new lines that would connect with those already under construction.[21] Moreover, specifications of route were often repealed or amended on request, giving railroads greater freedom to exploit rivalries among communities competing for a place on the line.[22]

The public-utility character of railroads was reflected also in provisions affecting traffic rules and rates. One of the earliest charters specifically reserved "to the state, or the citizens thereof, or any company hereafter to be incorporated" the right to build connecting lines. Another required the railroad to accept the vehicles and cargo of "any other company, person or persons," subject only to the company's published rate charges.[23] An even more significant restriction was formal reservation of the state's right to regulate rates. Many of the charters granted in the early thirties, when railroads were still sometimes regarded as modified turnpikes which could admit privately owned vehicles to the line, included provisions for maximum rates of "toll" as well as rates for "transportation."[24] But the railroads whose charters included rate restrictions often obtained amendments that either raised the maximum rates far above prevailing charges, or else removed the restriction altogether. Moreover, such charter changes were frequently obtained before the railroads had actually gone into operation, rendering regulation of rates an empty formality at best.[25]

The legislature's unwillingness to impose meaningful rate regulation was most apparent in the charters of railroads which, by virtue of their locations, would compete for the traffic of the state canals. In 1846, for instance, the Cleveland, Columbus & Cincinnati Railroad was required to reimburse the state for half the canal tolls lost on all freight that the road carried between cities located on the Ohio Canal.[26] And in 1847 the Cincinnati, Hamilton & Dayton was declared subject to a special tax, to be levied on all freight carried, sufficient to recapture revenues lost to the Miami Canal because of the railroad's operation.[27] However, the legislature soon afterward released each company from its obligations—in each case prior to completion of the railroad's construction. These reversals probably resulted from pressure on the legislature from the mercantile communities affected, which uniformly desired lower transport rates. Whatever the reason, the state did back down, and the elaborate restrictions of 1846–47 proved meaningless.[28]

From the standpoint of private railroad investors, perhaps the most ominous of all clauses in the typical Ohio charter was that which terminated the corporate privilege at a specified date, usually 20 years after charter. In practice the legislature never failed to renew the charter of a company that had actually built its line. But the termination clause did permit the legislature to reconsider powers and privileges granted in the original charter, and at the time of renewal concessions could be exacted from railroads (usually an imposition of taxes on companies formerly exempt) as *quid pro quo* for extension.[29]

Taken as a whole, then, the various curbs and regulations written into railroad charters in Ohio proved much less important than the special powers and immunities granted. But what explains the popular mood that supported so liberal a policy toward railroads? First of all, the pressures for railroads were essentially localistic. Railroad technology permitted construction of basic transport facilities at much lower cost per mile than was required for canals, so that local promoters saw the possibility of achieving their ambitions independently of the state-as-enterpriser. No longer did they feel the need to appear before the legislature as supplicants, seeking places in a larger system of public works that fused the goals of many local regions and neglected others. Instead, local promoters now asked the state only to give free play to private enterprise. Closely related to the localistic emphasis in railroad promotion was a more general decline of faith that the state could plan and operate a transport system efficiently— especially after the vexing experience with Ohio's expanded program after 1836. Third was the fact that in the 1840's the Ohio canals were not producing revenues sufficient to support amortization of the state debt. Had the canals' operating revenues been larger, the popular mood might well have been different—or so, at least, the comparable situation in New York suggested. For in the same period New York's Erie Canal was producing large annual surpluses, over and above the cost of amortizing the canal debt, and the funds were used to build ancillary (branch) canal lines. When local communities in that state sought new transport facilities, they usually demanded construction of a branch canal at state expense—and together with professional canal contractors, they helped form an effective lobby that pushed through a series of laws which for many years restricted railroad traffic and imposed special taxes on railway freight.[30]

But it was not so in Ohio, where the ambitions of local communities for new transport lines tended to support the private railroad promoters. Symptomatic of why pressures to regulate railway development failed, even when the canal interests were directly threatened, was the editorial stance of the *Toledo Blade*. On June 27, 1845, the journal's editor deplored railroad agitation at Cleveland, where local businessmen—using capital they had

"accumulated by the use of [the] state works"—wanted to build
a rail line to Columbus, a project which if successful would be
"fatal to the business of the state canal." He urged that the legislature adopt a policy to protect the public works "from ruinous
competition . . . while yet the danger threatens, and before the
evil is upon us." Six months later, however, the same editor was
promoting a railroad planned to run from Toledo westward,
parallel to the Wabash & Erie Canal![31] Clearly, laws that would
defend canal traffic and revenues were attractive only so long as
the railroad fever had not struck close to home.

A favorable public policy was not in itself sufficient to assure
that railroads would be built in Ohio. For the West was still a
capital-deficient region; and it was difficult in the best of circumstances to attract private investment from the East so long as
abundant opportunities for profit were open in land speculation,
townsite promotion, and banking. Therefore, despite the liberal
state railroad policy, construction of railways languished until
private capital became more readily available in the mid-forties.
Of seventy-seven railroad companies chartered in Ohio during
the 1830's, only six actually opened lines to traffic prior to 1841.
Moreover, the companies that did commence operations relied
heavily upon public funds to accomplish construction.

Ohio's first railroad was the Erie & Kalamazoo, a thirty-three-
mile line from Toledo northwest to the town of Adrian, Michigan.
It began operations in 1836, using horse-drawn cars at first.[32]
Four additional railways opened lines to traffic in 1838. Two were
of little importance—a six-mile line from Cleveland to New-
burgh, which also used horse-drawn cars and ran for only a few
years; and a four-mile line built by the Painesville & Fairport,
which failed in 1845. But the other two were fated to become
the first links in larger railroad lines: the Mad River & Lake Erie,
which opened sixteen miles between Sandusky and Bellevue; and
the Monroeville & Sandusky, which inaugurated traffic on a
twenty-mile track.[33]

The only other line built prior to 1841 was the Little Miami,
organized by Cincinnati entrepreneurs and designed to connect
their city with the Mad River & Lake Erie's projected southern

terminus at Springfield. The Little Miami was chartered in 1836, completing a fourteen-mile track between Cincinnati and Milford in 1841, aided by $250,000 in stock subscriptions from the Cincinnati municipal government and by Greene County, as well as $115,000 of state aid given under the Loan Law.[34]

Probably none of the longer lines—the Little Miami, the Mad River, or the Monroeville & Sandusky—would have completed any construction had they not received government aid. For the panic in 1837 and the post-1839 depression had made it impossible for these companies to attract substantial private investment. Yet all three continued to build new track in the early 1840's— the only railroads in the state to do so. In none of the three did private stockholders supply as much as half the funds expended.[35]

When the national business depression gave way to economic revival in the mid-forties, however, eastern capitalists became interested in western railroad stocks. Here, after all, was a chance to gain control of potentially valuable property at prices driven to low levels by the western promoters' difficulties. A new flow of eastern money into Ohio railway enterprises was signaled in 1845 when the Little Miami, the Mad River, and the Monroeville & Sandusky (now the Sandusky & Mansfield) successfully marketed issues of common stock or bonds in the East.[36] (The resultant increase in mileage is shown in Table 11.1.)

The 1845 stock sales whetted the appetites of western railroad promoters. But so too did the prospect of connections with the big eastern trunk lines—the Erie, the New York Central, the Pennsylvania, and the Baltimore & Ohio—that were beginning in earnest their moves to the west. Everywhere in Ohio, promoters planned railroads that might connect with the trunk lines and give the latter access through the state. And not least, the westerners hoped to obtain financial support for their own projects from the trunk lines that would benefit from such connections.[37] Some local railroad organizers advertised their projects as potential links in a transcontinental system that would carry the trade with the Far West and Asia through their towns. Others, less pretentious, merely sought to assure their communities of a place on one of the new lines. But however they boosted their schemes, railroad organizers made local needs and local objectives their

TABLE 11.1

OHIO RAILROAD MILEAGE COMPLETED AND
TOTAL IN OPERATION 1847–1860

YEAR	NEW MILEAGE COMPLETED	TOTAL IN OPERATION
1847	—	275
1848	32	307
1849	16	323
1850	132	455
1851	333	788
1852	292	1,080
1853	500	1,580
1854	587	2,167
1855	385	2,552
1856	133	2,685
1857	129	2,814
1858	0	2,814
1859	174	2,988
1860	16	3,034

Source: Paxson, "Early Railways of the Old Northwest," pp. 268–74. From a check of statistics
on individual companies available in annual
reports, Paxson's statistics appear to be entirely
reliable. Other estimates of railroad mileage
completed in 1850 range as high as 575, and in
1860 as high as 3,057. (See G. R. Taylor, in
National Bureau of Economic Research,
Trends in the American Economy in the 19th
Century, pp. 526–27.)

main point of reference. Few men spoke in terms of a state program of railroad construction. Instead railroads were planned,
and presented to the public, as a means of fulfilling parochial,
localistic ambitions.[38]

The increased availability of private investment capital, during
the recovery of the late 1840's, impelled railroad promoters to

redouble their efforts for public aid: all recognized that a tangible expression of support by government authorities, in the form of stock subscriptions, loans, or guarantees, would be the most effective lure for foreign or eastern capital. As one Cincinnati leader asserted, "The public [must] bear a leading part in the first introduction of improvements requiring such vast sums of money. . . . The burdens and the risk, as well as the benefits [of railroads] can thus be equalized."[39] The kind of government assistance that railroads sought in the mid-forties indicated the new localistic emphasis in their promotion as well as the growing disillusionment with public works. Rather than seeking outright government construction or even a coordinated plan of state aid based on a system of priorities, promoters sought special state laws authorizing the agencies of local government to borrow funds for investments in railroad securities. The legislature responded favorably to nearly all such requests, authorizing some ten million dollars in local bond issues for railroad aid during the forties. In this way, the legislature permitted the locus of power to shift from the state to the local governments, thus duplicating, on a smaller stage, the shift of power that had occurred in the 1820's when Congress had permitted the planning of national transportation development to devolve upon the states.[40]

By surveying alternate routes for their projected lines, Ohio's railroad organizers shrewdly exploited the hopes and fears of those who advocated public aid by local governments. With much publicity attending most of the railroad surveys, and with local expectations aroused, the railway promoters implied—or promised outright—that they would build through the towns which voted the largest total of public and private subscriptions. Because all the state laws authorizing local aid required prior approval by referenda of the voters, the question of railroad aid became an intense political issue in many local communities. To citizens who feared higher taxes or who opposed public support of private companies, the railway advocates responded that their roads were planned as a matter of "public consideration, and not . . . mere private cupidity."[41] Railroad companies, one group of organizers pleaded, "are not selfish and soulless corporations, to be controlled by a few capitalists for their benefit alone, but are rather the 'people's lines,' to be owned and managed by and in behalf of the various counties which take a majority of the stock."[42]

Although some communities did resist such blandishments and vote against public aid, usually the popular response was favorable. As a consequence, public aid became a critical determinant of the pace and location of new railroad construction in Ohio after 1846. Indeed, local governments contributed nearly half of an estimated 12.8 million dollars invested in Ohio's railroads up to 1850.[43] One can trace the routes of many railways built during this period by naming the towns and counties that issued bonds for public subscriptions to their stock. One railroad president admitted in 1850 that no railway line in the state, excepting only the Cincinnati, Hamilton & Dayton, had been constructed "without mainly depending . . . upon either State credit or [local aid]."[44] By the mid-fifties even the railroad companies, then suffering from fierce competition, denounced "the dangerous tendency, with mere local interests, to combine in construction of unnecessary lines which must divide or destroy the traffic of existing routes." And one prominent Ohio railroad organizer deplored "the present system of making roads by subscriptions paid in county and city bonds" because it actually discouraged private risk capital.[45]

Even before the movement for local aid had reached its apogee, evidence of opposition to the "railroad mania" had begun to appear. In some localities, an urban-rural conflict developed when farmers opposed bond issues for railroad aid, believing that the main benefit would accrue to urban merchants and manufacturers. Some of the urban spokesmen for local aid also became disillusioned, however, when parallel roads were planned in close proximity to one another.[46] Opposition to local-aid schemes deepened when communities began to see their public investments dissipated on roads never built. Local citizens of modest means, it was said, were drawn into "delusive schemes" into which private and government capital was poured heedlessly. "Then the concern comes to a stand. Then come in the wealthy men—the real capitalists, and . . . the big fish turn in and eat the little ones up."[47]

The rising hostility to public aid reached a climax in the Ohio

state constitutional convention of 1850. A bloc of conservative
delegates, opposed to any extension of public debt, successfully
joined forces with a group of radicals who harbored a bias against
all business corporations, to vote a constitutional prohibition
against further borrowing by local authorities for investment in
private companies. Only a small number of delegates, all from
localities still lacking railroad connections, fought against the prohibition.[48] The new constitution, including the ban on new local
borrowing for aid to private companies, became effective in 1851;
but many towns and counties which had been authorized earlier to
hold referenda on railroad aid had not yet voted on the issue.[49]
Their right to vote such aid, on the basis of legislative acts that
predated the new constitution, was upheld by the Ohio supreme
court in 1852—although the court's opinion condemned the policy
itself, inveighing against "the indiscriminate prodigality with
which grants of this kind had been made."[50] This decision proved
crucial, for about three million dollars of local railroad aid was
voted after the new constitution went into effect. This brought the
total of local government assistance to private railroads up to
nearly eight million dollars by the mid-fifties.[51]

The combination of eastern capital and local government aid
produced a distinct change in the structure of transportation in
Ohio. Effective railroad competition for the canal trade had
already begun in 1848, when the Mad River & Lake Erie connected with the Little Miami Railroad and opened a direct rail
route between Cincinnati and Lake Erie.[52] But the railroad revolution became manifestly decisive in 1851 with completion of
three new lines, each of which tapped the canal traffic at one or
more port towns.

The first of these lines was the Sandusky, Mansfield & Newark
Railroad. Its 116-mile route ran from Sandusky City on the lake
to the town of Newark, a major port near the center of the Ohio
Canal. This route to Lake Erie was fifty miles shorter than the
176-mile canal line between Newark and Cleveland. At once the
railroad began to challenge the canal by instituting low freight
rates and offering special warehouse services to shippers of agricultural produce.[53]

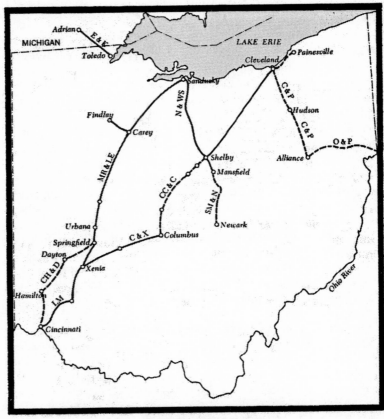

OHIO RAILROADS IN 1851

———— Railroads in operation before Jan. 1, 1851

– – – – Railroads completed during 1851

C & P   Cleveland & Pittsburgh
CC & C   Cleveland, Columbus & Cincinnati
CH & D   Cincinnati, Hamilton & Dayton
C & X   Columbus & Xenia
E & K   Erie & Kalamazoo
LM   Little Miami
MR & LE   Mad River & Lake Erie
O & P   Ohio & Pennsylvania (N.B. Passenger service only,
     on line from Alliance eastward several miles, temporarily
     operated with horsedrawn coaches. Full service began
     ca. Jan. 15, 1852.)

*Sources: Base map from George R. Taylor and Irene D. Neu, *The American Railroad Network, 1861-1890* (Cambridge: Harvard University Press, © Copyright 1956 by the President and Fellows of Harvard College). Reprinted by permission of the Harvard University Press.

Other data from annual reports of the railroad companies; also, F.L.Paxson,"Railroads of the Old Northwest,"256.

Map 11-A*

Also completed in 1851 was the Cincinnati, Hamilton & Dayton Railroad. Unique among the state's early railroads, the C. H. & D. was financed without government assistance of any sort. One-fifth of its $800,000 of common stock was sold in New York and the rest was purchased by residents of Cincinnati and the contractors who built the road. The C. H. & D. was planned as the first link of a line between Cincinnati and central Indiana. Its immediate significance, however, derived from the fact that it ran parallel to the Miami Canal, serving three of the canal's leading port towns. Moreover, it provided a second rail route between Cincinnati and Sandusky by means of a feeder road from Dayton to the main line of Mad River & Lake Erie at Springfield.[54]

The third major line completed in 1851 ran between the state's two largest cities, Cincinnati and Cleveland. Its first division comprised the Columbus & Xenia Railroad, which was completed in 1850 from the capital city to a connection with the Little Miami Railroad just east of Dayton. Meanwhile, a group of Cleveland and Columbus promoters, headed by Alfred Kelley (who was also president of the Columbus & Xenia) and fortified by substantial local public aid, built the Cleveland, Columbus & Cincinnati Railroad between the lake city and Columbus. The railroads that made up this through line were closely allied in their financing and management, and an interlocking directorate assured that they would compete vigorously with both the Mad River & Lake Erie and the state canals in western and central Ohio.[55]

In addition to the three new roads which thus challenged the trade of the state canals, two others were built in 1851 which would have a major impact upon the future pattern of Ohio transportation. One was the Cleveland, Painesville & Ashtabula, also headed by Alfred Kelley and designed to connect the line of the C. C. & C. at Cleveland with Erie, Pennsylvania. At Erie, it would meet the New York Central system's Buffalo-Erie extension road and also the western line of the Erie Railroad. The C. P. & A. was completed in 1851 to Ashtabula, and a year later it connected with the New York railroads at Erie.[56] Because it was designed to provide an all-rail route from Ohio to the eastern seaboard, the C. P. & A. best symbolized the strategy which would shape the character of railroad development in the state during the ensuing decade.

While the C. P. & A. was building along the Lake Shore, the Cleveland & Pittsburgh Railroad Company built a line from Cleveland southeast toward the Ohio River. In 1851 it was completed to Alliance, Ohio; and a year later it was connected there with the Ohio & Pennsylvania Railroad to Pittsburgh, giving the Pennsylvania Railroad access to the Lake Erie shore. Thus the Pennsy met the dual challenge of the New York Central system and the Erie Railroad, which formed their western connection with the C. P. & A. at Erie in 1852.[57] But for all three eastern lines, as well as their competitor the Baltimore & Ohio, this was only the first thrust into the West. The rich agricultural regions of Indiana, Illinois, and the Mississippi Valley lay beyond, and the race to tap their trade was beginning.

Situated athwart the routes of the great railroad lines building westward from the Atlantic coast, and with its own local communities more than eager to extend public aid, Ohio had become by the early fifties the scene of almost frantic railroad promotion. Between 1852 and 1855, the state's railway mileage expanded from 1,000 miles to over 2,500. Although the rate of new mileage added annually tapered off quickly after 1855, by 1860 the state had a railroad network of more than 3,000 miles of line, as shown in Table 11.1. Unlike the lines constructed up to 1851, most of the railroads built in the fifties ran on an east-west axis; and they were designed, in most cases, to be integrated into the railroad systems that were forming between the Atlantic seaboard cities and the Mississippi Valley.[58]

One of the major east-west systems built in Ohio during 1853–60 was the Lake Shore railroad group, composed of the Cleveland, Columbus & Cincinnati and its sister roads between Erie, Pennsylvania, and Toledo. The C. C. & C. was instrumental in financing a second integrated group of east-west roads, which gave Cleveland direct rail connections into central Indiana via the Columbus, Piqua & Indiana and the Bellefontaine & Indiana lines. A third group, associated with the Pennsylvania Railroad, consisted of numerous small lines which merged to form the Pittsburgh, Fort Wayne & Chicago system; their construction was accomplished with heavy financial aid from the Pennsylvania Railroad and from local governments along the route.

OHIO RAILROADS
AND CONNECTING LINES, 1861

C and IJ	Cincinnati and Indianapolis Junction
C and M	Cleveland and Mahoning
C and O	Carrollton and Oneida
C and P	Cleveland and Pittsburgh
C and T	Cleveland and Toledo
C and X	Columbus and Xenia
CC and C	Cleveland, Columbus and Cincinnati
CE and R	Cincinnati, Eaton and Richmond
CH and D	Cincinnati, Hamilton and Dayton
CO	Central Ohio
CP and A	Cleveland, Painesville and Ashtabula
CP and I	Columbus, Piqua and Indiana
CW and Z	Cincinnati, Wilmington and Zanesville
CZ and C	Cleveland, Zanesville and Cincinnati
D and M	Dayton and Michigan
DX and B	Dayton, Xenia and Belpre
F and I	Fremont and Indiana
G and M	Greenville and Miami
I	Iron Railroad
LM	Little Miami
M and C	Marietta and Cincinnati
PC and C	Pittsburgh, Columbus and Cincinnati
S and C	Springfield and Columbus
S and HV	Sciota and Hocking Valley
SD and C	Sandusky, Dayton and Cincinnati
SM and N	Sandusky, Mansfield and Newark
SMV and P	Springfield, Mt. Vernon and Pittsburgh
T and W	Toledo and Western

Source: Base map from George R. Taylor and Irene D. Neu, *The American Railroad Network, 1861-1890* (Cambridge: Harvard University Press, ©Copyright 1956 by the President and Fellows of Harvard College).Reprinted by permission of the Harvard University Press.

Map II-B

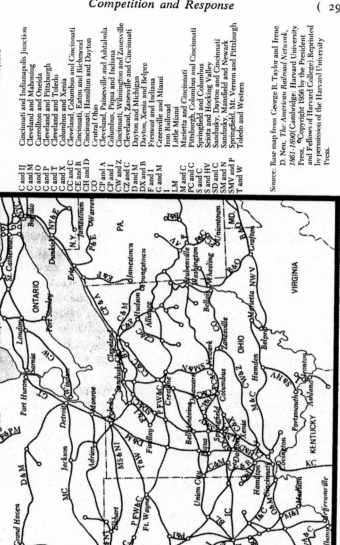

The Baltimore & Ohio had been first among the major eastern railroads to build westward, as early as 1827. But it was one of the last to complete its connections through Ohio to the Mississippi Valley. Its system in Ohio was built from the Ohio River westward through Zanesville, Newark, and Columbus. A connecting road to Marietta gave the B. & O. access to the Marietta & Cincinnati and by that road to Cincinnati. The B. & O. system reached St. Louis in 1857, with completion of the Ohio & Mississippi Railroad.

In the northwest corner of the state, new railroad construction challenged the Wabash & Erie Canal trade, just as the big east-west systems associated with the Pennsylvania, the New York Central, and the B. & O. were by the mid-1850's taking traffic away from the Miami and Ohio canals and the Muskingum Improvement. The Pittsburgh, Fort Wayne & Chicago Railroad was completed—and intersected the Wabash & Erie Canal in Indiana —in 1854. Facing loss of their local commerce, the canal towns promoted and financed the Toledo, Wabash & Western Railroad, completed in 1856 between Toledo and Lafayette, Indiana. Meanwhile, another competitor appeared when the Michigan Southern company invested some three million dollars in the Northern Indiana line. Completed in 1857, the Northern Indiana provided still a third east-west railway to compete with Toledo's canal trade.

Unlike these railroads, the Cincinnati, Wilmington & Zanesville was an orphan road, bereft of support from the eastern trunk-line companies. Financed largely by local government subscriptions, it was completed in 1857. Since it lacked its own line into Cincinnati, it was at the mercy of the Little Miami, which diverted traffic from it and reduced it to the status of a local carrier only.

Northeastern Ohio did not lag in the frenzied race for new railroads. Not content with Cleveland's already ample railroad connections, the city's businessmen sought a more direct rail route to Pittsburgh and financed the Cleveland & Mahoning Railroad in the late fifties. The project foundered during the 1857 financial crisis, after it had been completed to Youngstown. Stranded there and beset with chronic operating deficits, the C. & M. ironically did achieve one triumph: it took away the Mahoning

Canal's trade, and later bought up majority control of the canal, effectively ending its career.

In southern Ohio's iron region, lying between the Scioto and Hocking rivers, mine owners pressed for new railroads in order to exploit known iron resources located inland from the natural streams. In 1853 they completed the Scioto Valley & Hocking Railroad, subsidized with a subscription by Jackson County, which connected Portsmouth (the Ohio Canal's southern terminus) with the iron region. A thirteen-mile short line, the Ironton Railroad, was meanwhile built from a point on the Ohio River upstream from Portsmouth into the iron district of Lawrence County.

The only other major Ohio railway built in the late 1850's and not planned as part of an east-west system was the Dayton & Michigan. This company was designed to extend the Cincinnati, Hamilton & Dayton route northward to Toledo and Detroit, and it received handsome financial support from the parent road. Completed in 1859, it was operated under joint management with the C. H. & D.

Although local aid continued to play a role in railroad construction, it was overshadowed in the 1850's by an influx of private risk capital. One major source of funds was the eastern trunk-line railroad companies, which were themselves the instruments of a great commercial rivalry that pitted New York against Philadelphia, Baltimore, and later Boston. For Ohio was "the transit ground, where the commercial contest for the trade of the West must be waged between the great northern Atlantic cities." Thus the Pennsylvania, the Baltimore & Ohio, and the New York Central lines all purchased stock and bonds outright, or else guaranteed bond issues, of their connecting roads in Ohio.[59] Outside capital also came into the state in the form of bond purchases by individuals and financial institutions who sought more conservative types of investment: eastern and foreign (mainly English) investors bought nearly all the 74 million dollars of bonds issued by Ohio's railroads up to 1860.[60]

Of less importance than outside capital, but nonetheless a crucial determinant of the pace and location of new railroad construction, was investment in sister companies by the more successful early Ohio railroads. The wealthier Ohio companies played a "dowager" role, helping to finance connecting lines and branch roads which they sometimes absorbed, sometimes operated as separate corporations under joint management.[61]

The inpouring of new investment that produced a 3,000-mile railroad network in the state by 1860 also created financial difficulties for many of the Ohio roads. Of 140 million dollars invested in the state's railways up to 1860, 40 million dollars represented capitalization of lines that were in bankruptcy by that time.[62] For there had been much watering of stock, and many of the railroad bonds had been issued at heavy discounts.[63] In addition, the large number of roads in operation, many of them built on closely parallel routes, had led to cutthroat competition and a general rate decline. Although some of the roads completed early in the 1850's still enjoyed adequate profits at mid-decade, conditions became desperate for most of them after the 1857 panic, when freight charges and railroad profits declined precipitously under the combined impact of intense competition and price deflation.[64] (See Table 11.2.)

As one means of salvaging their finances, the railroads attempted to consolidate connecting lines and formed agreements for joint management or division of profits. At the same time, they launched a more direct attack on rate competition as such: on several occasions between 1852 and 1860 they held conventions at which all the major lines agreed upon set rate scales and banned such sharp practices as drawbacks, false advertising, and the issue of free passes to editors and politicians. In every case, however, the agreements were violated and quickly collapsed. What proved to be a more effective means of reducing competition was the intercompany "compact," often secret, by which companies pooled traffic, fixed rates, or divided revenues.[65]

Rate-fixing and similar anticompetitive practices evoked angry reactions from farmers and merchants. Local resentment sometimes developed, too, into a more generalized suspicion of railroads as exploitative corporations controlled by easterners. A Zanesville editor thus warned that "the people of this country are jealous of all monopolies," and he wished that a recently concluded rate-fixing agreement would "explode of its rottonness."

TABLE 11.2

ESTIMATES OF OHIO RAILROADS' OPERATING RECEIPTS AND

EARNINGS, 1839–1859

(thousands of dollars)

YEAR	TOTAL RECEIPTS	NET EARNINGS	PASSENGER RECEIPTS	FREIGHT RECEIPTS	NET RETURN[a] (%)
1839	$ 15.0	$ 7.5	$ 4.0	$ 11.0	n.a.
1849	770.1	399.9	403.9	345.1	7.5%
1855–56	9,927.1	5,217.0	4,739.6	4,853.5	6.4
1858	13,903.2	5,204.6	n.a.	n.a.	4.5[b]
1859	12,927.1	4,923.6	5,679.1	6,447.1	3.7

[a] Net dollars earnings as percentage of cost of construction.
[b] That estimated net earnings (percentages) subsume a large range of earnings performance is well illustrated by the report of individual Ohio railroad companies in 1858. Only a few of the companies in the state declared dividends that year, and others made large profits. For instance, among the roads that did register earnings were the Cleveland, Painesville & Ashtabula, 15%; the Cleveland, Columbus & Cincinnati, 12%; the Little Miami-Columbus & Xenia, 8%; the Cincinnati, Hamilton & Dayton, 7%; the Celeveland & Pittsburgh, 3½%; the Cleveland & Toledo, 6%; the Indianapolis & Cincinnati, 7%; the Central Ohio, 2½%; and the Bellefontaine & Indiana, 4%.

Sources: 1858: Ohio Commissioner of Statistics, *AR*, in *Exec. Docs.*, 1858–59, Part II, pp. 583ff. 1839, 1849, 1855–56, 1859; Albert Fishlow, *American Railroads and the Transformation of the Ante-bellum Economy* (Cambridge, 1965), 178, 322, 326, 328, 337.

Denouncing another intercompany rate agreement, a Cincinnati observer pointed out that "nine tenths of the stock in these great corporations is not held by the original subscribers, but by speculators in stocks who have little claim on public sympathy." Similarly, a Cleveland newspaper warned that legislation might be needed to protect "the local interests" against the "monopolizing and overbearing corporations" which had virtually taken over Ohio's railroads.[66] It was precisely because Ohio railroads had initially been promoted to fulfill localistic ambitions that the reaction against anticompetitive practices was so bitter. The communities that expressed the deepest disillusionment were those which had subsidized railways by means of bond issues, only to be victimized by rate-fixing practices. Towns dependent upon a single railroad were the hardest hit, for they were subjected to blatant short-haul discrimination as the railroads charged them high rates to offset losses incurred at more competitive shipping points.[67]

Rising popular resentment of railroads did produce some regulatory legislation, though it was modest at best. In 1848 the assembly enacted a "general railroad law," intended to subject railroad companies to taxation and to eliminate disparities in the numerous special charters under which the state's lines were operating. In practical terms, however, the law was permissive since any company might accept individual provisions at its discretion; the only restrictive aspect was a requirement that a company accepting any provision must, as *quid pro quo,* give up tax immunities it enjoyed under its original charter. Otherwise, the 1848 law was congenial to railroad interests: it empowered companies to build branch lines anywhere within counties through which they passed, it perpetuated the principle of "offsetting benefits" in eminent domain actions, it authorized local governments to convey public streets to railroad companies, and it provided that railroad property would be taxed at rates no higher than were imposed on other forms of property. Although one section of the act provided for maximum rate charges of 5 cents per ton-mile on freight carried more than thirty miles, it too was entirely permissive: the only companies likely to accept this provision were those whose charters had provided for lower rates.[68]

The only Ohio law enacted in the 1850's that even approached a meaningful regulatory policy was an act of May 1852 that outlawed long-haul rate discrimination and prescribed adherence to published rate schedules. But the law provided no penalties for violation, offering only court injunctions as remedy for abuse. Moreover, both the railroad managers and those who favored state regulation questioned the constitutionality of the law because it clearly abridged charter rights. In fact, the act was never enforced nor brought to a test in the courts.[69]

Neither the Democratic nor the Republican party, each of

which controlled the legislature at various times in the 1850's, was united on the question of railroad policy. And because nativism, the slavery question, and anticorporate radicalism factionalized the major parties in Ohio politics, the legislature probably was easy game for railroad managers lobbying at Columbus and for businessmen who feared legislation that might generally discourage new railroad investment.[70] Thus, even with ample evidence of popular sentiment favoring regulatory legislation and with sister states adopting such measures, the Ohio assembly failed to bring the state's railroad interests under control. If the Ohio railroad network did not exactly grow "like Topsy," the framework of legal authority and explicit public policy in the state did little to confine its growth and a great deal to encourage it.

A major cause of the weakness manifested by the movement for railroad regulation was the more general decline of popular faith in state policy as the proper instrument for fulfilling the interests of the commonwealth.

The erosion of faith in the active state was manifested dramatically in the convention called in 1850 to revise the Ohio constitution. Nearly all the delegates spoke against public internal improvements, and few defended the record of the active state or the canal system. The radical Democratic faction, which was hostile to private corporations of all sorts and stood for strong regulatory powers generally, was not a defender of the active state. This group denounced the public debt as an onerous burden, and some radicals denied outright that past expenditures on canals had contributed to the state's economic growth.[71] The conservative Democrats disagreed with their radical brethren on corporation policy, but had no substantial differences on public enterprise. Only among the Whigs were to be found three outspoken defenders of the state's old canal policy, but even they were ready to concede that private capital had become more than adequate to supply basic transport needs.[72] Delegates of all political persuasions who represented "neglected" districts, which lacked adequate transport, denounced the existing public debt, which involved taxation of all the state's citizens in the interest of a favored few. On the whole, this group sought authority for local governments to build roads or aid turnpikes and railroad companies, thereby avoiding the need to formulate overall state plans that produced unequal benefits.[73] Repeatedly the delegates listened, without protesting, to claims that "the exact economy of commercial men" would provide improvements far more efficiently than could the state.[74] Though in the 1830's praise for state transport projects had been the stock-in-trade of nearly all Ohio politicians, now there was wide agreement that the state policy had proved a disaster.

It was no surprise, therefore, when the convention wrote into the new constitution a prohibition against any further increase of state debt. And, as noted earlier, even borrowing by local governments for aid to private corporations (including railroads) was banned, despite objections from representatives of the neglected districts.[75] It was, in short, a victory for doctrinaire opponents of the active state. And this boded ill for the future of the state canals. For if the ideological basis for public enterprise was eroding, then only a pragmatic rationale for the canals remained. And once tonnage of canal traffic declined or deficits were incurred, as happened only a few years later, the pragmatic basis of support too would be undermined.

THE ADMINISTRATIVE DEFENSE

Even though many of their political associates denounced the active state during the constitutional debates, the Democrats who dominated the board of public works from 1849 to 1857 did all possible to strengthen the canal enterprise. They courted popular opinion with strong statements praising the canals; they sought the legislature's approval for new expenditures to improve navigation on the canal system; and they used the state rate-making power aggressively in competition with the railroads.

In pleading the case for the canals in its public reports, the board recalled the condition of the Ohio economy in 1825, asserting that transport improvement had been fundamental to development of "real civilization" in the state.[76] The best way to assure a continued progressive role for the canals, the board argued, was

to keep them in good repair and enlarge them so as to encourage
heavier traffic. Employing its discretionary administrative powers,
the board ordered extensive repairs in 1850, and rebuilt nineteen
heavy locks on the Ohio Canal. The following year, the board
proposed to the legislature that Ohio emulate New York and
undertake a major program of reconstruction, enlarging and
deepening the entire Portsmouth-Cleveland line.[77] But the legislature refused to make such appropriations in 1851, and repeatedly turned down similar requests afterward. The last major
renovation that the assembly did approve involved replacement
in 1851 of decaying wooden locks, originally built as "temporary"
a decade earlier. From that time forward, the deterioration of
reservoir facilities, aqueducts, culverts, and other installations
rendered navigation on the canals increasingly hazardous and
uncertain.[78]

Though it won little support for improving or enlarging the
canals, the board acted independently to protect the canal traffic
by imaginative manipulation of canal tolls as a rate-making device.
In 1848 the first lake-to-river railroad line was opened between
Cincinnati and Sandusky. Then in 1851 the threat of the iron
horse became more imposing as the Mansfield & Sandusky
reached Newark, an Ohio Canal port; the Cincinnati, Hamilton &
Dayton was completed parallel to the Miami Canal line; and the
Cleveland, Columbus & Cincinnati transected the state, threatening the trade of both the Miami and Ohio canal systems. To meet
these challenges, the board reduced tolls by an average of 30 per
cent. It also instituted "local discrimination," by which preferential, low canal tolls were established at port towns served by
both rail and canal lines. Individual board members were also
permitted to adjust tolls on portions of the canals that they super-
vised, in order to meet the day-to-day exigencies of railway
competition.[79]

Dayton and Newark were the principal focal points of rate
warfare in 1851–52. The Cincinnati, Hamilton & Dayton Railroad
proposed to the canal board a pool arrangement, whereby the
railroad and the Miami Canal would share equally in traffic
between Dayton and Cincinnati. The canal board quickly publicized the railroad managers' cynical attitude toward competition,
and refused to accept the arrangement. A rate war ensued, so

intense that the board was forced to reduce the flour toll between Dayton and Cincinnati to a nominal level of one mill per ton-mile.[80] At Newark, the Mansfield & Sandusky Railroad threatened the business of the canal with special services and rate cuts. In response, the canal board reduced Newark-Cleveland tolls on flour, wheat, pork and whiskey from the old maximum of one dollar per ton to 90 cents in March 1852; and a month later the commissioner in charge ordered further reductions to 80 and 70 cents.[81]

Canal officials admitted that the local-discrimination policy in tolls was "a very odious one, not to be tolerated at all if it can possibly be avoided." But forwarding merchants in the towns that profited from railroad-canal competition gave the board little comfort. Although they pleaded it was only "by the necessity of self-protection" that they gave freight to the railroads, in practice they played one side against the other, finally demanding complete removal of canal tolls.[82]

As railroad competition intensified, the board reduced tolls repeatedly. Maximum charges on wheat and flour, which had been $2.50 per ton on the Ohio Canal in 1850, were cut to between 70 cents and $1.20 in 1853. Maximum tolls on corn were reduced from $1.50 per ton in 1850 to $1 in 1853, and toll charges of merchandise fell from $5 to $1.50 in the same period. On the Miami and Wabash & Erie canals, merchandise tolls were reduced from a maximum of $3 per ton in 1850 to $1.40 in 1853, and tolls on pork from $1.50 to 80 cents.[83] From 1853 to 1860, tolls fluctuated according to commodity and locality, but the trend continued downward. Increases were attempted in 1855 and 1858, in hopes that the railroad companies would respond by raising their own charges to remunerative levels. In each case, the increase was quickly rescinded; and in June 1858 the board finally adopted maximum toll rates of 50 cents per ton for canal shipments of any distance on farm produce, whiskey, meat, flour, and other staples.[84]

While warfare with the railroads continued, the board of public works developed new rhetorical arguments in defense of the canals. The board's annual reports continually reiterated that the canals ought to be judged not alone by their revenues, but also by their contribution to the economy: the public welfare was "the only legitimate object of a system of public improvements," and the benefits of state canals were not confined to financial returns. In a more aggressive vein, the board condemned outright the competitive techniques being used by railroad management. The railroads' ultimate purpose, the board contended, was not to undertake a "fair competition" but rather to destroy the canal trade and induce the state to abandon its public works. Once freed from the discipline of competition, railroad monopolies would force local shippers to pay for their folly with ruinously high rate charges.[85]

To avert such a disaster, the board proposed in March 1852 that the state enact harsh legislation designed to "protect its revenues from being destroyed." Specifically, the board requested: (1) repeal of laws protecting railroad rights-of-way from vandalism, so that "the companies would soon sue for mercy"; (2) an act requiring removal of railroad bridges built across the canal lines, so that the companies would need to "submit to a system of freightage required by their own true interests and the interests of the State"; (3) a law prohibiting railroads from acting as forwarders or dealing in produce on their own account. a means by which they had realized profits on freight even while losing on the transportation itself; and (4) a pro-rata law that forbade discriminatory railroad charges favoring towns also served by canals.[86]

To angry merchants and editors in the towns that would be affected adversely, such proposals smacked of "utter jacobinism." Derision greeted the doctrine of fair competition which would force the people to market their produce only by such routes as "God, Nature, and the State of Ohio, under the guardian care of the Board of Public Works, have supplied them with."[87] Nonetheless, the legislature did enact a pro-rata law as proposed by the board. No penalties were attached, however, and the law could not be enforced. All the more extreme proposals of the board were ignored.[88] The unwillingness of the legislature, and even of the hard-core faction of doctrinaire anticorporation radicals, to put teeth in regulatory legislation was an ominous portent for the state canals.

When tonnage carried by the canals began to decline after

TABLE 11.3

REVENUES AND AGGREGATE TONNAGE OF THE OHIO STATE CANALS
1849–1860
(selected years)

| YEAR | AGGREGATE TONNAGE[a] | | NET REVENUES[d] |
	MIAMI & ERIE[b]	OHIO ERIE[c]	
1849	275,601	295,737	$278,525
1851	403,022	494,065	493,018
1853	542,578	570,363	172,836
1855	352,499	384,530	93,421
1857	355,477	284,346	(—12,944)
1859	199,501	264,219	(—52,900)
1860	323,440	256,214	(—107,761)

[a] Combined tonnage of arrivals and clearances at termini (Cleveland, Portsmouth, Cincinnati, Toledo). This is, of course, only a rough measure of total tonnage carried, as it takes no account of way freight that did not arrive or leave from terminal cities. In terms of relative change, however, tonnage measured as clearances and arrivals from *all* ports moved in almost exactly the same magnitudes as those indicated above.
[b] Includes Miami Canal, Miami Extension Canal, and Wabash & Erie Canal.
[c] Includes Ohio Canal, Muskingum Improvement, Walhonding, Hocking Valley, and minor feeder canals. Does not include Mahoning Canal except as its trade was reported at Cleveland, having passed onto the Ohio Canal.
[d] Gross receipts less tolls refunded, expenses of collection, superintendence and repairs (including items sometimes accounted for as "construction" and not set off against earnings), salaries of officers, and incidental expenses.

Sources: Tonnage from annual reports of Board of Public Works, 1848–1860. Financial data from *Executive Docs.*, 1861, Part I, 499.

1853, the premises on which discussion of their fate was based had to change. No longer was it possible to maintain that the canals served an economic function of growing importance by virtue of freight carried. Now, the board of public works began to emphasize instead that the canals—even if they suffered outright deficits—were valuable because they provided competition for the railroads and averted railway monopoly.[89] But the legislature took a less sanguine view. In 1853 it voted to sell for a nominal sum the Warren County, which produced no revenues; and a year later it ordered the National Road in Ohio to be leased to private operators for only six thousand dollars a year.[90] Gross receipts on the trunk-line canals fell from their peak in 1851, when $850,000 was collected, to about half a million dollars in 1854. Maintenance costs meanwhile were rising as the ravages of time, wear, and neglect became more troublesome. Rising expenditures for operation of the canals were often regarded as evidence of bureaucratic inefficiency. And so the board yielded to the "well settled view that individuals can do everything in the way of labor required by Governments, cheaper and better than it can be done under the public supervision";[91] and in 1855 it concluded a five-year contract for maintenance and repair of the canals by private firms. This plan was well received in the newspaper press even though the board had awarded contracts to prominent Democrats despite lower bids by some Whig-affiliated businessmen.[92]

The plan was doomed from the start. Far from demonstrating the efficiency of private enterprise, the contracts—because they were to terminate after five years—merely induced the contractors to neglect all but emergency repairs. As a result, the canals reached a nadir in 1856, as mud was allowed to slip down the banks into the water, culverts collapsed, and vegetation clogged reservoirs, feeder lines, and the main ditches themselves. Never had navigation been so uncertain or difficult, and this was disastrous at a time when the railroads were competing successfully against even the best of America's canals. The crisis might have been avoided, for the canal board had reserved the right to make repairs at the contractors' expense when negligence was evident. But the legislature had cut the board's budget so sharply in 1856 that adequate supervision of the lines by state officials proved impossible.[93]

The fiasco ended in 1857, when a committee of the legislature discovered that fraud and collusion had occurred during the original negotiations. The committee, which was dominated by Republicans, blamed the whole affair on the canal board and said nothing of the contractors' negligence. Its report led the general assembly to repudiate the 1855 contracts as fraudulent. This unusual action was supported by the courts, but only after a protracted suit during which the canals were left to deteriorate still further.[94]

During the debate on the legality of the 1855 contracts, one faction of legislators sought to rid the state of its canals altogether by their outright sale to private interests. Opponents of the move blocked it successfully, however, arguing that the railroads would inevitably obtain control and close down the canals. Even at this late date, some spokesmen were still insisting that the canals "amply repay the interest of the public debt in the benefits to commerce."[95]

SURRENDER

By the late 1850's sentiment for disposal of the public works to private enterprise had become one of the principal political questions in Ohio, often crowding even the slavery issue from the front pages of the state's newspapers.[96] At no time had there been much public sympathy in Ohio for maintaining the canals if they produced insufficient revenues, and after 1856 annual operating deficits led to rising public pressure for sale of the public works. Meanwhile, the sharp decline in railroad rates during the post-1857 depression was undermining the old argument that the canals helped keep railroad shipping charges competitive. Then, a series of floods in 1858 and 1860 did major damage to the already antiquated canal lines, virtually forcing the legislature to face either a costly program of reconstruction or else the alternative of complete abandonment.[97] This cycle of miseries had important political ramifications. As one astute editor summarized the issue in 1860, many sections of the state were "restive under the present [tax] burden"; recurring deficits were an embarrassment to the party in power; "repairs actually demanded by judicious economy" were being postponed; and yet sale of the canals to private interests would involve dismantling a sizable and important political-patronage device.[98] The political difficulties of the canal issue were even more prickly because the state's major parties were both under pressure from factions divided on other questions, especially slavery and abolitionism.[99]

Eager to remove this troublesome question from state politics, the leaders of all the parties concluded that the canals must be sold. In 1859 a Democratic legislature finally pushed through a bill for lease of the canals to private parties for five years, but the terms were too harsh and no bidders came forward.[100] This left the issue to the Republicans when they captured a majority in the legislature during the 1859 state elections. Although the official Republican newspaper press favored sale or lease of the canals, the party came under heavy pressure from chambers of commerce in the canal towns, and also from "republican babes" who held canal jobs, to maintain the public works. Delay proved safer than decision; and so the assembly adjourned in 1860 without taking action.[101]

When the legislature convened in December 1860 the Republican governor, William Denison, provided no real leadership. In an ambiguous recommendation on the canal issue, Denison deplored the taxation of "unimproved" counties to maintain deficit-ridden public works. On the other hand, he feared that sale of the canals would "conflict with the well established policy of every commercial State to multiply rather than lessen the avenues of trade."[102]

From the board of public works came divided, though less ambiguous, counsel. The sole Democratic member declared in principle against continued public enterprise, claiming that the canals had lost traffic because the state's private railroads were run with such "energy, economy, [and] close and vigilant business management."[103] The Republican majority, on the other hand, opted in favor of continuing state operation of the canals or else leasing them to private parties with close safeguards against their control by the railroad interests. Finally, the Republican legislature decided in favor of the leasing proposal. On June 2, 1861, the Ohio canals were leased to a syndicate of six operators for a ten-year term, with a nominal rental of only $20,075 per year charged.[104]

And so culminated the movement for liquidation of Ohio's public works. To have maintained the canals as a public enterprise would have required large-scale appropriations (probably at least two million dollars) for basic reconstruction of locks and dredging of the lines. It would also have required public tolerance of annual operating deficits, however, and there was no evidence of popular willingness to accept this inevitability. For by 1860 there was an evident, widespread acceptance of the notion that only private enterprise could operate the canals profitably; and if this failed, it would merely prove that artificial waterways had been rendered obsolete by the railroads and were an expensive monument to an earlier era. "Every one who observes," a Republican editor declared in defense of the canal lease, "must have learned that private enterprise will execute a work with profit, when a government would sink dollars by the thousand."[105] This homely maxim would have been irrelevant in 1825, when only the state could command capital in sums sufficient to support canal construction; but by 1861 it had become an accepted truism.

In subsequent years, the leasing arrangement was renewed by the state, and then in 1877 the canals reverted to public management. Afterward, all segments of the canal system except the two main trunk lines were either sold to railroad corporations, ceded to abutting landowners, or else simply abandoned by gross neglect, which permitted their preëmption. In the 1890's a movement began for reconstruction of the canals as a means of forcing competitive rates upon Ohio railroads, but the realistic occasion for such a measure had long since passed.[106] Finally, in the Progressive era of the early twentieth century, the major canal reservoir sites were converted into public parks. In the 1960's small segments of the major canal lines survived for local water supply or pleasure boating, while some portions lying within cities had become rights-of-way for water and sewer lines. Except for scattered locks, whose ruins served as a poignant reminder of a once great state enterprise, the Ohio canals had been reclaimed by the landscape of the country.

NOTES

1. On early eastern promotion, see Julius Rubin, "An Imitative Public Improvement: The Pennsylvania Mainline," in *Canals and American Economic Development*, ed. Carter Goodrich

(New York, 1962), 82ff.; George R. Taylor, *The Transportation Revolution, 1815–1860* (New York, 1951), Chap. 5; and R. E. Carlson, "British Railroads and Engineers and the Beginnings of American Railroad Development," *Business History Review*, XXXIV (1960), 137–49.

2. Delaware *Patron*, Jan. 5, Jan. 19, 1826. The British experiments in question were the famous Stockton and Darlington trials of 1825.

3. Hamilton *Intelligencer*, Jan. 29, 1835. For an instructive account of varying early views on the nature of railways, see Stephen Salsbury, *The State, the Investor, and the Railroad* (Cambridge, 1967), 37–61. In Ohio, during ensuing years, James Kilbourne changed his views several times on the comparative merits of canals, railroads, and turnpikes. (See Delaware *Patron*, Sept. 14, 1826; Columbus *Ohio State Journal & Gazette*, Jan. 12, 1836; and Columbus *Ohio Statesman*, Jan. 7, 1839.)

4. Of special importance were the Mad River & Lake Erie and the Monroeville & Sandusky projects. (See Chap. 4, above.)

5. Lebanon *Western Star*, Nov. 13, 1835, quoted in E. O. Porter, "Financing Ohio's Pre-Civil War Railroads," *OAHQ*, LVII (1948), 218.

6. *Western Hemisphere* (Columbus), Feb. 1, 1837 (deploring "little local works"); see also Hamilton *Intelligencer*, Nov. 19, 1831; and broadside "Internal Improvement Meeting," Jan. 9, 1836, in CC Papers.

7. Lancaster *Gazette*, Aug. 4, 1829. On the Charleston project, see Ulrich B. Phillips, *A History of Transportation in the Eastern Cotton Belt* (New York, 1908), 169–71.

8. Computed from annual laws, local and general, of Ohio. A slightly different computation is given in G. H. Evans, *Business Incorporations in the U. S.* (New York, 1943), 18, Table 10.

9. 1802 Ohio Constitution, Art. viii, sec. 27.

10. See James Willard Hurst, *Law and the Conditions of Freedom in the 19th Century U. S.* (Madison, 1956), 17. The doctrine of public purpose did not always lead to limited liability. Indeed, in many states, this became a subject of considerable conflict, explained by Edwin M. Dodd, in *American Business Corporations until 1860* (Cambridge, 1954), 84ff.

11. One charter of 1836 required appraisers to assess "the true amount of damages, over and above the benefits arising from

said road." 34 L.O.L. (*Laws of Ohio: Local*) 533, sec. 8.
See also 30 L.O.L. 15, sec. 15; 34 L.O.L. 576, sec. 13. (The
charters of Ohio railroads are reproduced in full in Commissioner of Railroads, *AR*, 1870, Vol. I.) On eminent domain
and railroad seizures of property generally, see Hurst, *Law
and the Conditions of Freedom*, 63–64. Eminent domain law
varied greatly, however, from state to state in the early nineteenth century. Ohio's statutory provisions allowing offsetting
benefits in computation of damages, as they appeared in railroad charters, followed the formula established in the state's
1825 canal law, which had directed "a just and equitable appraisal of the loss or damage, if any, over and above the
benefit and advantage to the respective owners and proprietors." (Quoted in 6 Western Law Journal 353.) On the transition from law centered on government's exercise of eminent
domain for its own enterprises, to law relative to devolution
of the power on private corporations, see Arthur Lenhoff,
"Development of the Concept of Eminent Domain," *Columbia
Law Review*, XLII (1942), 599–600 and citations. Leonard
W. Levy's discussion of railroads and eminent domain, in
The Law of the Commonwealth and Chief Justice Shaw (Cambridge, 1957), 117ff., is flawed by his contention (at p. 120 n.)
that "the first and only mention of 'eminent domain' in an
American decision before 1834" came in a New York case
of 1831. See, for instance, the numerous cases cited by J. A. C.
Grant, "The 'Higher Law' Background of Eminent Domain,"
Wisconsin Law Review, VI (1930–31), 67–85.

12. 1850 Constitutional Convention, *Official Reports of the Debates and Proceedings*, ed. J. V. Smith (Columbus, 1851),
372, 893; Gregory *v.* C.C. & C. Railroad, 4 Ohio State Rep.
675 (1855).

13. 45 L.O.L. 178, sec. 4. This instance was called to my attention by Walter Marvin, "Columbus and the Railroads of Central Ohio" (Ph.D. diss., Ohio State University, 1953), pp.
20–21.

14. For example, 34 L.O.L. 404, sec. 19.

15. See text at n. 68, below.

16. Willyard *v.* Hamilton, 7 Ohio Reports at 450 (1836).

17. Matter of Cincinnati, Hamilton, and Dayton Railroad, 6
Western Law Journal (Court of Common Pleas, Hamilton
County) at 352 (1849).

18. Cincinnati, Wilmington & Zanesville Railroad Co. *v.* Clinton

County, 1 Ohio State Rep. 77, at 94–95 (1852). The courts stretched their beneficent hand still further over railroad interests by ruling that a railroad was "presumed to be a benefit" unless proved otherwise. Sargent *v.* Ohio & Mississippi Railroad, 1 Handy (Cincinnati Superior Court) at 61–62 (1854). It was ruled that railroads engaging in eminent domain proceedings, because they embodied a public purpose, could not be made subject to common law remedies as public nuisances, in Hueston *v.* Railroad, 4 Ohio State Rep. 685 (1855). The Hueston decision in effect applied to railroad officials the same tort immunity in eminent domain operations as had been extended to state canal officials in Bates *v.* Cooper, 5 Ohio Reports 115. On the origins and ramifications of tort immunity in public internal improvements projects, see J. W. MacDonald, "The Administration of Tort Liability Law in New York," *Law and Contemporary Problems,* IX (1942), 262–64.

19. Matter of C. H. & D. Railroad, cited n. 17, at 354.

20. 30 L.O.L. 15, sec. 13; 34 L.O.L. 576.

21. 43 L.O.L. 280, sec. 1; 46 L.O.L. 256, sec. 1.

22. For example, 48 L.O.L. 267.

23. 30 L.O.L. 15, sec. 24; 34 L.O.L. 533, sec. 11; 34 L.O.L. 404, sec. 16.

24. See 34 L.O.L. 533, sec. 11; 34 L.O.L. 404, sec. 15; 34 L.O.L. 452.

25. For example, 37 L.O.L. 61; 30 L.O.L. 146; 43 L.O.L. 405.

26. 44 L.O.L. 167, sec. 7.

27. 44 L.O.L. 28; 45 L.O.L. 81.

28. This was because the railroads involved became subject only to the loose rate controls of the general railroad law enacted in 1848.

29. See 34 L.O.L. 404.

30. David M. Ellis, "Rivalry between the New York Central and the Erie Canal," *New York History,* XXIX (July 1948), 276. See also Frederick Merk, "Eastern Antecedents of the Grangers," *Agricultural History,* XIII (Jan. 1949), 1–8. The strength of popular sentiment favoring canals in New York was demonstrated by the results of a constitutional-amendment referendum in 1854. See Ronald Shaw, *Erie Water West* (Lexington, 1966), 395; also *ibid.,* 305ff.

31. Toledo *Blade,* June 27, Dec. 5, 1846. See also H. Scheiber, "Urban Rivalry and Internal Improvements," *OH,* LXXI (1962), 295ff.

32. Because Toledo was situated in territory then claimed by both Michigan and Ohio, the charter for the Erie & Kalamazoo was issued by the Michigan legislature. See Francis P. Weisenburger, *The Passing of the Frontier, 1825–1850* (Columbus, 1941), 113; Thomas D. Odle, "The American Grain Trade of the Great Lakes," *Inland Seas,* VIII (1952), 100.

33. L. Klein, "Rail-roads in the United States," *Journal of the Franklin Institute,* new series, XXVI (1840), 100; Cleveland *Herald & Gazette,* July 2, 1838; Cleveland *Herald,* Jan. 28, 1840; Weisenburger, *Passing of the Frontier,* 113.

34. Robert L. Black, *The Little Miami Railroad* (Cincinnati, n. d. but 1941), 13–31.

35. The Little Miami's subscribers paid not more than $132,000 in cash prior to completion of the first segment; the Mad River stockholders paid largely in land rather than cash; and the Monroeville & Sandusky apparently did little better since it was still using horsepower in 1845. (Black, *Little Miami, passim;* Mad River & Lake Erie Railroad Co., *Annual Report, 1853* [Sandusky, 1854], 4; A. D. Chandler, Jr., "Patterns of American Railroad Finance, 1830–1850," *Business History Review,* XXVIII [Sept. 1954], 258–59.)

36. Chandler, *ibid.,* 258–59; Arthur M. Johnson and Barry E. Supple, *Boston Capitalists and Western Railroads* (Cambridge, 1967), 84–86. The substantial stock and bond sales of these two roads in the East in 1845 controvert Paul Cootner's thesis, in "The Role of Railroads in United States Economic Growth," *Journal of Economic History,* XXIII (1963), 497–98, that the great foodstuffs export boom of 1847 was critical to the revival of interest in east-west railroads. But Cootner's more embracing interpretation, that the steady rise in western shipments to the Atlantic Coast in the early forties awakened expectations that railway investment could be made profitable, is entirely persuasive. (Compare Johnson and Supple, *Boston Capitalists,* 79.)

37. George R. Taylor and Irene D. Neu, *The American Railroad Network, 1861–1890* (Cambridge, 1956), 38ff.; Pennsylvania Railroad Company, *5th Annual Report* (1852), 19.

38. Scheiber, "Urban Rivalry," 237ff.; John Pixton, *The Marietta Cincinnati Railroad, 1845–1883* (Pennsylvania State University Studies, #17, 1966), 12, 22–23, 42.

39. Alphonso Taft, *A Lecture on Cincinnati and Her Rail-roads* (Cincinnati, 1850), 12.

40. Charles Francis Adams observed in 1840: "The tendency to improvements of a local and wholly useless character, instead of being counteracted by the separate action of the States, [was] infinitely increased." (*North American Review*, LI [1840], 320–21.) See also Carter Goodrich, *Government Promotion of American Canals and Railroads, 1800–1890* (New York, 1960), 45.

41. 1850 Const. Conv., *Debates*, 1268.

42. Zanesville *Courier* (weekly), Oct. 3, 1851.

43. Size of local debt for railroad aid in 1850 given as five million dollars in 1850 Const. Conv., *Debates*, 958; the estimate of 12.8 million dollars total Ohio railroad investment is by George R. Taylor, in National Bureau of Economic Research, *Trends in the American Economy in the Nineteenth Century* (Princeton, 1960), 539.

44. 1850 Const. Conv., *Debates*, 950–51.

45. Marietta & Cincinnati Railroad, *6th Annual Report* (1856), pp. 21–22; John H. James to S. Kenner, Nov. 22, 1852, John H. James Papers, OHS.

46. Zanesville *Daily Courier*, Sept. 21, 1847; see also the heavy rural vote against public aid, reported in Lancaster *Gazette*, April 10, 1851; and the discussion of rural opposition in Zanesville *Courier* (weekly), Sept. 25, 1851. Marvin, "Columbus and the Railroads of Central Ohio," pp. 104ff., discusses opposition to railroad aid in Franklin County.

47. 1850 Const. Conv., *Debates*, 258.

48. The vote is in *ibid.*, 960. Only twelve delegates opposed the prohibition, and their statements during the debate indicate they were all from counties contemplating railroad aid; the vote cut across party lines, despite the fact that some radical Democrats wished to make opposition to local debt a partisan issue.

49. Cincinnati, Wilmington & Zanesville Railroad *v.* Clinton County, 1 Ohio State Rep. 77 (1852).

50. *Ibid.*, at 90, 94–95, 105. A related decision (1 Ohio State Rep. 105) held township subscriptions under pre-1851 authorizations to be legal on identical grounds.

51. The 1860 estimate of total local debt is in *Executive Docs.*, 1860, Vol. II, pp. 497–98.

52. F. L. Paxson, "Railways of the 'Old Northwest' before the Civil War," Wisconsin Academy of Sciences, Arts and Letters, *Transactions*, XVII, Pt. 1 (Oct. 1912), 248–49.

53. Board of Public Works, special report in *Executive Docs.*, 1851–52, No. 39, pp. 641–42.

54. *Executive Docs.*, 1850–51, No. 34, pp. 675–76; Cincinnati, Hamilton & Dayton Railroad Co., *1st Annual Report* (Cincinnati, 1850), 7; S. S. L'Hommedieu, in *Cincinnati Pioneer*, III (April 1874), 18; Black, *Little Miami*, 74–75.

55. Cleveland, Columbus & Cincinnati Railroad Co., *1st Annual Report* (Cleveland, 1852), 5–6; Marvin, "Columbus and the Railroads of Central Ohio," 168–91; William G. Rose, *Cleveland: The Making of a City* (Cleveland, 1950), 145ff.

56. Cleveland, Columbus & Cincinnati Railroad Co., *1st Annual Report*, 9; J. H. Kennedy, "The Early Railroad Interests of Cleveland," *Magazine of Western History*, II (1885), 594–619 (a useful brief history of Cleveland's early lines); and, on the efforts of the Pennsylvania legislature to frustrate the plans to connect at Erie, Donald H. Kent, "The Erie War of the Gauges," *Pennsylvania History*, XV (Oct. 1948), 253–75; and Laura G. Sanford, *The History of Erie County, Pennsylvania* (n. p., 1894), 120.

57. Cleveland & Pittsburgh Rail Road Co., *Report upon the Survey, Location and Estimates* . . . (Pittsburgh, 1847); *id.*, *Report of the President and Directors*, Jan. 7, 1852 (Hudson, Ohio, 1852); see also William K. Schusler, "The Railroad Comes to Pittsburgh," *Western Pennsylvania Hist. Mag.*, XLIII (Sept. 1960), 254–55; and R. Richard Wohl, "Henry Noble Day," in *Men in Business*, ed. William Miller (Cambridge, 1952), 175.

58. No effort is made here to document the history of Ohio railroads in the 1850's. No single published work is adequate, but the best introduction is Marvin, "Columbus and the Railroads of Central Ohio," cited earlier. On the Lake Shore roads, see the useful chapters in Randolph C. Downes, *History of Lake Shore Ohio* (3 vols., New York, 1952), Vol. I; on the Cincinnati roads, Black, *Little Miami;* on the B. & O. connections, William P. Smith, *Book of the Great Railway Celebrations of 1857* (New York, 1858); on the Pennsylvania Railroad's connections, Pixton, *The Marietta and Cincinnati*, and H. W. Schotter, *Growth and Development of the Pennsylvania Railroad Company, 1846–1926* (Philadelphia, 1927); and on the roads of northwest Ohio, H. L. Kerlin, "History of the Railroads that Entered Toledo before the Civil War" (M.A. thesis, Ohio State University, 1938). Railroad development

in Southern Ohio's iron district is treated in Vernon D. Keeler, "An Economic History of the Jackson County Iron Industry," *OAHQ*, XLII (1933), Chap. 3.

59. Pennsylvania Railroad Co., *6th Annual Report* (Philadelphia, 1853), 32–33; see also Pennsylvania Company, *Corporate History of the Pittsburgh, Fort Wayne and Chicago Railway Company* (Pittsburgh, 1875), 3–9. The Pennsylvania Railroad expended nearly two million dollars to finance connecting roads on three alternate routes across the state; the Michigan Southern put some three million dollars into the Northern Indiana; and the Baltimore & Ohio invested nearly $500,000 in the Central Ohio Railroad and still more in the Marietta & Cincinnati.

60. *Executive Docs.*, 1859–60, Vol. I, pp. 792–93.

61. The most prominent Ohio dowager lines were the Cleveland, Columbus & Cincinnati, which invested about one million dollars in other Ohio roads; the Cincinnati, Hamilton & Dayton, which put $500,000 into two lines connecting its route with interior points in Indiana, and put an equal amount into the Dayton & Michigan; and the Little Miami, which invested about $600,000 in the financing of connecting roads. See Smith, *Book of Great Railway Celebrations*, part 2, pp. 19–20, 23; various annual reports of the C. C. & C. Railroad; Black, *Little Miami, passim;* Cincinnati, Hamilton & Dayton Railroad, *4th Annual Report* (Cincinnati, 1854), 8–9. The term "dowager" railroad was suggested by E. C. Kirkland, in *Men, Cities, and Transportation* (2 vols., Cambridge, 1948), I, 330.

62. Ohio Senate, *Report of the Standing Committee on Railroads* (1861), 2.

63. *Proceedings of a Meeting of . . . Railroad Companies . . . Cleveland, Nov. 28, 1854* (Cleveland, 1854), 14–15.

64. Thomas S. Berry, *Western Prices before 1861* (Cambridge, 1943), 92ff.; *Railroad Record* (Cincinnati), II, 647 (Nov. 23, 1854); J. R. Swan to N. Wright, May 14, 1860, Nathaniel Wright Papers, CHS; Sandusky, Mansfield & Newark Railroad Co., *1st Report of the President and Directors* (Sandusky, 1857), 9ff.

65. Railroad conventions, a neglected subject, are treated briefly in A. L. Kohlmeier, *The Old Northwest as the Keystone of the Arch of American Federal Union* (Bloomington, 1938), 165 *et passim*. Pools, intercompany profit-sharing agreements,

etc., are treated in various annual reports. On two of the most ambitious pooling arrangements, cf. Mad River & Lake Erie Railroad Co., *Annual Report, 1853* (Sandusky, 1853), 10–11; and Sandusky, Dayton & Cincinnati Railroad Co., *Report of a Committee . . . on the Difficulties between Said Road and the Cincinnati, Hamilton and Dayton Road* (Columbus, 1858), 21.

66. Zanesville *City Times*, Nov. 4, 1854; and quotations of Cincinnati and Cleveland papers in William F. Gephart, *Transportation and Industrial Development in the Middle West* (New York, 1909), 174, 183–84.

67. See William Smith, ed., *Annual Statement of the Trade and Commerce of Cincinnati, 1860* (Cincinnati, 1860), 25; and Ohio Board of Agriculture, *6th Annual Report* (1852), 342–43, in which a Logan County correspondent reported the Mad River road's charges of 11.76 cents per mile for 100 bushels of wheat between Bellefontaine and Sandusky, as against only 7.6 cents between Dayton and Sandusky.

68. 46 L.O. 40 (Feb. 11, 1848).

69. 50 L.O. 205 (May 1, 1852). "The law has never been enforced; its requirements are generally disregarded by railroad companies, and no decisions have been made under it." (Commissioner of Railroads, *AR, 1870,* Vol. I, p. 34n.) See also p. 301, below.

70. See *Newark Advocate*, March 24, 1852; and BPW, *17th AR,* in *Executive Docs.*, 1854, Vol. I, No. 3, p. 48. Eugene H. Roseboom, *The Civil War Era* (Columbus, 1944), 255ff., treats Ohio politics in the fifties. The legislature did enact a law in April 1856 prohibiting any new railway construction in counties that had given public aid to other railroads. (Pixton, *Marietta and Cincinnati,* 22.) But the law was aimed specifically at protection of the Marietta & Cincinnati from a projected competitor, and apparently it was either not applied generally or else enacted so late in the decade that it had little effect. See also Gephart, *Transportation,* 195.

71. 1850 Ohio Constitutional Convention, *Official Reports of the Debates and Proceedings,* ed. J. V. Smith (2 vols., Columbus, 1851), 217.

72. *Ibid.*, 349, 444.

73. *Ibid.*, 445.

74. *Ibid.*, 450; see also *ibid.*, 455, 752, 784-87, 1199.

75. Ohio Constitution (1851), art. 8, art. 12. For a summary of

political divisions and issues in the convention, cf. Roseboom, *The Civil War Era,* 126–35.

76. *Executive Docs.,* 1848–49, No. 11, pp. 146, 153. Portions of the ensuing sub-chapter first appeared in slightly different form in my article, "The Rate-Making Power of the State in the Canal Era," *Political Science Quarterly,* LXXVII (Sept. 1962), 408–13.

77. *Executive Docs.,* 1848–49, No. 11, pp. 141–42; *Executive Docs.,* 1850–51, No. 34, pp. 654, 675–76.

78. *Executive Docs.,* 1852–53, I, No. 19, pp. 219–20.

79. *Executive Docs.,* 1851–52, I, No. 22, pp. 293–95.

80. *Ibid.,* I, No. 39, p. 641.

81. Board of Public Works, Minutes (MSS., Dept. of Public Works, Records Rooms, Columbus), Vol. V, pp. 127, 130; James George to Jno. Wheeler, April 15, 1852, BPW Papers.

82. George W. Manypenny to H. Beard, April 2, 1852, BPW Papers, on local discrimination; petition of warehousemen, forwarding and commission merchants, Newark, to BPW, March 31, 1852, *ibid.,* on professed allegiance of merchants to the canal; Manypenny to Levi J. Haughey, April 2, 1852 (copy), BPW Papers.

83. See Appendix 2. Table C, on 1850 tolls; 1853 tolls are in BPW Minutes, Vol. V, pp. 355ff.

84. *Executive Docs.,* 1855–56, I, No. 33, p. 440; BPW Minutes, Vol. VI, pp. 215, 244–45.

85. *Executive Docs.,* 1853–54, I, No. 3, p. 45; Special BPW Report, March 10, 1852, *Executive Docs.,* 1851–52, I, No. 39, pp. 640–41; cf. also *ibid.,* 1850–51, No. 22, pp. 295–96. The board received little help from forwarders in attempting to assure "fair competition." Thus one canal official wrote from Dayton: "While the State has made every reduction in order to retain the trade on the canal I do not hear of the commission men abating one cent from their old rates, but on the contrary holding on to them religiously in every instance." (B. W. Ayres to A. P. Miller, April 17, 1854, BPW Papers.)

86. BPW Report, *Executive Docs.,* 1851–52, I, No. 39, pp. 641–42. The board had exchanged bitter charges with officials of the Central Ohio Railroad, which was in 1852 bridging the canal lines without regard for effects upon the towpath or navigation. Finally, in March, just before the special report was published, the board ordered state crews at Newark to fill in the pits dug for foundations of a bridge then being

built over the Ohio Canal by the C. O. Railroad. (Cf. William
Spencer to Manypenny, March 14, 1852, Stanbery and Wright
to Mr. Blaney, March 29, 1852, BPW Papers.)

87. Cleveland *Herald,* copied in *Zanesville Weekly Courier,* March
26, 1852; the charge of "utter jacobinism" is reported in Lewis
W. Sifford to Manypenny, March 19, 1852, BPW Papers.

88. 50 *Laws of Ohio: General* 205. The law applied to railroad
rates charged by any company "whose line of road extends
. . . to any place in the vicinity of, or to a point of intersection
with, any of the navigable canals or other works of internal
improvement belonging to this state." (*Ibid.,* sec. 1.) The
charge of "capricious tyranny" was levied by a public meeting led by railroad men at Zanesville, reported in *Zanesville
Weekly Courier,* March 25, 1852. On the general history of
pro-rata railroad laws in the 1850's, see Merk, "Eastern Antecedents of the Grangers." See also n. 69, above.

89. *Executive Docs.,* 1853–54, I, No. 3, p. 47. "It is our deliberate
conviction," the board asserted, "that the control of canal
navigation which the people of Ohio wisely retain in themselves, will, during the next 25 years, force the freightage of
our products to a reduced scale of prices, which otherwise
would not be tolerated by the railroad 'fusion' now so manifestly in progress." (*Ibid.*) See also E. L. Bogart, *Internal
Improvements and State Debt in Ohio* (New York, 1924), 101
et passim; Bogart's study (pp. 96–104) treats briefly of railroad-canal competition in the state.

90. *Report of the Joint Committee of the General Assembly on
the Public Works of Ohio* (Columbus, 1857), 54 (hereafter
cited *1857 Joint Committee Report*); *Executive Docs.,* 1855–
56, Vol. I, No. 33, p. 433.

91. The board also asserted: "A distrust has always existed in
the public mind, of the expenditure of public money in the
construction of public works by Government." (*Executive
Docs.,* 1855–56, I, No. 33, p. 439.)

92. *1857 Joint Committee Report,* 3, 14–15; *Ohio State Journal*
clipped in Defiance (Ohio) *Democrat,* No. 24, 1855; Zanesville *City Times,* No. 17, 1855.

93. *Executive Docs.,* 1856–57, I, No. 12, p. 489. For formal bills
of grievances about condition of the canals in 1856, see Cleveland *Leader,* Jan. 20, Feb. 14, 1857. Boatmen on the Ohio
Canal complained that in earlier days, when the canal was in
good repair, the Cleveland-Portsmouth run took 8 to 9 days

with 50-ton loads, costing them an average of $1.44 per ton plus tolls; in 1856 fifteen days was considered good time for the same trip, and costs were four dollars a ton plus tolls because of delays, the need to run with only 30 to 40 tons, and extra expenses for horses and labor. (Cleveland *Leader,* Feb. 12, 1857.)

94. *1857 Joint Committee Report,* 32. "It has been so long the custom to use the public funds *liberally* that it has grown into a vice that can hardly be cured unless the State be cut loose from the whole system of improvements." (*Ibid.*) See also Report of the Attorney General in *Executive Docs.,* 1857–58, II, No. 6, pp. 260–61; *ibid.,* I, No. 12, pp. 481–82; *ibid.,* 1858–59, I, pp. 125, 134; Lima (Ohio) *Western Gazette,* April 22, 1858.

95. *Railroad Record,* 4:817 (Feb. 19, 1857); see also *Zanesville City Times,* April 3, 1858; and the argument against leasing of the canals given by the editor of the Lima (Ohio) *Allen County Democrat,* May 11, 1859. The Cleveland editor, a spokesman for mercantile interests, warned, "It has always been the policy of railroad companies to control all competition," and predicted they would acquire control of the canals in some way. (*Leader,* Feb. 6, 1857.)

96. See, for example, the front-page articles in the Columbus *Ohio State Journal,* 1860–61, *passim.*

97. See *Executive Docs.,* 1859–60, I, pp. 589–90, 596.

98. *Ohio State Journal,* March 13, 1860.

99. Roseboom, *The Civil War Era,* Chaps. 9–11, treats shifts in the political structure during the 1850's.

100. *Ibid.,* 104; *Ohio State Journal,* March 13, 1860.

101. *Ohio State Journal,* Feb. 9, 1860; also *ibid.,* Feb. 25, March 13, March 28, 1860.

102. *Ibid.,* Jan. 7, 1861.

103. Abner Backus's minority statement, cited in *ibid.,* Jan. 10, 1861.

104. *Executive Docs.,* 1861–62, I, pp. 491–92. There were only two bids, apparently collusive. (Bogart, *Internal Improvements,* 110.)

105. *Ohio State Journal,* May 6, 1861.

106. Bogart, *Internal Improvements,* 111–39; C. P. McClelland and C. C. Huntington, *History of the Ohio Canals* (Columbus, 1905), pp. 47–56.

CHAPTER 12

Transportation and Economic Change 1850–1860

THE 1850's were years of swift growth and sweeping structural change in the American national economy. Impetus was given to growth by the opening of California's mining fields, by surges in foreign demand for American exports, by reorganization and quickened growth of eastern manufacturing, and by renewed expansion of settlement and farm-making in the West. More than two and a half million immigrants came into the country, their demand for urban housing contributing to an upswing in urban construction, while their labor provided a vital response to the work-force needs of the railroad construction industry and manufacturing. So dramatic was the increase in railway mileage and traffic—the mileage in operation rose from less than 9,000 in 1850 to 30,000 ten years later, much of the new construction being concentrated in the western states—that the fifties have been termed the period of "railroadization" of the economy. Some have termed the decade the period of the "take-off" into self-sustained economic growth: for in the years from the mid-forties to 1860, there was a major shift in the composition of commodity output, with the share provided by manufacturing rising from about 20 per cent to about one-third; and there was a quickening of urban development, as both commercial and manufacturing cities led in the pattern of overall economic expansion.[1]

The Industrial Revolution, then, was in full progress, and changes in the Ohio economy reflected the larger transformation of American economic life. As in the national economy, urban population in Ohio grew more quickly than rural population; and some of Ohio's commercial cities became more deeply committed to manufacturing, with factory production displacing household crafts and small-scale manufacturing by artisans. Ohio agriculture also reflected national changes. In the United States, the area of land in farms increased by one-third, and farm output rose by half as the fertile lands of the Mississippi Valley were brought into production and mechanization took hold. Confronted now with competition from newly opened regions farther west, Ohio farmers in some districts were forced to shift their pattern of production or even to abandon the land altogether. But in other areas of the state, transportation developments brought the same kind of response from agriculture as they did in the states farther west: more land was improved, new settlement encouraged, and the staple crops (corn and wheat) produced in increasing quantities.

The new lines of transport linking Ohio with both East and West affected the state's merchants as well. To survive, many mercantile firms had to shift either the location of the business or the old style of operations. Manufacturers in Ohio obtained better access to supplies of raw materials, and also more direct transport facilities to an expanding consumer market. But they also confronted more vigorous competition in their local markets from eastern manufacturers, giving an important advantage to those in Ohio who achieved greater efficiency by moving into production on a larger scale.

Not least important of the economic changes in Ohio during the 1850's was the success of railroads in capturing an ever larger share of the state's commerce from the canals. The volume of tonnage carried by the state canals had gone into decline by the mid-fifties, and soon canal revenues dropped below the annual cost of operations.[2] The shift from canal to railroad dominance was effective both in intrastate commerce, within Ohio, and in the trade between the state and outside markets.[3]

Some modern students have argued that canal technology has been underrated, and the superiority of the railroad exaggerated. In the absence of the railroad, it is claimed, the canal lines built prior to 1850 (together with some new canals and river improvements, and a system of feeder-line wagon roads) would have been adequate to perform nearly all the transportation services required by the national economy in the nineteenth century.[4] Interesting as this hypothesis may be to the modern student, it would not have had much relevance for the farmer, merchant, or traveler who in 1850 had to choose between canal and railroad alternatives. Above all, the railroads offered him speed. Several weeks were required to ship goods by the all-water routes between Ohio and the Atlantic coast, whereas railroad shipment usually took only a few days. Railroad transport was available all year long as well, while the canals and Lake Erie were closed by ice for as much as four or five months annually. Even when the canals were navigable, sudden floods, water shortages, or damage to the banks and locks might interrupt traffic for weeks at a time.[5] Hazards of fire, flood, and accident were of course not uncommon on the railways. But when a railroad bridge or right-of-way was closed, traffic usually could be rerouted expeditiously through connecting lines. Moreover, as telegraphic communication came into use, railroads permitted merchants and farmers to take advantage of short-term price movements in distant markets; and many of the more aggressive railroad lines further enhanced their attractiveness to shippers by providing storage and warehouse facilities along their routes.[6]

Although the other advantages of the railroads were numerous, the structure of rate charges naturally continued to be a critical factor in the rivalry with canals. Throughout the fifties, it was least expensive to ship heavy products on the canal-and-lake routes to the East from northern and central Ohio; but in southern Ohio after 1856, it was often most economical for farmers and merchants to use the direct railroad lines to the East. When, in the mid-fifties, the railroad companies concluded arrangements with steamboat lines on the Ohio River and Lake Erie, this brought additional reductions in rates on the rail-and-water routes. And at towns where the rail lines crossed the canals, the

railroads consistently charged less on most products than prevailing canal rates.[7]

The decline in the relative importance of the canals inevitably
affected the major terminal cities. The trade in grain products
between the farm regions of the interior and the major terminal
cities, shown in Table 12.1, illustrates the small proportion of

TABLE 12.1

EXPORTS OF FLOUR, WHEAT, AND CORN FROM THE MAJOR OHIO
EXPORT CITIES: AND PROPORTION OF TOTAL
RECEIVED BY CANAL 1851, 1860

	FLOUR (000 BBL)		WHEAT (000 BU.)		CORN (000 BU.)	
	1851	1860	1851	1860	1851	1860
A. CLEVELAND						
Exports	656	455	2142	912	905	146
Canal receipts	646	158	2530	212	998	89
B. TOLEDO						
Exports	243	808	1640	5341	2775	5387
Canal receipts	197	150	1250	1162	2563	1799
C. CINCINNATI						
Exports[a]	487	428	—	322	102	97
Canal receipts	317	99	130	34	270	170

[a] Years ending Aug. 31, 1851, 1860.

Sources: Exports for 1851: Table 9.3, *supra*.
Exports for 1860: (a) Cleveland. Ohio Commissioner of Statistics, *Annual Report, 1861*, p. 31. (b) Toledo. U. S. Secretary
of the Treasury, *Statistics of the Foreign and Domestic Commerce of the U. S.* (Washington, 1864), p. 155.
Canal receipts: Ohio Board of Public Works, *Annual Reports.*

grain products being received at the termini by canal in 1860,
as compared with the proportion ten years earlier. In the shipment of products from Ohio to outside export markets, the
increasing role of the railroads was similarly manifest (see
Table 12.3).

When central Ohio gained access by direct rail routes to the
East, farmers there began to ship wheat directly to the Atlantic

TABLE 12.2

MAJOR EXPORTS FROM CINCINNATI,
1846–50 AND 1856–60

| COMMODITY (UNIT) | EXPORTS (000 UNITS) | |
	1846–50	1856–60
Flour (bbl.)	269	515
Whiskey (bbl.)	164	336
Pork and bacon (lb.)	1576	705
Pork and bacon (bbl.)	149	108
Grease (bbl.)	4	6
Hides (units)	10[a]	94
Soap (boxes)	8	53
Candles (boxes)	31	181
Lard oil (bbl.)	9	48
Sundry merchandise (packages)	283	1428
Cooperage (pieces)	45	124
Iron and Steel (pieces)	63	679
Coffee (sacks)	18[a]	63
Sugar (hhd.)	9	26
Cotton (bales)	4[a]	34
Molasses (bbl.)	18[a]	45

[a] 1847–1850 only.

Source: Berry, *Western Prices before 1860*, pp. 166, 257, 320.

Coast, instead of selling to local merchants and millers or else having the wheat ground locally for export as flour.[8] The wheat they sent eastward, on the railroads that crossed central Ohio, thus by-passed Cleveland. And so between 1851 and 1860 Cleveland's flour exports declined slightly while her wheat exports fell by half. This development deprived Cleveland of its earlier position as the state's leading primary market for grain—a shift illustrated in Table 12.1.[9]

The effect of the railroads on Cleveland's trade in pork and bacon was somewhat different. First, the completion of the rail line from Cleveland to Cincinnati in 1851 led to a vast increase in the city's exports of salted meats, as the pork and bacon of southern Ohio was sent to Cleveland instead of down the Ohio River to New Orleans. In 1856 the railroad carried 50 million pounds of salted meat to Cleveland; at this time, the receipts on the Ohio Canal were only 2 million pounds. But the Pennsylvania Railroad and its connecting lines through Pittsburgh were already cutting rates in a bid for the western meat trade. Shipments of salted meat on the Pennsylvania road increased from 21 million pounds in 1853 to 40 million five years later, producing a decline by half in Cleveland's meat trade between 1856, the peak year, and 1858.[10]

Cleveland's canal trade in coal held up better than the traffic in farm products, and indeed by 1855 coal comprised two-thirds of all the canal tonnage arriving at the city. Similarly, iron receipts by canal, consisting mainly of Pittsburgh manufactures, increased in tonnage until 1856. In the last years of the decade, however, even these heavy commodities were shipped mainly by rail instead of canal.[11]

The import trade of Cleveland, which had traditionally consisted mainly of merchandise and salt from the East, grew in volume and changed in composition during the 1850's. The import tonnage passing through the Cleveland entrepôt increased enormously after 1850. Merchandise shipments on the canal had been declining since 1839 under competition first from the Ohio River route, then from the Miami Extension Canal, and later from the Sandusky railroads. Completion of the Cleveland-Cincinnati Railroad in 1851, however, gave the city's import trade a new boost. In its first year of operation, the road carried nearly 11,000 tons of merchandise inland from Cleveland, and by 1860 merchandise freight on the railroad had increased nearly threefold. But the new railroad reduced still further the canal's significance as a channel for importation of merchandise to the interior; throughout the decade, the tonnage of merchandise imports by canal fell steadily.[12] Imports by canal of the heavier, low-value commodities held up better. Iron tonnage, consisting mainly of Lake Superior ores destined for Pittsburgh, increased until 1854.[13] Lumber also reached the inland market via Cleveland from the newly opened forests of the Great Lakes area, until a decline in canal shipments began in 1854 under impact of railroad competition both at Cleveland and other lake ports in Ohio. In this manner, the Ohio Canal—once the lifeline of northern and central Ohio's import trade from the East—became in the fifties mainly a carrier of bulk products inland from the lake. Meanwhile, Cleveland's total import trade changed in its composition, consisting more of heavy bulk items, especially iron, for use by manufacturing industries, than had formerly been the case.

At Cincinnati the effects of new transportation were even more dramatic. Major changes occurred both in the composition of Cincinnati's exports and the direction of her export trade. Pork and bacon, which had long been the mainstay of Cincinnati's commerce, declined in significance as western livestock began to be sent by railroad directly east; and the amount of pork packed at the city declined from 475,000 hogs slaughtered in 1848 to an average of 400,000 during 1856–60. Before long, a whole-sale trade in livestock developed at Cincinnati, this too at the expense of the city's packing industry. In the late fifties, some twenty thousand head of cattle and ten thousand hogs were being sent eastward each year aboard railroad stock cars from the Queen City market.[14]

Because corn was being fed to livestock on farms, the export trade in corn from Cincinnati fell, declining by half between 1846–50 and 1856–60. Cincinnati exports of unprocessed wheat were not reported until 1857; but in the last years of the decade, wheat exports were nearly half a million bushels annually. Even so, the trade in grain was small in comparison with flour exports. Cincinnati's milling industries grew rapidly in the fifties, as farm-ers shipped wheat to the large-scale city mills instead of having it processed at small custom mills in the countryside. Exports of flour from Cincinnati nearly doubled during the decade, reaching half a million barrels annually in 1856–60. Hence the vigorous growth of milling and of flour exports partially offset Cincinnati's losses in the pork and bacon export trade.[15]

Cincinnati's exports of foodstuffs generally increased at a slower rate than her shipments of manufactured products and southern groceries, as shown in Table 12.2. Throughout the fifties, a rising percentage of the city's total export trade consisted of the products of her own burgeoning factory districts: furniture, clothing, soap and candles, leather, ironware, and machinery. The trade in cotton, sugar, molasses, and coffee also increased in volume, as reduced upriver charges from the South and improved rail connections with a wide area of Indiana, Illinois, and Wisconsin enhanced the city's marketing position. Indeed, fully one-sixth of Louisiana's sugar crop and one-eighth of all Brazilian coffee imports to the U.S. in 1858 were sent to the Cincinnati wholesale merchants.[16]

Accompanying the shift in the composition of Cincinnati's trade was an equally striking change, brought about by railroads, in the direction of the city's commerce. Even in 1853, fully eight years after the city's canal had been extended to Toledo, 80 per cent of Cincinnati's pork exports were still shipped by river to southern markets. But the advent of through-line railroads revolutionized the meat trade, and by 1860 some 60 per cent of the Queen City's pork exports were shipped directly eastward. During 1850–52, only 8 per cent of Cincinnati beef and 15 per cent of her whiskey went directly to eastern ports; by 1860 the proportions were 30 and 33 per cent, respectively.[17]

Although the Miami Canal played but a small role in the export trade, it did continue to carry bulky imported goods southward from the Lake Erie market at Toledo. Probably a third of the pig iron consumed by Cincinnati's manufacturers and also a large portion of the lumber used by the furniture industry came by way of Toledo in the early fifties. The Miami Canal was also a major channel for transportation of coal from Cincinnati to inland towns.[18]

In summary, despite the high hopes of the early canal promoters, it was the railroads and not the Miami Extension Canal that enabled Cincinnati to ship exports directly to eastern markets. Although rapid expansion of settlement in the states farther west reduced Cincinnati's importance both as a packing center and as a primary grain market, the same new settlement enlarged marketing opportunities for the Queen City's merchants and manufacturers. Construction of railroads westward from Cincinnati was instrumental in expanding the city's exports, from

an estimated 33 million dollars in 1852 to 77 million dollars in
1860, and in permitting her industrialists to reach the vast new
consumer markets in the region behind Ohio's western border.[19]

While Cleveland and Cincinnati were becoming less important in the foodstuffs trade and more prominent in other classes
of commerce, Toledo seized first position as a grain market in
Ohio. The new canal lines completed in 1842 and 1845 had
linked Toledo with western Ohio and the interior of Indiana;
then, progressive reductions of canal tolls in the mid-forties had
brought to Toledo vast quantities of grain from areas that had
formerly exported only to New Orleans. Now, in the mid-fifties,
new railroads built westward from Toledo tapped the rich farming regions of Illinois and the upper Mississippi.[20] The canal
continued to carry a major share of Toledo's receipts of grain
from the interior until late in the 1850's. But beginning in 1855
the railroads captured an increasing proportion of Toledo's trade.
They also forced a change in the city's import trade by canal to

TABLE 12.3

EXPORTS OF OHIO FOR THE COMMERCIAL YEAR 1857–58

ARTICLE (UNIT)	BY RAILROAD	BY LAKE	BY RIVER	TOTAL
Flour (ooo bbl.)	—a	475.9	227.5	703.4
Wheat (ooo bu.)	5,487.9	2,607.1	—	8,095.0
Other grain (ooo bu.)	956.6	1,990.7	40.0	2,987.3
Whiskey (ooo bbl.)	142.4	53.6	181.6	377.5
Beef (ooo bbl.)	6.0	0.3	14.2	20.4
Pork & bacon (ooo bbl.)	361.5	7.7	95.2	464.5
Butter (ooo lb.)	7,292.7	18.7	1,424.7	8,735.1
Cheese (ooo lb.)	3,541.3	14.8	3,180.0	6,736.1
Cattle (ooo units)	118.0	—	—	118.0
Hogs (ooo units)	341.6	—	—	341.6
Wool (ooo lb.)	5,332.0	1,321.4	919.4	7.572.8
Coal (ooo bu.)	—	5,600.0	3,000.0	8,600.0

a Railroad shipments of flour counted as wheat equivalent (1 bbl. = 5 bu.
wheat).

Source: Ohio Commissioner of Statistics, Annual Report, 1859, p. 578.

interior points, the railroads taking the merchandise trade and leaving lumber products and iron as the principal commodities for the canals to carry.[21]

By 1860 Toledo had reached a stage of commercial development comparable to Cleveland's in the mid-forties: its commerce was based mainly on the grain trade, with local manufacturing not yet important in its export trade. Toledo's exports of flour were nearly equal in 1860 to those of Cleveland and Cincinnati combined; and her shipments of wheat and corn far exceeded those from the rival cities. Indeed by 1860 Toledo flour exports made up one-fifth, wheat exports more than one-fourth, and corn exports nearly half the entire volume of receipts from the West at New York City.[22]

The decline in canal traffic at all the major terminal cities occurred in part because of the general advantages of railroads over water routes. But factors unique to the Ohio situation also contributed to the decrease of canal tonnage. In 1857, the Mahoning Canal, which previously had been the main feeder line for the Ohio Canal, was purchased by a competing railroad and in effect put out of business. Two years later, much of the Indiana portion of the Wabash & Erie Canal was abandoned by its operators. Although groups of local businessmen in Indiana assumed responsibility for its continued operation, the financing of its maintenance was thereafter uncertain, discouraging shippers from using the waterway.[23] Even the Ohio canals that remained in operation were in generally poor repair, and were thus vulnerable to crippling damage when natural disasters occurred—as happened in 1858 when floods washed away large portions of the Wabash & Erie Canal just west of Toledo. Droughts in 1851 and 1856 closed the major canals for weeks at a time, driving traffic to the railroads—and perhaps thereby helping to break down the inertia that might otherwise have kept many shippers faithful to the accustomed pattern of trade by canal.[24]

Highly significant in determining the outcome of rivalry between canals and railroads was the degree of competition among the railways themselves. In an often desperate quest for traffic, Ohio's thirty-three railroad companies, which by 1860 operated three thousand miles of line, provided middleman services in

competition wtih established commission merchants, built warehouses, and made impressive improvements in the handling of
goods and the speed of their service.[25] But their principal weapon
was rate-cutting. This they resorted to with frequently drastic
effect, especially after 1856. Along with the general decline of
railroad rates a great reduction of charges took place on the
combined rail-and-water routes; the resultant shift of long-haul
traffic away from the canals was so massive that it astonished
even the railroad executives who had worked to perfect their
long-haul arrangements with lake and river steamer companies.[26]

By 1858 the railroads had clearly won the contest with canals
in Ohio. The railways now carried half or more of Ohio's exports
of pork and bacon, dairy products, whiskey, wool, and unprocessed grain. Livestock exports were carried exclusively by
railroad. In only two major export trades, both out of the Lake
Erie port cities, were water shipments larger than shipments by
railroad: in coal and in grains other than wheat. Yet a large
portion of the coal and grain sent to the East by lake had arrived
from the interior at lake or river ports by railroad.[27] Indeed,
several railroad companies were operating their own lake steamers while all maintained regular rail-and-water service as well as
their all-rail service. Tie-in arrangements between lake shipping
companies and the railroads were so important by 1858 that
probably half the tonnage exported by ships from Lake Erie
ports went forward as part of rail-and-water shipping contracts.[28]

The structure of Ohio agriculture was altered markedly under
the impact of new railroad construction that placed the state's
farm sector in a new context of national production and market
advantages. The changing composition of Ohio exports is reflected
in Table 12.4, which indicates the value of commodities exported
in current prices. Among the most important shifts were the decline of wheat and flour between 1853 and 1858, when the actual
volume exported fell by about half; the exports of corn and other
grains also declined sharply, both in valuation and in volume.
Meanwhile, Ohio farm production of corn and other grains,
excepting wheat, was increasing. This indicated that a rising
proportion of the grain crop was being consumed in the cities,

TABLE 12.4

CURRENT VALUE OF OHIO'S AGRICULTURAL EXPORTS,
COMMERCIAL YEARS 1852–3, 1855–6, 1857–8
($ million)

COMMODITY GROUP	(1844)ª	1852–3	1855–6	1857–8
Flour and wheat	(9.58)	15.74	—	11.10
Other grains	(4.15)	3.27	—	1.75
Beef and cattle	—	2.39	4.37	6.17
Pork, lard and hogs	—	7.99	9.15	13.89
Butter, cheese, tallow				
and grease	—	0.75	0.94	1.73
Whiskey	—	2.85	—	5.11
Tobacco	(0.28)	1.62	—	2.20
Wool	—	2.10	3.00	2.65
Miscellaneous	—	3.50	—	3.80
TOTALᵇ	—	$40.22	—	$48.40

ª Estimated total value of Ohio agricultural production (not exports).
ᵇ U.S. wholesale price index (1850–59 = 100): 1853, 96; 1858, 98.
Sources: On 1844 total output, DeBow, *Industrial Resources*, Vol. 2, p.
346. On exports, for 1852–53 and 1857–58, *Executive Docs.*,
1858–59, II, p. 580. On exports, for 1855–56, *Railroad Record*,
4:65–66 (March 27, 1856).

fed to livestock, or else processed for export as liquor or meal.
That a shift into livestock feeding was a central feature of this
change was manifest from the increase in number of stock animals on Ohio farms (shown in Table 12.5). Exports of meat
and other animal products rose swiftly during 1853–58: live
cattle from 68,000 head to an estimated 118,000, hogs from
182,000 to 342,000, pork and bacon from 234,000 barrels to
464,000, and butter and cheese from 7 million to 14 million
pounds.[29]

The new emphasis on livestock production was largely a result of the railroads' operations. In the cattle trade, for example,
for half a century Ohio stock raisers had driven herds overland
to the Atlantic Coast market each year. But in the early fifties,
the railroads introduced rapid box car service for direct ship-

OHIO CANAL ERA

ment of cattle to the East, and the rates for shipping by rail
were only half the cost of driving. Moreover, the year-round
operations of the railroads and their speed permitted Ohio farm-

TABLE 12.5

STATISTICS OF OHIO AGRICULTURE, 1849, 1859

	NUMBER, 1849 (THOUSANDS)	NUMBER, 1859 (THOUSANDS)	RANK OF STATE IN U. S. 1849	1859
1. *Livestock on farms*				
Horses	463.4	625.3	1	1
Milk cows	544.5	676.6	2	2
Other cattle	749.1	895.1	2	4
Swine	1,964.8	2,251.7	5	6
Sheep	3,942.9	3,546.8	1	1

	PRODUCTION (MILLIONS) 1849	1859	RANK OF STATE IN U. S.	
2. *Crop production*				
Wheat (bu.)[a]	14.49	15.12	2	4
Corn (bu.)[b]	59.08	73.54	1	2
Oats (bu.)	13.47	15.41	3	3
Flax (lb.)	0.47	0.88	7	2
Barley (bu.)	0.35	1.66	2	3
Buckwheat (bu.)	0.63	2.37	4	3
Butter (lb.)	34.45	48.54	3	3
Cheese (lb.)	20.82	21.62	2	2

[a] The severe fluctuations in wheat output were reflected in the state data:
1850 = 32 million bushels, 1855 = 20 million, 1857 = 25 million.
[b] State data on corn output: 1850 = 57 million bushels, 1855 = 88 million, 1857 = 83 million.
Sources: 1849, 1859 data: *8th U.S. Census (Agriculture)*; data in notes
(a), (b): *Commissioner of Statistics*, annual reports.

ers to ship fattened stock on short notice, with rapid delivery
expected, as information of price changes in the East was received by telegraph. And so by 1854 the historic annual "long
drive" of cattle had abruptly ended.[30] Converging with the reduc-

tion in shipment costs were more favorable market prices on the Atlantic Coast, as the New York price for cattle doubled between 1849 and 1855. Sensitive to such changes, Ohio farmers shifted to stock raising, and total cattle on farms in Ohio rose from 1.1 million in 1852 to over 1.7 million three years later. A decline in eastern prices after 1855 similarly led to a decline in the number of cattle on Ohio farms by 1859, but only to 1.5 million.[31]

The new emphasis on livestock was also reflected in the sheep and dairy industries. Throughout the fifties, Ohio led the Union in the number of sheep on farms, but the peak year for both sheep raised and exports of wool came in 1858; afterward, the lower national protective tariff on wool began to discourage sheep raising. In 1856 the value of wool exports from Ohio was reported as 50 per cent higher than the 1853 level; and in 1858 more than 220,000 live sheep were exported from Ohio, for slaughter or feeding in the East.[32] As for dairying, the completion of railroad lines to the eastern seaboard coincided with rising markets for cheese in the Atlantic cities, in the growing urban centers of the West, and in California and Europe. The center of Ohio dairy production continued to be the old Western Reserve district of northeastern Ohio. Formerly tied closely to southern markets and dependent upon the river, however, the Western Reserve dairy producers now concentrated their export trade instead upon the East. Late in the decade, Cincinnati and the markets to the west served by Cincinnati wholesalers once again became attractive. "Since the opening of railway communication with the great cheese counties of Ohio," the Cincinnati chamber of commerce noted in 1855, "this article reaches the market in good order, and stocks [no longer] . . . accumulate in the warm months, and the loss by damaged cheese is now small."[33] The new transport facilities also caused a shift in local marketing patterns. In Lorain County, for example, the town of Huntington was the center for distribution of local cheese until 1849, when the C. C. & C. Railroad built its line through Wellington, located five miles away. Within a few years, nearly all the leading cheese merchants of the county had built new warehouses in the railroad town.[34]

Express companies that operated on the railroads expedited the sale of fresh butter to the growing urban centers in Ohio, expanding further the market available to dairy producers. An allied development was the small but increasing trade in fluid milk. Until well past 1860, urban consumers relied mainly upon city dairies for their notoriously unhealthful fresh milk; but at Cincinnati, the opening of railroads to both the Western Reserve and the Clark County dairying centers permitted shipment of fresh milk from country farms.[35]

The growth of Ohio's industrial and commercial cities during the 1850's similarly affected market-garden production on the farm. Garden crops were shipped mainly by wagon, and large-scale production was concentrated exclusively in the districts located near major cities and within ready access by road to the urban consumer.[36] Another specialty crop that gained in importance during the fifties was tobacco. In the rich "Miami bottoms" of Montgomery County, land was taken out of corn and other crops and given to production of seed leaf tobacco. Output was nearly 200,000 pounds in Montgomery in 1849 and increased steadily in the following decade.[37]

Throughout the fifties exports of swine and pork meats remained higher in dollar value than beef or wool exports. The number of hogs on Ohio farms increased by 10 per cent during the decade, and the value of pork and bacon exports doubled: in 1858 pork and hogs comprised nearly a third the value of the state's agricultural exports. The railroads transported all the hogs sent to out-of-state markets, and by the late 1850's three-fourths of packed pork products were also being shipped by rail. In this crucial segment of the farm economy, therefore, the railways held a manifestly central position.[38]

The increased role of livestock, dairy products, and specialty crops was at the expense of the traditional wheat crop in several areas of the state. Second in 1849 only to Pennsylvania in wheat output, by 1859 Ohio had fallen behind Illinois, Indiana, and Wisconsin; wheat production in the United States rose by nearly half during the fifties, whereas Ohio's output went from 14 million bushels in 1849 to a pre-Civil War high of 32 million the next year, slipping back to only 15 million in 1859. (See

Table 12.5.) Of basic importance in causing the shift away from wheat was a decline in average yields in eastern Ohio, which had long been a main center of wheat production in the state. Long years of inadequate crop rotation and devastating visitations of the midge disease in the late fifties resulted in far smaller wheat yields per acre—and financial ruin for many farmers. In each of fifteen counties of the eastern "Backbone" region, on the central division of the Ohio Canal, and in the upper Muskingum Valley, at least five thousand acres were taken out of wheat between 1852 and 1860.[39]

The state's wheat output would have lagged even further if northwestern Ohio had not been opened up to new settlement by the canals and railroads built after 1843. In this region, which still remained close to the frontier pattern of development in 1850, wheat and corn were the first staple crops that farmers planted. Also, in three counties of west-central Ohio (Fayette, Madison, and Union), land formerly devoted to range-type grazing of livestock was put into wheat production when railroads gave farmers access to outside markets. In northwest Ohio and the old grazing district, therefore, wheat production nearly doubled during the fifties, while statewide production increased only slightly.[40] Meanwhile, southwestern Ohio and the Scioto Valley were also adding heavily to their acreage sown in wheat. By 1860, the wheat belt had shifted to western Ohio. Whereas the ten leading wheat-growing counties in 1852 were in the eastern or central part of the state, in 1860 all but one of the ten leading counties were in southwestern Ohio.[41]

The operations of new railroads were closely linked to both the decline of wheat output in the older areas and the westward shift of Ohio's wheat belt. On the one hand, railroad and large-capacity lake vessels carried wheat and flour from the fertile, newly settled regions of Illinois, Iowa, and Wisconsin to the eastern markets at low cost; and this put pressure on farmers in areas of Ohio where yields were declining, forcing a shift to other types of production. In northwest Ohio and the old grazing counties, on the other hand, the new transport lines made it profitable to put land into arable production and farm-making went forward in previously unsettled localities. In southwest Ohio

CHANGES IN POPULATION AND FARMLAND VALUE, 1850–1860

 Population increase of 50% or more, and also increase of 100% or more in farmland values, 1850–60

 Increase in farmland values of 100% or more, 1850–60

 Population increase of 50% or more, 1850–60

COUNTY Underlining of county name indicates absolute population decrease.

Sources: U.S. Census, 1850, 1860 (Agriculture); Census population data.

Map 12–A

and the Scioto Valley, the railroad freed farmers from reliance upon the southern market, making possible a shift back to production of wheat, for direct shipment to the East.[42]

Although agricultural readjustment was often difficult, the 1850's were a period of sharply rising land values in Ohio. With the opening of northwest Ohio to new settlement and the move toward more intensive agriculture in the older-settled regions, the area of "improved" farmland rose from 10 million acres in 1849 to 12.6 million a decade later. The cash value of farms increased from 359 million dollars (or an average of $20 per acre) to 678 million dollars (more than $33 per acre) in the same period; and so by 1860, Ohio was second only to New York in valuation of land.[43]

Region by region, land valuation changes were hardly uniform. Four groups of counties (shown in Map 12.A) registered an increase of 100 per cent or more in values over the decade. They were: (1) the counties of northwest Ohio on the Miami Extension Canal line, between Montgomery and Lucas, and on the new railroads built in the mid-fifties; (2) the upland counties of western and northwest-central Ohio, which were supplied with no improved transport facilities until construction of the Mad River & Lake Erie and other railroad lines; (3) a group of counties in southern Ohio, including the Hocking Valley area and counties on the river between Washington and Lawrence, where newly opened coal and iron mines stimulated a rise in land values; and (4) a small group surrounding Cuyahoga County, where the dairy industry and market-gardening expanded rapidly in the fifties under the stimulus of swift urban growth in the area.

Despite their rapid *rates* of land-value increase, two of these four districts registered relatively small absolute gains: in both northwest Ohio and the Hocking-Ohio River mining district, the ten-year gains averaged only two million dollars or less per county. By contrast, the wealthiest districts of the state in 1850 reported gains of five million dollars or more per county over the decade: these included a bloc of counties in the Dayton-Cincinnati region of southwest Ohio, where urban growth and industrialization were intensive and agriculture prospered; and the

Ohio Canal and Mahoning Canal counties of central and northeast Ohio, similarly an area of urban growth and rising manufacturers in addition to being the seat of the dairy industry.[44] In short, the regions given access to outside markets for the first time during these years gained in land values at the fastest rate; but those with a head start were gaining most in dollar values over the decade.

Population trends during the 1850's were also marked by considerable regional variations. In the agricultural counties that were forced to reduce their wheat acreage, population growth was minimal; in fact, sixteen of the former wheat counties of eastern Ohio experienced an absolute population decline.[45] This was the result of painful agricultural readjustment; for some farmers presumably could not muster the capital to shift to livestock raising, while others either migrated to the cities or moved to more fertile lands farther west. Indeed, a total of some 400,000 native Ohioans left the state during the 1850's. Ohio had long been "a hive from which swarms of pioneers sought new homes"; but the exodus of this decade took more Ohioans to other states than had migrated from Ohio during the preceding four decades.[46] Yet in northwestern Ohio, every county registered a population increase of 50 per cent or more during the 1850's, and many of the new settlers were probably eastern or foreign-born emigrants, recently arrived in Ohio.[47]

The population growth of the state was only 18 per cent in the decade, from just under two million in 1850 to 2.3 million in 1860. But urban growth was much more rapid, with one-fourth of the statewide increase registered by only four cities: Cleveland, Cincinnati (including its neighboring industrial suburbs), Dayton, and Toledo.[48] Each of these communities enjoyed major advantages of location on both canals and railroads. When one considers urban growth in a broader framework, the stimulus of new transportation facilities is even more striking. In the Miami Valley, the towns situated on railroads underwent rapid population increases during the fifties, while those lacking railway connections grew more slowly or barely held steady. Among the railroad towns, moreover, those which were junctions or termini grew more quickly in population than those which were way stations.[49] If the Miami Valley was typical, as seems to have been true, then there was a firm basis in reality for the sense of urgency with which urban promoters had sought places for their towns on the new railroad lines.[50]

The opening of new transport lines created opportunities but also posed some major challenges for the Ohio mercantile community, no less than it had for the state's farmers. A constant factor in Ohio's commercial life, however, was the continuing dominance of Cincinnati. Long before 1850, the Queen City had won primacy in the West as a wholesale market for eastern and imported manufactures, and in the forties Cincinnati merchants regularly had sold in small lots to retail shopkeepers in the countryside. The new railroads emanating from the city enlarged her wholesale trade throughout Indiana and Illinois, as well as in the other states of the Mississippi Valley. Year-round reliability of railroad transportation rendered it unnecessary for country merchants to lay up a store of goods during the navigational season on the lakes and canals. Instead of tying up capital in inventory, they now were able to buy as needed on credit from the Cincinnati wholesale houses, which could deliver "in three or four days what [would] require as many weeks in a trip east."[51]

The more aggressive railroad companies went into competition with commission merchants at Cincinnati as well as at other commercial towns. Several railroads provided farm-produce dealers with storage and warehouse services; some went directly into the commission business; and at least one actually bought up farm produce on its own account—all at the expense of established Ohio merchants. The large wholesale grain dealers of Boston and New York invaded the western merchant's domain with equal ingenuity. Exploiting the telegraph and rapid rail service, they assigned agents to country districts of Ohio to buy up produce directly from the farmers, thereby circumventing customary middleman services.[52]

Ohio merchants also came under pressure from eastern manufacturers and from wholesalers of eastern and imported merchandise. The eastern firms persuaded many western country storekeepers (who had already learned to buy in small lots from

Cincinnati or other Ohio cities) to buy in retail quantity from the coastal cities. Direct factory sales to rural stores in Ohio thus became common in the fifties; and the structure of railroad rates, with charges for long-haul shipments often no higher than rates for shipment a third of the distance, gave a major advantage to the eastern dealers.[53] Thus many an Ohio farm wife bought at local stores retail goods and hardware that a fortnight earlier had been loaded on railroad cars from a Connecticut Valley factory or a New York importer's warehouse.

Ohio merchants as a group apparently held their own in this difficult situation, since mercantile inventories in the state rose from 18 million dollars in 1852 to 26 million dollars in 1860. Cincinnati, meanwhile, had increased her lead as a commercial center, with an even higher concentration of inventories there in 1860 than eight years earlier.[54] Although Cincinnati was therefore not typical of commercial operations in Ohio during the 1850's, the city's experience did reflect the basic statewide changes in trade: a more intensive competition between the large Ohio wholesale centers and eastern interlopers, more steady year-round purchasing from the wholesale houses by country stores, and a highly unstable transport rate structure that included long-haul discrimination—sometimes to the advantage, but often at the expense, of Ohio merchants.

The manufacturing sector of Ohio's economy grew more rapidly than either agriculture or trade during the 1850's: it was a period of accelerating industrialization in the national economy. and Ohio was keeping pace. National output of manufactured products rose by a reported 86 per cent in value during the fifties, while Ohio's rate of increase was 94 per cent. Population in the state meanwhile rose by less than one-fifth, so that the value of Ohio's manufactures went from 32 dollars per capita in 1850 to about 53 dollars a decade later. During the same period, the value of farm products exported from the state increased by only one-fourth.[55]

Urbanization was, of course, a stimulus to industrial development as well as a concomitant of it. The population of cities of four thousand or larger rose by 48 per cent during the decade; and Cincinnati, the principal manufacturing center, experienced an increase of more than 50,000. The flow of displaced farming families, emigrants from the East, and foreign immigrants into Ohio's cities provided a growing labor force for the state's factories. These newcomers were attracted to urban locations by expanding employment opportunities in industry. But urban workers were also consumers: they enlarged the market for foodstuffs produced on the state's farms; and the major urban centers, well supplied by the late fifties with transport facilities into the countryside, created rising demand for fluid milk, garden crops, and other special products. The urban dwellers also generated demands for housing, and urban construction amounted to nearly 40 million dollars in Ohio between 1851 and 1860—for purposes of comparison, equivalent to the entire value of farm products exported in 1853.[56]

Together with urbanization came large-scale factory production of consumer goods that took the place of products formerly made in the home. Representative of the new consumer industries was the manufacture of men's clothing, concentrated mainly in Cincinnati. Output of clothing increased from 2.8 million dollars in 1850 to nearly 9 million dollars in 1860, by which time this had become the state's largest employing industry.[57] Having the advantage of a large German and Jewish immigrant work force skilled in tailoring, Cincinnati's clothing manufacturers sold in a market that stretched from the South's plantation country to the remotest parts of the new West.[58] Like the clothing industry, the manufacture of soap, candles, and lard-oil more than tripled its output over the decade, from 1 million dollars to nearly 4 million dollars, so that by 1860 one-sixth of all national production was supplied by Ohio.

The growth of heavy manufacturing in Ohio was especially rapid during the fifties. A group of eight Ohio industries manufacturing mainly machinery and metal products increased their output from 4 million dollars to 11.5 million dollars between 1850 and 1860. Within this group, the manufacturers of agricultural implements and machinery—serving a western farming region that was mechanizing heavily in the fifties—increased output from half a million dollars to nearly 3 million dollars; in 1860, they accounted for a sixth of national output. Just as the expansion of western farming stimulated production of agricultural machinery, so did urban growth affect the industries related to construction: the value of builders' supplies increased from half a million dollars in 1850 to 2.6 million dollars in 1860.[59]

The state's mining industries also recorded rapid growth during this period. Coal mined in Ohio rose from 3.5 million bushels in 1840 to 8 million in 1850, but then production surged to an estimated 46 million bushels in 1857. Output of pig iron rose from 53,000 tons in 1850 to more than 100,000 tons in 1857.[60]

Growth of heavy industries, mining, and factory-based manufacture of consumers' goods all bespoke an emerging industrial society. However, the basic composition of the state's industrial output (measured by value of product) shifted only slightly during the decade. As shown in Table 12.6, Ohio's manufacturing product in 1860 still consisted mainly of processed farm and forest products. Flour-milling, the largest industry, accounted for nearly a fourth the value of industrial output in 1850 and a fifth in 1860. Fully one-third of total output in 1860 was still accounted for by liquor, meat products, and flour. Even many of the more important light industries—such as paper and printing, furniture, and leather goods—consisted of the manufacture of crude or finished products from animal materials or wood.

The industries associated with farm or forest products did undergo major *internal* structural changes during the 1850's, with a marked shift toward larger-scale production and more concentrated location of plants in the major urban centers. Flour milling was the prime case in point. In the five counties with the largest flour product, the average 1860 output per mill was $46,000; in all the other counties, however, output averaged only $18,000 per mill.[61] Also, a widening difference emerged between the "mix" of manufacturing in the largest urban centers and the pattern in less urbanized regions. More than half the industrial product of Cincinnati, for example, consisted of light manufactures; but statewide, only one-fifth of output was of this class.[62] Moreover, the eight leading industrial counties produced more than half the value of Ohio's manufactured goods; indeed, Hamilton County alone produced nearly a third of the 122 million dollars of manufacturing product in 1860.[63]

There was no simple cause-and-effect relationship between

TABLE 12.6

GROWTH OF OHIO INDUSTRIES, BY GROUPS, AND THEIR SHARE IN
STATEWIDE TOTAL INDUSTRIAL PRODUCT 1850, 1860

INDUSTRY GROUP	OUTPUT ($ MILLION) 1850	OUTPUT ($ MILLION) 1860	1850–60 INCREASE	SHARE OF TOTAL OHIO INDUSTRIAL PRODUCT 1850	SHARE OF TOTAL OHIO INDUSTRIAL PRODUCT 1860
(1) Flour and meal	14.4	24.8	72%	23%	20%
(2) Animal products	6.9	12.0	78	11	10
(3) Finished leather products	3.4	4.9	44	5	4
(4) Forest products	4.6	7.5	63	7	6
(5) Finished wood products	4.8	9.2	92	8	8
(6) Liquors	3.5	11.2	220	6	9
(7) Men's clothing	2.8	8.8	214	4	7
(8) Builders' supplies and hardware	0.5	2.6	420	1	2
(9) Heavy industries: metals and durables	6.3	15.9	152	10	13
Total, Groups (1)–(9)	47.2	96.9	103%	75%	80%
Total Ohio industrial product	62.7	121.7	94%	100%	100%
Total U.S. industrial product	1019.1	1885.9	86%	—	—

(1) Flour and meal; (2) provisions, leather, soap, lard oil, candles; (3) Saddlery and harness, boots and shoes, trunks and valises; (4) Lumber (saw and plane), paper; (5) Furniture, carriages, wagons, sashes and doors, spokes and hubs, cooperage, turning, woodware; (6) malt, distilled and rectified liquors; (7) men's clothing; (8) alcohol, carpenters' tools, white lead, hardware, linseed oil, varnish; (9) brass foundings, sheet-metalware, pig iron, agricultural implements, machinery, bridges, railroad cars, plumbing and gasfitting, sewing machines, type and stereotype foundings, and bar, sheet and railroad iron.
Source: 1850, 1860 U. S. Census of Manufactures.

transport changes of the fifties, urbanization, and the development of Ohio manufacturing.[64] But in the case of certain industries, the stimulative impact of the new transportation was immediate and direct. For example, the Hanging Rock iron region of southern Ohio had been engaged in iron manufacture since early in the 1820's.[65] Until the mid-forties, however, the furnaces had been concentrated near the Ohio River because shipping facilities were lacking at locations farther inland, where iron deposits were known to exist.[66] Then the construction of the Scioto and Hocking Valley railroad, from Portsmouth northeast into the interior, led to heavy new investment both in furnaces and in coal mines. Of twenty-five blast furnaces located on the railroad line in 1854, a year after it was opened to traffic, fifteen had been constructed during 1853 and 1854. When the railroad obtained a direct connection with Cincinnati in 1855, another six furnaces were built on the line in Jackson County alone. Construction of the Marietta & Cincinnati Railroad through Vinton County in 1856 similarly led to opening of new furnaces along its route; and the Iron Railroad, a short line built in 1851 from the Ohio River inland to Center Furnace in Lawrence County, stimulated iron production in its trade area and established the industry at Ironton, later the leading iron city in Ohio.[67]

From new railroad construction in southern Ohio's mining district flowed a series of structural and locational changes of major significance: the railroads not only determined, to a large extent, the location of new furnaces in the iron region, but they also impelled urban growth—for example, the town of Jackson built more than one hundred new structures in 1853–54, and Portsmouth increased its population by 50 per cent in the fifties as its iron industry expanded rapidly. The new rail facilities expanded the markets for Hanging Rock iron by opening routes to Columbus, Chicago, and other distant industrial centers, freeing the iron-makers from exclusive reliance on the river market. Also, by reducing the cost of coal freightage, railroads expedited the initial shift from charcoal to coal-burning furnaces, making possible larger-scale furnace operations. As an incidental consequence, the railways thereby contributed to overexpansion of capacity which led to a sharp price deflation and lay-offs in the Ohio iron region during the post-1857 depression; but the Hanging Rock region was also ready to profit from suddenly enlarged demands for iron during the Civil War.[68]

In a larger context, the railroads aided the emergence of large-scale, urban-based manufacturing in Ohio by carrying raw materials at lower rates and by expanding the market areas of the major industrial cities. The remarkable growth of consumer-goods industries at Cincinnati and other centers was stimulated by the railroad network that linked Ohio with the fast-growing agricultural regions of the West. Thus iron stoves built in Cincinnati were carried to country stores as far west as Wisconsin and Iowa, and furniture manufactured in the Queen City was shipped unassembled at special carload rates throughout the West.[69] The important trend toward greater concentration of the food-processing industries in the major cities was also given impetus by new transportation lines: as the railroads connected industrial cities like Cincinnati with an expanding hinterland, they permitted farmers to ship unprocessed grain to the large city mills; and even when farmers chose to ship grain directly east instead, this too was principally at the expense of the country gristmills, rather than of the urban-based millers.[70] The growth of particular industries can be traced to the markets created by railroads as consumers: thus, manufacturers of locomotives, parts, railroad cars, and chairs established themselves at Zanesville, Cincinnati, Columbus, Troy, and other cities. In addition, the railroads must have consumed a significant proportion of the iron, lumber, and coal produced in Ohio in the 1850's.[71]

Whatever the extent to which the striking industrial progress of Ohio in the fifties was directly attributable to transportation changes, the state had established by 1860 a viable base for a modern industrial economy. Her new transport facilities had expedited exploitation of Ohio's rich mineral and lumber resources, had forced adjustments—including some very profitable adjustments—in the state's farm sector, and had enabled Ohio manufacturers to tap an expanding western market. But the industrialization of the fifties, and indeed the growth of the Ohio railroad network in the first place, had been made possible by the large existing population of the state, the earlier agricultural prosperity, the capital accumulation generated by a thriving commercial sector, and the prior development of natural resources— in short by the legacy of the canal era.[72]

NOTES

1. For summaries of American growth in the fifties, see Douglass C. North, *The Economic Growth of the United States, 1790–1860* (Englewood Cliffs, N.J., 1961), Chap. 15; and H. N. Scheiber, "America in the World Economy: A Retrospect," *America, Purpose and Power*, ed. Gene M. Lyons (Chicago, 1965), 61ff. The basic data on commodity output are Robert Gallman's statistical construct, in National Bureau of Economic Research, *Trends in the American Economy in the 19th Century* (Studies in Income and Wealth, Vol. 24, Princeton, 1960), 13ff., esp. Table 4 at p. 26; see also George Rogers Taylor, *The Transportation Revolution, 1815–1860* (New York, 1951), 79, 85 *et passim*. The "take-off" concept is, of course, Walt Rostow's, from his *Stages of Economic Growth* (Cambridge, England, 1960). The "railroadization" theory is Joseph Schumpeter's, presented in his *Business Cycles* (New York, 1939), Vol. I, 327.
2. See Chap. 11, above.
3. See Tables 12.1, 12.2, below.
4. A thesis argued by Robert William Fogel in various studies, especially his *Railroads and American Economic Growth* (Baltimore, 1964).
5. *Eighth Census of the United States: Agriculture (1860)*; p. clvii, New York, State Engineer and Surveyor, *Annual Report on Canals, 1853* (Albany, 1854), 32–33; Louis Hunter, *Studies in the Economic History of the Ohio Valley* (Northampton, Mass., 1934), 31. Boasting of the transforming effects of the railroad on Cleveland's commerce, for example, a city editor declared: "We have no longer an annual hybernation, but reckon time by the same almanac which serves as a guide to other civilized communities." (*Cleveland City Directory, 1853* [n. p.], pp. 30–33. See also Columbus *Western Hemisphere*, Feb. 1, 1837, praising railroads because to the farmer "it is of first importance to get his produce to market, and upon *the time* that he gets it there, often depends its price.")
6. Thomas S. Berry, *Western Prices before 1861* (Cambridge, 1943), 93.

7. H. Scheiber, "Rate-Making Power of the State," *Political Science Quarterly*, LXXVII (1962), 408ff.; A. L. Kohlmeier, *The Old Northwest* (Bloomington, 1938), 164ff. Erie Canal charges on flour from Buffalo to Albany reflected the sharp post-1856 rate decline on water and rail routes. Averaging 58¢ per barrel in 1856, they fell to 46¢ in 1857 and 31¢ in 1859. (U. S. Secrtary of the Treasury, *Statistics of the Foreign and Domestic Commerce of the U. S.* [Washington, 1864], p. 179.)

8. The rapidity of rail transport reduced the risks of spoilage in transit and also made it possible for farmers and merchants to take advantage of short-term price changes on the basis of year-round transportation—advantages magnified by the railway companies' efforts to improve their handling facilities. (See text at n. 52, below.) Closely related to, and interacting with, transport improvement was the rising importance of large-scale mills at the major eastern cities: for as their area of feasible supply of grain widened, their economies-of-scale advantages over small country mills became decisive. (See text at n. 61, below.) For an excellent discussion of how an expansion of the transport "net" interacts with agglomeration effects in such a situation, see Allan Pred, *The External Relations of Cities during "Industrial Revolution"* (University of Chicago, Dept. of Geography Research Paper #76, 1962), 29ff. See also Charles B. Kuhlmann, "Processing Agricultural Products in the Pre-Railway Age," in *The Growth of the American Economy,* ed. Harold F. Williamson (2nd edition, Englewood Cliffs, N.J., 1951), 162ff.

9. Thomas D. Odle, "The American Grain Trade of the Great Lakes," *Inland Seas*, VII (1951), 240–41.

10. Statistics from annual reports of the Cleveland, Columbus & Cincinnati Railroad and the Pennsylvania Railroad. See also Appendix 3, Table 1. Cleveland pork exports were 27,000 barrels in 1847, 14,000 in 1851, and 10,000 (by lake only—shipments by railroad not available) in 1860. (*Andrews Report*, pp. 166ff.; Ohio Commissioner of Statistics, *AR*, 1861.)

11. See Appendix 3, Table 1. As early as 1855, the Cleveland & Pittsburgh Railroad carried over 75,000 tons of coal; and in 1860, when canal receipts of coal were only 70,600 tons at Cleveland, the Cleveland & Mahoning Railroad carried 135,000 tons to the city. (Cleveland & Mahoning R.R., *Annual Report, 1861,* p. 13; Cleveland & Pittsburgh R.R., *Annual Report, 1856,* p. 4.)

12. In its first year of operation, the C. C. & C. Railroad carried twice as much merchandise tonnage from Cleveland as the Ohio Canal. In 1860 the road's merchandise shipments from Cleveland alone were nearly equal to the *entire* import tonnage of the canal. (See Appendix 3, Table 1.)

13. The Cleveland & Mahoning carried 18,000 tons of iron ore in 1858 and nearly 46,000 tons in 1860. By contrast, the peak of canal shipments was 16,000 tons, in 1853. (C. & M. R.R., *Annual Report, 1860*, p. 3; *ibid., 1861*, p. 13.)

14. See Table 12.2, on pork and bacon exports. The pork pack at Cincinnati is in Auditor of State, *AR, 1859*, p. 645. On livestock, cf. Berry, *Western Prices*, p. 222; *ASTC, 1859*, p. 11; *ASTC, 1860*, p. 14.

15. *ASTC*, 1860, p. 24. Also, Table 12.2.

16. *ASTC*, 1859, p. 3. There was a lag in growth of the southern-groceries trade after 1856. (Berry, *Western Prices*, p. 337.)

17. Berry, *Western Prices*, 91; *ASTC*, 1860, p. 8. The changing direction of Cincinnati's meat exports was naturally reflected in coastwise exports of pork from New Orleans to the Atlantic Coast cities. From nearly 250,000 barrels of pork in 1846, New Orleans' exports to the coast ports declined to about 150,000 in 1856 and less than 80,000 in 1859. (U. S. House, 50th Cong., 1st Sess., 1888, *Exec. Doc.* No. 6, pt. 2, serial 2552, p. 286; P. W. Bidwell and J. I. Falconer, *History of Agriculture in the Northern United States* [New York, 1941], p. 310.)

18. See Appendix 3, Table 2. On Cincinnati's lumber trade, cf. *ASTC, 1860*, p. 6; on iron imports, Berry, *Western Prices*, p. 257; and on the coal trade, *ASTC, 1857*, p. 10.

19. After 1851, when the through-line railroad to Cleveland was completed, northward exports of all major farm staples from Cincinnati on the Miami Canal fell sharply. Statistics of export values are as given in Henry E. White, "An Economic Study of Wholesale Prices at Cincinnati, 1844–1914" (mimeographed, Cornell University, 1935), pp. 83–84. Estimates are conflicting; e.g., *ASTC, 1860*, p. 43 gives an official figure (computed on a different basis from pre-1858 statistics) of 119.6 million dollars.

20. Scheiber, "Rate-Making Power," pp. 403–4.

21. See Table 12.1, and Appendix 3, Table 3.

22. U. S. Secretary of the Treasury, *Statistics of Foreign and Domestic Commerce* (1864), p. 161.

23. *Executive Docs.*, 1859–60, Vol. I, pp. 572–73; *ibid.*, 1857–58, Vol. I, No. 12.

24. *Ibid.*, 1851–52, No. 22, p. 263; 1857–58, No. 12, pp. 477–78; 1858–59, Vol. I, pp. 112–13; 1859–60, Vol. I, pp. 589–90.

25. *Ibid.*, 1850–51, No. 34, p. 675.

26. On the first railroad venture in operation of lake shipping, see E. Dowling, "The Erie Fleet," *Inland Seas*, VII (1951), 204.

27. See Table 12.1 and Appendix 3.

28. C. C. & C. R.R., *3rd AR* (1854), 11; Berry, *Western Prices*, 92; *Proceedings of the Rail Road Convention . . . March 23, 1859* (Columbus, 1859); Odle, "American Grain Trade," *Inland Seas*, VIII, 187; Leola M. Stewart, "Sandusky: Pioneer Link between Sail and Rail," *OAHQ*, LVII (1958), 231–33.

29. The percentage changes in absolute volume of exports are estimated from data and discussion in *Railroad Record*, I (1853), 82; and *Executive Documents*, 1859, Pt. II, 570–82. It is important to note that the 1857 wheat crop, 25.4 million bushels, was one of the highest of the decade. In 1858 the Ohio crop was only 18 million bushels, and in 1859 about 15 million bushels. (*Ibid.*, 1861, Pt. II, 439–41.) Some 221,000 sheep were exported live in the commercial year 1857–58, with none reported (and probably few exported on the hoof) in 1853. There was a sharp decline in barreled beef exported between 1853 and 1858, but the decline measured by weight represented was more than offset by the increase in export of live cattle. (See *Railroad Record* and 1858 data, cited above, this note.) The increase in value of beef and cattle exports is shown in Table 12.4. I make no brief for the absolute accuracy of data in these sources; the proportions of change in exports are only estimates.

30. Paul W. Gates, *The Farmer's Age* (New York, 1960), pp. 212–13; Robert Leslie Jones, "The Beef Cattle Industry in Ohio prior to the Civil War," *OHQ*, LXIV (1955), 314.

31. Number of cattle given in Auditor of State, *AR*, 1852, 1855, 1860. On New York prices, see Paul C. Henlein, *Cattle Kingdom in the Ohio Valley* (Lexington, 1959), p. 147; and on Ohio's share of eastern markets for livestock, estimated at nearly one-third of New York's cattle purchases in 1857 and one-fourth of Philadelphia's the same year, see Commissioner of Statistics, *AR* in *Exec. Docs.*, *1857–58*, Vol. II, p. 499.

32. Jones, "Beef Cattle Industry," p. 316; Commissioner of Statistics, *AR*, 1860, pp. 16–17.

33. *ASTC*, *1855*, p. 17. See also Robert L. Jones, "The Dairy Industry in Ohio prior to the Civil War," *OAHQ*, LVI (1947), 51–52.

34. F. C. Van Cleef, "The Rise and Decline of the Cheese Industry in Lorain County," *OHQ*, LXIX (1960), 37–38.

35. *ASTC, 1859*, p. 10; Jones, "The Dairy Industry," p. 68.

36. Market-garden crop production exceeding $20,000 was reported in the 1860 Census only for Hamilton, Montgomery, Lucas, Franklin, Belmont, and Cuyahoga counties—all embracing or contiguous to major urban centers.

37. Robert L. Jones, "Special Crops in Ohio before 1850," *OHQ*, LIV (1945), 140–41.

38. See Tables 12.3, 12.4, 12.5.

39. And in each of these counties, the number of cattle increased 10,000 head or more during the same period. (From annual reports of Auditor of State.) Average yields fell from 18 bushels of wheat per acre in 1850 to 7.3 per acre in 1859; in the eastern counties, the decline in yields was even more precipitous. (Commissioner of Statistics, reports in *Exec. Docs.*, 1857–58, Vol. II, pp. 495–96; *ibid.*, 1860–61, Vol. II, pp. 439–41.)

40. This refers to a fourteen-county area of northwest Ohio and the grazing districts (Allen, Auglaize, Defiance, Fulton, Henry, Mercer, Paulding, Putnam, Van Wert, Williams, Lucas, Fayette, Madison, and Union); output reported in the *U. S. Census: Agriculture*, 1850, 1860. On rising land values and their impact upon the former grazing counties, see Jones, "The Beef Cattle Industry," pp. 314–18.

41. Computed from U. S. Census data, by output. See dot-type maps of farm output in Census years, in W. A. Lloyd *et al.*, *The Agriculture of Ohio* (Wooster, 1918).

42. On earlier production patterns and retardation of settlement and growth in northwest Ohio and the Scioto region, see Chap. 8–9, *supra*.

43. Lloyd, *Agriculture of Ohio*, pp. 199–200; *U. S. Census: Agriculture*, 1860, p. xii. Values include *all* farmland.

44. Based on 1850, 1860 U. S. agricultural census, data on value of farms.

45. Interestingly, this group included three counties (Portage, Medina, Knox) where land values increased despite depopulation and painful agricultural readjustment.

46. Lloyd, *Agriculture of Ohio*, p. 218; quotation from F. J. Turner, *The United States, 1830–1850* (New York, 1935), p. 259. See also E. Lang, "Ohioans in Northern Indiana before 1850," *Indiana Magazine of History*, XLIX (1953), 391–404.

47. Many of the purchasers of canal lands in northwest Ohio in

the forties and fifties had distinctly Irish or German names; some were no doubt construction laborers on the canals. (MSS. land-entry books, Ohio Land Offices, Auditor of State Records Room, Columbus.)

48. The increase for these four cities, including Cincinnati's industrial suburbs, was about a hundred thousand.

49. Sherry O. Hessler, "Patterns of Transport and Urban Growth in the Miami Valley" (M.A. thesis, Johns Hopkins, 1959), 44–45. For similar examples, see William T. Utter, *Granville* (Denison, 1956), 214–25; and L. Goggins, "The Economic Development of the Xenia, Ohio, Area" (M.A. thesis, Ohio State University, 1955), 35.

50. Of the twenty largest cities in Ohio in 1860, all but two were on either railroad or canal lines.

51. Charles Cist, quoted in Fred M. Jones, *Middlemen in the Domestic Trade of the United States* (Urbana, 1937), 52–53. See also Berry, *Western Prices*, 318–29; and Lewis Atherton, *The Pioneer Merchant in Mid-America* (Columbia, Missouri, 1939), 77. In 1859 more than one-third of the local merchants in western Ohio maintained credit accounts with Cincinnati wholesalers. The same was true of twelve hundred merchants in Illinois, four thousand in Indiana, two thousand in Kentucky, and about five hundred each in Tennessee and Missouri. (Henry E. White, "An Economic Study of Wholesale Prices at Cincinnati," mimeographed, Cornell University, 1935, p. 97.)

52. J. R. Robinson to J. Brasee, March 22, 1852, John T. Brasee Papers, OHS (asserting the railroad would provide warehouse and forwarding services); W. B. Thomas to J. A. Trimble, Aug. 7, Aug. 26, Sept. 22, 1858, and responses of Aug. 13, Aug. 17, 1858, Trimble Family Papers, OHS (on eastern grain dealers buying directly through western agents); Mad River & Lake Erie R.R. Co., *Annual Report, 1849*, p. 3; *ibid.*, 1853, pp. 7–8; Cleveland & Pittsburgh R.R. Co., *Annual Report, 1854*, pp. 4–7, 27; *ibid.*, 1859, pp. 8–9. In 1858–59, in severe trouble under pressure of competition, the Sandusky, Dayton & Cincinnati (formerly Mad River & Lake Erie) announced it was giving up its elaborate system of warehousing at way stations in an effort to cut its payroll—suggesting that for some railroad companies, at least, their providing such services was a costly competitive technique. (S. D. & C. Railroad Co., *Report, 1858*, pp. 5–7.)

53. Cincinnati merchants, for example, complained in 1860 that

the railroads carried cabinetware as cheaply from the Atlantic seaboard to Indiana as from Cincinnati to the same places. *ASTC*, 1860, p. 25; see also Cleveland *Leader*, April 30, 1859; and C. P. Wight to G. W. Venneman, Aug. 15, 1853, Misc. MSS., OHS (a Boston firm advertising direct sales to western retailers). The mercantile house of Phelps Dodge in New York, specializing in metal, sold through three agencies in Cincinnati, but elsewhere in Ohio and throughout the West they shipped in small lots directly to retailers and manufacturers. On their complex operations, see Richard Lowitt, *A Merchant Prince of the 19th Century: William E. Dodge* (New York, 1954), 37–38 and Chap. 2, *passim*.

54. Reporting 25 per cent of statewide mercantile stock in 1852, Cincinnati accounted for more than 40 per cent in 1860. (Auditor of State, *AR*, 1852, 1860.)

55. Commissioner of Statistics, *AR*, 1860, p. 24; processed animal products such as candles, soap, and lard-oil are here excluded from valuation of "farm exports."

56. *Ibid.*, pp. 46–47. See also Table 12.6.

57. The men's clothing industry employed over 13,000 workers in 1860. The next largest employing industry (lumber) reported less than six thousand workers. This and all other data relating to manufacturing from the 1850 Census (*Digest of the Statistics of Manufactures according to the Returns of the Seventh Census*, 35th Cong., 2d. Sess., Senate Ex. Doc. No. 39, serial 984) and the Census of 1860, *Manufactures of the U. S. in 1860* (Washington, 1865).

58. Isaac Lippincott, *History of Manufactures in the Ohio Valley* (New York, 1914), pp. 168–69; Commissioner of Statistics, *AR*, 1860, p. 25.

59. See Table 12.6. The eight industries mentioned were the last eight of the eleven listed in Group 9, Table 12.6. For purposes of analysis, in an effort to represent urban industrialization as it interacted with the changing hinterlands of Cincinnati and other centers, I have cited in Table 12.6 and in the text the data on value of output to portray industrial structure. The Census data on value-added in manufacture would support an even greater emphasis on the structural shift toward "new" industries, including production of durables, finished consumer goods such as clothing, etc., which reflect modernization of the manufacturing sector. In short, improved access to coal and

metal ores, widening of spatial areas from which urban manufacturers could draw raw materials, intensification of market demand as agricultural expansion went forward and farm income rose, and intensification as well of "intraurban" demand (as for construction material) all reveal—whichever set, of data are adduced—that the leading industrial districts (see n. 63, below) were breaking away from the old manufacturing structure. Some scholars have cast analysis of this sort in terms of the "take-off" into self-generating industrialization, contrasted with an older urban economy based on "commerce-related" and "entrepôt" manufacturing which were adjuncts to agriculture and trade; see Allen R. Pred, *The Spatial Dynamics of U. S. Urban-Industrial Growth, 1800–1914* (Cambridge, 1966), 167ff. *et passim.* Application of Pred's categories would not significantly alter the interpretation of manufacturing shifts presented here.

60. *Exec. Docs.,* 1857–58, Vol. II, p. 514.

61. These counties were Hamilton, Cuyahoga, Montgomery, Butler, and Miami.

62. Light manufactures are here defined as industries in classes 3, 5, 7, and 8 in Table 12.6. These industries, in nearly all the leading industrial counties, were more important than flour milling; elsewhere in the state, milling was almost uniformly the largest industry.

63. The eight leaders were Hamilton, Cuyahoga, Montgomery, Franklin, Lucas, Mahoning, Muskingum, and Stark. Only in Lucas and Montgomery did food processing and forest products dominate. All eight were canal counties.

64. See generally Eric Lampard in H. S. Perloff *et al., Regions, Resources, and Economic Growth* (Baltimore, 1960), 109–20.

65. This region embraced Scioto, Lawrence, Gallia, Jackson, Vinton, and Hocking counties.

66. Wilber E. Stout, "The Charcoal Iron Industry of the Hanging Rock District," *OAHQ,* XLII (1933), 82.

67. Frank H. Rowe, *History of the Iron and Steel Industry in Scioto County, Ohio* (Columbus, 1938), 22; Vernon D. Keeler, "An Economic History of the Jackson County Iron Industry," *OAHQ,* XLII (1933), 162, 167; Stout, "Charcoal Iron Industry," 99–100.

68. Keeler, *ibid.,* 166, 176, Chap. 3, *passim;* Rowe, *History of Iron and Steel,* 23. Noting increased shipments of coal to the iron

furnaces, the Marietta & Cincinnati Railroad Company reported in 1856 that the ironmongers no longer needed to rely upon the proximity of extensive stands of timber for charcoal; "not only is the *cost* of manufacture reduced, but the *extent* to which it may be profitably carried [on], is indefinitely increased." (*6th Annual Report*, p. 13.)

69. *ASTC, 1857,* pp. 24–25; Berry, *Western Prices,* 258n.

70. As noted earlier, however, direct rail shipment of livestock to the East adversely affected Ohio packers.

71. See City of Zanesville, *Report . . . in relation to the Management of the Central Ohio Railroad* (n. p., 1854), on railroad shops in the Zanesville urban economy; also, L. L. Unstad, "A Survey of Industrial and Economic Development in Central Ohio" (Ph.D. diss., Ohio State University, 1937), 374–76. In 1858, 21 Ohio railroads (out of 30 in the state) reported consumption of 209,416 cords of wood for fuel. (*Exec. Docs.,* 1858, Pt. II, p. 626.)

72. On this point, see Albert Fishlow, *American Railroads and the Transformation of the Ante-Bellum Economy* (Cambridge, 1965), 164, 172–73; also, Chap. 11, note 36, above.

CHAPTER 13

Conclusion

THE preceding chapters have explored the manifold dimensions of public policy in one state, as men of the early nineteenth century grappled with the problem of providing themselves with transportation facilities essential to economic growth. But there still remain some issues that touch the larger significance of Ohio's experience, issues concerning the broader patterns of governmental interaction with the private sector in American development.

PLANNING—OR MERE INTERVENTION?

Historians of government's role in the pre-Civil War economy disagree sharply as to the character of state policy. It is established beyond doubt that the states *intervened* in economic affairs, both to support the efforts of private enterprise and to regulate various activities based in the private sector. Many state governments, including Ohio, undertook public construction of some major transport facilities as well; and most of the states developed a program of subsidies, either direct or indirect, to encourage transportation development.[1]

Disagreement centers upon whether such interventions represented conscious "planning," that is, the pursuit of well-defined programs on some rationalized basis of priorities for resource allocation. At one end of the spectrum of scholarly opinion is the view that when the Federal government—constrained by sectional rivalries, fiscal problems, and Constitutional disputes—failed to seize the lead in planning of transport development, the state governments filled the void. The states "assumed the job of shaping decisively the contours of economic life;" and indeed, "far from being limited, the objectives of the state in the economic field were usually so broad that they were beyond its administrative power to achieve."[2] Historians propounding this view assert that a theory of governmental planning dominated policy-making until the 1850's.[3] This progovernmental theory made the public interest, or the interest of "the commonwealth," the validating principle of state action; and its influence diminished only when the conflicting *laisser-faire* ideology became ascendent just before the Civil War.

At the other end of the spectrum, some scholars have portrayed the early state governments as merely responding—passively, as it were—to whatever forces in the private sector demanded supportive public action. Government's role "was typically that of facilitating the financing of projects whose origin and conception were private;" and in transportation, the public sector was called into play only "when convenient, and in particular when national, regional, or local ambitions coincided with private profit, or could be made to seem to do so."[4] One historian generalizes from a case study of Massachusetts to say: "The states did not follow well thought through plans for the guidance and stimulation of economic development. Assistance to a few key projects and widely scattered speeches of local politicians to influence votes on a specific measure are not evidence of a theory of government aid."[5] The eminent legal historian Willard Hurst has offered a subtle variant of this view. He contends that state economic policy consisted largely of *ad hoc* responses to private initiatives and special interests. But policy took this form, first, because of the society's insistence on maximizing productivity in the short-run, rather than out of any well-defined commitment to limited intervention. Secondly, the structure of state government was ill-suited to the job of formulating commonwealth goals or pursuing "the public interest." The legislatures met for only brief sessions and were understaffed, so that lawmakers undertook no systematic fact-finding; administrative agencies lacked professional staffs and adequate funding; and the courts did not subject broad policy questions to searching scrutiny. Therefore, basic policy decisions were not decisions at all: they were "taken mostly in silence and largely by default."[6]

Ohio's record in making transportation policy suggests, above all, the perils of generalizing about any single pattern of early nineteenth century policy. For as in New York, Pennsylvania, and other major canal states, government did play a conscious developmental role and engaged in calculated planning. Unlike Massachusetts, where the initiatives for intervention all originated with private entrepreneurs, in Ohio it was a public agency—the canal commission of 1822–25—which formulated the state's transport plan and built up a political coalition strong enough to get the measure enacted in 1825.[7] And unlike Wisconsin, where the government's policies conformed to the model of "drift and default," in Ohio—at least until the mid-thirties—both lawmakers and administrative officials displayed a strong commitment to planning concepts.[8] To be sure, when the Ohio legislature formulated its railroad policy, drift and default did prevail. But this development warns us that we must focus on explaining why such basic changes in the accepted premises of policymaking occurred, instead of attempting to categorize all of the pre-1860 state programs in essentially static terms.

The people of early nineteenth century Ohio were motivated by "theories" of active government, I think, but not all of them by a single conception. Instead, there were several competing theories. First, the "commonwealth" conception was amply evident, especially in the proposals of the first canal commission in 1825, which argued for mobilizing public resources because a distinct public interest required collective action. Similar to mercantilist theory of the eighteenth century, the commonwealth idea proposed that only through definition of collective interests could the state provide the essential prerequisites for growth. Of course, the commonwealth idea was no more fixed or solidly objective than any definition of "the public interest," then or today.[9] (That is why local promoters in the 1820's and 1830's found it easy, as we have seen, to invoke commonwealth ideals to justify their pet local projects.) But even as late as the 1850's, men were explicitly concerned with redefining "public and private as well as corporate rights."[10]

A second theory, closely related to the first, which was present in policy debates and also in concrete state policies well into the 1840's, was the theory of planning, which called for the systematic ordering of growth by the state government itself. Planning concepts underlay the 1825 canal law; they were championed by the canal commission during the late twenties, when new projects were being debated; and they were the basic rationale for the canal officials' allocation of markets through rate-making policies designed to achieve balanced growth.

Still a third theory articulated in the canal era was the doctrine of equalized benefits. It was antithetical to the planning concept, for it decreed that equal distribution of costs and benefits among all members of the polity was a higher goal than rational definition of priorities aimed primarily at stimulating growth. It is impossible to say definitively whether men were sincerely motivated by the doctrine itself, or merely used egalitarian rhetoric for selfish purposes. Yet if repetition and reiteration of a theory permits the historian to make "a presumption of commitment," then this ideology was a factor in the policy process of the day.[11] In the Ohio case, moreover, the specific form given the Loan Law of 1837 for aid to private companies was consistent with the ideology; and certainly considerations of equity, on egalitarian lines, were frequently adduced to justify administrative decisions as well.

The record in Ohio reveals as a central theme tension among these competing theories; but also tension between theory and the parochial pursuit of local ambition. It was not until the mid-thirties that localism overwhelmed planning concepts. Yet the canal officials continued to pursue rate-making policies that reflected planning ideas; and similarly, in the early 1840's, the board of fund commissioners attempted to make state banking policy consistent with the more embracing objectives of developmental policy. Even the feeble move toward adoption of a general railroad law in 1848, though it came too late to be effective, revealed a concern for definition of uniform policy in the public interest. But the evolution of Ohio's railroad policy through the medium of special charters reveals that by the 1840's "the public interest" had come to rest on the definition of local, not state, collective interests.

ADMINISTRATIVE UNDERDEVELOPMENT

One reason why rationalized planning broke down during the mid-thirties was the weakened autonomy of the Ohio canal commission, which had played the central role in articulating and defending the planning principle.[12] The men who had directed the building of the first canals had been as competent and purposeful as they were audacious: in addition to their technical and managerial skills, they had brought to the project a deeply felt "proprietary sense," which they sought to inspire in their staff as well. As a result, those concerned with directing the enterprise shared an élan which became an important source of strength.

Once the original canals were nearly completed, the magnitude and complexity of the tasks performed by the agency diminished considerably: the operation of working canals required far less formal organization than had been needed when thousands of construction laborers, scores of contractors, and a large engineering staff all needed coordination.[13] The agency responded to this by introducing considerable decentralization of responsibilities and by routinizing tasks. But when new construction was approved by the legislature, the canal board did not reinstitute centralized control of operations, of the kind that had been maintained under Williams and Kelley; instead, responsibilities remained decentralized, and the board did not institute adequate inspection or accounting procedures. Lost now was the proprietary sense which had characterized direction of the enterprise in the early period.

Under such conditions, the commission and its successor agency, the board of public works, ceased to be an effective champion of planning concepts. The board approved new projects in 1836 without seriously considering an exercise of the potential veto power that it enjoyed; and in administering the 1837 Loan Law, the commissioners seemed more interested in evading policy choices than in exercising their statutory powers in the public interest. The board was therefore a feeble instrument for resisting policy demands based on "entrepreneurial imperatives," localism, egalitarian ideology, and the like. Moreover, after corruption was discovered in the board's direction of new canal construction, the agency lost its autonomy even in the conduct of internal affairs: the legislature interfered with its policymaking, imposed new (and demoralizing) personnel policies, and permitted absorption of the board's staff into the machinery of party patronage.

Historians have generally recognized that "administrative underdevelopment" was an obstacle to effective economic planning before 1860.[14] But the weakness of state agencies is usually attributed simply to understaffing, the absence of a civil service, and inadequate funding. The Ohio case suggests that poorly considered administrative decisions—such as the decentralization instituted by the canal commissioners themselves in Ohio—contributed to such weakness. Moreover, faults in the structure of organization were exaggerated because the legislature insisted that administrative officials perform a political function, as when the district system of representation was adopted in appointment of board members. Once administrative autonomy began to erode, the process became cumulative; and the record of canal administration in Ohio may be interpreted as a case of arrested bureaucratic development, rather than as one of simple administrative underdevelopment.

DISILLUSIONMENT

Administrative failures, engineering errors, and the loss of prestige suffered by the canal board, all contributed during the 1840's to a growing public reaction against active state enterprise. The idealistic impulses and commonwealth theories which had been invoked earlier were now downgraded; and in retrospect it appeared that the state had merely "turned canal digger and turnpike builder by wholesale" and had "got as crazy as the rest of mankind upon these subjects."[15] With once-honored theoretical justifications stripped away, the canal policy was reinterpreted as one based only upon the "selfish principle."[16]

Perhaps more important still, alternatives to state initiatives were beginning to appear: eastern capital began to move into western railroad finance in the 1840's, while European investors stood ready to purchase railroad bond issues, especially those backed with the credit of local governments. The quest for private railroad facilities led to a generally permissive railroad policy in Ohio. Not only did massive local aid play a key role in financing railway construction during the late forties and early fifties; the state also granted liberal charters and left the companies virtually free to establish freight charges on traffic. It is especially revealing of popular attitudes that corruption, profligate waste, and fraud were certainly as much a feature of private railroad enterprises as they had been of public canal construction—and yet the railroads never suffered the same kind of criticism as was directed against the state canal authorities. Also, because most Ohio shippers and consumers enjoyed major economic advantages from the rapid service, year-round operation, and declining rates of railroad transportation, their attention was directed to promoting railroad enterprise rather than to regulating it in the public interest. Expressions of concern that railroads' operating practices were becoming increasingly arbitrary did not result in significant regulatory measures.

TRANSPORT AND ECONOMIC GROWTH

The relationship between transport innovations and economic development in Ohio fulfilled in many respects the predictions of the original promoters. But development was not uniform in all the regions served by new transportation facilities; and the structure of rates proved fully as important as the construction of new lines both in the canal era and the early railroad period. An often-neglected feature of canals was that, for some localities favored by topography, they furnished waterpower for industry and had a formative influence in the location of mills and the composition of regional labor forces. The state's protectionist rate-making policies afforded an additional advantage to manufacturers situated in the interior regions of the state, so long as the canals held a monopoly position in the carriage of heavy commodities such as salt. Destruction of this protectionist system was one of the subtler effects of private railroad construction in the 1850's. Another neglected feature of transport development in the canal era was the great intensification of competition among rival (and proliferating) water routes in interregional commerce, with an accompanying decline in rates during the 1840's, prior to the completion of east-west railroads.

The dawning of the railroad age forced new adjustments upon the Ohio economy: the comparative advantages of individual cities were altered, the structure of wholesaling changed, and a group of "modern" industries began to flourish (notably in Cincinnati) while some of the older food-processing industries lagged. Some of the state's older farming regions that had failed to diversify were now forced to shift out of arable farming and into livestock production. The railroads developed a thriving trade in carrying unprocessed grain to eastern milling centers, meanwhile destroying abruptly the old pattern of driving cattle and hogs overland, substituting transportation by rail.

The tempo of economic activity quickened, once the railroads came: New York City's wholesale shops no longer drew their shades halfway to announce the winter closing of the canals, and full way to indicate that ice had shut down the Hudson River as well, ending their "season." Already the smoke of steam engines rose from Ohio factories; the coal trade burgeoned, and hundreds of men went down into mines; and the iron and other minerals that portended a modern industrial era were now carried across the Great Lakes to such old canal ports as Cleveland, which had once reported commerce only in barrels of flour and salt, cartons of "merchandise" and sacks of "southern groceries."

INSTITUTIONAL AND POLITICAL CONTINUITIES

The impact of early nineteenth century transport innovations, both public and private, was also manifest in the changing character of institutions; and one can identify important institutional continuities that originate early in the canal era, bridging the years of Civil War that otherwise might appear to have forced a distinct break in patterns of development.

The financing of the canal projects illustrates one such continuum. In the 1820's, a small number of banking houses on the Atlantic seaboard purchased state bonds, including Ohio's, and developed lines of credit for these operations with the great investment bankers of London. Their role as intermediaries in governmental finance led logically to their taking a leading part in underwriting railroad stock and bond issues in the 1840's and 1850's. The success with which New York and other eastern investment banks handled the Federal government's Civil War bond issues had its precedents in these developments; and by the end of the century, when American manufacturing corporations were ready to finance expansion through public issues of their equity stock, banking institutions capable of responding had gained a long experience in marketing both governmental and railroad securities.[17]

Conscious, well-considered policies pursued by the Ohio board of fund commissioners also had a major effect on the growth of banking institutions within the state. For many years, while the canals were being constructed, the fund board deposited in selected Ohio banks the capital funds acquired by bond issues. This enabled the banks to expand the scope of their operations, and it provided reserves on which the banks predicated expansion of their note issues and provisions of credit to Ohio land speculators, farmers, and manufacturers. Therefore, the history of American state government's interaction with privately owned banks—usually considered only in terms of the state's promotional role in issuing charters and its regulatory role—had another dimension in the banks' handling of the funds employed to build public works. And the latter was in turn closely interrelated with the early history of bank regulation, especially after the Ohio banks became major sources of capital as purchasers of canal bonds. In light of this record, the Federal government's reliance on banks to provide investment capital when national bonds were marketed during 1862–65 may be viewed as a variant, though, on a much larger scale, of a scenario already played out in the canal states.

In the evolution of managerial techniques for the organization and operation of railroads—which were the first giant corporate

enterprises of the nineteenth century—there was a significant
carryover, in terms of both administrative precedents and personnel, from the public canal enterprises.[18] The methods for
organizing construction through use of private contractors and
for recruiting a labor force were pioneered by the canal builders;
the practical education of managers and engineers in the direction
of large-scale undertakings had been provided by the canal agencies; and the transfer of individual entrepreneurs from public
canal management to similar roles in the private railroad companies was often critical to the success of railroad ventures. Thus
Alfred Kelley, after leaving the state service, became president of
the Cleveland, Columbus, & Cincinnati Railroad and was a principal architect of the Lake Shore railway system. In negotiating
bond sales or short-term loans for his railroad, Kelley dealt with
the same eastern and British bankers with whom he had collabo-
rated in his role as a fund commissioner; in planning the C. C. &
C., Kelley encountered problems precisely comparable to those he
had confronted in the early 1820's as a canal commissioner; and
no doubt he traversed districts where he had once trudged, carrying his surveying instruments, when those areas were still virtual
wilderness.

An intangible quality that men such as Kelley brought to private
enterprise was a long experience in mapping strategies of transport development that embraced the entire West, whereas the
typical entrepreneur still dealt with the problems of local markets
and small-scale operations. By dint of his earlier prominence in
state enterprise, Kelley was easily identifiable as part of a new
business élite in the West. This was true as well of Micajah T.
Williams, who became the organizer and first president of the
Ohio Life & Trust, one of the region's largest banks. In his role
as banker, Williams drew his associates from the circle of men
who had been his colleagues in the canal enterprise and in state
financing; and he obtained the bulk of his capital from eastern
investors with whom he had formed contacts while still in state
service. Williams and Kelley were representative of a small group
of men who moved readily in and out of state-government posts,
and who transferred a valuable fund of managerial experience
and personal business relationships to the private sector.[19]

Other strands of continuity may be discerned in politics and in law. In the pre-1860 period, voting in the Ohio legislature on transportation policies took the form of coalitions and logrolling, and party discipline was less important than the struggle between "have" and "have-not" local districts. The same was true of the cleavages on transportation questions in the 1850 constitutional convention. Here then were striking precedents for the post-Civil War debates over railway regulation in the Granger states, where communities suffering from adverse railroad rate practices demanded state controls, while the "have-not" localities wanted a liberal policy. Transportation was well enough developed by the Granger era to make regulatory policy rather than promotional schemes the main focus of debate, but the localistic organization of political forces was the same as in both the canal period and the 1850's. Nor was the concept of state-dictated rates without pre-Civil War precedents, as demonstrated by the rate-making activities of state canal officials.

In the 1850's, in addition, private railroad managers engaged in many of the strategies usually associated with the post-Civil War era. Efforts at pooling of traffic, rate-fixing through inter-company agreements, and efforts to control connecting lines were followed by a quest for private reordering of a highly competitive system by means of joint management or consolidation of firms. From state political leaders and business groups, these actions drew forth cries of "monopoly" and warnings that predatory out-of-state capitalists were gaining control of lines originally built, with state and local aid, for state and local purposes. Compare the historian Robert H. Wiebe's description of the profound social changes that he identifies with the 1870's: "Towns that had tied their future to a local [railroad] line almost never owned it. Nor did they have any part in deciding the rates charged, the services offered, the distant connections made or not made. That power lay elsewhere, in 'alien' hands. Moreover, crops were increasingly processed well beyond the farmer's ken, and the goods he needed came more often from strange, remote places." Hence it was out of a desire to somehow restore "community self-determination" that Americans of the 1870's advocated antimonopoly laws.[20]

But this same sense of social crisis was manifest in some of the public debates of the 1850's. Indeed, one may guess that men's sense of loss, when they realized that "alien" capitalists controlled their transportation and processed their farm products at distant places, was all the more painful because only a few years earlier the state—their own state government—had controlled the basic arteries of commerce. But in the fifties, this gathering sense of disturbing social change and loss of communities' power of "self-determination" produced neither an effective antimonopoly movement nor forceful pressure for effective state regulation—only a distressing perception that the private sector was outrunning the capacity of government to control it.

When the society finally did demand state regulation in the 1870's, however, the instruments were ready at hand, embedded in the confusing welter of statute law and court decisions that comprised early railroad law. For when the state gave private railroad companies the same power of eminent domain as had been exercised by the public canal authorities, the courts early upheld such grants of power—on grounds that railroads were chartered for a public purpose. This very doctrine contained the legal foundation for bringing railroads under public control in the post-Civil War decades: for if railroads were given extraordinary privileges in the public interest, they could be regulated in the same interest.[21] By that time, the wheel had gone full circle, and the commonwealth doctrine was reasserted.

In the 1850's, however, the time for revival of commonwealth ideals had not yet come. Indeed the success of Ohio's railroads in taking traffic from the canals seemed to reinforce an already powerful disillusionment with the active state. Repeatedly the board of public works called for maintenance of the canals, whatever the cost, to provide a yardstick for rates and to prevent railroad monopoly of commerce. But the slim public support it enjoyed was based entirely on a pragmatic willingness to keep the public works in operation only so long as no operating deficits were incurred. Once annual deficits began to plague canal operations, the case for public enterprise was lost.

Therefore, while the drama at Fort Sumter engaged a concerned people's attention in 1861, the Ohio canals were turned over to

private operators. A forty-year venture in public enterprise had
come to an end.

NOTES

1. See James Willard Hurst, *Law and the Conditions of Freedom
   in the 19th Century United States* (Madison, 1964); other general works on government's role are cited in the Bibliography,
   below.
2. Louis Hartz, *Economic Policy and Democratic Thought: Pennsylvania, 1776–1860* (Cambridge, 1948), 289, 292. These brief
   quotations from Hartz's study do not do justice, it must be
   said, to the subtleties of his larger analysis of Pennsylvania's
   state policy; see, for example, *ibid.*, 9–17, on localism.
3. See the admirable critical discussion by Robert A. Lively, "The
   American System," *Business History Review*, XXIX (March
   1955), 81–96. In Currin V. Shields, "The American Tradition
   of Empirical Collectivism," *American Political Science Review*,
   XLVI (1952), 104–20, the author contends that collective
   (governmental) problem-solving has gone forward pragmati-
   cally, but with distinct preferences for individual (private) action, for minimal interference in private affairs, and for local
   or state instrumentalities instead of Federal. Definition of these
   neatly defined tendencies is based mainly, however, on the
   writings of theorists, of commentators such as Tocqueville and
   Bryce, and of a few leading national political spokesmen.
4. Hugh G. J. Aitken, review in the *Business History Review*,
   XXXV (Summer 1961), 291–92.
5. Stephen Salsbury, *The State, the Investor, and the Railroad:
   The Boston & Albany, 1825–1867* (Cambridge, 1967), 34.
6. Hurst, *Law and Economic Growth: The Legal History of the
   Lumber Industry in Wisconsin, 1836–1915* (Cambridge, 1964),
   278. Hurst makes this statement in reference to taxation and
   public lands policies in Wisconsin, but it is consistent with his
   interpretation of public economic policy more generally. (See
   ibid., 102–7, 171–72, 248–76.)

7. The record in Massachusetts is reappraised in Salsbury, *The State, the Investor, and the Railroad.*

8. See Hurst, *Law and Economic Growth,* cited n. 6. The term "planning" as used here connotes active pursuit of commonwealth interests and the vesting of important discretionary power in governmental officials for allocation of resources. Of course, in present-day industrial societies the planning process ordinarily involves such attributes as a high degree of centralization of power and the elaborate coordination of various public agencies. In pre-Civil War America, neither social nor governmental institutions were geared to this type of implementation. See Jan Tinbergen, *Central Planning* (Studies in Comparative Economics, Vol. IV, New Haven, 1964), 42–43; and Andrew Shonfield, *Modern Capitalism: The Changing Balance of Public and Private Power* (New York, 1965), 301–6. Lawrence M. Friedman, in *Contract Law in America* (Madison, 1965), 142ff., provides a highly original and persuasive analysis of the goals and functions of early American state governments as they were analogous to those of modern governments.

9. This classic problem is considered in Pendleton Herring, *Public Administration and the Public Interest* (New York, 1936). A redefinition of its terms, prescribing for its solution political debate and elections that make possible meaningful coalitions and an expression of "majority will," is in William H. Riker, *Democracy in the United States* (2nd edn., New York, 1965), 98ff. For different perspectives, however, see J. R. Pennock, "Responsiveness, Responsibility, and Majority Rule," *American Political Science Review,* XLVI (Sept. 1952), 790ff.; and G. A. Schubert, Jr., " 'The Public Interest' in Administrative Decision-Making," *ibid.,* LI (June 1957), 346ff.

10. Ohio Board of Agriculture, *6th AR* (1852), 21; Ohio Senate, Special Committee on Railroads, *Report* (1861), 2.

11. Harold D. Lasswell, "The Study of Political Elites," *World Revolutionary Elites,* ed. Lasswell and D. Lerner (Cambridge, 1965), 18. The "public interest" and the effects of "equal benefits" and related egalitarian doctrines are treated in their relationship to both interventionist and *laisser-faire* ideology, in two highly useful articles by Wiley E. Hodges: "The Theoretical Basis for Anti-Governmentalism in Virginia, 1789–1836," *Journal of Politics,* IX (1947), 325–54; and "Pro-Governmentalism in Virginia, 1789–1836," *ibid.,* XXV (1963), 333–60.

12. The commission's commitment to planning principles may be compared usefully to some modern governmental agencies' similar ideological rationales, as for instance the Tennessee Valley Authority's espousal of the "grass roots" planning variant. See Philip Selznick, *TVA and the Grass Roots* (2nd edn., New York, 1966), 47–48, 76.

13. In 1858, for example, the Board of Public Works reported the full-time equivalent of well under 200 employees regularly employed on Ohio's public works. (BPW, *20th AR*, 125ff.)

14. Carter Goodrich, "American Development Policy: The Case of Internal Improvements," *Journal of Economic History*, XVI (Dec. 1956), 456–57; Hurst, *Law and Economic Growth, passim.*

15. See Chap. 4, note 10, above. In the 1850 convention, one delegate deplored internal improvements for local purposes, as "mere legalized plunder and robbery." 1850 Constitutional Convention, *Debates and Proceedings* (Columbus, 1851), 349.

16. *Ibid.,* 752.

17. See Appendix I, below. For a different view, stressing relative immobilities of capital for interregional investment outside the public sector, see Lance E. Davis, "Capital Immobilities and Finance Capitalism, . . . 1820–1920," *Explorations in Entrepreneurial History/ 2nd Series, I* (Fall 1963), 91 *et passim.*

18. In a sense, the tremendous managerial requirements of the canal enterprise in the *construction phase* were comparable to the organizational problems posed by railroad operation; canal *operation,* because control of the commodities and vessels was in hands of men and firms other than the canal officials, was far less demanding in organizational terms. Cf. Alfred D. Chandler, Jr. and Stephen Salsbury, "The Railroads: Innovators in Modern Business Administration," *The Railroad and the Space Program,* ed. Bruce Mazlish (Cambridge, 1965), 127ff., esp. at 133–34, where the authors insist that railroad organization was absolutely without precedent; but compare the canal-management organization adopted in Ohio, discussed in Chap. 3, above.

19. Others associated with the Ohio canal enterprise who became prominent in the private transport sector include Jesse Williams, a junior engineer who became Indiana's chief state engineer and later chief engineer for the Ft. Wayne & Chicago Railroad and other lines; Increase Lapham and Francis Cleveland, also

engineers; Samuel Forrer, who became chief engineer for several private turnpike companies; Sebried Dodge, who headed the Mahoning Canal engineering staff; and Daniel Kilgore, who became an organizer of the Steubenville & Indiana Railroad. (See Scheiber, "Entrepreneurship and Western Development," *Business History Review*, XXXVII [Winter 1963], 368 *et passim.*)

20. Robert H. Wiebe, *The Search for Order, 1877–1920* (New York, 1967), 7, 52.

21. Leonard W. Levy, *The Law of the Commonwealth and Chief Justice Shaw* (Cambridge, 1957), 120–26, 255.

APPENDICES,
BIBLIOGRAPHY
AND INDEX

Appendix 1

THE SOURCES OF CAPITAL: FOREIGN AND DOMESTIC INVESTMENT IN OHIO STATE BONDS, 1825–1840

During the period of canal construction in Ohio, from 1825 to 1845, the state was one of the leading public authorities borrowing in American and foreign money markets. During 1815–34, an estimated $41.2 million was expended by American governments (Federal, state, and municipal) for canal construction, and of that amount Ohio was responsible for 11 per cent. During 1834–44, total American governmental expenditures for canal construction were $57.3 million, of which investment by the Ohio state government was $9.7 million in outright public construction, with an additional $400,000 of state funds invested in Mahoning Canal stock and with the City of Cincinnati expending another $400,000 in the Whitewater Canal project.[1] Ohio's prominent role in public canal investment of this period raises the question of what were the sources of Ohio's capital.

It is well known that in the 1820's investment capital in Great Britain and Continental Europe began to flow into the United States, and mainly into state securities issued to finance canal construction, as the end of European borrowing to finance wars and a slowdown in European government debt-financing generally released funds for overseas opportunities. In the period 1815–34 alone, bankers and individual investors in Europe placed some $43 million of their capital in American canal bonds; and in the 1830's the flow of capital across the Atlantic to the U.S. continued to swell.[2] The American state governments competed with one another for available funds, and interest rates gradually rose (witness Ohio's issues of 5 per cents at prices as high as 24 per cent above par in 1832, as compared to sales of 6 per cents at only slightly above par in the late thirties). The Anglo-American banking houses regularly accepted consignments of state bonds from the investment banks of New York, Philadelphia, and Baltimore; and they re-sold the bonds in the broad-based investment market in London and on the Continent. Thus the Anglo-American bankers developed a mechanism for the orderly flow of funds into what was then regarded as relatively high-yield, low-risk government paper. After the 1837 panic and with the onset of a serious depression in 1839, American foreign-trade earnings from cotton and other exports fell off dramatically; the Bank of England raised its own rediscount rates to stem the flow of specie funds across the Atlantic; and the Anglo-American houses perforce tightened the reins of credit. By late 1840 there was a serious crisis in the securities markets, stranding many of the American state governments as they struggled to complete ambitious canal projects first undertaken in the late 1830's.

The defaults and repudiations of Pennsylvania, Michigan, and other states in the forties led to panic selling by some European investors, and more important produced much bitterness and mistrust of American state securities—a mistrust not overcome until the 1850's, when foreign capital once again found an outlet in American paper, this time with heavy emphasis on railroad bonds and commercial paper supporting sales of iron rails on short-term credit.[3]

In the case of New York, the pioneering public-canal state, the intial bonds of 1817 were sold in the domestic market, and only in the early 1820's did British investors emerge as important sources of capital—that is, as the original purchasers, directly from the state, of its Erie Canal bonds.[4] But in the case of Ohio, never in the period 1825–32 (during the first canal program) did the state sell directly to European investors. All the bonds of that period, amounting to $4.5 million, were marketed in

New York and Philadelphia. During the second phase of Ohio borrowing, during 1836–45, bond sales were mainly to Ohio banks and to investment firms and wealthy individuals in New York—except for the direct sales to Baring Brothers of London.[5]

This did not mean that in Ohio's case no significant contribution to financing was made by the foreign investor. On the contrary, it is well known that the firms and individuals who gave Ohio support by virtue of their direct bond purchases—Rathbone & Lord, Prime, Ward & King, the Ohio Life & Trust, John Jacob Astor, William Bucknor, and the rest—regularly consigned their American state securities to Anglo-American bankers such as Baring for re-sale in the European money market. The relative importance of European *versus* American investment in supporting Ohio's public works program fortunately can be documented up to 1840. An analysis of investment up to that time is presented in the tables below.

Of $4.5 million in bonds sold during 1825–32, nearly two thirds had been marketed abroad by 1840, mainly in England. Of the 5 per cents issued in 1825 (Table A), none of the $308,-

---

TABLE A

HOLDERS OF RECORD, FEB. 1840, OF 5% BONDS
(REDEEMABLE IN 1850), ISSUED IN 1825

CLASS	NUMBER OF INVESTORS	AMOUNT HELD
Foreign	28	$308,244
American	26	88,141
Unknown	2	3,615
TOTAL	56	$400,000

Source: State of Ohio, *Exec. Docs.,* 1839–40, No. 91, pp. 37–52. This is the source also for data in remaining Tables of Appendix I.

---

244 in bonds owned by foreign holders was in the hands of the large investment houses: the holders were mainly small individual investors—that is, upper-class and bourgeois government officials, professional people, managers of trusts, widows and rentiers

who are known to have comprised the popular market for gilt-edged public securities in Europe. No doubt the original purchaser of the 5 per cents (Rathbone & Lord of New York) had consigned the bonds to an English house, probably Baring, and the latter in turn had marketed them in London. Of the $88,141 held by Americans in 1840, none was in Rathbone & Lord's possession.

Of the 6 per cents sold initially during 1826–32 (Table B),

TABLE B

HOLDERS OF RECORD, FEB. 1840, OF 6% BONDS
(REDEEMABLE IN 1850), ISSUED 1826–32

CLASS	NUMBER OF INVESTORS	AMOUNT HELD
Foreign	166	$2,664,158
American	121	1,185,161
Unknown	12	158,896
Unreported	—	91,785
TOTAL	299	$4,100,000

$1,185,161 had remained in the United States. Of this portion, one third ($362,552) was owned by the Bank for Savings in New York, an institution which solicited the savings deposits of small tradesmen and other petty savers in order to put their money to work in gilt-edged investment stock.[6] Aside from the Bank for Savings lot, nearly all the 6 per cents were held by small-scale individual investors in America; and of the larger portion, $2,664,158, in foreign hands, nearly all had been widely diffused, similarly, among small purchasers.

The $150,000 bond issue of 1837, comprised of 5 per cents, was originally sold to the Bank of Marietta, which in February, 1840, still held $25,000 of the securities. (See Table C.) The other American holders listed were Prime, Ward & King ($13,-000) and Goodhue & Co. ($15,000), so that the entire issue was still owned by institutional investors. By contrast, however, the 14 foreign holders were all individuals, nine owning $5,000 or less each while the largest held only $20,000. From this, we may

TABLE C
HOLDERS OF RECORD, FEB. 1840, OF 5% BONDS
ISSUED IN 1837

CLASS	NUMBER OF INVESTORS	AMOUNT HELD
American	3 (all institutions)	$ 53,000
Foreign	14 (all individuals)	97,000
TOTAL	17	$150,000

infer that the Marietta bank sold or consigned its holdings to the New York firms, which in turn sold them to individual investors in England through the Anglo-American banking houses.

During 1838 and 1839 Ohio issued $1,826,000 in 6 per cent bonds. The fund commissioners had sold most of this issue to three firms, the Ohio Life & Trust ($715,000), the North American Trust ($500,000), and Prime, Ward & King ($300,000); they had marketed the remainder to banks in Ohio. As of 1840 (shown in Table D) there were only nine American bondholders;

TABLE D
HOLDERS OF RECORD, FEB. 1840, OF 6% 1860 BONDS
ISSUED IN 1838–1839

CLASS	NUMBER OF INVESTORS INDIVIDUALS	INSTITUTIONS	AMOUNT HELD
American	1	8	$ 799,000
Foreign	28	4	842,500
Foreign & U.S.	0	2	179,500
Unknown	1	0	5,000
TOTAL	30	14	$1,826,000

and only one, owning $25,000, was an individual. The others were banks or investment houses, including two of the original purchasers, the Ohio Life & Trust ($440,000) and the Urbana Bank ($86,000). The remainder of the American holders in 1840 were investment firms in the Atlantic Coast cities, including John Ward & Co., Jacob Reese, and Peter Harmony. Nor did the category listed as "Foreign and American" differ from the picture; here again, the bonds were held by investment firms and institutions, not yet having been sold in the broad-based securities market. The two "Foreign & U.S." holders were the Anglo-American banks Ralston & Co. and Roskill, Ogden & Co. Some $842,500 were held overseas: the Barings owned $320,000 and another $60,000 was owned by three other banks. But the remainder had found its way into the hands of smaller investors, including Thomas Cotterill (who had invested heavily in Erie Canal bonds and who owned $35,000 of the Ohio 6 per cents in Table D) and a brief catalogue of English nobles and commoners, with pensions, livings, or inheritances—ministers, government officials, and so on.[7] In summary, while the smaller English investors had purchased a considerable portion of the total issue ($460,000), by far the largest portion of all the 1838–39 6 per cents was still owned by the original purchasers or other investment-banking firms. The heavy holdings still in the hands of Baring, the Ohio Life & Trust, and others indicate that by early 1840 these firms were already encountering resistance in the broad-based money market. In any event, it is consistent with what we know of the Barings' operations, that they enjoyed modest success in marketing Ohio bonds in late 1839 and early 1840, following which they were to encounter a two-year period of negligible demand and sharply reduced sales.[8]

An additional $3,164,638 of 6 per cents were issued in 1836–39, as shown in Table E. Of the original purchasers, Prime, Ward

TABLE E
HOLDERS OF RECORD, FEB. 1840, OF 6% 1856 BONDS
ISSUED 1836–1839

| CLASS | NUMBER OF INVESTORS | | AMOUNT HELD |
	INDIVIDUALS	INSTITUTIONS	
American	28	16	$1,223,872
Foreign	112	5	1,925,766
Unknown	3	0	15,000
TOTAL	143	21	$3,164.638

& King and the Ohio Life & Trust together had taken $1,490,000. As of February, 1840, the two firms together still held $456,000, apparently having found no market for that portion of their purchase—and indeed it might have been their entire purchase on their own account, as possibly they had bought originally on behalf of other investors who formed a syndicate. The other American holders of record in 1840, in any event, included 14 institutions (holding $598,000) and 28 individuals (holding some $170,000). Thus all but a very small proportion of the American bondholders at that time were institutions.

A very different pattern characterized the foreign list, shown in Table E. There was not the same degree of concentration in a few hands as in the case of American holders, nor did institu-

---

TABLE F
BONDHOLDERS OF RECORD, FEB. 1840,
SECURITIES ISSUED 1836–1839
(Summary, Tables C, D, E)

CLASS	NUMBER OF INVESTORS*	AMOUNT HELD
American	56	$2,075,872
Foreign	163	2,865,266
Foreign & U.S.	2	179,500
Unknown	4	20,000
TOTAL	225	$5,140,638

* Multiple holders not discounted.

---

tions dominate to the same extent. Some sizeable blocs of the bonds were held by institutions: the Barings ($110,000), Hope & Co. ($85,000), and N. M. Rothschild & Sons ($48,000). Investment groups headed by Abraham Q. Henriques and Samuel P. Labouchere held $48,259 and $120,000 respectively. But in addition, more than a hundred individual investors had purchased holdings in amounts ranging from $170 owned by one Elizabeth Frazer to the more substantial sums in hands of such notables as Prince Napoleon Bonaparte ($17,000), Sir Francis Chantrey ($42,000), Thomas Cotterill ($46,000), Lord William Fitz Roy

($10,000), and Sir Robert Peel ($30,000). Withal, the foreign holders were precisely the type that one would expect to find, in light of what we know of the Anglo-American bankers' clientele. It was a conservative investor, on the whole, who sought out American governmental securities, hoping for regular income and (mistakenly, as it proved with the bonds of Pennsylvania and other American states) assured safety. The fund board in Ohio thus assessed very accurately the prospects for further overseas sales, when they declared in 1841 that "the European demand for our stocks, which of course regulates that at home, is rarely of a speculative character. The stock is absorbed in sums comparatively small, by persons seeking . . . income."[9]

From the standpoint of Ohio canal finance in early 1840, the situation illustrated by these tables was ominous indeed. Approximately $2 million of the bonds issued since 1837 still remained the property of large institutional investors, most of them having been the original purchasers—Prime, Ward & King, the Barings, the Ohio Life & Trust, and a few others—and their willingness or ability to take on additional risks was severely limited by these holdings. Considering the continuous depreciation of Ohio securities from 1840 to 1842—in the summer of 1842 a leading commercial journal reported Ohio bonds selling at 50 per cent of par value and the state's fiscal position "going rapidly to decay"—it was all the more remarkable that the Ohio Life & Trust and others should have continued to sustain the state in those desperate years.[10] Of course, during 1840–42 investment in Ohio paper was no longer a matter of gilt-edged stock purchasing: the probability of repudiation appeared high. Moreover, when the Barings extended further aid, it was on their own terms: their purchase at 60 per cent of par was hedging their bet. On the other hand, the prominent role of European investors as the ultimate market for Ohio's bond issues—and the fact that their role was publicized in 1840, when the data on current bondholders was issued—renders more easily understood the position of the Locofoco repudiationists in Ohio. With their hatred of the English nobility and their fear of foreign "economic imperialism," these radicals found repudiation congenial, as a policy that would hurt "merely" some foreigners and a pack of corrupt bankers who had picked up the state's securities at bargain-counter prices.[11]

NOTES

1. Harvey Segal, "Cycles of Canal Construction," *Canals and American Economic Development,* ed. Carter Goodrich (New York, 1962), 215. On Ohio expenditures, see Chapters 2, 5, and 6, *supra.* On capital flows and American net indebtedness to foreigners, see Douglass C. North's estimates, "The U. S. Balance of Payments, 1790–1860," *Trends in the American Economy in the 19th Century* (National Bureau of Economic Research, Studies in Income and Wealth, Vol. 24, Princeton, 1960), 622ff.

2. The standard account is Leland H. Jenks, *The Migration of British Capital to 1875* (New York, 1927), but see also R. C. McGrane, *Foreign Bondholders and American State Debts* (New York, 1935), and R. C. O. Matthews, *A Study in Trade Cycle History* (Cambridge, Eng., 1954).

3. Ralph W. Hidy, *The House of Baring in American Trade and Finance* (Cambridge, 1949), *passim;* Muriel Hidy, "The Capital Markets" (1789–1865), *Growth of the American Economy,* ed. H. F. Williamson (2nd edition, Englewood Cliffs, 1951), 256–78.

4. Nathan Miller, *Enterprise of a Free People* (Ithaca, 1962), 77–111. Miller's is a detailed study of canal-bond issues by New York and the sources of capital.

5. See Chapter 6, *supra.*

6. On the Bank for Savings, cf., Miller, *Enterprise,* 88–89.

7. On Cotterill, cf. *ibid.,* 106.

8. Hidy, *House of Baring,* 289ff.

9. *Executive Docs.,* 1840–41, No. 66, p. 4.

10. *Hunt's Merchants' Magazine,* VII (1842), 287–88, 550.

11. For example, *Ohio Statesman* (Columbus), Jan. 20, Feb. 21, 1840.

Appendix 2

TOLLS ON THE OHIO CANALS

Given in the tables of this appendix are the schedules of tolls adopted by the canal commission and its successor agency, the board of public works. In her index to economic materials in documents of the American states, Adelaide Hasse asserts that the 1830 schedule is the earliest known. In the *History of the Ohio Canals* by McClelland and Huntington (Columbus, 1905), pp. 163–65, there is reprinted an accurate table of tolls in effect as of February 21, 1833. Schedules given in Bogart's *Internal Improvements and State Debt in Ohio* (New York, 1924) unfortunately are inaccurate. What follows in Tables A, B, and C of this appendix are the tolls as they were recorded, beginning in 1827, in the manuscript minutes of the canal commission and board of public works proceedings. The data in the tables underlie much of the analysis in Chapter 10, above, which treats in detail the timing of toll adjustments and the reasons for discrimination in favor of long hauls and "domestic" (Ohio) manufactures and mineral products. Table D presents tolls in effect in 1854 and—following some relatively short-lived upward adjustments—in 1855. Table E lists some of the subsequent actions of the board, which are treated, in the context of the railroad competition of the 1850's, in Chapter 11.

At least until the 1850's, Ohio tolls generally were higher than tolls on similar commodities on main-line canals in other states, just as the mercantile community of Ohio asserted in various petitions seeking downward adjustments (see Chapter 10). To

TABLE A
TOLLS ON THE OHIO CANALS, 1827, 1841

ITEM	RATE PER TON-MILE (CENTS)						MAXIMUM CHARGE PER TON 1841
	1–100 MILES		101–200 MILES		OVER 200 MILES		
	1827	1841[a]	1827	1841[a]	1827	1841[a]	
Grain, flour, whiskey, provisions	1.5	1.8	1.0	1.2	—	0.8	$3.12
Merchandise[b]	4.0	4.8	3.0	3.6	—	2.4	6.88
Corn	1.5	1.2	1.0	0.8	—	—	2.00
Ohio salt	1.5	1.0	1.0	0.5	—	—	3.00
'Foreign' salt[c]	1.5	2.0	1.0	1.0	—	—	3.00
Coal	0.5	0.5[d]	0.3	0.2	—	—	—

[a] 1841 tolls, except for maximum charges, same as in effect since 1837 for produce moving north on Ohio Canal; merchandise moving south from Cleveland had remained at 1827 toll level until 1841.

[b] Domestic (Ohio) manufactures, specified, reduced to half toll, 1829.

[c] 1841 schedule provided for rebate of 20¢ per bbl. on "foreign" (i.e., out-of-state) salt shipped through from Cleveland to Portsmouth for re-shipment on the Ohio River. Coal used by domestic salt producers was exempt from toll in 1841.

[d] 1841 coal charges 0.5 cents for first 50 miles, 0.2 cents thereafter.

Source: "Rates of Toll," January 10, 1827, broadside in M. T. Williams Papers, Ohio State Library; Canal Commission and Board of Public Works, Minute Books (MSS.), Vol. I, pp. 34–35, 76–77; *ibid.*, Vol. III, pp. 340–341, 444–446.

TABLE B

TOLLS ON THE OHIO CANALS, JULY 1845

| | RATE PER TON-MILE (CENTS) | | | MAXIMUM CHARGE PER TON | |
ITEM	MILES 1–100	101–200 MILES	OVER 200 MI.	RIVER TO LAKE	LAKE TO RIVER
Flour (general)	1.8	1.2	0.8	$2.50	$2.50
Flour and pork (shipped toward L. Erie)	1.5	1.0	0.6	—ᵃ	—ᵃ
Pork (general)	1.8	1.2	0.8	2.00	2.00
Corn (general)	1.8	1.2	0.8	—	—
Wheat (general)	1.8	1.2	0.8	2.50	2.50
Wheat (Wabash & Erie Canal)	1.5	1.0	0.6	—	—
Merchandise	4.0	3.0	none	—	5.00ᵇ
Ohio salt	1.0	0.5	0.5	—	—
'Foreign' salt	2.0	1.6	1.0	3.00	3.00ᶜ
Salt at Portsmouth or Harmar	4.0	1.0	0.5	—	—

ᵃ Maximum toll on flour on the Wabash and Erie and Miami Extension, $2.00.

ᵇ Maximum toll on merchandise on the Wabash & Erie and Miami Extention, from Toledo, $6.00.

ᶜ Maximum toll on salt shipped through from Toledo to Cincinnati, $1.20.

Source: BPW, Minute Books, Vol. IV–A, pp. 9ff. Tolls on all articles passing in either direction between Cleveland and the Mahoning Canal were to be the same as charged by the Mahoning (generally about 25% lower for short hauls than Ohio Canal tolls).

T A B L E   C
TOLLS ON THE OHIO CANALS, 1850
Part I. The Ohio Canal and Branches

| ITEM | RATE PER TON-MILE (CENTS) | | | MAXIMUM CHARGE PER TON | |
	1–100 MILES	101–200 MILES	OVER 200 MI.	GENERAL	BETWEEN TERMINI
Flour, wheat	1.8	1.2	none	$2.50	$2.50
Flour, pork, to Lake Erie	1.5	1.0	0.6	—	—
Corn	1.2	0.8	none	1.50	—
Corn, to L. Erie	1.0	0.6	0.6	—	—
Salt	2.4	1.0	none	—	—
Merchandise	4.0	3.0	none	—	5.00ᶜ
Coalᵃ	0.6	0.1	0.1	—	—
Coffee, sugar, molasses	4.0	2.0	—	4.00	2.50ᵇ

ᵃ Coal used by salt manufacturers exempt.
ᵇ Maximum toll on southern groceries from Portsmouth to Cleveland, $2.00.
ᶜ Cleveland-Columbus maximum.

Part II. The Miami-Wabash and Erie Canal

| ITEM | RATE PER TON-MILE (CENTS) | | | MAXIMUM CHARGE PER TON | | |
| | NORTH-BOUND | FROM TOLEDO SOUTH[a] | | EITHER WAY | LAKE TO RIVER | RIVER TO LAKE |
		1–100 MI.	OVER 100 MI.			
Flour	1.2	1.4	1.2	$1.50	$1.00	—
Corn	1.2	1.2	—	1.00	1.00	$1.00
Pork	1.2	1.4	1.2	1.50	1.50	1.50
Salt (south-bound)	—	1.5	1.0	2.00	2.00	2.00
Merchandise	3.0	4.0	—	3.00	3.00	3.00
Wheat	1.5	1.4	1.2	2.00	1.50	1.50
Southern groceries[b]	2.0	3.0	—	2.00	1.50	1.50

[a] All agricultural products coming from Indiana to Cincinnati to be charged same rates as specified for same articles if cleared from Toledo.

[b] Rate on southern groceries cleared from Toledo, 4.0 to 50 miles, 2.0 each mile thereafter; maximum charge to places in Indiana, $2.70; maximum to places in Ohio, $2.50.

Source: BPW Minutes, Vol. IV–A, 415ff. The Ohio Canal branches include the Muskingum Improvement, the Walhonding Canal, and the Hocking Valley Canal. The Miami-Wabash and Erie Canal (Miami & Erie Canal) includes the Miami and Miami Extension and Wabash and Erie Canals; no tolls were charged on the Warren County Canal.

TABLE D
TOLLS ON THE OHIO CANALS, 1854, 1855

| | 1854 | | | | 1855 | |
| | MIAMI-WABASH & ERIE | | OHIO CANAL & BRANCHES | | ALL CANALS | |
ITEM	TON/MILE	MAXI-MUM	TON/MILE	MAXI-MUM	TON/MILE	MAXI-MUM
Flour	1.0¢	$1.00	0.8¢	$1.20	1.2¢	$1.20
Pork	1.0	1.00	0.8	1.20	1.0	1.40
Corn	0.8	.80	0.6	.80	0.8	1.00
Wheat	1.0	1.00	0.8	1.20	1.2	1.20
Merchandise	1.6	1.80	1.6	1.80	1.6	2.00
Salt	0.8	.80	1.0	1.00	1.0	1.00
Coal	0.4	.30	0.5	.30	0.5	.24

Source: BPW, *AR,* in *Executive Docs.,* 1855–56, I, No. 33, pp. 446–450.
N.B. In 1852, Miami-Wabash tolls on flour, corn, pork, and salt had been set at 0.8¢ per ton-mile, maximum charge $0.80; on wheat, 0.8¢ and $1.00. (Minutes, V, p. 129)

TABLE E
TOLL ADJUSTMENTS IN 1858[a]

1. On flour, fish, corn, pork, salt, wheat, and whiskey on all clearances from ports south of Carroll (including Columbus, Zanesville, and ports on the Hocking Canal) on the Ohio Canal, a maximum toll of 50¢ per ton. June, 1858.
2. On fish and salt from Cleveland to Akron and Massillon, 50¢ per ton maximum. June, 1858.
3. On corn, flour, pork, salt, wheat, and whiskey, from Akron and Massillon to the Lake (Cleveland), 50¢ per ton maximum. June, 1858.
4. On all flour on the Miami-Wabash & Erie Canal, 50¢ per ton maximum. September, 1858.
5. On any wheat shipped on the Ohio Canal and branches to Ohio mills for grinding, 50¢ per ton maximum. September, 1858.

[a] These adjustments followed a brief increase in tolls, instituted when navigation commenced in early 1858.
Source: BPW, Minutes, VI, pp. 244–46.

cite only a few examples, in 1840 Pennsylvania charged on its Mainline System tolls of 4 mills per ton-mile on corn (the Ohio toll in 1841 was in no case less than 8 mills on corn and on the average haul was more than 1 cent per ton-mile); Pennsylvania charged 7 mills per ton-mile for pork (the Ohio toll was 1.8 cents for distances of less than 100 miles, and 1.2 cents per mile over 100 miles); and Pennsylvania charged 3 cents on dry goods (in Ohio, the toll was an average of nearly 4.2 cents and in no case less than 2.4 cents for short hauls, though the effective maximum charge on the 309-mile Ohio Canal was 2.6 cents).[1] In 1848, the New York toll on Erie Canal shipments of flour was 8 mills per ton-mile, whereas in Ohio it was 1.5 cents on the Miami Canal and its connecting lines and 1.8 cents on the Ohio Canal lines, for short hauls; for long hauls, the Ohio Canal rates were comparable to the New York tolls.[2] For tolls prevailing on other lines, printed schedules are available in various secondary works.[3]

NOTES

1. Compilation of the Laws of Pennsylvania relative to the Internal Improvements, together with the Canal and Railway Regulations (Harrisburg: Barrett and Parke, 1840), Appendix, pp. 27ff. (Copy in Library of Congress.)
2. State of New York, Canal Commissioners, Annual Report, 1852 (Albany, 1853), pp. 11–32.
3. Walter S. Sanderlin, The Great National Project (Baltimore, 1946), pp. 312–14, for the Chesapeake & Ohio Canal; Chester L. Jones, "The Economic History of the Anthracite-Tidewater Canals," Publications of the University of Pennsylvania, Series in Political Economy and Public Law, No. 22 (1908), pp. 54, 69, et passim, for the coal lines; James W. Putnam, The Illinois and Michigan Canal (Chicago, 1918), 166ff., on 1848 tolls.

Appendix 3

TONNAGE OF CANAL COMMERCE, 1850–1860

TABLE 1
CANAL COMMERCE OF CLEVELAND, 1850–1860
(thousands of tons)
Part I. Arrivals

YEAR	WHEAT & FLOUR	CORN	PORK, BACON & LARD	COAL	IRON & NAILS	LUMBER	TOTAL[a]
1850	75.9	23.3	4.8	83.9	8.9	1.1	232.8
1851	146.2	27.9	3.3	107.2	8.5	1.1	355.7
1852	170.0	24.2	3.4	141.2	7.6	2.0	425.1
1853	118.2	4.7	3.5	174.7	6.2	11.7	461.1
1854	51.3	13.9	7.5	171.0	9.3	1.8	320.9
1855	22.7	7.4	0.6	221.9	12.5	0.9	309.7
1856	36.4	6.2	2.0	181.5	22.8	0.9	286.5
1857	25.7	4.6	0.9	141.9	9.2	1.0	215.0
1858	38.0	7.8	1.2	78.5	1.2	0.2	154.3
1859	18.3	0.8	1.2	67.2	1.5	1.3	118.0
1860	23.4	2.3	0.1	70.6	1.8	1.2	122.5

Part II. Clearances

YEAR	MERCHAN-DISE	SALT	LUMBER	IRON & NAILS	TOTAL[a]
1850	5.5	9.1	11.9	8.5	52.0
1851	5.4	8.6	14.4	5.9	86.7
1852	4.2	7.0	19.9	10.5	66.8
1853	3.7	6.0	19.6	15.7	64.0
1854	3.0	5.8	15.9	9.1	54.8
1855	1.7	5.9	13.7	6.2	42.6
1856	1.6	4.4	10.0	3.1	42.4
1857	0.8	3.2	11.5	0.5	33.7
1858	0.7	2.8	13.9	0.4	34.4
1859	0.7	3.8	15.0	0.3	38.2
1860	0.8	1.9	12.5	0.1	34.2

[a] Total includes unspecified classes of tonnage.

Source: BPW *Annual Reports,* 1850–1860. Figure for peak year during 1850–60 period is shown in bold-face type.

TABLE 2
CANAL COMMERCE OF CINCINNATI, 1850–1860
(thousands of tons)
Part I. Arrivals

YEAR	FLOUR & WHEAT	CORN	PORK, BACON & LARD	IRON	MER-CHAN-DISE	LUMBER	TOTAL[a]
1850	14.3	17.3	7.8	0.5	**3.4**	—	117.7
1851	**27.8**	7.6	4.3	2.6	2.8	—	120.9
1852	20.0	9.0	4.5	4.0	0.9	—	103.3
1853	15.9	9.2	4.6	**13.1**	1.8	—	153.8
1854	9.1	14.5	4.5	0.7	1.1	4.8	122.2
1855	6.7	10.7	2.7	0.4	0.5	2.7	93.3
1856	8.6	1.3	1.5	1.2	0.6	4.8	69.4
1857	9.1	**78.5**	1.3	0.2	1.1	5.3	152.4
1858	12.1	7.3	1.4	0.3	0.9	6.3	118.8[b]
1859	8.0	3.3	1.5	0.5	0.2	4.1	38.2
1860	11.7	5.6	1.6	0.3	0.5	**8.1**	130.1[b]

Part II. Clearances

YEAR	COAL	SALT	PORK, BACON & LARD	IRON	MER-CHAN-DISE	LUMBER	TOTAL[a]
1850	6.7	—	3.3	3.1	2.7	—	42.8
1851	5.7	—	4.4	**8.3**	2.8	—	45.4
1852	—	—	4.4	6.9	2.2	—	50.1
1853	—	—	**8.4**	6.6	2.4	—	60.9
1854	13.0	0.7	7.4	6.9	2.1	2.1	61.8
1855	17.5	1.1	0.4	5.3	1.1	1.9	50.9
1856	8.0	0.2	2.1	3.1	0.9	3.0	35.8
1857	**51.9**	**1.2**	0.5	3.0	1.9	1.8	74.3
1858	15.6	0.8	1.0	2.4	2.0	**3.3**	38.0
1859	20.5	—	1.1	2.2	1.4	1.2	63.3
1860	23.2	1.1	0.5	3.7	2.3	2.3	44.8

[a] Total includes unspecified classes of tonnage.
[b] Unspecified tonnage for 1858 was 84,900, for 1860 109,900. This may indicate inclusion of substantial factory-machinery or railroad equipment.

Source: See note, Table 1. Figure for peak year, 1850–60, shown in bold-face type.

TABLE 3
CANAL COMMERCE OF TOLEDO, 1850–1860
(thousands of tons)
Part I. Arrivals

YEAR	WHEAT AND FLOUR	CORN	PORK, BACON AND LARD	LUMBER	TOTAL[a]
1850	14.3	44.6	13.1	1.5[b]	122.6
1851	58.6	71.8	13.2	1.5[b]	163.5
1852	77.5	108.6	11.7	—	237.1
1853	86.8	66.3	26.1	4.0	225.3
1854	22.0	113.9	20.3	55.5	246.5
1855	32.3	79.8	9.5	2.8	148.5
1856	42.2	63.2	9.7	3.6	151.7
1857	31.0	28.2	2.4	2.1	88.5
1858	56.6	32.3	1.5	0.6	107.1
1859	40.5	3.4	1.8	3.6	67.1
1860	51.0	50.4	0.9	2.2	112.7

Part II. Clearances

YEAR	SALT	MERCHAN-DISE	IRON	LUMBER	TOTAL
1850	—	6.4	1.3	—	61.4
1851	—	6.7	13.1	—	73.9
1852	—	5.0	22.2	—	85.3
1853	21.7	6.1	31.9	9.7	102.6
1854	16.8	3.6	27.4	24.7	89.1
1855	22.2	2.4	12.7	8.1	59.8
1856	11.3	3.8	15.8	10.5	56.6
1857	10.9	9.0	1.0	16.7	40.3
1858	9.8	0.9	0.3	16.3	36.4
1859	10.7	0.5	0.7	22.5	40.9
1860	8.4	1.9	0.2	16.0	35.8

[a] Total includes unspecified classes of tonnage.
[b] Estimated.
Source: See note, Table 1. Figure for peak year, 1850–60, shown in bold-face type.

Appendix 4

A NOTE ON THE PROBLEM OF ESTIMATING "INDIRECT RETURNS"

One of the principal arguments of canal promoters in the nineteenth century—as it is today a major argument in the rhetoric of highway and airport promoters—was that transport facilities generate "indirect benefits"; and hence the returns they might yield on the capital invested to build them can exceed what the government itself recaptures through user fees. In recent years, economists have devoted much attention to devising means of quantifying such indirect benefits, and a school of cost-benefit analysis has attracted the interest of many. In cost-benefit analysis, the projected construction cost of a facility is set against (1) the estimated revenues from user fees (direct returns), and (2) the estimated external benefits (indirect returns, or "social savings") that accrue to the society but are not recaptured by the investing agency itself. This kind of analysis can yield data that is valuable in two respects: first, it can provide a quantitative basis for establishing priorities among alternative projects competing for available funds; and second, it can offer a quantitative measure of total benefits (direct and indirect) that will be generated by any single project—a measure that is useful when a government has established a certain minimum return as prerequisite for any appropriation of funds for social-overhead investments.[1]

Economic historians recently have seized upon cost-benefit analysis as an instrument for making retrospective judgments concerning the benefits that were derived from various investments in the past. For instance, Douglass North has asserted that the social savings derived from pre-1860 state canal investments (many of which did not generate direct returns, from tolls, sufficient to carry interest and amortization of principal on their cost) probably in fact were not very large—or at best were not large enough to have represented the best use of the society's available investment capital. In a parallel but substantively different and more thorough argument, Robert William Fogel has asserted that the U. S. investment in railroads, up to 1890, did not pay large social returns. He states that if the society had lacked railroads and instead used its capital to build a comprehensive system of waterways and ancillary wagon roads, then it would have sacrificed at most 5 per cent of Gross National Product in 1890. Fogel's is an elaborate exercise in hypothetical history: he hypothesizes the feasibility, construction cost, and operating costs and revenues of an imaginary system of waterways and roads; and he obtains his 5 per cent social-saving estimate by comparing the cost of moving all goods on facilities actually operating in 1890 with the cost of moving the same goods the same distances on his hypothetical (imaginary) system. The burden of his argument is that canals and other waterways were nearly (within 5 per cent of GNP in 1890) sufficient to perform the transport services necessary to the nineteenth century U. S. economy.[2]

The assertions of North and Fogel raise questions relevant to the subject of this book. First of all, what were the social returns from Ohio's investment in canals and other public transport facilities? And do the quantified returns suggest that Ohio made the best use of its investment capital? To explore this issue, the author and Roger L. Ransom have used a theory of rent (developed by Ransom) to measure the impact of the Ohio Canal's operations during 1827–60. This analysis finds that the Ohio Canal paid very satisfactory social returns until the advent of railway competition in the early 1850's.[3] Our finding accords with the conclusions of a similar analysis by the Ohio canal commissioners: in a report of 1833, the commission computed the costs of operating the state canals and amortizing the canal debt, setting off costs against the returns (*direct* as measured by revenue from tolls, and *indirect* as measured by the price differential on Ohio export commodities before and after the canals were built). The commissioners concluded that during 1832 some $169,000 in social savings had been generated "in consequence of the canals."[4] If applied consistently over the next two decades, the commission's formula for measuring benefits would have shown that the canal investment was highly "profitable" to the society, even if it failed to produce direct returns (in revenues) sufficient to pay interest and principal on the canal debt.

I strongly doubt that cost-benefit analysis, intriguing as it is, and despite its appeal of quantification producing solid-looking numbers, suffices to explain *either* the full range of benefits from the canal investment *or* the extent to which the benefits fulfilled the goals of the men who had planned the investment. For in the first place, canal construction induced new private investment in the state; encouraged entrepreneurship in mining and manufacturing; encouraged (by dint of state borrowing in the East and Europe) an inflow of specie funds that enabled Ohio banks to expand their circulation (with a stimulative impact on local economies); and, not least, permitted the state to pursue certain mercantilistic goals—through protectionist tolls—that protected in-state manufacturing firms in the short run and may (or may not) have stimulated local development in the long run. The range of variables incorporated in this incomplete list defies quantification, as a practical matter if not in theory. For some of these impacts are not readily reducible to quantifiable measures in any event; most certainly, they do not appear in the range of benefits ordinarily measured by cost-benefit analysis, be it contemporary or historical. In the second place, even if one found that the investment did not generate returns of 5 per cent on capital invested (or, alternatively, some percentage of private income in Ohio, the "local" counterpart of GNP) it does not mean that Ohio would have done better to have invested the $15 million in iron mills, government securities, or some other outlet. For one cannot assume that the capital would have been forthcoming for purposes other than social-overhead investment.

And in any case, the men of Ohio did not decide to invest in canals and other public works merely with a view toward getting higher-than-market-rate returns: instead, they had in mind broad "developmental goals." They were confronted with a serious barrier to economic development, the lack of improved transportation to outside cash markets. They were, as a commonwealth, competing with other western states (and eastern and southern states) for scarce capital and scarce labor (*qua* settlement, *qua* entrepreneurial talent, *qua* expertise, etc.).[5] They postulated that if they did *not* provide potential investors and settlers with social-overhead facilities such as transport, then the flow of capital and people from the East would move to other states that did. And no doubt they were right. In this sense, American federalism may have bred an inefficient pattern of government investment and overall development. But to unravel all the multiple threads of duplicating facilities and investments, and to measure the marginal efficiencies of each investment in every state of the Union, is a task which—if it is ever performed —will probably be approached best with conventional instruments of qualitative analysis and not with "high-powered" quantitative tools. Like Professor Fogel's study of 1890 railroads, such a study will need to make elaborate assumptions about a world that never was; it will be an exercise in hypothetical history. But to succeed, it will have to take account of a wide range of complexities in the process—the long-term process— that we call economic growth, and not merely the question of what a single innovation contributed to GNP in a single year.[6]

A second broad issue concerns whether, as a matter of hypothesis, Ohio might have achieved all or some of its developmental goals by using a prior technology instead of canal technology. (There seems little question that they should have opted for *railroad* technology by the mid-thirties; but here we have reference only to the investment decision of 1825.) I find considerable evidence that one might "demonstrate" that, theoretically, the notoriously high costs of overland wagon transportation could have been reduced greatly had Ohio systematically expended its funds on road improvement—if funds so expended had been equivalent in magnitude to the capital invested in canals. The most compelling evidence derives from empirical examples of canals in competition with roads that *were* actually constructed in Ohio. Roads could be built on more direct routes than canals, in many cases; and in nearly all cases would have been at less cost per mile than canals. One such direct road route—between Lebanon and Cincinnati—put an entire halt to canal trade on the competing Warren County Canal, even though the state removed all tolls on that canal's trade. Similarly, the port city of Milan traded with a wide area of north-central Ohio—including the Walhonding Valley region, which was served by a branch of the Ohio Canal that gave it an all-water route to Cleveland; farmers found it more profitable to move their produce by wagon to Milan than to ship by canal on the longer route to Cleveland.[7] Moreover, in 1844 the Ohio board of public works found it necessary to impose high rates on the National Road (which it controlled) in order to protect the competing canal trade; and it forced private turnpike companies likewise to increase their tolls, to protect competing state canals.[8]

These facts lead us into a complex maze of questions that would need to frame our hypothetical model: how low would canal tolls need to have been cut in order to restore the competitive position of the canals *vis-à-vis* roads? what premium would shippers have been willing to pay for the savings in time and convenience that roads offered, if transfer charges were equivalent on canals and roads? what would have been the capital costs, direct returns, and indirect returns, of building roads sufficient to substitute for canals in Ohio? And so on.

If we engaged in this complex exercise, we might be able to calculate fairly readily for one year, say 1835, the social savings (or costs) of Ohio's use of canals in lieu of the hypothetical alternative of roads—just as Professor Fogel calculated social savings attributable to railroads in 1890. But to understand the process of economic development in Ohio over a long period, say 1820–35, or better still 1820–50, such a calculation on cost-benefit principles would avail us little. For we cannot assume that the savings or losses of using roads in the absence of canals in 1835 would have been proportional to savings or losses in every year before and after 1835. This would be *ceteris paribus* with a vengeance. It would assume that the Ohio economy actually would have developed, in the absence of canals, just as it did in the presence of canals—that transfer costs would have been different, but that no adjustments over time to a differential between canals and roads, as they served the economy, would have been made.

NOTES

1. For a technical survey and critique, see Otto Eckstein, essay in *Public Finances: Needs, Sources, and Utilization* (Conference of the Universities—National Bureau Committee for Economic Research, Princeton, 1961), 439–94.
2. Douglass North's comment is in *Growth and Welfare in the American Past* (Englewood Cliffs, N.J., 1966), 104. Robert Fogel's major work is *Railroads and American Economic Growth: Essays in Econometric History* (Baltimore, 1964).
3. "External Benefits from Public Transport Investment," by Ransom and Scheiber. For an earlier effort, cf. Harvey H. Segal in *Canals and American Economic Development*, ed. Carter Goodrich (New York, 1962), 241ff.
4. The commission's analysis is conveniently reprinted in C. P. McClelland and C. C. Huntington, *History of the Ohio Canals* (Columbus, 1905), 172–74.
5. On the important differences between developed societies planning public investments on a cost-benefit basis and societies combatting underdevelopment planning investments to remove bottlenecks to growth, to stimulate private sectors, etc., see the excellent study by Timothy King, "Development Strategy and Investment Criteria: Complementary or Competitive?" *Quarterly Journal of Economics*, LXXX (Feb. 1966), 108–20.
6. I have argued this caveat at length in my essay, "On the New Economic History," *Agricultural History*, XLI (October 1967), 383–95.
7. Again, the canal port of Massillon was connected by a road to the Ohio River in the mid-forties, and immediately overland commerce to the river cut deeply into the merchandise trade by

canal from Cleveland to Massillon. ("Memorial of forwarders of Akron, Massillon &c," April 10, 1847, MS. in BPW Papers, Ohio State Archives.) And salt was carried by wagon from Zanesville and Columbus overland to the upper Miami Valley, in competition with the canal-river route, in 1838. (Canal Commission, *15th AR*, 1839, p. 9.) On the Warren County Canal and Milan cases, cf. Scheiber, "Rate-Making Power of the State," *Political Science Quarterly*, LXXVII (Sept. 1962), 399ff.

8. *Ibid.*, 401. For a thorough technical critique of Professor Fogel's study and of social savings estimates of an entirely different order, focused on 1859 only, see Peter D. McClelland, "Railroads, American Growth, and the New Economic History," *Journal of Economic History*, XXVIII (March 1968), 102–23. In his distinguished presidential address before the Economic History Association, Prof. Alexander Gerschenkron has observed that elaborate hypothetical constructs are highly useful for analysis of relatively short-term economic changes, less so as the time period analyzed lengthens. ("The Discipline and I," *ibid.*, XXVII [Dec. 1967], 457.)

Bibliography

THE unusually rich archival collections of Ohio supported the
emphasis in this book on administrative aspects of canal
construction, financing, and management. Abundant documenta-
tion of all the major decisions and operations of the state agencies is available in the vast files of the Ohio canal commissions
and board of public works, and in the slimmer but ample records
of the fund commissioners. These materials, few of which had
been examined by earlier scholars, held many surprises; and they
supported numerous interpretations quite different from what one
would have expected from consulting only the published agency
reports. For instance, on canal finance the archives documented
the complex interplay of state banking, public bank policy, and
interregional capital transfers, a main theme in Chapters 2 and 6.
The canal commission records revealed the milieu in which basic
policies were formulated during planning of the 1825 and 1836–
38 investment decisions, and also during the long history of canal
management. Readily recaptured was the set of assumptions,
aspirations, information, and misinformation in which each policy
was made or in which drift substituted for policy. Moreover, the
state officials of that time, before the advent of the telephone,
filled intra-agency correspondence with "private" messages,
so marked. Indeed, some of the most informative letters that survive were designated to have been destroyed.

History written exclusively from such evidence risks all the
pitfalls of "court history" or "company history," in which the historian shares so intimately the information (and only the information) available to decision-makers—and often comes to share,
despite himself, the decision-makers' aspirations as well—that his
perspective becomes identical to that of the men and organizations

that are his subject. Therefore, contemporary comment originating outside the state agencies was especially important. Newspaper reports and editorials were extremely diverse in their assessments of the state agencies, reflecting both their political commitments and the astonishing lack of restraint that marked journalistic mores of that day. In petitions of special interest groups, aggrieved individuals, and the like; in business correspondence, records, and journals; and above all, in the debates, investigations, and reports of the legislature, I found both data and perspectives that proved invaluable. But I sought to inform my interpretations as well by studies of government activism in other American states and in the developing countries today; and also by consulting sociological theory on formal organization and the writings of economists and historians on entrepreneurial roles and functions. Court decisions and published legal briefs proved highly important as well. For the lawyers of that day spoke eloquently on the ambitions and assumptions of the society; and they also provided perceptive criticism of the means employed in the pursuit of social and political goals.

I have attempted also to measure the ambitions of the men who had formulated economic policy against the actual performance of the economy. The core of evidence for this was in the statistical reports of state agencies and the ample (though hardly unfailingly accurate) data in the published U.S. Census reports. I have become painfully aware of the accuracy of William N. Parker's observation that when a researcher adduces statistics on the nineteenth century economy, he constructs a statistical universe but not necessarily the statistical universe that actually existed. However, I have analyzed economic change not only on a statistical base of evidence, but also by giving attention to institutional interrelationships through study of business records, chamber of commerce reports, railroad reports, and the like.

In this bibliography, Part I treats all manuscript collections consulted and the most useful printed primary sources. In Part II is a discussion of relevant secondary studies, but for a fuller discussion I must refer the reader to the fine bibliographic essay in George Rogers Taylor, *The Transportation Revolution, 1815–1860* (New York: Holt, Rinehart, 1951); to Harry Stevens, "Re-

cent Writings in Midwestern Economic History," *OHQ,* LXIX
(Jan. 1960); and to standard bibliographic reference works.

I: PRIMARY SOURCES

A. MANUSCRIPTS

In the Ohio State Archives, a division of the Ohio Historical
Society, are the Canal Commission Papers and the Board of
Public Works Papers, 1825–1861, a voluminous collection of
correspondence, petitions, reports, pamphlets, and other material
relating to construction and management of the canals and other
public works. Also in the Archives is a "Stock Issue Book," listing
the original purchasers of Ohio bonds, 1826–1839; three volumes
of letter-books of the Board of Canal Fund Commissioners, the
basic source for canal-bond issues and management of canal
funds; and the Correspondence of the Treasurer of State, a small
but valuable group of letters including many between the Treasurer and the banks that held canal fund deposits. The Canal Commission and Board of Public Works Minute Books are in the
Records Room, Ohio Department of Public Works (Columbus).

The most important sources in the rich manuscripts collection
of the Ohio Historical Society (Columbus) were the Canal Commission Letters, 1822–1852, two boxes of correspondence, mainly
on the pre-1825 surveys; and the Official Governors' Papers, an
extensive body of correspondence treating diverse economic and
policy questions for the pre-1860 period. The private papers of
several figures prominent in western transport history complement
the archival records. In the Ohio Historical Society are Ethan
Allen Brown Papers; Thomas Worthington Papers; Benjamin
Tappan Papers; Alfred Kelley Papers; and Daniel Kilgore Papers.
All contain letters bearing directly upon canal administration and
finance, and in the extensive Worthington, Tappan, and Kilgore
materials there is much data on economic and business conditions
in the state. The Erasmus Gest Papers include the memoirs of an
early canal commission engineer, and also letters and clippings
on Ohio railroads in the fifties. The Society also maintains type-

script copies of Ohio material from two collections in the State Historical Society of Wisconsin: the John Johnston Papers and the Increase Lapham Papers; there are some additional Lapham manuscripts as well.

Other Ohio Historical Society manuscripts that proved useful were the memoir and letters of Samuel Williams, valuable for descriptions of the Scioto Valley and of travel conditions; the Charles Rice Collection and the Charles Hammond Papers, both of which contain letters on Ohio politics and internal improvements; the Joshua Reed Giddings Papers; the Thomas Ewing Papers; and the Thomas Corwin Papers. A large collection of Trimble Family Papers includes business and personal correspondence, as well as political materials. The Wildman Family Papers contain correspondence on early Sandusky and on the Sandusky promoters' role in canal politics; also, material on the Mad River & Lake Erie Railroad project. The Jacob Barker Papers concern the townsite promotion at Manhattan, Ohio—a rival to Toledo, one whose proprietors were active in Wabash & Erie Canal promotion.

Business records in the Ohio Historical Society that proved useful on the economic impact of canals and railroads include the Lancaster Lateral Canal Company Papers, containing the journals and minutes of a private canal enterprise; the John T. Brasee Papers, which illuminate marketing mechanisms as revealed in the operations of a major milling firm; the Hocking Valley Mills Letterbook, 1852–1854, and the H. B. Hunter Letterbook, 1852–1853, both of which contain freight-rate and price data; the John H. James Papers, which include letters on railroad promotion and flour milling; and the Urbana Banking Company Papers, the records of a firm which became involved in promotion of the Mad River & Lake Erie. The Charles Wetmore Papers have material on the Ohio state lands and their administration; and the Alfred Edgerton Papers are the records of a northwest Ohio land speculator. The Land Office Records and Correspondence concern early Ohio land disposal more generally. The John Piatt Papers, 1817–1822, and the manuscript Autobiography of Sheldon Ingalls (1871), concern Cincinnati business affairs. Data on canal labor, wages, and working conditions are in the Avery and Whitaaker Labor Records, a canal contractors' accounts; and the Hugh Beale Account Book, a general-store ledger.

The Ohio State Library (Columbus) houses in its manuscripts collection three sizable groups of correspondence that complement the Canal Commission Papers for the pre-1836 period: the Micajah T. Williams Papers, which include correspondence with contractors and laborers, private promoters, and state officers during 1822–1832, and also reveal Williams' later role in Maumee Valley land speculation and in the Ohio Life Insurance & Trust Company; the Thomas Worthington Papers, containing letters written and received while Worthington served as a canal commissioner; and the Ethan Allen Brown Papers, which are a basic source on canal planning, construction, and finance. Also in the State Library are an unpublished history of Massillon, a canal town, by R. H. Folger; and the manuscript U.S. Army Engineers Survey Report for the Maumee River, July, 1835.

Complementary to the pre-1825 records of the Ohio canal project are the De Witt Clinton Papers, in the Columbia University Library. In the Cincinnati Historical Society Library are Letters on Canals, a small collection of official letters that fills some gaps in the archival records; the Robert Lytle Papers, valuable on Ohio politics in the 1830's; the James McBride Papers, which document the work of one of the canal commission's boards of appraisers, as it operated under eminent domain procedures; the John Woods Papers; and the Nathaniel Wright Papers, which concern Cincinnati's railroad projects of the 1850's. In the Dayton and Montgomery County Public Library (Dayton) are the papers of Samuel Forrer, a canal engineer and after 1832 a commissioner, who was also associated with turnpike and railroad promotion in western Ohio.

A major collection on canal finance, though important also for materials on Ohio banking and land speculation, is the Simon Perkins Papers, in the Western Reserve Historical Society Library (Cleveland). In the same library are the Elisha Whittlesey Papers, which have correspondence with Perkins, Micajah T. Williams, and Alfred Kelley on canal finance, on the promotion of the Mahoning Canal (formally, "the Pennsylvania & Ohio Canal

Company"), and on Ohio politics; the Commercial Bank of Lake Erie Letterbooks, the records of a bank that managed canal funds as a depository of the fund commission; and a Miscellaneous Manuscript File, while includes some letters of Jacob Blickensderfer, a land speculator and general entrepreneur who later became a member of the board of public works.

Glimpses of life in the early farming regions of Ohio, supplementing material in the Trimble, Samuel Williams, Lapham, Gest, and archival papers, are in the following: the Delano Family Papers (Baker Library Archives of Dartmouth College), the correspondence of a family that migrated from Vermont to Chillicothe; the Moses Quinby Diary (Regional History Collection, Cornell University Library), the journal of a trip by the Ohio Canal through northeast Ohio in 1831; the McNeill Family Papers (West Virginia University Library), containing letters on the Ohio River trade, cattle-raising in the Scioto Valley before 1820, and the flatboat trade; and the Jared Warner and Henry F. Young Papers (State Historical Society of Wisconsin), which include notebooks and account books of a flatboatman. Also in the Wisconsin society's holdings are the John F. Seymour Papers, which provide data on Great Lakes marketing and freight charges; and the complete papers of Increase Lapham, who left the Ohio canal commission's service to manage Micajah Williams' real estate speculations at Milwaukee, where Lapham became a leading promoter as well as one of the West's leading scientists.

Other manuscripts consulted include the Charles Ellet Papers (University of Michigan Transportation Collection), the papers of a prominent early engineer; Miscellaneous Manuscripts on Ohio Canals, 1836–1845 (Vermont State Library, Montpelier), which have data on the Wabash & Erie's construction; the correspondence of Frederick Huth & Co. (Huth Papers, Packet D-13, Business Archives Council, London) with the North American Trust Company on marketing of American state bonds; and the Duncan McArthur Papers and the Thomas Worthington Notebooks (both in the Library of Congress). Also, materials in the U.S. National Archives, including Letterbook marked "Canals, 1833–49" and box marked "Ohio Canals" in the Treasury Department Records; General Land Office Records relating to Ohio canal lands, and the Piqua, Bucyrus, and Lima land office cor-respondence; and selected letters and documents (microfilm copy in the Ohio Historical Society), Office of the Chief of Engineers papers regarding the National Road in Ohio, War Department Records.

B. PUBLISHED PRIMARY MATERIALS

1. Statutes and Official State and Federal Documents:

Ohio state laws, both "General" and "Local" series, relevant federal statutes, the journals of the House and the Senate of the Ohio General Assembly, and the annual *Executive Documents* (occasionally termed *Legislative Documents*) of Ohio for 1820 to 1860, were all of basic importance to this research. So too was J. V. Smith, ed., *Official Reports of the Debates and Proceedings of the Ohio State Convention Called to Alter, Revise or Amend the Constitution of the State* (1850 Convention, 2 vols. pag. consec., Columbus: Scott & Bascom, 1851). The annual reports for the period before 1861 were used for the following state offices: Auditor of State, Board of Agriculture, Board of Canal Fund Commissioners, Board of Public Works, Canal Commission, Commissioner of Statistics, Commissioners of the Sinking Fund. The 1870 *Annual Report* of the Commissioner of Railroads con-tains a summary of all legislation to that time pertaining to Ohio railroads, with annotated reprints of the laws. The Congressional documents series was consulted, volume by volume, in a search for materials relating to Ohio and western transportation; the most valuable material uncovered was in Army Engineers' reports and surveys, although occasional petitions for Federal aid for transportation were also important. Also consulted were the an-nual reports of the New York State canal commission, 1849–1863; the annual reports on canals of the New York State Engineer and Surveyor, 1850–1861; and the reports of the Super-intendent of the Onondaga Salt Springs, 1849–1861. All pre-1870 volumes of the United States Census reports on population, agriculture, and manufacturing were used, as were the U. S. Patent Office reports, covering Ohio agriculture, 1849–61.

2. *Court Decisions:*

The judicial history of law on eminent domain, state regulatory power, and state activity in transportation was traced in the state supreme court *Ohio Reports* and *Ohio State Reports,* the *Superior Court of Cincinnati Reports* (1, 2 Handy; 1, 2 Disney), and *Ohio Decisions Reprints* (which includes the important *Western Law Journal*).

3. *Newspapers and Periodicals:*

Newspapers and periodicals proved, on the whole, much more illuminating on political and ideological questions than on problems of the Ohio economy. A notable exception is *The Railroad Record* of Cincinnati, which reported not only railroad matters (and these with unusual perceptiveness) but also larger issues of economic development as it was affected by transportation; it reflected too the learned and often brilliant activity of its editor, Edwin Mansfield, in the collection and analysis of economic statistics. The informed statistical studies that appeared in his annual reports, when he became Ohio's commissioner of statistics in 1857, are presaged in the columns of his newspaper. The other newspapers that showed the best understanding of economic affairs were the Cleveland *Herald* and its successors; the *Cincinnati Price Current,* most of the best articles in which are reprinted or summarized in Henry E. White's "Economic Study of Wholesale Prices at Cincinnati, 1844–1914" (Ithaca: Cornell University, 1935, mimeographed); and the *Toledo Blade* in its early years, while under Jesup Scott's editorship. A complete listing of papers and journals consulted follows: Cincinnati *Liberty Hall and Cincinnati Gazette,* 1824–25; Cincinnati *Daily Commercial,* 1845–46; *Cincinnati Pioneer,* I–VI (1873–1885); *Cincinnati Price Current,* 1850–60, scattered; Cleveland *Herald,* 1839–1844; Cleveland *Herald Gazette* and *Leader,* 1823–1860, as compiled in *Annals of Cleveland* (U. S. Works Progress Admin. project, mimeo.); Columbus *Capital City Fact,* 1857–58; Columbus *Gazette* (later *Ohio State Journal*), 1824–28; *Gazette,* 1856–60; Columbus *Ohio State Journal* (various names), 1834–61; Columbus *Ohio Statesman,* 1837–43, 1850–51; Columbus *Western*

Hemisphere, 1833–37; *DeBow's Review*, 1846–60; *Delaware Patron*, 1825–26; *Hamilton Intelligencer*, 1831–37; *The Hesperian*, I (1838–39); *Hunt's Merchants' Magazine*, 1839–60; *Kalida Venture*, 1850–54 (scattered); *Lancaster Gazette*, 1826–35, 1850–60 (scattered); Lima *Allen County Democrat*, 1859–60; Lima *Reporter and Advertiser*, 1844–47; Lima *Western Gazette* (and *Weekly Gazette*), 1856–61; Maumee City *Maumee Express*, 1837–39; *Newark Advocate*, 1850–54; *North American Review*, 1840–48; *Piqua Courier and Enquirer*, 1835–40; Piqua *Gazette*, 1821–22, 1827, 1830–34; *Piqua Register* (also *Weekly Register, Tri-weekly Register*), 1849–61 (incomplete); *Portsmouth Tribune*, 1841, 1843–47 (scattered); *Railroad Record*, I–VIII (1853–60), published at Cincinnati; Sandusky *Clarion*, 1824–26; Sandusky *Commercial Register*, 1851–60; St. Mary's *Sentinel*, 1843–44; Steubenville *Western Herald and Steubenville Gazette*, 1823, 1824 (scattered); *Toledo Blade*, 1845–50 (complete), 1850–60 (scattered); Warren *Western Reserve Chronicle*, 1843–44, 1854–55; Zanesville *City Times* (weekly), 1852–57; Zanesville *Courier* (weekly), 1846–52; *Daily Courier*, 1847, 1851; Zanesville *Gazette*, 1844–45, 1850–54 (scattered).

A few articles that appeared in the periodicals listed above require special comment. First, in *Hunt's Merchants' Magazine*, XXXI (1854), 123ff. and subsequent installments, is conveniently reprinted the "McAlpine Report," an extended analysis of canal transportation, its costs and potential costs, in New York State and the West. Occasionally scholars have cited data from this report as if all the rates McAlpine computed were actually effective in the mid-1850's; but in fact, the report (which McAlpine presented to the New York legislature in his capacity as State Engineer and Surveyor) touches both actual and *estimated potential rates*, and it must be read with care. Second, in the *Railroad Record*, I (April 7, 1853), 81–82 is Mansfield's excellent study of Ohio exports in 1852, computations in which I checked against the sources that he used; in his annual reports as Ohio Commissioner of Statistics after 1857, Mansfield frequently cited his 1852 study as a point of reference for discussion of subsequent commercial changes. Both *Hunt's* and *De Bow's Review* published frequently articles on the trade of specific Ohio ports, on prevailing freight rates and canal tolls, and on trends in western commerce and manufacturing. In the *Toledo Blade,* during the period of Scott's editorship, informed articles and editorials on western urban growth and trade often appeared; the essence of Scott's ideas of urbanization and western development, as expressed in these writings and also his numerous articles in *Hunt's,* is treated ably by Charles Glaab in an article in *Ohio History,* LXXIII (Winter 1964).

4. *Corporation and Other Reports:*

The annual volumes of William Smith, ed., *Annual Statement of the Trade and Commerce of Cincinnati,* 1855–61, are invaluable not only for local trade data in tabular form but also for Smith's excellent articles on contemporary trends in commerce, manufacturing, and transportation—withal an essential complementary source to the *Cincinnati Price Current.* The *Toledo Blade* published a similar, though less ambitious, annual statement of trade and commerce, from the mid-fifties on. Annual and special reports of the Portsmouth Dry Dock and Steam-Boat Basin Company, which cast light on navigational problems at the Ohio Canal's southern terminus, are available in the New York Public Library. Useful as an example of industrial promotion in the canal period—a precursor, and very similar to, the modern "industrial park" movement—are the materials presented in the Portage Canal and Manufacturing Company, *Charter . . . and Other Papers Relating Thereto* (New York, 1837). The annual reports of the Pennsylvania & Ohio Canal Company (which I term the Mahoning Canal in this book) are available in the *Executive Documents* of Ohio, and contain trade data, information on financing of a quasi-private canal enterprise, and comments on the quickly changing competitive situation in western transport after 1845. Because so little analysis of Ohio railroad development is available, I was driven to rely heavily on the published annual reports of individual lines, and these sources underlie much of the basic analytic framework in Chapter 11. The individual reports actually consulted, together with reports of special conventions, are as follows:

Bellefontaine and Indiana Rail Road Company: *Report on the Preliminary Surveys* (Pittsburgh, 1850); 1st-4th Annual Reports (Cleveland, 1851–54).

Belpre and Cincinnati Railroad Company: William P. Cutler, *A Report Exhibiting Some Statistical Facts and Arguments* (Chillicothe, 1848).

Cincinnati, Hamilton and Dayton Railroad Company: 1st, 2nd, 4th, 6th Annual Reports (Cincinnati, 1850–56).

Cleveland and Mahoning Rail Road Company: *Exhibit, Oct. 1, 1853* (New York, 1853); Annual Reports for 1852, 1854, 1860–63 (Cleveland); *To the Stockholders . . . November 14, 1857* (n. p.); "Office of the Cleveland & Mahoning Rail Road Co., Cleveland, January 20, 1859," broadside; *Lease . . . to the Atlantic & Great Western Railway Line, October 7, 1863, 99 Years* (Cleveland, n.d.).

Cleveland and Pittsburgh Rail Road Company: *Report of the Survey* (Akron, 1845); *Report of the Survey* (Philadelphia, 1846); *Report upon the Surveys* (Pittsburgh, 1847); Annual Reports, 1851–1861 (variously published at Hudson, Cleveland, and New Haven).

Cleveland and Pittsburgh Railroad: *Report of the Chief Engineer* (Hudson, 1849).

Cleveland and Pittsburgh Railroad, Akron Branch: *Report of the Chief Engineer* (Hudson, 1852).

Cleveland and Warren Railroad: *Further Proceedings* (n. p., n. d. but 1836).

Cleveland, Columbus & Cincinnati Rail Road Company: Annual Reports, 1852–61. (Include annual tabulations of arrivals and clearances from Cleveland.)

A Committee from Steubenville, Ohio. *Letter to Thomas Bakewell, Esq. . . . on the Subject of Connecting Pittsburgh and Philadelphia with Cincinnati* (1848).

Mad River and Lake Erie Rail Road Company: Annual Reports, 1849–53 (Sandusky).

Marietta & Cincinnati Rail Road Company: *Exhibit of the Affairs* (New York, 1852); *Exhibit of the Affairs* (Paris, France, 1854); 1st-6th Annual Reports (various places).

Marietta, Hillsboro and Cincinnati Rail Road Company: *Cor-*

respondence between a Committee of Citizens of Cincinnati and the President (Cincinnati, 1856).

Ohio and Mississippi Railroad: *Geographic, Geological and Statistical Relations* (n.d. but 1853); *Report of the Present Conditions* (Cincinnati, 1852); *The Ohio and Mississippi Railroad: Its Vital Importance* (Cincinnati, 1855).

Pennsylvania Railroad Company: 1st-12th Annual Reports (Philadelphia, 1847–59). (Contain abundant comment on progress of western roads and on competitive situation.)

Railroad conventions: *Report of the Proceedings of the Ohio Railroad Convention . . . 1852* (Columbus, 1852); *Proceedings of a Meeting of Representatives of the Several Railroad Companies . . . 1854* (Cleveland, 1854); *Proceedings of a Convention of the Representatives of the Various Railroad Companies . . .* 1856 (Cincinnati, 1856).

Sandusky, Dayton & Cincinnati Railroad Company: *Report . . . to adjourned meeting, July 10, 1855* (New York, 1855); Annual Reports, 1858–61 (Sandusky); *Report of a Committee . . . on the Difficulties . . . [with] the Cincinnati, Hamilton and Dayton Road* (Columbus, 1858).

Sandusky, Mansfield and Newark Railroad Company: 1st Report (Sandusky, 1857); *Report of a Committee* (N.Y., 1855).

5. Miscellaneous Published Primary Sources:

An effort was made to consult the major travel accounts, reminiscences of travel and social life, surveys and engineering reports and accounts, and published correspondence of prominent political figures bearing on the Ohio scene for the period covered in this book. No doubt many were overlooked, but those found most useful (including a few government reports) were as follows:

Barton, James L. *Lake Commerce* (4th edition, Buffalo, 1846).

Cist, Charles. *Sketches and Statistics of Cincinnati in 1859* (n.p., 1859).

DeBow, J. D. B. *Industrial Resources and Statistics of Southern and Western States* (3 vols., New Orleans, 1852–53).

Drake, Daniel. *Natural and Statistical View, or Picture of Cincinnati and the Miami Country* (Cincinnati, 1815).

Gerstner, F. A. C. de. "Letters from the United States of North America," *Journal of the Franklin Institute,* n. s. XXVI (1840), and 3rd ser., I (1841), various instalments.

Hall, James. *The West: Its Commerce and Navigation* (Cincinnati, 1848).

Hamlin, L. B., ed. "Selections from the Follett Papers," *Quarterly Publication of the Historical and Philosophical Society of Ohio,* V (1910), IX (1914), XIII (1918). Three instalments, including letters of Follett, a board of public works commissioner, and of Thomas Corwin and S. P. Chase on Ohio affairs.

Howells, W. C. *Recollections of Life in Ohio from 1813 to 1840* (Cincinnati, 1895).

Jones, R. L., ed. "Flatboating Down the Ohio and Mississippi, 1867–1873: Correspondence and Diaries of the William Dudley Devol Family," *Ohio State Arch. and Hist. Quar.,* LIX (July 1950), 287–309. (A valuable, compressed introduction.)

Kilbourn (also Kilbourne), John. *Public Documents Concerning the Ohio Canals* (rev. edn., 1832).

Klein, L. "Rail-roads in the United States," *Journal of the Franklin Institute,* n. s., XXVI (1840). Three instalments.

Maxwell, James D. "Journal." Ed. Doris M. Reed, *Indiana Magazine of History,* XLVI (March 1950), 73–81.

Ogden, George W. *Letters from the West* (1821). Reprinted in R. G. Thwaites, ed., *Early Western Travels* (Cleveland, 1904–07), Vol. XIX.

Paulding, James K. *The Letters of James Kirke Paulding,* ed. Ralph M. Aderman (Madison, Wis., 1962).

Peabody, Charles. "Diary" (1845–46), ed. W. E. and O. D. Smith, Historical and Phil. Society of Ohio, *Bulletin,* XI (Oct. 1953), XII (April 1954).

Phelps, Edwin. "Memoirs," ed. Francis P. Weisenburger, *Northwest Ohio Quarterly,* XVIII (1945), 72–124. (Contains much valuable data on social life and canal digging in northwest Ohio.)

Smith, William Prescott. *The Book of the Great Railway Celebrations of 1857* (New York, 1858).

Southward, W. R. *Chillicothe: 1811* (Chillicothe, 1950).

Stucklé, Henri. *Voies de Communication aux Etats-Unis* (Paris, 1847).

Taft, Alphonso. *A Lecture on Cincinnati and Her Rail-roads* (Cincinnati, 1850).

Tanner, H. S. *A Description of the Canals and Rail Roads of the United States* (New York, 1840).

Titus, Leo G., ed. "Swiss Emigrants Seek Home in America," Hist. and Phil. Soc. of Ohio, *Bulletin,* XIV (July 1956), 167–185.

Trotter, Alexander. *Observations on the Financial Position and Credit of Such of the States of the North American Union as Have Contracted Public Debts* (London, 1839).

U. S., 32nd Cong., 1st Sess., Senate *Executive Doc.* No. 112 (serial 622, Washington, 1853): Israel D. Andrews, *Report . . . on the Trade and Commerce . . .*

U. S., 50th Cong., 1st Sess., House *Executive Doc.* No. 6, pt. 2 (serial 2552, Washington, 1888): William Switzler, *Commerce of the Mississippi and Ohio Rivers . . .*

II: SECONDARY SOURCES

George Rogers Taylor's superb study of government, transportation, and industrialization from 1815 to 1860, *The Transportation Revolution* (New York: Holt, Rinehart, 1951), provides the indispensable framework for studies of public policy and their impact.

Since the Taylor study was published, the interpretation of American development during the early nineteenth century has been much enriched by the theme explored in Douglass C. North, *Economic Growth in the United States, 1790–1860* (New York: Norton, 1966), that the foreign trade sector was the major determinant of national growth patterns. The forces of change in agriculture, however, are explored more thoroughly in Paul W. Gates, *The Farmer's Age, 1815–1860* (New York: Holt, Rinehart, 1960); and Gates, *Agriculture and the Civil War* (New York: Knopf, 1965). Articles on commodity output by Robert Gallman, on federal government activity by Paul B. Trescott, and on transport investment by E. R. Wicker, Jerome Cranmer, and others, in National Bureau of Economic Research, *Trends in the American Economy in the Nineteenth Century* (Vol. 24 in Studies in Income and Wealth, Princeton: Princeton University Press, 1960), all have an important bearing on problems treated in this book. A discussion of major interpretive themes and controversies in the recent literature is provided by Stuart Bruchey in *The Roots of American Economic Growth, 1607–1861* (New York: Harper and Row, 1965).

Since 1960, the study of pre-1890 transportation has been much influenced by one set of studies that emphasizes the importance of governmental initiatives and another that focuses on the social returns of transport investments. The central study of public policy is Carter Goodrich's learned, comprehensive survey of federal, state, and local governments' roles, *Government Promotion of American Canals and Railroads, 1800–1890* (New York: Columbia University Press, 1960). I place more emphasis on ideological factors in the policy process than does Professor Goodrich, and I have given more attention to administrative history; but my own work represents research in themes that he opened up. Recent efforts to explore the social returns from transport investments include Albert Fishlow's excellent book, *American Railroads and the Transformation of the Antebellum Economy* (Cambridge: Harvard University Press, 1965); and Robert William Fogel, *Railroads and American Economic Growth* (Baltimore: Johns Hopkins Press, 1964), both of which have produced lively controversies, discussed in my review article, "On the New Economic History—and Its Limitations," *Agricultural History,* XLI (Oct. 1967). Also important are essays in Carter Goodrich, ed., *Canals and American Economic Development* (New York: Columbia University Press, 1962).

The themes pursued by Professor Goodrich have been elaborated in other important studies of government transport policy: Forest Hill, *Roads, Rails, and Waterways* (Norman, Okla.: University of Oklahoma Press, 1957), a study of the Army Engineers; Nathan Miller, *Enterprise of a Free People* (Ithaca: Cornell University Press, 1962), a richly documented account of the Erie Canal Fund's management, and the fullest study available to date of an early state agency's internal operations and its impact on local and regional economic change; Julius Rubin, *Canal or Railroad?* (American Philosophical Society, *Transactions,* new series, Vol. 51, Part 7, Philadelphia, 1961), a discussion of diverse responses to the Erie Canal in the eastern seaboard cities; and Ronald Shaw, *Erie Water West* (Lexington: University of Kentucky Press, 1966), a study mainly of the Erie Canal in New York politics. Stephen Salsbury, *The State, the Investor, and the Railroad: The Boston and Albany, 1825–1867* (Cambridge: Harvard University Press, 1967); Robert S. Hunt, *Law and Locomotives: The Impact of the Railroad on Wisconsin Law* (Madison: State Historical Society of Wisconsin, 1958); and Leonard W. Levy, *The Law of the Commonwealth and Chief Justice Shaw* (Cambridge: Harvard University Press, 1957), all probe the interrelationships of law and railroad promotion. William Appleman Williams, *The Contours of American History* (Chicago: Quadrangle, 1966) offers a provocative interpretation of interest group conflicts and overarching mercantilistic ideology in policymaking. Henry W. Broude, "The Role of the State in American Economic Development, 1820–1890," in *The State and Economic Growth*, ed. Hugh G. J. Aitken (New York: Social Science Research Council, 1959); and Robert A. Lively, "The American System," *Business History Review*, XXIX (1955), are incisive overviews.

The economic impact of early canals and railroads is a subject first opened up, in many respects, by Arthur L. Kohlmeier, *The Old Northwest as the Keystone of the Arch of American Federal Union* (Bloomington: Principia Press, 1938); and A. H. Sadove, "Transport Improvement and the Appalachian Barrier" (Ph.D. diss., Harvard University, 1950), a study on which other scholars have drawn heavily, as in the essays by Harvey H. Segal in *Canals and American Economic Development*, ed. Goodrich. *The Growth of the Seaport Cities, 1790–1825*, ed. David T. Gilchrist (Charlottesville: University of Virginia Press, 1966); Roger L. Ransom's study, "Interregional Canals and Economic Specialization in the Antebellum United States," *Explorations in Entrepreneurial History: Second Series*, V (Fall 1967); Stanley Lebergott, "United States Transport Advance and Externalities," *Journal of Economic History*, XXVI (December 1966), with discussion, *ibid.*; and Lance E. Davis and John Legler, "The Government in the American Economy, 1815–1902," *ibid.*, XXVI (Dec. 1966), all have contributed to discussion of the question of economic impact.

Localism in state politics is a theme treated brilliantly by Louis Hartz in *Economic Policy and Democratic Thought: Pennsylvania, 1776–1860* (Cambridge: Harvard University Press, 1948), as well as in studies of Massachusetts government policy by Oscar and Mary Handlin, *Commonwealth . . . 1774–1861* (New York: New York University Press, 1947), and of Georgia by Milton Heath, *Constructive Liberalism* (Cambridge: Harvard University Press, 1954). Other lines of inquiry were suggested by Wiley E. Hodges, "Pro-Governmentalism in Virginia, 1789–1836: A Pragmatic Liberal Pattern," *Journal of Politics*, XXV (May 1963); Currin V. Shields, "The American Tradition of Empirical Collectivism," *American Political Science Review*, XLVI (1952); and Theodore J. Lowi, "American Business, Public Policy, Case Studies, and Political Theory," *World Politics*, XVI (1964).

Unique for its breadth of learning as it treats the interrelationships of policy with social and economic change is Edward Chase Kirkland's monumental *Men, Cities, and Transportation* (2 vols., Cambridge: Harvard University Press, 1948), a New England regional study. Another anchor for students of government policy is James Willard Hurst's *Law and the Conditions of Freedom in the Nineteenth Century United States* (Madison: University of Wisconsin Press, 1961). Hurst has elaborated his thesis that "drift and default" marked the policy processes, in *Law and Economic Growth* (Cambridge: Harvard University Press, 1964), an exhaustive study of legal factors in development of the Wisconsin lumber industry. Indispensable for the study of eminent domain concepts are J. A. C. Grant, "The 'Higher Law' Background of the Law of Eminent Domain," *Wisconsin Law Review*, VI (1931); Arthur Lenhoff, "Development of the Concept of Eminent Domain," *Columbia Law Review*, XLII (1942); and Joseph Cormack, "Legal Concepts in Cases of Eminent Domain," *Yale Law Journal*, XLI (1931).

The notion of "administrative underdevelopment" in state enterprises, explored by Hurst and Goodrich, is treated in a fresh context by Lawrence Friedman, in *Contract Law in America* (Madison: University of Wisconsin Press, 1965). My own treat-

ment of entrepreneurial-style leadership in the Ohio public enter-
prise was much aided by Arthur H. Cole's many studies, notably
Business Enterprise in Its Social Setting (Cambridge: Harvard
University Press, 1959); by G. H. Evans, Jr., "A Century of
Entrepreneurship in the United States," in *The Entrepreneur*
(Cambridge: Harvard University Research Center in Entre-
preneurial History, 1958); and by Fritz Redlich, "The Business
Leader in Theory and Reality," *American Journal of Economics
and Sociology,* VIII (1949). Arthur M. Johnson and Barry E.
Supple make a contribution to entrepreneurial theory as well as
to early western railroad history, in *Boston Capitalists and West-
ern Railroads* (Cambridge: Harvard University Press, 1967).
Studies which treat the theory of modern, complex bureaucracies,
but which also suggest parallels with development of the early
state agencies, include: J. D. Thompson and W. J. McEwen,
"Organizational Goals and Environment," *American Sociological
Review,* XXIII (1958); and Victor Thompson, "Bureaucracy
and Innovation," *Administrative Science Quarterly,* X (1965);
more directly relevant is Peter Blau et al., "The Structure of Small
Bureaucracies," *American Sociological Review,* XXXI (1966).
Daniel H. Calhoun's *The American Civil Engineer* (Cambridge:
The Technology Press of MIT, 1960) provided well the national
context for consideration of Ohio's uses of engineering expertise.

My own views on how the public enterprises of the states
affected the distribution of real power in the federal system are set
out in *The Condition of American Federalism* (89th Cong., 2nd
Sess., Senate Committee on Government Operations print, 1966);
but for an entirely different interpretation, see Daniel Elazar,
The American Partnership (Chicago: University of Chicago
Press, 1962).

On canal technology in general, I found invaluable Ralph D.
Gray's various articles in *Delaware History,* now incorporated
into his book, *The National Waterway: A History of the Chesapeake & Delaware Canal, 1769–1965* (Urbana: University of
Illinois Press, 1967). Also helpful are the more general articles
on transport and engineering in *Technology in Western Civilization,* ed. Melvin Kranzberg and C. W. Purcell (2 vols., New York:
Oxford University Press, 1967), Volume I.

The student of Ohio history is fortunate to have a rich literature on which to draw, for probably no state has had so much attention lavished on it by professional historians of the first standing. Of unique importance is Thomas Senior Berry's monumental study of the Cincinnati market, *Western Prices before 1861* (Cambridge: Harvard University Press, 1943); but also invaluable are the volumes in Carl Wittke, editor, *History of the State of Ohio* (Ohio Historical Society) that bear on the period treated here: William T. Utter, *The Frontier State, 1803–1825* (Columbus, 1943); Francis P. Weisenburger, *The Passing of the Frontier, 1825–1850* (Columbus, 1941); and Eugene H. Roseboom, *The Civil War Era, 1850–1870* (Columbus, 1944). R. Carlyle Buley, *The Old Northwest: Pioneer Period, 1815–1840* (2 vols., Bloomington: Indiana University Press, 1954), establishes the regional framework; and the earlier era is treated by Beverley W. Bond, Jr., *The Civilization of the Old Northwest . . . 1788–1812* (New York: Macmillan, 1934). Two scholars whose work illuminates important aspects of Ohio's social and economic history are Robert Leslie Jones and Harry Stevens. Professor Jones is author of a number of definitive article-length studies of Ohio agriculture, cited below. Professor Stevens has written perhaps twoscore articles on social and economic subjects, as well as *The Early Jackson Party in Ohio* (Durham: Duke University Press, 1953); and an entrepreneurial case study, "Bank Enterprisers in a Western Town, 1815–1822" (Cincinnati), *Business History Review,* XXIX (1955), which provided essential background for the section of this book on banking and canal financing. John G. Clark, *The Grain Trade in the Old Northwest* (Urbana: University of Illinois Press, 1966), provides a comprehensive analysis of grain production, the shifting demand pattern, and mechanisms of interregional trade.

On Ohio transportation in general, the best introduction is still William F. Gephart, *Transportation and Industrial Development in the Middle West* (New York: Columbia University, 1909); and on the Ohio canals, the more limited study by C. P. McClelland and C. C. Huntington, *History of the Ohio Canals* (Columbus: Ohio Historical Society, 1905). More ambitious but much less accurate, and indeed often internally inconsistent, is Ernest

L. Bogart, *Internal Improvements and State Debt in Ohio* (New York: Longmans, Green, 1924). A more useful work is Bogart's *Financial History of Ohio* (Urbana: University of Illinois Studies in the Social Sciences, Vol. I, 1912). Article-length studies on the Ohio project include Arthur Hirsch, "The Construction of the Miami and Erie Canal," *Proceedings* of the Mississippi Valley Historical Assoc., X (1918–21); John J. George, Jr., "The Miami Canal," *OAHQ*, XXXVI (1927); George W. Dial, "Construction of the Ohio Canals," *ibid.*, XIII (1904); and, more reliable and detailed, John Still, "Ethan Allen Brown and Ohio's Canal System," *ibid.*, LXVI (Jan. 1957); and Ernest M. Teagarden, "Builders of the Ohio Canal, 1825–1832," *Inland Seas*, XIX (1963), on laborers. Thomas D. Odle, "The American Grain Trade of the Great Lakes, 1825–1873," published in five parts, *ibid.*, VII–VIII (1951–52), is a full and detailed account of marketing and forwarding on the canal-and-lake system, and it treats the development of canal-boat operating firms and their contacts with eastern merchants and forwarders. Lee Newcomer, "Construction of the Wabash and Erie Canal," *OAHQ*, XLVI (1937) is suggestive but uses evidence that does not bear entirely on the canal that is purportedly his subject. Charles R. Morris, "Internal Improvements in Ohio, 1825–50," in American Historical Association, *Report of Proceedings*, III (1889) is completely superseded by later studies.

By far the best scholarly work on economic aspects of the canal enterprise is in two unpublished theses: Harvey H. Segal, "Canal Cycles, 1834–1861" (Columbia University Ph.D. diss., 1956), which treats financing entirely from published sources but is sound so far as it goes; and Sherry O. Hessler, "Patterns of Transport and Urban Growth in the Miami Valley, Ohio, 1820–1880" (Johns Hopkins University M.A. thesis, 1961). Similarly, the best introduction to Ohio's railroad history is unpublished: Walter R. Marvin, "Columbus and the Railroads of Central Ohio before the Civil War" (Ohio State University Ph.D. diss., 1953). The essence of some of this work has appeared in scattered articles: Segal's study in Goodrich, ed., *Canals and American Economic Development;* Hessler, "The Great Disturbing Cause and the Decline of the Queen City," *Bulletin* of the

HPSO, XX (July 1962); and Marvin, "The Steubenville and Indiana Railroad," *OHQ*, LXVI (Jan. 1957). John E. Pixton, Jr., "Faith vs. Economics: The Marietta and Cincinnati Railroad," *ibid.*, LXVI (Jan. 1957), is a useful survey, elaborated in his book, *The Marietta and Cincinnati Railroad, 1845–1883* (Penn. State Univ. Studies, #17, 1966). Eugene O. Porter, "Financing Ohio's Pre-Civil War Railroads," *OHQ*, LVII (July 1948) was found less useful and in particulars inaccurate. Leola Stewart, "Sandusky: Pioneer Link between Sail and Rail," *ibid.*, LVII (1948) is a useful local study.

On privately promoted and financed canals, most helpful were R. Max Gard and W. H. Vodrey, *The Sandy and Beaver Canal* (East Liverpool, Ohio: East Liverpool Historical Society, 1952); and Harold E. Davis, *The Pennsylvania-Ohio Canal, 1823–1877* (Hiram [Ohio] Historical Society *Publications*, No. 1, 1929), on the Mahoning canal project. Davis is author also of "Social and Economic Basis of the Whig Party in Ohio, 1828–1840" (Western Reserve University Ph.D. diss., 1933), some main themes of which are summarized in his article, "The Economic Basis of Ohio Politics, 1820–1840," *OAHQ*, XLVII (Oct. 1938).

The interrelationships of canal financing, state banking, and public policy were much illuminated by Ralph W. Hidy, *The House of Baring in American Trade and Finance, 1763–1861* (Cambridge: Harvard University Press, 1949); and I have treated in detail one bank that profited from the deposit of canal funds, in "The Commercial Bank of Lake Erie, 1831–1843," *Business History Review*, XL (Spring 1966). The economic conditions and Federal policies that interacted with local problems in the post-1836 period of canal finance in Ohio are treated in Hidy and Nathan Miller, works already cited; in R. C. O. Matthews, *A Study in Trade Cycle History* (Cambridge: Cambridge University Press, 1954); R. C. McGrane, *Foreign Bondholders and American State Debts* (New York: Macmillan, 1935); Scheiber, "The Pet Banks in Jacksonian Politics and Finance, 1833–1841," *Journal of Economic History*, XXIII (June 1963); and Leland Jenks, *The Migration of British Capital to 1875* (New York: Knopf, 1927).

Local studies of Ohio in the traditional geneological vein

abound, but still outstanding among them is Henry Howe, *Historical Collections of Ohio, Centennial Edition* (Cincinnati: The State of Ohio, 1888). For the Miami country, especially useful were Frank P. Goodwin, "Building a Commercial System," *OAHQ*, XVI (April 1907); and Goodwin, "The Rise of Manufactures in the Miami Country," *American Historical Review*, XII (July 1907). Randolph C. Downes, *History of Lake Shore Ohio* (3 vols., New York: Lewis Publishing Co., 1952), and William T. Utter, *Granville: The Story of an Ohio Village* (Granville: Denison University, 1956), provide respectively, a model regional study and a model local history. Both contain much on the canal era. H. S. Knapp, *History of the Maumee Valley* (Toledo, 1872) covers well the history of northwest Ohio; the impact of federal and state land policies on the region are the subject of my article "State Policy and the Public Domain: The Ohio Canal Lands," *Journal of Economic History*, XXV (March 1965). Also useful was James F. Winter, *A History of Northwest Ohio* (3 vols., New York: Lewis Publishing Co., 1917). Harlan Hatcher, *The Western Reserve* (Indianapolis: Bobbs-Merrill, 1949) treats northeastern Ohio, though only in a general way. A more thorough study is Elbert Jay Benton, *The Cultural Story of an American City: Cleveland* (2 vols., Cleveland: Western Reserve Historical Society, 1944, 1946), supplemented by William G. Rose's compendious study, *Cleveland: The Making of a City* (Cleveland: World Publishing Co., 1950). Northeast Ohio is covered also, from a geographer's angle of vision, in James S. Matthews, *Expressions of Urbanism in the Sequent Occupation of Northeastern Ohio* (Chicago: University of Chicago, Dept. of Geography, Research Papers, #5, 1949). A vivid portrayal of early farming and farm-making in the Western Reserve is provided by John J. Horton, *The Jonathan Hale Farm: A Chronicle of the Cuyahoga Valley* (Western Reserve Historical Society, Publication #116, Cleveland, 1961). Trade and development on the Ohio River shore are the subject of Josephine E. Phillips, "Flatboating on the Great Thoroughfare," *Bulletin* of the HPSO, V (June 1947); Louis Hunter, *Steamboats on the Western Rivers* (Cambridge: Harvard University Press, 1949); Hunter, *Studies in the Economic History of the Ohio Valley* (Smith College Studies in History, XIX, 1933–34); Thomas W. Lewis, *History of Southeastern Ohio and the Muskingum Valley* (3 vols., Chicago: S. J. Clarke Co., 1928); and, for the Cincinnati food-processing industries and their development, two articles by Charles T. Leavitt, "Some Economic Aspects of the Western Meat-Packing Industry," *Journal of Business,* IV (1931), and "Transportation and the Livestock Industry of the Middle West," *Agricultural History,* VIII (Jan. 1934).

The livestock industry of the Scioto Valley and west-central Ohio is treated in Paul C. Henlein, *Cattle Kingdom in the Ohio Valley* (Lexington: University of Kentucky Press, 1959); and more fully in Robert Leslie Jones, "The Beef Cattle Industry in Ohio prior to the Civil War," *OHQ,* LXIV (April, July 1955). Jones's study of "The Dairy Industry in Ohio Prior to the Civil War," *ibid.,* LVI (Jan. 1947) treats the Western Reserve in particular but also considers changing marketing patterns. His "Special Crops in Ohio before 1850," *ibid.,* LIV (1945) is a systematic regional survey. Stephen L. Stover, "Early Sheep Husbandry in Ohio," *Agricultural History,* XXXVI (April 1962) is also useful.

Other special studies of regional change include two on southern Ohio's mining and iron-making region: Frank H. Rowe, *History of the Iron and Steel Industry in Scioto County, Ohio* (Columbus: *Ohio Historical Collections,* Vol. X, 1938), and Wilber E. Stout, "The Charcoal Iron Industry of the Hanging Rock Region," *OAHQ,* XLII (1933). Norris F. Schneider, *Y-Bridge City: The Story of Zanesville and Muskingum County* (Cleveland: World, 1950) is sketchy but suggestive nonetheless. Catherine E. Reiser, *Pittsburgh's Commercial Development, 1800–1850* (Harrisburg: Pennsylvania Historical and Museum Commisison, 1951), is the basic source on that city's trade with northeastern Ohio and with Cleveland. Lyder L. Unstad, "A Survey of the Industrial and Economic Development of Central Ohio" (Ohio State University Ph.D. diss., 1937), concentrates on Columbus' pattern of industrialization to 1873. William T. Hutchinson, "The Bounty Lands of the American Revolution in Ohio" (University of Chicago Ph.D. diss., 1927), is of basic importance to an understanding of how landownership patterns, first set by Virginia's disposal of its military reserve, affected the Scioto Valley's development. The Scioto region's economy is explored in the context of Worthington's many business enterprises in Alfred B. Sears, *Thomas Worthington, Father of Ohio Statehood* (Columbus: Ohio Historical Society, 1958). Cincinnati's development to 1830 is considered in a comparative analysis of urbanization by Richard C. Wade, *The Urban Frontier: The Rise of Western Cities* (Cambridge: Harvard University Press, 1959). One of Wade's main themes is urban rivalry, a subject considered in the larger setting of politics by Stanley Elkins and Eric McKitrick, in "A Meaning for Turner's Frontier," *Political Science Quarterly,* LXIX (1954).

Private capital flowed into the American West and was an essential factor conditioning development in the region. As we have seen, public financing was one mechanism by which investment capital came into the West, but how private investment entered and was managed is a problem still largely unexplored. A valuable preliminary study is Bernard M. Olsen, "A Representative Study of Capital Origins," *Economic Development and Cultural Change,* VI (1958), which treats Indiana manufacturing but has implications for Ohio's manufacturing development. How one group of Massachusetts investors were stimulated to place capital in Ohio, and how they managed their enterprise, is the subject of a parallel study, in my "A Jacksonian as Banker and Lobbyist: New Light on George Bancroft," *New England Quarterly,* XXXVII (Sept. 1964). Alfred D. Chandler, Jr., opens up the history of railroad-investment flows in "Patterns of American Railroad Finance, 1830–1850," *Business History Review,* XXVIII (Sept. 1954); and the role of short-term lending by the British bankers is treated in Ralph W. and Muriel E. Hidy, "Anglo-American Merchant Bankers and the Railroads of the Old Northwest, 1848–1860," *ibid.,* XXXIV (1960). Johnson and Supple, *Boston Capitalists and Western Railroads,* is a full study of its subject. On urbanization, see also Alan R. Pred, *The Spatial Dynamics of U.S. Urban-Industrial Growth, 1800–1914* (Cambridge: MIT Press, 1966).

There must be a category, too, for works that are seldom cited in the text or whose importance is not immediately obvious because it inheres in the personal way that an author developed his subject. Most important in this respect is Hugh G. J. Aitken's study of *The Welland Canal Company* (Cambridge: Harvard University Press, 1954), a gem of a book that offers important parallels to the role of entrepreneurs as public officials in the Ohio enterprise. York Willbern's "The States as Components in an Areal Division of Powers," *Area and Power,* ed. Arthur Maass (Glencoe: Free Press, 1959); and E. A. J. Johnson, "Federalism, Pluralism, and Public Policy," *Journal of Economic History,* XXII (Dec. 1962) lent substance to intuitions concerning the importance of state administrative activity in the context of nineteenth-century federalism. In a similar manner, Paul W. Gates, *The Illinois Central Railroad and Its Colonization Work* (Cambridge: Harvard University Press, 1934) provided a model of what localized history at its best can offer. Finally, I could not have formulated much of my research on state mercantilism without having had the benefit of Curtis P. Nettels' lectures, at Cornell University, now cast in book form in his *Emergence of a National Economy, 1775–1815* (New York: Holt, Rinehart, 1962).

Index

Administration, public, 61ff, 164ff
  and party patronage, 147ff, 166–70, 358
  and planning, 171ff
  and bureaucratic development, 357–358
  See also Board of Canal Fund Commissioners, Canal Commission
Agriculture
  impact of canals on, 198, 201, 220, 319
  impact of railroads on, 328–36
  See also specific crops (grain, etc.), farmers
Akron, 48
Aqueducts, 41
Astor, John Jacob, 38, 46, 373
Athens (Ohio), 102. See also Hocking Valley

Baltimore & Ohio Railroad, 276, 283, 292
Bank for Savings (N.Y.), 49, 374
Bank of England, 372
Banking law (Ohio)
  of 1816, 8
  of 1839, 145, 147–48
  of 1840, 149, 151
Banking policy (Ohio), 187, 356
  and transport financing, 135, 141
  See also Board of Canal Fund Commissioners
Banks, Ohio state-chartered, 5, 7, 142–45, 153–54, 361
  canal loans, 46, 149–51
  and canal bonds, 77–78, 143–50, 157
  capitalization of, 160n
  See also Ohio Life Insurance and Trust Company

Baring Brothers of London, 144–47, 149, 152, 157, 373–74, 376–78
Barter system, 189
Bates, David S., 21, 23, 64, 75
Bayard, William, 21
Beasley, Nathaniel, 28, 62
Bellefontaine & Indiana Railroad, 290
Benson, Lee, 90
Biddle, Thomas, 49
Blackburn, William, 69
Board of Canal Fund Commissioners, 29, 37, 52, 126, 140, 149–150, 356, 361, 378
  and bond issues,
    1825, 38–39
    1826–27, 46, 48
    1828, 49
    1830, 50–51
    1832, 50–51
    1836–41, 141–52
    1842, 152
    1843, 154
  administration, 141–45
  membership, 148–49
  policy after 1840, 150–53
Board of Public Works, see Canal Commission
Bonaparte, Prince Napoleon, 377
Bonds, Ohio canal, 21–22, 37–39, 46, 52, 143–49, 152–53, 189, 372–378
  issue of 1825, 37
  issue of 1826, 46–47
  issues of 1836–38, 110–11, 124, 140, 142, 374
  issues of 1841–44, 140–41, 151–55
  "domestic," 151, 153, 155
  See also Board of Canal Fund Commissioners, capital investment
Brier Hill coal mines, 215–16, 222

Brown, Ethan Allen, 3–5, 7, 11, 15–
    17, 29, 37, 80
Buckingham, Ebenezer, 17, 29, 37,
    81n
Bucknor, William, 38, 49, 50, 373
Bureaucracy, *see* administration, pub-
    lic

Calhoun, John C., 79
Canal board, *see* Canal Commission
Canal Commission (succeeded by
    Board of Public Works)
  first commission established (1822),
    17–18
  1820's surveys by, 19–28, 30, 66–
    67, 355
  1823 report of, 20
  1824 report of, 21–22
  1825 report of, 25–28, 164
  personnel, 28–29, 61–62, 66–67,
    165–67, 174, 355
  plans construction, 40–45, 47–48,
    171
  relationship with contractors, 44–
    45, 69–73, 125, 171
  public relations, 49–50, 67–69
  organization and procedures, 61–
    64, 166–68, 171–72, 357–58
  and legislature, 65–66, 67, 88, 173–
    74, 177, 301–05
  labor relations, 69, 72–74
  technical training of personnel, 75–
    76
  attitude toward new projects (1828–
    1833), 107–08
  reorganization of, and politics,
    164–70
  1832 report of, 165
  and 1837 Loan Law, 110–11, 172–
    73. *See also* Loan Law of 1837
  and canal maintenance, 175–76,
    298–99, 303–04
  routes, 189
  sets canal tolls and allocates mar-
    kets, 248–58, 298–301
  and merchants, 253–54
  See also eminent domain, specific
    canals (Ohio Canal, etc.)
Canal contractors, 44–45, 62, 142,
    144, 174
  as entrepreneurs, 69–75
  relations with state, 69–70, 72ff,
    124–26
  and laborers, 72–74, 124–26
Canal debt, repudiation threatened
    for Ohio's, 152, 156–58. *See*

also Board of Canal Fund
    Commissioners
Canal finance, 36–40, 53–54, 108,
    120–26, 128, 135, 140–42,
    149–58, 304, 361, 371–78
  expenditures, 72–73, 112, 120, 371
  revenues, 92, 108, 127, 141, 152,
    154, 156–57, 171–72, 185, 213–
    214, 223, 236–38, 261, 302
  See also Board of Canal Fund
    Commissioners; bonds
Canal labor, 69, 72–74, 190
  shortage of, 48–49, 124–25
Canal locks, 41–42, 121, 123, 176,
    299
Canal plan
  of 1822, 167
  of 1825, 36–38, 67–68, 80, 88, 91–
    92, 97, 156–57, 188, 248, 275–
    276, 356
  of 1836, 126–30, 133–35, 167–68,
    170, 357
Canal routes, 15–25, 40, 187, 212–13
Canal technology, 53, 62–63, 112n,
    135, 235–38, 275
  navigational technique, 40–42, 175,
    320–21
  maintenance problems, 172, 174ff,
    303–06, 357
  See also canals, construction of;
    engineering
Canal trade, 187–206, 215–16, 218–
    219, 222, 224, 226–31, 255,
    258, 287, 300, 323–29
Canal traffic, 215, 236, 238, 301–03
  passenger, 235–37
  forwarders, 249, 252, 261
Canals
  construction of, 23, 42, 44–45, 47–
    50, 52, 78, 113, 126, 171–72,
    238, 276. *See also* Canal tech-
    nology
  and railroad competition, 96, 289,
    298–303
  deterioration of, 319–20, 327
Capital investment, 8–9, 297–98,
    371–78
  eastern, 27, 36, 38, 45, 97, 103–04,
    153–55, 189, 283, 285, 289,
    358–59, 361, 371–78
  British, 38, 49, 144–47, 149, 152,
    157, 293, 371–78
  for Mahoning Canal, 102–03
  for Lancaster Lateral Canal, 102
  foreign, 285, 359, 371–78
  See also banks, Ohio state-char-
    tered; bonds

Central Ohio Railroad, 315n
Chantrey, Sir Francis, 377
Chesapeake & Delaware Canal, 70
Chesapeake & Ohio Canal Company, 13
Chevalier, Michel, 89, 164
Chillicothe, 49–52
  Bank of, 150
  See also Scioto Valley
Cincinnati, 10, 105, 130, 220–22
  canal trade, 11, 13, 22, 201–06, 220ff, 224–35, 324–26
  meat-packing, 205–06
  as wholesale market, 337–38
Cincinnati & Whitewater Canal Company, 131
Cincinnati Chamber of Commerce, 253
Cincinnati, Hamilton & Dayton Railroad, 280, 289
Cincinnati, Wilmington & Zanesville Railroad, 292
Clay, Henry, 61, 75, 79
Cleveland, 206
  canal trade, 48, 192ff, 196, 215–17, 258–59, 322–24
Cleveland & Mahoning Railroad, 292
Cleveland & Pittsburgh Railroad Company, 290
Cleveland, Columbus & Cincinnati Railroad, 280, 289, 323, 362
Cleveland, Francis, 367n
Cleveland, Painesville & Ashtabula Railroad, 289
Clinton, De Witt, 3, 14, 20, 23, 25, 30, 35n, 37, 52, 79
Coal, 215–16, 222, 323
Colden, Cadwallader, 21
Columbus & Xenia Railroad, 289
Columbus, Piqua & Indiana Railroad, 290
"Commonwealth" concept, xvii, 272, 355. *See also* Ideology
Competition
  of water routes in 1840's, 212ff
  among railroads, 294–95
  of railroads and canals, 96, 238, 259, 273, 280, 287, 289, 298–303, 320–28
Constitution, Ohio
  1851, 155, 177
  1802, 277
Constitutional Convention of 1850, 287, 297–98
Cootner, Paul, 310n
Corn, 203, 218–19, 224, 227, 230–31, 258, 300, 321–22, 324, 328

Corporations, *see* railroads, private enterprise
Corruption, *see* Canal Commission
Cotterill, Thomas, 376–77
Cotton, 10
Cozad, Elias, 71

Dairy products, 215–16, 331–32
Dayton, 200–01, 203, 205, 221–22
Dayton & Michigan Railroad, 293
Democrats, 166, 170, 298
  in Ohio General Assembly, 92–94, 169, 305
  anti-bank, 144
  radical faction, 145–48, 157–58, 169, 297, 301
  and fund board, 145ff, 151–52
  on Canal Commission, 168
  railroad policy, 296–97
Denison, William, 305
depression of 1839–43, 125–26, 140, 250, 372
district representation system, 167, 168
Dresden, 101, 121
  side-cut, 108

Economic development, 221–22, 318–319, 325, 339–40, 353
  and state transport, 11–14, 237, 340–43, 359–60
  cash economy, 189–90
  See also canal trade, land values, manufacturing, urbanization
Egalitarianism, 89–94, 109, 111, 168, 248, 272, 276, 356
Elections, state
  1824, 24–25
  1841, 151
  1859, 305
Emigration to Ohio, 4–5, 10, 190–92, 220, 235, 237, 336, 339
Eminent domain, doctrine of, 65, 67–68, 189, 277–78, 296, 364
Engineering, 47, 64, 65, 76, 78, 89, 123, 164–65
  surveys, 19–21
  difficulties in, 127, 129
  and politics, 169, 174
  See also canal technology
Entrepreneurial spirit, 93, 121
Entrepreneurship, and management of private enterprise, Ch. 3, *passim*; Ch. 7, *passim*; 362
  in management of canals and railroads, 367n

See also Canal Commission, Administration, Private enterprise, Railroads
Equal benefits doctrine, 90–93, 109, 131, 135, 356, 366n. *See also* egalitarianism
Erie (Pennsylvania), commerce, 251
Erie & Kalamazoo Railroad, 282
Erie Canal (New York), 3, 7n, 14–16, 20, 56n, 212
  financial success of, 25, 30, 281
  bonds, 36, 38, 39, 372
  technology, 40–42
  organization, 62, 69, 70
  rates, 251, 260
Erie Railroad, 89, 283, 289

Farmers, 4, 5, 11–13, 72, 192, 221
  as canal laborers, 72, 190
  import gypsum, 197–98
  and canal rates, 252, 255–56, 294
  and railroads, 286, 294
Fishlow, Albert, 246n, 295 (table), 352
Fitz Roy, Lord William, 377
Flatboats, 9, 123, 213
Flour, *see* Grain trade
Fogel, Robert W., 344n, 391ff
Forrer, Samuel, 21, 64, 165, 368n
Franklin Bank of Columbus, 150
Frazer, Elizabeth, 377
Fund board, *see* Board of Canal Commissioners
Furs and hides, 10

Geddes, James, 20–21, 23
General Assembly (Ohio), 7–8, 37, 354, 363
  canal policy, 8–9, 14–16, 27–29, 45–46, 50, 88–89, 299, 305–06
  relations with Canal Commission, 65–66, 88, 165–74, 177, 303–304
  and public enterprise, 88–94, 108
  and Miami Extension Canal, 98, 100
  and Wabash and Erie Canal, 99
  and Muskingum Improvement, 101
  and private enterprise, 103–04, 276–78
  and Mahoning Canal, 103–04
  and roads, 106
  transport program of 1836, 110–11
  repeals Loan Law, 133
  enacts bank reform (1837), 145
  financial policy, 147, 149–53, 157–58, 160

land policy, 233
  reduces salt tolls, 258
  grants railroad charters, 272, 276–78
  and railroad routes, 279
  regulation of railroads, 279–81, 285, 295–97, 301–04, 355
Grain
  trade, 192–95, 201, 217–21, 224–25, 227, 230, 258, 300, 321–22, 324, 328, 332–35
  milling, 203, 340–41
  See also agriculture
Granger Law agitation, 263, 363
gypsum, 197–98

Haines, Charles, 3–5, 38
Harmony, Peter, 375
Hartz, Louis, 365n
Hemp, 10
Henriques, Abraham Q., 377
Hessler, Sherry O., studies by, 205
Hocking Valley, 101–02
Hocking Valley Canal, 102, 110, 122, 127, 135, 151
Hope & Company, 377
Hurst, James Willard, 93, 354

Ideology, 27, 90–94, 127, 135, 353–354. *See also* egalitarianism
Illinois & Michigan Canal, 163n, 251
Indiana, 213
  Wabash and Erie Canal in, 99–100
  Whitewater Canal in, 105, 107, 135, 224
Indirect benefits doctrine, in cost-benefit analysis, 27, 92–93, 112, 173, 238, 304, 391ff. *See also* social savings
Indirect returns, *see* social savings
Industrialization, *see* economic development
Interest groups
  regional, 11–14, 24
  functional, 254–56
  See also localism, merchants, farmers, transport rates, etc.
Interest rates, 141–42, 146, 372
Interventionism, 90
Investment capital, *see* capital, investment
Iron and iron products, 221, 293, 323, 325

Jackson, Andrew, 75, 114n, 166–67
Jenks, Leland H., 206n
John Ward & Company, 375

Johnston, John, 28, 62, 67, 97–98
Judicial review, *see* law

Keelboats, 10–11
Kelley, Alfred, 17, 20–21, 23, 40, 62, 66, 69, 71, 80, 109, 132, 162n, 165, 167, 172, 289, 357, 362
Kilbourne, James, 275
Kilgore, Daniel, 141, 148, 368n

Laborers, *see* canal labor
Labouchere, Samuel P., 377
Laissez-faire, 7, 28, 90, 94
Lake, Joseph, 148, 151
Lake shipping, 328
Lake Shore railroad group, 290
Lancaster Lateral Canal, 102, 107, 110, 127
Land values, 187–89, 198, 335
Lapham, Increase, 367n
Law
    and power of eminent domain, 68, 278. *See also* Eminent domain
    evasion of banking, 149
    respecting canal administration, 173ff
    relief, for canal contractors, 174
    of railroad corporations, 276ff
    and local aid to railroads, 287
    of tort immunity, 309n
    See also Banking, Planning
Levy, Leonard W., 308n
Licking Summit, 23, 43–45, 50–51, 54, 175
Limited liability, for railroads, 277
Little Miami Railroad, 131–33, 282–283, 287, 289
Livestock, 10, 218–19, 231, 324–25, 328–32
Loan Law of 1837, 110–13, 130–33, 135, 147, 156, 172–73, 271, 283, 356–57
    repealed, 152
Local governments, issue railroad bonds, 285, 287
Localism, 9, 11–13, 14, 88–91, 118n, 122, 156, 165, 356
    and new canal projects, 66–67, 94, 101–02
    and private enterprise, 102–06
    public works expansion and, 107–108
    and canal tolls, 253–54
    and railroads, 271–72, 281, 283–285, 295–96
    See also district representation, interest groups

Logrolling, 109. *See also* localism
Louisville, Falls at, 9, 32n
Lucas, Robert, 100, 166
Lumber, 197–98, 203, 222, 323–25, 352n

Maccracken, Samuel, 141, 148
Mad River & Lake Erie Railroad, 95–99, 110, 132–33, 213, 225, 227, 233, 237, 253, 282–283, 287
Mahoning Canal (Pennsylvania and Ohio Canal), 102–04, 107–08, 131, 134–35, 213, 215–17, 250–251, 327
Mansfield & Sandusky Railroad, 132
Manufacturing, 187, 198, 203, 237, 254, 319, 338–43, 350n. *See also* economic development, waterpower
Marietta, 101, 121
    Bank, 75
Marietta & Cincinnati Railroad, 314n, 352n
Market–garden production, 332
Maumee Valley, 121–22
Meat-packing industry, 205–06
Mercantilism, 247, 355. *See also* ideology
Mercer County Reservoir, 174–75
Merchandise trade, 10, 194, 196, 223, 237, 300, 323
Merchants, 252–53, 294–95, 319, 336–38
Miami Canal, 27–28, 30, 48, 53, 75, 77, 188, 191, 213, 224, 237, 325
    route, 25–26
    construction of 42–45, 48–50
    Extension, 23, 27, 66–67, 96–99, 100, 105, 108, 110, 123–25, 129–30, 147, 153, 171, 173–76, 188, 220–21, 253, 258–59, 323
    Lebanon branch of, 104–05
    trade, 200–06, 253
    railroad competition for, 280, 289
Miami Extension Canal, *see* Miami Canal
Miami Valley, 11–12, 19, 95, 97, 190, 200ff, 220ff, 230. *See also* Cincinnati canal trade; Miami Canal
Middletown, 205
Milan Canal Company, 104–05, 106–107, 110, 227
Mill-sites, location of, *see* waterpower
Miltonville, 189

Mining industries, 340, 342
Minor, Isaac, 17, 28, 62
"Mixed" enterprise, 111, 130–33. *See also* Loan Law, private enterprise, public enterprise
Monroeville & Sandusky Railroad, 282–83
Morrow, Jeremiah, 17, 25
Muskingum River Improvement, 110, 122–23, 127, 134, 151, 175–176, 213, 217–18, 230
Muskingum Valley, 100–01

National Road, 10–11, 13, 48, 167, 303
New Orleans trade route, 9–10, 11, 213, 323
New York, *see* canal trade, Erie Canal, capital investment
New York & Erie Railroad, *see* Erie Railroad
New York Central Railroad, 283, 289
North American Trust and Banking Company, 145–46, 375
North, Douglass, 392
Northern Indiana Railroad, 292
Notice to Labourers, 73–74

Ohio Canal, 75, 77, 101, 164, 188, 212–13
  plans for, 3–5, 49–50
  route, 23–26
  construction, 28, 43–44
  costs, 53–54
  trade, 134, 232, 256–57
  maintenance, 176, 299
  as monopoly, 191–92, 194, 196–200
  waterpower sites on, 200
  passenger traffic on, 235–37
  rates, 250–52, 259, 261
  railroad competition for, 280, 287, 324
  See also canal trade, Portsmouth terminus, grain trade, and specific commodities
Ohio Life Insurance and Trust Company of Cincinnati, 141, 144–146, 149, 151–54, 157, 362, 373–78
Ohio–Mississippi River trade route, 105, 185, 196, 206, 225, 230–231, 333, 335
Ohio Railroad, 132
Ohio River settlements, 9
  trade, 227
Onondaga salt works, 256–57

Packet lines, *see* canal traffic, passenger
Panic of 1819, 4, 5, 7; of 1837, 125, 140, 142, 171, 201, 250, 372
Patronage, political. *See* Administration
Peel, Sir Robert, 378
Pennsylvania
  and canal bonds, 46–47
  public works, 48
Pennsylvania & Ohio Canal, *see* Mahoning Canal
Pennsylvania Mainline system, 96, 249, 251
Pennsylvania Railroad, 283, 290, 323
Perkins, Simon, 37, 141, 148
Philadelphia bankers, *see* capital investment
Piqua, 201, 221
Pittsburgh, 196
Pittsburgh, Fort Wayne & Chicago Railroad, 292
Planning, 355–56
  transport policy, 353–55
  and canal board, 357–58
  See also canal plan, ideology, mercantilism
Policy-making, *see* Canal Commission, General Assembly, ideology
Politics
  1820's, 11
  and economic development, 13–14
  and construction priorities, 109, 156
  and loans, 133
  partisanship and finances, 157–58, 177
  and canal commission, 165–72, 177
  and rate-making, 256, 259–63
  and transport policy, 271–72, 304–306
  and railroad policy, 272, 285–86, 363
Pomeroy mines, 222
Population growth, 5, 192, 198–99, 205, 224, 231, 233, 319, 336
Pork and pork products, 194, 201–03, 219, 224, 225, 227, 230, 258, 300, 322–23, 332
Portage Summit, 45, 48, 175
Portsmouth terminus, 50–52, 54, 60n, 175, 180n, 194, 196
Pred, Allan R., 345n, 351n
Price, William H., 64, 76
Prices, local, 125–26

Prime, Ward & King, 38, 48–50, 142, 144, 146, 154, 157, 373–78
Private enterprise, 4, 15, 33n, 35n, 82n, 135, 172–73, 281, 353–55
    railroads, 271–73, 359
    canals, 303. *See also* Mahoning Canal, Sandy & Beaver Canal, Whitewater Canal
Protectionism, 254–57
Public enterprise, 7–8, 11–12, 16, 26–27, 135, 353–55
    vs. private enterprise, 26–27, 305–306
    disillusionment with, 176–77, 297–298, 358–59
    See also Canal Commission, canal plan

Railroads, 135, 212, 305
    promotion of, 95, 97, 106–07, 275–276, 282ff, 290–93
    public aid to, 110, 131–33, 173, 278, 282–87, 293
    and canal board, 171
    trade, 225, 319–28
    passenger traffic, 237–38
    compete with canals, 238, 259, 273, 280, 287, 289, 298–303, 320–328
    rates, 262–63, 294–96, 320–31, 328, 338
    agitation for, 271, 276, 281–82, 286
    general law of 1848, 276, 356
    corporate charters for, 276–77, 280
    state regulation of, 275–82, 298, 356, 359, 363–64
    eminent domain right devolved on, 277–78
    tax exemptions for 278, 296
    public policy toward, 275–78
    routes, 279, 285
    private investment in, 279, 282–85, 293–94, 359
    technology, 275, 281
    invest in sister companies, 293–94
    consolidation, 294
    self-regulation of, 294–96, 314n, 328
    impact on agriculture, 328–36
    impact on merchants, 336–38
    stimulate industries, 341–43
    operation, 362
Ralston & Company, 376
Ransom, Leander, 165
Rathbone & Lord, 38–39, 46, 373–74
Reese, Jacob, 375

Republicans, 305
    and railroad policy, 296–97
Reservoirs, 41, 43, 174–75
River improvement, 122. *See also* Muskingum River Improvement
River trade, *see* Ohio–Mississippi River trade route
Roads, 8–9, 11, 29, 106, 227. *See also* turnpikes, Three Per Cent Fund
Roskill, Ogden Company, 376
Rothschild, N. M., & Company, 376
Ruggles, Samuel, 89

Salt trade, 196–97, 222, 255–57
Sandusky, 95–99, 227
Sandusky, Mansfield & Newark Railroad, 287
Sandy and Beaver Canal, 103–04, 107, 233
Scioto Valley, 13, 44, 50–52, 196, 199–200, 218, 233
Scioto Valley & Hocking Railroad, 293
Seward, William H., 89
Shannon, Wilson, 148
Sheep, 331. *See also* wool
Shields, Currin V., 365n
Social savings, and transportation, 237, 391ff
Southern groceries trade, 222–23
Southern route, *see* Ohio–Mississippi River trade route
State administration, *see* administration, public
State bonds, *see* Bonds, Board of Canal Fund Commissioners
Steamboats, 10, 101, 123, 212, 213
Stock, railroad, 279, 283. *See also* railroads

Tappan, Benjamin, 17, 20–21, 28, 62
Taxation, Ohio, 8, 25–26, 28–30, 156–157, 208n, 209n, 278, 296
Three Per Cent Fund, 8–9, 11
Tobacco, 332
Toledo, 220–25, 258, 326–27
Toledo, Wabash & Western Railroad, 292
Tolls, canal, *see* transport rates and canal tolls
Trade routes, interregional, 213
Transport policy, Ohio, 7–9, 14–19, 88–94, 353–56
Transport rates, and canal tolls, 92, 127, 152, 154, 171, 185, 186,

215, 223, 247–63, 356
1840's and 1850's, 212–14, 215,
    217, 238, 247–48, 250–52, 260,
    299–300, 304, 360
criteria for, 248
1827 toll schedule, 249
interstate agreements on, 249
discriminatory,   249–52,   254–55,
    257, 261, 300
and merchants, 252–53, 255, 259,
    280
1829 toll schedule, 254
and manufacturers, 254–55
farmer demands, 255–56
salt tolls, 256–57
determine market patterns, 258–59
and politics, 259–61
and routes, 261–62
state regulation of, 279–80, 295–97
protectionist, 359–60
See also railroads, rates
Transportation Revolution
    and social change, 89ff
    second phase of, in 1840's, 212ff
Trimble, Allen, 29, 37
Turnpikes,   106,   110–11,   127,   131,
    135. *See also* roads

United States government
    and Ohio canals, 15–16
    grants Ohio federal lands, 49, 98–
        99, 106, 151, 191–92, 233
    and egalitarian ideology, 91
    General Land Office of, 98, 100
    distributes surplus funds, 108, 153
    Treasury Department of, 142
Urbanization, 198, 205, 223–25, 319,
    336, 338–40

Van Buren, Martin, 168
Vance, Joseph, 92
Virginia Military District, 199

Wabash and Erie Canal, 99–100, 108,
    111, 121, 123, 125, 127–30,
    134, 151, 171, 188–89, 204,
    220–21, 237, 327
tolls, 258, 262
railroad challenge to, 292
Wages, 72–74, 124–25. *See also* canal
    labor
Walhonding Canal, 106, 110, 121,
    127, 135, 175, 217–18
Warren County Canal, 107, 110,
    126–27, 302–03
Waterpower, 24, 188, 200, 237
    in Scioto Valley, 199–200
    See also manufacturing
Water supply, for Ohio Canal, 41
Welland Canal, 55n, 208n
Western Reserve and Maumee Road,
    111–12
Wheat, *see* grain trade, agriculture
Wheat Belt, 230
Whigs, 93–94
    and state finance, 150, 157–58
    canal policies of, 165–70, 266n, 297
Whiskey trade, 10, 194, 201–03, 225,
    227, 230, 258, 300
Whitewater Canal, 105, 107, 135, 224
Wiebe, Robert H., 363
Williams Committee Report, 16–17,
    20
Williams, Jesse, 367n
Williams, Micajah T., 16, 20–21, 23,
    28, 40, 51, 62, 74–80, 165, 172,
    357, 362
Wool, 215–16, 227, 230
Woolsey, William, 49
Wooster Bank, 151–52
Workers, *see* canal labor
Worthington, Thomas, 14–15, 17, 24,
    28, 62, 66, 80n, 81n

Zanesville, 101, 121